ISSN 1538-6686

GROWING OLD IN AMERICA

D1441465

Barbara Wexler

INFORMATION PLUS® REFERENCE SERIES
Formerly Published by Information Plus, Wylie, Texas

GALE
CENGAGE Learning™

Detroit • New York • San Francisco • New Haven, Conn • Waterville, Maine • London

GALE
CENGAGE Learning

Growing Old in America

Barbara Wexler
Kepos Media, Inc.: Paula Kepos and Janice Jorgensen, Series Editors

Project Editors: Elizabeth Manar, Kathleen J. Edgar

Rights Acquisition and Management: Margaret Abendroth, Jennifer Altschul

Composition: Evi Abou-El-Seoud, Mary Beth Trimper

Manufacturing: Cynde Lentz

© 2010 Gale, Cengage Learning

ALL RIGHTS RESERVED. No part of this work covered by the copyright herein may be reproduced, transmitted, stored, or used in any form or by any means graphic, electronic, or mechanical, including but not limited to photocopying, recording, scanning, digitizing, taping, Web distribution, information networks, or information storage and retrieval systems, except as permitted under Section 107 or 108 of the 1976 United States Copyright Act, without the prior written permission of the publisher.

This publication is a creative work fully protected by all applicable copyright laws, as well as by misappropriation, trade secret, unfair competition, and other applicable laws. The authors and editors of this work have added value to the underlying factual material herein through one or more of the following: unique and original selection, coordination, expression, arrangement, and classification of the information.

For product information and technology assistance, contact us at
Gale Customer Support, 1-800-877-4253.
For permission to use material from this text or product,
submit all requests online at **www.cengage.com/permissions.**
Further permissions questions can be e-mailed to
permissionrequest@cengage.com

Cover photograph: Image copyright Cassiede Alain, 2009. Used under license from Shutterstock.com.

While every effort has been made to ensure the reliability of the information presented in this publication, Gale, a part of Cengage Learning, does not guarantee the accuracy of the data contained herein. Gale accepts no payment for listing; and inclusion in the publication of any organization, agency, institution, publication, service, or individual does not imply endorsement of the editors or publisher. Errors brought to the attention of the publisher and verified to the satisfaction of the publisher will be corrected in future editions.

Gale
27500 Drake Rd.
Farmington Hills, MI 48331-3535

ISBN-13: 978-0-7876-5103-9 (set)
ISBN-10: 0-7876-5103-6 (set)
ISBN-13: 978-1-4144-4119-1
ISBN-10: 1-4144-4119-3

ISSN 1538-6686

This title is also available as an e-book.
ISBN-13: 978-1-4144-7002-3 (set)
ISBN-10: 1-4144-7002-9 (set)
Contact your Gale sales representative for ordering information.

Printed in the United States of America
1 2 3 4 5 6 7 14 13 12 11 10

TABLE OF CONTENTS

PREFACE

Growing Old in America is part of the *Information Plus Reference Series*. The purpose of each volume of the series is to present the latest facts on a topic of pressing concern in modern American life. These topics include the most controversial and studied social issues in the 21st century: abortion, capital punishment, crime, the environment, health care, immigration, minorities, national security, social welfare, women, youth, and many more. Even though this series is written especially for high school and undergraduate students, it is an excellent resource for anyone in need of factual information on current affairs.

By presenting the facts, it is the intention of Gale, Cengage Learning to provide its readers with everything they need to reach an informed opinion on current issues. To that end, there is a particular emphasis in this series on the presentation of scientific studies, surveys, and statistics. These data are generally presented in the form of tables, charts, and other graphics placed within the text of each book. Every graphic is directly referred to and carefully explained in the text. The source of each graphic is presented within the graphic itself. The data used in these graphics are drawn from the most reputable and reliable sources, such as from the various branches of the U.S. government and from major independent polling organizations. Every effort has been made to secure the most recent information available. Readers should bear in mind that many major studies take years to conduct and that additional years often pass before the data from these studies are made available to the public. Therefore, in many cases the most recent information available in 2010 is dated from 2007 or 2008. Older statistics are sometimes presented as well if they are of particular interest and no more-recent information exists.

Even though statistics are a major focus of the *Information Plus Reference Series*, they are by no means its only content. Each book also presents the widely held positions and important ideas that shape how the book's subject is discussed in the United States. These positions are explained in detail and, where possible, in the words of their proponents. Some of the other material to be found in these books includes historical background, descriptions of major events related to the subject, relevant laws and court cases, and examples of how these issues play out in American life. Some books also feature primary documents or have pro and con debate sections that provide the words and opinions of prominent Americans on both sides of a controversial topic. All material is presented in an even-handed and unbiased manner; readers will never be encouraged to accept one view of an issue over another.

HOW TO USE THIS BOOK

The percentage of Americans over the age of 65 has increased over the past century, and it will continue to increase as the children born during the mid-20th-century baby boom age. This book explores the current condition of growing old in the United States. Included is a general overview on growing old in the United States; the economic status of older people; the Social Security program; Medicare and Medicaid; the living arrangements of older adults; working and retirement; and the education levels, voting trends, and political behavior of older Americans. Physical and mental health problems, drug and alcohol abuse, care for older adults, and crime and victimization of older adults are also covered.

Growing Old in America consists of 11 chapters and 3 appendixes. Each chapter is devoted to a particular aspect of aging. For a summary of the information covered in each chapter, please see the synopses provided in the Table of Contents at the front of the book. Chapters generally begin with an overview of the basic facts and background information on the chapter's topic, then proceed to examine subtopics of particular interest. For example, Chapter 3: Living Arrangements of the Older Population, observes that the living arrangements of older adults are important because they are closely associated with their health, well-being, and economic status. It then goes on to detail where older adults live. This is followed by discussion of long-term care, supportive housing, and other residential alternatives. Many older Americans live in nursing homes, so quality of care issues associated with these facilities are examined along with innovative approaches to nursing home care. Assisted living, cohousing, board-and-care facilities, and public housing are also described. Readers can find their way through a chapter by looking for the section and subsection headings, which are clearly set off from the text. They can also refer to the book's extensive index if they already know what they are looking for.

Statistical Information

The tables and figures featured throughout *Growing Old in America* will be of particular use to readers in learning about this issue. These tables and figures represent an extensive collection of the most recent and important statistics on growing old and related issues—for example, graphics cover the living arrangements of older adults, the marital status of older Americans, chronic health conditions, crimes against older Americans, health care costs paid by Medicare and Medicaid, health insurance coverage, and motor vehicle accidents. Gale, Cengage Learning believes that making this information available to readers is the most important way to fulfill the goal of this book: to help readers understand the issues and controversies surrounding growing old in the United States and to reach their own conclusions.

Each table or figure has a unique identifier appearing above it for ease of identification and reference. Titles for the tables and figures explain their purpose. At the end of each table or figure, the original source of the data is provided.

To help readers understand these often complicated statistics, all tables and figures are explained in the text. References in the text direct readers to the relevant statistics. Furthermore, the contents of all tables and figures are fully indexed. Please see the opening section of the index at the back of this volume for a description of how to find tables and figures within it.

Appendixes

Besides the main body text and images, *Growing Old in America* has three appendixes. The first is the Important Names and Addresses directory. Here, readers will find contact information for a number of government and private organizations that can provide further information on growing old. The second appendix is the Resources section, which can also assist readers in conducting their own research. In this section, the author and editors of *Growing Old in America* describe some of the sources that were most useful during the compilation of this book. The final appendix is the detailed index, which facilitates reader access to specific topics in this book.

ADVISORY BOARD CONTRIBUTIONS

The staff of Information Plus would like to extend their heartfelt appreciation to the Information Plus Advisory Board. This dedicated group of media professionals provides feedback on the series on an ongoing basis. Their comments allow the editorial staff who work on the project to make the series better and more user-friendly. The staff's top priority is to produce the highest-quality and most useful books possible, and the Information Plus Advisory Board's contributions to this process are invaluable.

The members of the Information Plus Advisory Board are:

- Kathleen R. Bonn, Librarian, Newbury Park High School, Newbury Park, California
- Madelyn Garner, Librarian, San Jacinto College, North Campus, Houston, Texas
- Anne Oxenrider, Media Specialist, Dundee High School, Dundee, Michigan
- Charles R. Rodgers, Director of Libraries, Pasco-Hernando Community College, Dade City, Florida
- James N. Zitzelsberger, Library Media Department Chairman, Oshkosh West High School, Oshkosh, Wisconsin

COMMENTS AND SUGGESTIONS

The editors of the *Information Plus Reference Series* welcome your feedback on *Growing Old in America*. Please direct all correspondence to:

Editors
Information Plus Reference Series
27500 Drake Rd.
Farmington Hills, MI 48331-3535

CHAPTER 1

OLDER AMERICANS—A DIVERSE AND GROWING POPULATION

Old age is the most unexpected of all the things that happen to a man.

—Leon Trotsky

THE UNITED STATES GROWS OLDER

The United States is aging. Throughout the 20th century and the first decade of the 21st century the country's older population—adults aged 65 and older—increased significantly. According to Saadia Greenberg of the U.S. Administration on Aging (AoA), in *A Profile of Older Americans: 2008* (2008, http://www.mowaa.org/Document.Doc?id=69), the number of older adults grew from 34.1 million in 1997 to 37.9 million in 2007 (the most recent year for which comprehensive data, as opposed to estimates or projections, were available as of mid-2009), which represented 13% of the U.S. population. In the press release "An Older and More Diverse Nation by Midcentury" (August 14, 2008, http://www.census.gov/Press-Release/www/releases/archives/population/012496.html), the U.S. Census Bureau projects that by 2030 one out of five U.S. residents will be aged 65 and older and that by 2050 the population of people aged 65 and older will number 88.5 million. Figure 1.1 shows projections of the growth in the population of older adults from 2010 through 2050. Figure 1.2 shows how older adults will make up an increasing percentage of the total U.S. population.

The Census Bureau reports in the press release "Older Americans Month: May 2009" (March 3, 2009, http://www.census.gov/Press-Release/www/releases/archives/cb09ff-07.pdf) that in 2009 there were 518 million people aged 65 and older worldwide and that this population will grow to 1.6 billion by 2050. Table 1.1 shows Census Bureau projections of the increasing percentage of people aged 65 and older worldwide from 7.7% in 2010 to 16.7% in 2050. Throughout the world, the growth in the population of older adults will outpace the growth of any other segment of the population. Figure 1.3 compares the average annual growth rates of the total populations and older adult populations of various regions of the world; it reveals that between 2002 and 2025 the older adult population will be the fastest growing segment of the world population.

Fewer children per family and longer life spans have shifted the proportion of older adults in the population. Growth in the population segment of older adults in the United States, often called "the graying of America," is considered one of the most significant issues facing the country in the 21st century. The swelling population of people aged 65 and older affects every aspect of society—challenging policy makers, health care providers, employers, families, and others to meet the needs of older Americans.

Many of the findings and statistics cited in this chapter, as well as a number of the tables and figures presented, are drawn from *Older Americans 2008: Key Indicators of Well-Being* (March 2008, http://www.agingstats.gov/agingstatsdotnet/Main_Site/Data/2008_Documents/OA_2008.pdf), a report prepared by the Federal Interagency Forum on Aging-Related Statistics. This forum consists of 13 federal entities—the Census Bureau, the AoA, the Agency for Healthcare Research and Quality, the Centers for Medicare and Medicaid Services, the National Center for Health Statistics, the National Institute on Aging, the Office of the Assistant Secretary for Planning and Evaluation, the Substance Abuse and Mental Health Services Administration, the U.S. Bureau of Labor Statistics, the U.S. Department of Veterans Affairs, the U.S. Environmental Protection Agency, the Office of Management and Budget, and the Social Security Administration—that are dedicated to encouraging cooperation and collaboration among federal agencies to improve the quality and utility of data on the aging population. Other data are drawn from Greenberg's *A Profile of Older Americans*.

To understand the aging of the United States, it is important to not only consider the current population of older adults but also to look at how the older population will fare

FIGURE 1.1

Projected U.S. population aged 65 and older, 2010–50

[In millions]

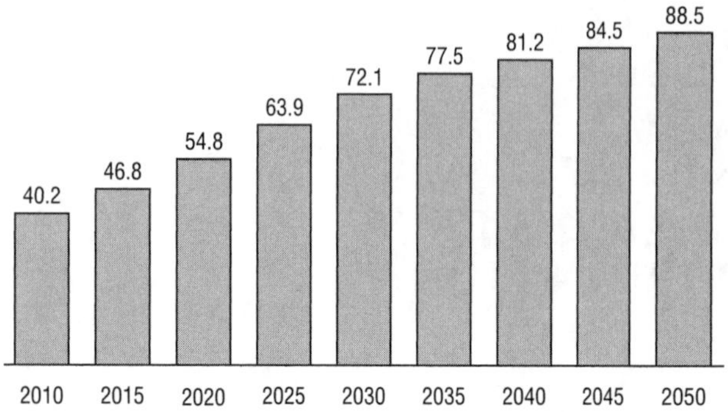

SOURCE: "Projected U.S. Population Aged 65 and Older: 2010 to 2050," in *2008 National Population Projections Tables and Charts*, U.S. Census Bureau, Population Division, August 2008, http://www.census.gov/population/www/projections/tablesandcharts/chart_5.pdf (accessed April 15, 2009)

FIGURE 1.2

Projected percent of the U.S. population aged 65 and older, 2010–50

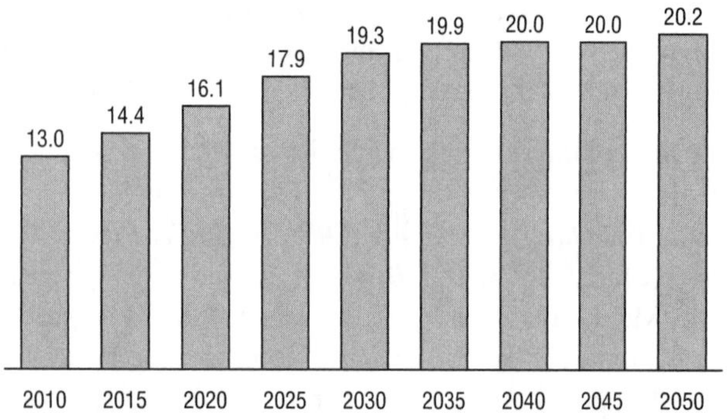

SOURCE: "Projected Percent of the U.S. Population Aged 65 and Older: 2010 to 2050," in *2008 National Population Projections Tables and Charts*, U.S. Census Bureau, Population Division, August 2008, http://www.census.gov/population/www/projections/tablesandcharts/chart_6.pdf (accessed April 15, 2009)

TABLE 1.1

Older adults worldwide, by age and sex, 2010 to 2050

	Percent both sexes	Percent male	Percent female
World/2010			
Total, all ages	**100.0**	**100.0**	**100.0**
65–69	2.6	2.4	2.7
65+	7.7	6.7	8.7
70–74	2.1	1.9	2.3
70+	5.1	4.3	5.9
75–79	1.5	1.3	1.7
75+	3.0	2.4	3.6
80+	1.5	1.1	2.0
World/2020			
Total, all ages	**100.0**	**100.0**	**100.0**
65–69	3.4	3.2	3.6
65+	9.5	8.4	10.7
70–74	2.5	2.3	2.7
70+	6.1	5.2	7.0
75–79	1.6	1.4	1.9
75+	3.6	2.9	4.3
80+	2.0	1.4	2.5
World/2030			
Total, all ages	**100.0**	**100.0**	**100.0**
65–69	4.0	3.8	4.2
65+	12.0	10.6	13.4
70–74	3.1	2.8	3.4
70+	8.0	6.8	9.2
75–79	2.3	2.0	2.6
75+	4.9	3.9	5.8
80+	2.6	1.9	3.2
World/2040			
Total, all ages	**100.0**	**100.0**	**100.0**
65–69	4.4	4.3	4.6
65+	14.7	13.1	16.4
70–74	3.8	3.6	4.0
70+	10.3	8.8	11.8
75–79	2.9	2.5	3.2
75+	6.5	5.3	7.7
80+	3.7	2.8	4.5
World/2050			
Total, all ages	**100.0**	**100.0**	**100.0**
65–69	4.6	4.5	4.7
65+	16.7	14.9	18.5
70–74	3.9	3.7	4.1
70+	12.1	10.4	13.7
75–79	3.3	3.0	3.6
75+	8.2	6.7	9.7
80+	4.9	3.8	6.1

SOURCE: "Table 094. Midyear Population, by Age and Sex," in *International Data Base (IDB)*, U.S. Census Bureau, Population Division, December 2008, http://www.census.gov/ipc/www/idb/tables.html (accessed April 15, 2009)

over time. To anticipate the needs of this growing segment of society, policy makers, planners, and researchers rely on projections and population estimates. Population estimates and projections are made at different times and are based on different assumptions. As a result, it is not surprising to find considerable variation in the statistics cited by different agencies and investigators. This chapter contains estimates and projections of demographic changes from several different sources, and as a result there is some variability in the data presented.

HOW DO POPULATIONS AGE?

Unlike people, populations can age or become younger. There are key indicators of the age structure of a given population. Populations age or grow younger because of changes in fertility (birth rates expressed as the number of births per 1,000 population per year) and/or mortality (death rates expressed as the number of deaths per 1,000 population per year) or in response to migration—people entering or leaving the population.

FIGURE 1.3

Growth of older population and total population by region, 2002–25

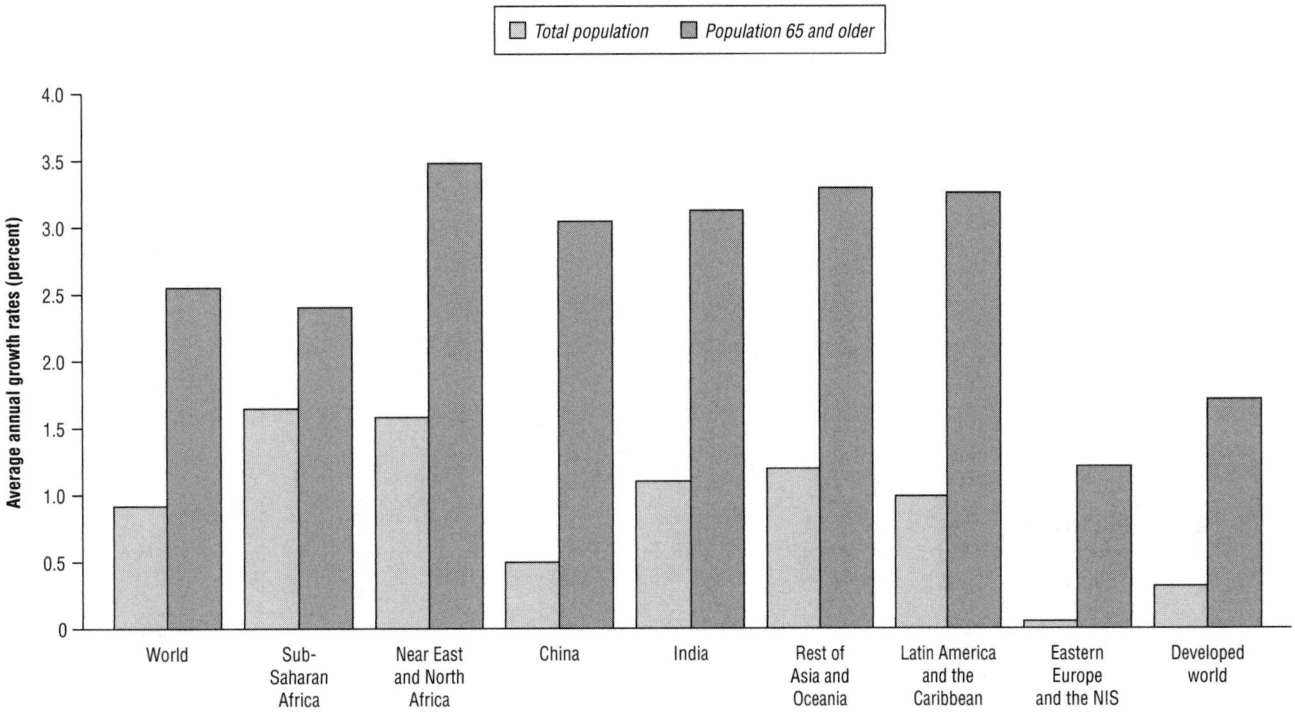

SOURCE: "Figure 38. Change in the Elderly Population and Total Population by Region: 2002–2025," in *Global Population Profile: 2002*, U.S. Census Bureau, Population Division, 2002, http://www.census.gov/ipc/prod/wp02/wp-02004.pdf (accessed April 15, 2009)

The aging of the United States resulted from changes in fertility and mortality that occurred over the past century. Such shifts in birth and death rates are called demographic transitions. Generally, population aging is primarily a response to long-term declines in fertility, and declining fertility is the basic cause of the aging of the U.S. population. Reduced infant and child mortality, chiefly as a result of public health measures, fueled the decline in the fertility rate; that is, the increased survival of children prompted families to have fewer offspring. The birth of fewer babies resulted in fewer young people.

According to the Central Intelligence Agency (CIA), in *The World Factbook: United States* (April 30, 2009, https://www.cia.gov/library/publications/the-world-factbook/geos/US.html), in 2009 the total fertility rate in the United States was two children born per woman. This rate, which has not changed significantly since the mid-1980s, is sharply lower than the fertility rates between 1946 and 1964, following the end of World War II (1939–1945). Victorious U.S. soldiers returning home after the war were eager to start families, and this was facilitated by the relatively prosperous postwar economy.

Census Bureau statistics indicate that during this period, which came to be known as the baby boom, U.S. fertility rates exploded, at one point approaching four children born per woman. Children born during the baby boom became known as baby boomers, and it is this huge cohort (a group of individuals that shares a common characteristic such as birth years and is studied over time) that is responsible for the tremendous increase projected in the number of people aged 65 and older, and especially aged 65 to 74, after 2010. The older adult segment of the population is expected to swell between 2010 and 2030 as the baby boom cohort completes its transition from middle age to old age.

The decline in death rates, especially at the older ages, has also contributed to the increase in the number of older adults. The death rates of older adults began to decrease during the late 1960s and continued to decline through the first decade of the 21st century. Advances in medical care have produced declining death rates for all three of the leading causes of death: heart disease, malignancies (cancer), and cerebrovascular diseases that cause strokes. The Centers for Disease Control and Prevention (CDC) reveals in the press release "U.S. Mortality Drops Sharply in 2006, Latest Data Show, National Center for Health Statistics" (June 2008, http://www.cdc.gov/nchs/pressroom/08newsreleases/mortality2006.htm) that the age-adjusted death rate in the United States reached an all-time low in 2006 of

FIGURE 1.4

Number of people aged 65 and over, by age group, selected years 1900–2006 and projected 2010–50

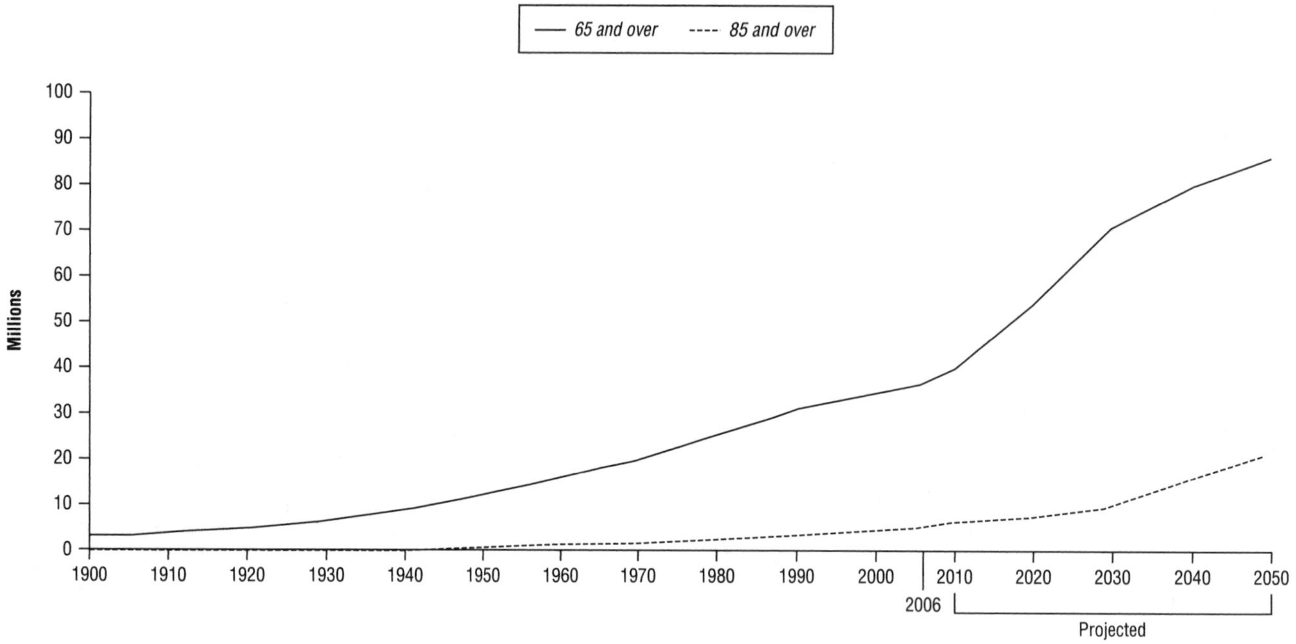

Note: Data for 2010–2050 are projections of the population.
Reference population: These data refer to the resident population.

SOURCE: "Number of People Age 65 and Over, by Age Group, Selected Years 1900–2006 and Projected 2010–2050," in *Older Americans 2008: Key Indicators of Well-Being*, Federal Interagency Forum on Aging-Related Statistics, March 2008, http://www.agingstats.gov/agingstatsdotnet/Main_Site/Data/2008_Documents/OA_2008.pdf (accessed April 15, 2009)

776.4 deaths per 100,000 population, down from 799 deaths per 100,000 in 2005.

Projections of an increasing proportion of older adults from 2010 to 2030 are based on three assumptions: historic low fertility and the prospect of continuing low fertility until 2030, aging of the baby boom cohort, and continued declines in mortality at older ages and low mortality until 2030. Demographers (those who study population statistics) expect that when the entire baby boom generation has attained age 65 in 2030, the proportion of older people in the U.S. population will stabilize. (See Figure 1.2.)

DEFINING OLD AGE

Forty is the old age of youth; fifty the youth of old age.

—Victor Hugo

When does old age begin? The challenge of defining old age is reflected in the terminology used to describe adults aged 50 and older: for example, middle aged, elder, elderly, older, aged, mature, or senior. The AARP (formerly the American Association of Retired Persons), a national advocacy organization for older adults, invites people to join its ranks at age 50. Many retailers offer senior discounts to people aged 50 or 55 and older, and federal entitlement programs such as Social Security (a program that provides retirement income and health care for older adults) and Medicare (a medical insurance program for older adults and people with disabilities) extend benefits to people at age 62, 65, or 67. Despite the varying definitions of old age and the age at which one assumes "older adult" status, in this text, unless otherwise specified, the term *older adults* is used to refer to people aged 65 and older.

Gerontology (the field of study that considers the social, psychological, and biological aspects of aging) distinguishes among three groups of older adults: the young-old are considered to be those aged 65 to 74, the middle-old includes those aged 75 to 84, and the oldest-old are those aged 85 and older. Figure 1.4 shows that the oldest segment of older adults, the oldest-old, grew from just over 100,000 in 1900 to 5.3 million in 2006 and is projected to steadily increase between 2010 and 2050.

LIFE EXPECTANCY

In *Health, United States, 2008* (2009, http://www.cdc.gov/nchs/data/hus/hus08.pdf), the National Center for Health Statistics indicates that life expectancy (the anticipated average length of life) has increased dramatically since 1900, when the average age of death for men and women combined was 47.3 years. Most projections see life expectancy continuing to rise; according to the CIA, in *World Factbook*, the life expectancy of a baby born in the United States in 2009 was 75.7 years for males and 80.7 years for females.

However, some researchers caution that the historic trend of increasing longevity has ended, with life expectancy at birth beginning to decline by as much as five years as a direct result of the obesity epidemic in the United States. Nancy E. Adler and Judith Stewart of the University of California, San Francisco, suggest in "Reducing Obesity: Motivating Action While Not Blaming the Victim" (*Milbank Quarterly*, March 2009) that the rise in obesity in the United States may slow or even reverse the long-term trend of increasing life expectancy.

Adler and Stewart base their projections on an analysis of body mass index (a number that shows body weight adjusted for height) and other factors that could potentially affect the health and well-being of the current generation of children and young adults, and they observe that obesity currently reduces life expectancy at age 18 by 7.2 years for obese women and 4.4 years for obese men. The researchers assert that unless individual and society-wide actions taken to address the obesity epidemic are effective, younger Americans will likely face a greater risk of mortality throughout life than previous generations.

Global Life Expectancy

The more developed regions of the world have lower death rates than the less developed regions and, as such, have higher life expectancies. In *World Factbook*, the CIA observes that some nations more than doubled their life expectancy during the 20th century. In 2009 the projected life expectancy at birth in Macau was 84.4 years, and it was at least 79 years in many developed countries. (See Table 1.2.) Many less developed countries have also seen a steady increase in life expectancy, except for countries in Africa that have been hard hit by the human immunodeficiency virus–acquired immunodeficiency syndrome (HIV/AIDS) epidemic. Table 1.2 shows ranks of the top 50 countries in terms of life expectancy in 2009.

Even though the United Nations' Department of Economic and Social Affairs predicts in *World Population Prospects: The 2008 Revision* (2009, http://www.un.org/esa/population/publications/wpp2008/wpp2008_highlights.pdf) that the gap in life expectancy will narrow during the first half of the 21st century, the developed world will still be far ahead. From 2045 to 2050 the more developed regions will have a life expectancy of 83 years, compared with 74 years for the less developed regions. Table 1.3 shows the ranks of the 25 countries with the lowest estimates of life expectancy in 2009. Swaziland and Angola had the lowest life expectancy at 31.9 and 38.2 years, respectively.

TABLE 1.2

Estimated life expectancy at birth by country, 2009

Rank	Country	Life expectancy at birth (years)
1	Macau	84.36
2	Andorra	82.51
3	Japan	82.12
4	Singapore	81.98
5	San Marino	81.97
6	Hong Kong	81.86
7	Australia	81.63
8	Canada	81.23
9	France	80.98
10	Sweden	80.86
11	Switzerland	80.85
12	Guernsey	80.77
13	Israel	80.73
14	Iceland	80.67
15	Anguilla	80.65
16	Cayman Islands	80.44
17	Bermuda	80.43
18	New Zealand	80.36
19	Italy	80.20
20	Gibraltar	80.19
21	Monaco	80.09
22	Liechtenstein	80.06
23	Spain	80.05
24	Norway	79.95
25	Jersey	79.75
26	Greece	79.66
27	Austria	79.50
28	Faroe Islands	79.44
29	Malta	79.44
30	Netherlands	79.40
31	Luxembourg	79.33
32	Germany	79.26
33	Belgium	79.22
34	Saint Pierre and Miquelon	79.07
35	Virgin Islands	79.05
36	United Kingdom	79.01
37	Finland	78.97
38	Jordan	78.87
39	Isle of Man	78.82
40	Korea, South	78.72
41	European Union	78.67
42	Puerto Rico	78.53
43	Bosnia and Herzegovina	78.50
44	Saint Helena	78.44
45	Cyprus	78.33
46	Denmark	78.30
47	Ireland	78.24
48	Portugal	78.21
49	Wallis and Futuna	78.20
50	United States	78.11

SOURCE: Adapted from "Country Comparison: Life Expectancy at Birth," in *The World Factbook*, Central Intelligence Agency, April 2009, https://www.cia.gov/library/publications/the-world-factbook/rankorder/2102rank.html (accessed April 15, 2009)

OLDER ADULTS IN THE UNITED STATES

According to U.S. census estimates, in 2010 there will be an estimated 40.2 million people aged 65 and older living in the United States. (See Table 1.4.) The young-old bracket (aged 65 to 74) will account for 53% (21.5 million) of the 65 and older population. Thirty-two percent (13 million) of the older adult population will be in the middle-old bracket (aged 75 to 84), and 14% (5.8 million) will make up the oldest-old (aged 85 and older).

TABLE 1.3

Countries with lowest estimated life expectancy at birth, 2009

Rank	Country	Life expectancy at birth (years)
200	Burkina Faso	52.95
201	Uganda	52.72
202	Niger	52.60
203	Burundi	52.09
204	Tanzania	52.01
205	Sudan	51.42
206	Namibia	51.24
207	Rwanda	50.52
208	Mali	50.35
209	Somalia	49.63
210	South Africa	48.98
211	Guinea-Bissau	47.90
212	Chad	47.70
213	Nigeria	46.94
214	Zimbabwe	45.77
215	Afghanistan	44.64
216	Central African Republic	44.47
217	Malawi	43.82
218	Djibouti	43.37
219	Liberia	41.84
220	Sierra Leone	41.24
221	Mozambique	41.18
222	Lesotho	40.38
223	Zambia	38.63
224	Angola	38.20
225	Swaziland	31.88

SOURCE: Adapted from "Country Comparison: Life Expectancy at Birth," in *The World Factbook*, Central Intelligence Agency, April 2009, https://www.cia.gov/library/publications/the-world-factbook/rankorder/2102rank.html (accessed April 15, 2009)

By 2015 the number of young-old is projected to rise to 26.2 million, the middle-old will be nearing 13.6 million, and the oldest-old will be 6.3 million. (See Table 1.4.) Older women are expected to outnumber men in all three age brackets. Greenberg indicates that in 2007 the female-to-male sex ratio increased with advancing age, from about 114 for the young-old to 210 for the oldest-old. Longer female life expectancy, combined with the fact that men often marry younger women, contributes to a higher proportion of older women living alone—widowed or unmarried.

The Oldest-Old

Greenberg states that in 2006 adults who reached "age 65 had an average life expectancy of an additional 19.0 years (20.3 years for females and 17.4 years for males)." The 85 and older population will grow from 4.2 million in 2000 to an estimated 5.7 million in 2010, an increase of 36%, and this population is expected to increase by 15% to 6.6 million in 2020.

In *Older Americans 2008*, the Federal Interagency Forum on Aging-Related Statistics notes that some researchers believe death rates at older ages will decline more rapidly than is reflected in Census Bureau projections, which will result in even faster growth of this population segment. The Census Bureau reports that among the oldest-old, women dramatically outnumber men—in 2010 there will be more than two times as many women aged 85 and older than men. (See Table 1.4.) Because it is anticipated that women will continue to live longer into the middle of the 21st century, they will make up an even larger proportion of the older population and the overall U.S. population in the future.

THE WORLD'S 80-PLUS POPULATION. According to the Census Bureau, in the press release "Older Americans Month Celebrated in May" (April 25, 2003, http://www.census.gov/Press-Release/www/releases/archives/facts_for_features_special_editions/001626.html), in 2003 the United States was second only to China in terms of the number of people aged 80 and older. The United States contained just 5% of the world's population but 13% of the U.S. population was aged 80 and older. Furthermore, people aged 85 and older made up the fastest-growing population segment in the world. In the United States the 85 and older population grew from just over 100,000 in 1900 to an estimated 5.8 million in 2010. (See Table 1.4.)

Centenarians

During the first half of the 21st century the United States will experience a centenarian boom. Living to age 100 and older is no longer a rarity. The chances of living to age 100 have increased by 40% since 1900. The centenarian population more than doubled during the 1980s, and the Census Bureau estimates in "Older Americans Month: May 2009" that in November 2008 the country had 96,548 centenarians. By 2050 the number of centenarians will increase more than sixfold to 172,000. (See Table 1.4.) The National Centenarian Awareness Project (NCAP; June 2009, http://www.adlercentenarians.org/), a nonprofit advocacy organization for older adults, observes that the number of centenarians is growing steadily and is "predicted to more than quadruple by 2030, reaching 1.15 million by 2050." The NCAP also asserts that "at least one out of three women age 50 today will reach 90" and that "high school students of today have a good chance of reaching the century mark."

As the numbers and percentages of all older adults increase, the shape of the U.S. population pyramid (also called the age-sex pyramid and the age structure diagram), which graphically displays the projected population by age, will change. Figure 1.5 shows the projected population distribution in 2025; Figure 1.6 and Figure 1.7 contain comparable data for 2050 and 2100, respectively.

Racial and Ethnic Diversity

The older population is becoming more ethnically and racially diverse, although at a slower pace than the overall population of the United States. In 2006 the older population was made up by approximately 81% of non-Hispanic whites, 9% of African-Americans, 6% of Hispanics, and 3% of Asian-Americans. (See Figure 1.8.) By 2050 the

TABLE 1.4

Projections of the population by age and sex, 2010–50

[Resident population as of July 1. Numbers in thousands]

Sex and age	2010	2015	2020	2025	2030	2035	2040	2045	2050
Both sexes	**310,233**	**325,540**	**341,387**	**357,452**	**373,504**	**389,531**	**405,655**	**422,059**	**439,010**
Under 5 years	21,100	22,076	22,846	23,484	24,161	25,056	26,117	27,171	28,148
5 to 9 years	20,886	21,707	22,732	23,548	24,232	24,953	25,893	26,998	28,096
10 to 14 years	20,395	21,658	22,571	23,677	24,567	25,319	26,105	27,108	28,274
15 to 19 years	21,770	21,209	22,554	23,545	24,723	25,682	26,501	27,354	28,422
20 to 24 years	21,779	22,342	21,799	23,168	24,191	25,408	26,408	27,272	28,171
25 to 29 years	21,418	22,400	22,949	22,417	23,804	24,855	26,102	27,138	28,039
30 to 34 years	20,400	22,099	23,112	23,699	23,216	24,647	25,745	27,040	28,126
35 to 39 years	20,267	20,841	22,586	23,645	24,279	23,848	25,321	26,462	27,799
40 to 44 years	21,010	20,460	21,078	22,851	23,944	24,612	24,224	25,726	26,897
45 to 49 years	22,596	21,001	20,502	21,154	22,943	24,061	24,759	24,411	25,933
50 to 54 years	22,109	22,367	20,852	20,404	21,087	22,884	24,025	24,750	24,445
55 to 59 years	19,517	21,682	21,994	20,575	20,186	20,903	22,703	23,867	24,621
60 to 64 years	16,758	18,861	21,009	21,377	20,080	19,760	20,513	22,305	23,490
65 to 69 years	12,261	15,812	17,861	19,957	20,381	19,230	18,989	19,776	21,543
70 to 74 years	9,202	11,155	14,452	16,399	18,404	18,879	17,906	17,754	18,570
75 to 79 years	7,282	7,901	9,656	12,598	14,390	16,249	16,771	16,016	15,964
80 to 84 years	5,733	5,676	6,239	7,715	10,173	11,735	13,375	13,925	13,429
85 to 89 years	3,650	3,786	3,817	4,278	5,383	7,215	8,450	9,767	10,303
90 to 94 years	1,570	1,856	1,976	2,047	2,360	3,044	4,180	5,007	5,909
95 to 99 years	452	546	669	739	795	952	1,270	1,803	2,229
100 years and over	79	105	135	175	208	239	298	409	601
Median age (years)	36.9	37.1	37.7	38.2	38.7	39.0	38.9	38.9	39.0
Male	**152,753**	**160,424**	**168,258**	**176,102**	**183,870**	**191,609**	**199,434**	**207,465**	**215,825**
Under 5 years	10,779	11,278	11,671	11,996	12,341	12,797	13,338	13,876	14,374
5 to 9 years	10,654	11,074	11,596	12,011	12,358	12,724	13,202	13,764	14,322
10 to 14 years	10,421	11,049	11,514	12,076	12,527	12,906	13,304	13,811	14,403
15 to 19 years	11,159	10,844	11,513	12,016	12,612	13,095	13,506	13,934	14,472
20 to 24 years	11,100	11,378	11,072	11,749	12,266	12,878	13,379	13,810	14,259
25 to 29 years	10,873	11,353	11,624	11,321	12,004	12,531	13,154	13,669	14,115
30 to 34 years	10,308	11,182	11,674	11,962	11,682	12,384	12,930	13,574	14,110
35 to 39 years	10,191	10,506	11,399	11,913	12,223	11,969	12,689	13,255	13,918
40 to 44 years	10,509	10,247	10,581	11,486	12,014	12,340	12,107	12,840	13,420
45 to 49 years	11,165	10,447	10,210	10,560	11,469	12,009	12,348	12,136	12,878
50 to 54 years	10,827	10,977	10,302	10,091	10,456	11,364	11,915	12,267	12,079
55 to 59 years	9,450	10,524	10,700	10,078	9,898	10,278	11,184	11,745	12,111
60 to 64 years	8,024	9,023	10,079	10,283	9,727	9,584	9,981	10,878	11,448
65 to 69 years	5,747	7,449	8,412	9,434	9,665	9,189	9,090	9,502	10,380
70 to 74 years	4,191	5,109	6,660	7,564	8,529	8,787	8,406	8,356	8,782
75 to 79 years	3,159	3,480	4,285	5,635	6,452	7,331	7,610	7,341	7,345
80 to 84 years	2,302	2,342	2,622	3,275	4,363	5,056	5,810	6,096	5,952
85 to 89 years	1,297	1,409	1,466	1,681	2,144	2,913	3,437	4,017	4,282
90 to 94 years	473	591	663	713	844	1,110	1,551	1,879	2,251
95 to 99 years	108	142	186	218	244	302	413	599	753
100 years and over	15	21	29	40	51	62	81	114	172
Median age (years)	35.5	35.9	36.5	37.0	37.5	37.7	37.7	37.7	37.8
Female	**157,479**	**165,116**	**173,128**	**181,349**	**189,634**	**197,922**	**206,221**	**214,594**	**223,185**
Under 5 years	10,320	10,798	11,175	11,488	11,820	12,259	12,779	13,296	13,775
5 to 9 years	10,232	10,633	11,136	11,537	11,874	12,229	12,691	13,234	13,773
10 to 14 years	9,975	10,609	11,057	11,601	12,040	12,412	12,802	13,297	13,872
15 to 19 years	10,611	10,365	11,041	11,529	12,112	12,587	12,995	13,420	13,950
20 to 24 years	10,680	10,963	10,728	11,419	11,926	12,530	13,029	13,462	13,913
25 to 29 years	10,545	11,048	11,325	11,096	11,800	12,324	12,948	13,469	13,925
30 to 34 years	10,092	10,917	11,438	11,737	11,534	12,263	12,814	13,466	14,015
35 to 39 years	10,076	10,335	11,186	11,732	12,056	11,879	12,632	13,206	13,881
40 to 44 years	10,500	10,214	10,497	11,365	11,929	12,272	12,117	12,886	13,477
45 to 49 years	11,430	10,553	10,292	10,594	11,474	12,052	12,411	12,275	13,056
50 to 54 years	11,282	11,390	10,550	10,313	10,632	11,520	12,111	12,483	12,366
55 to 59 years	10,067	11,158	11,293	10,497	10,288	10,625	11,519	12,122	12,509
60 to 64 years	8,733	9,838	10,929	11,094	10,353	10,176	10,532	11,428	12,043
65 to 69 years	6,514	8,364	9,449	10,524	10,715	10,041	9,899	10,273	11,163

composition of the older population is projected to be more racially and ethnically diverse, with 61% being non-Hispanic white, 18% being Hispanic, 12% being African-American, and 8% being Asian-American. Even though the older population will increase among African-Americans, Asian-Americans, and Hispanics, the older Hispanic population will grow the most dramatically, from 6.4% in 2006 to 17.5% in 2050. (See Table 1.5.) During this same period non-Hispanic whites will decline from 80.8% to 61.3%.

TABLE 1.4

Projections of the population by age and sex, 2010–50 [CONTINUED]

[Resident population as of July 1. Numbers in thousands]

Sex and age	2010	2015	2020	2025	2030	2035	2040	2045	2050
70 to 74 years	5,011	6,046	7,791	8,835	9,875	10,092	9,500	9,398	9,788
75 to 79 years	4,123	4,421	5,371	6,962	7,937	8,918	9,161	8,674	8,619
80 to 84 years	3,431	3,334	3,618	4,440	5,810	6,679	7,565	7,830	7,477
85 to 89 years	2,353	2,376	2,351	2,598	3,239	4,302	5,013	5,750	6,021
90 to 94 years	1,097	1,265	1,312	1,334	1,515	1,934	2,629	3,128	3,657
95 to 99 years	344	404	484	521	551	650	857	1,203	1,476
100 years and over	65	84	106	134	156	177	217	295	429
Median age (years)	38.2	38.4	38.9	39.4	39.9	40.2	40.2	40.2	40.2

SOURCE: "Projections of the Population by Age and Sex for the United States: 2010 to 2050," in *2008 National Population Projections*, U.S. Census Bureau, Population Division, August 2008, http://www.census.gov/population/www/projections/summarytables.html (accessed April 15, 2009)

FIGURE 1.5

Projected U.S. population in 2025

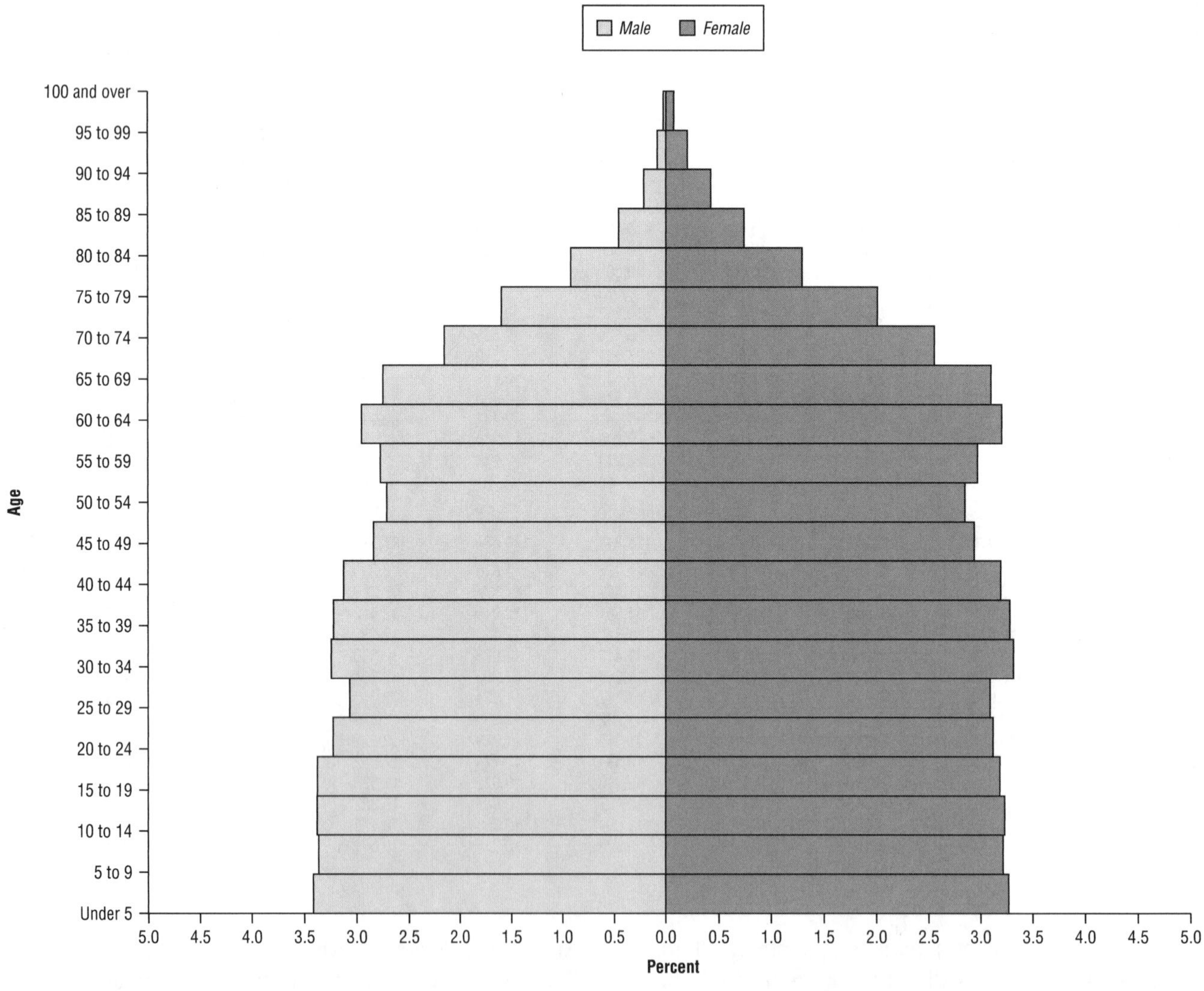

SOURCE: "(NP-P3) Projected Resident Population of the United States as of July 1, 2025, Middle Series," in *National Population Projections III. Population Pyramids: Total Resident Population of the United States by Sex, Middle Series*, U.S. Census Bureau, Population Division, Population Projections Branch, August 2002, http://www.census.gov/population/www/projections/np_p3.pdf (accessed April 1, 2009)

FIGURE 1.6

Projected U.S. population in 2050

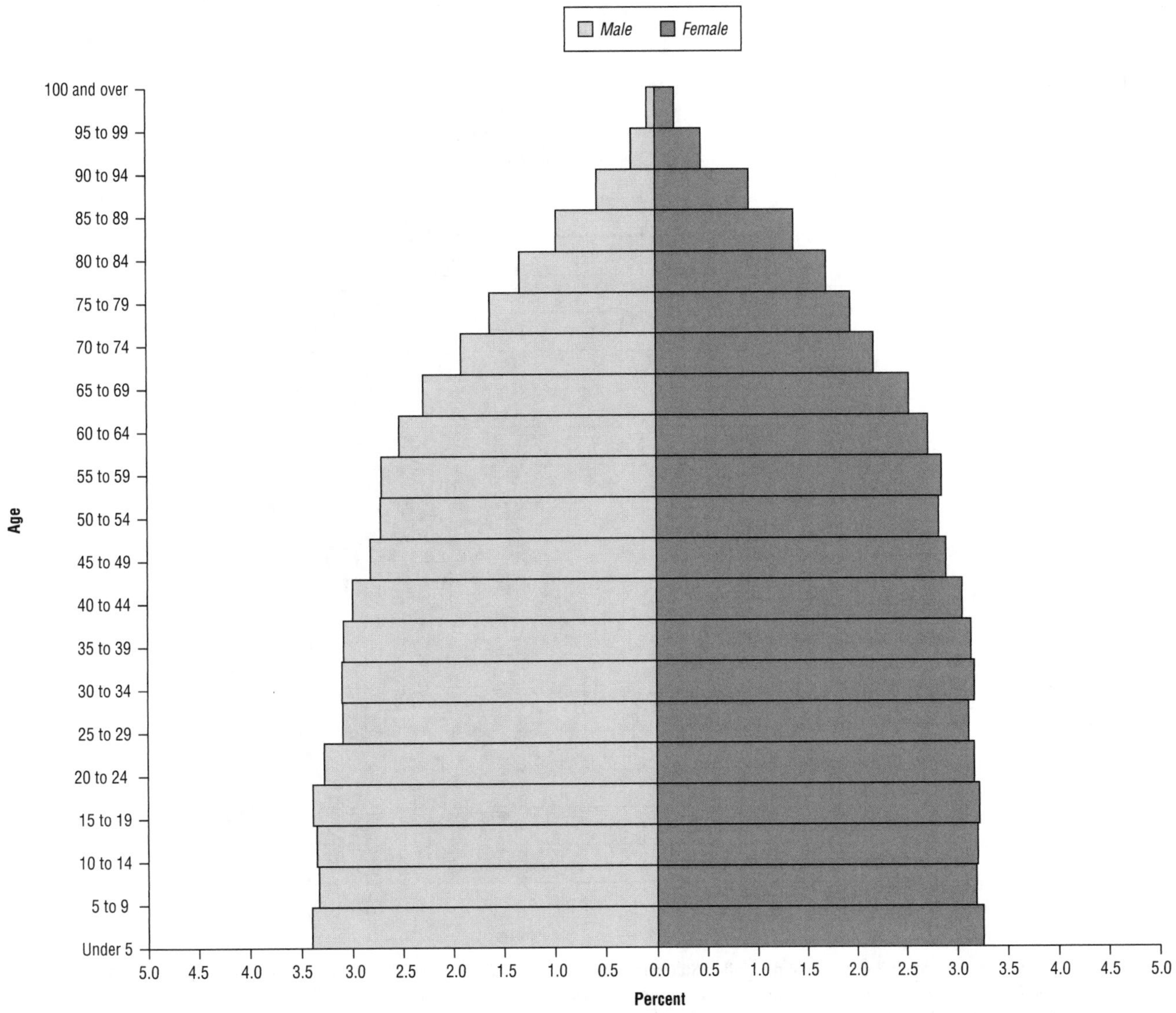

SOURCE: "(NP-P4) Projected Resident Population of the United States as of July 1, 2050, Middle Series," in *National Population Projections III. Population Pyramids: Total Resident Population of the United States by Sex, Middle Series*, U.S. Census Bureau, Population Division, Population Projections Branch, August 2002, http://www.census.gov/population/www/projections/np_p4.pdf (accessed April 15, 2009)

Marital Status

As in previous years, in 2007 older men were much more likely than women to be married. More than three-quarters (78%) of men aged 64 to 75 were married, compared with 57% of women in the same age group. (See Figure 1.9.) The proportion married decreases with advancing age. In 2007, 38% of women aged 75 to 84 and 15% of women aged 85 and older were married. Among men the proportion that were married decreased with advancing age but not as sharply. Even among the oldest-old, most men (60%) were married.

As older women outnumber older men in all age groups, it is not surprising that there are more widows than widowers. In 2007 more than three times as many women as men aged 65 to 74 were widowed—26% of women, compared with 8% of men. (See Figure 1.9.) Even though the gap narrows in the older age groups, there were still more than twice as many women as men aged 85 and older who were widowed—76% of women as opposed to 34% of men. A fairly small proportion of older adults were divorced, whereas an even smaller proportion had never married.

Foreign-Born Older Adults

The Census Bureau reports that in 2007 the nation's foreign-born population numbered 37.3 million, accounting for 12% of the population. (See Table 1.6.) Of this

FIGURE 1.7

Projected U.S. population in 2100

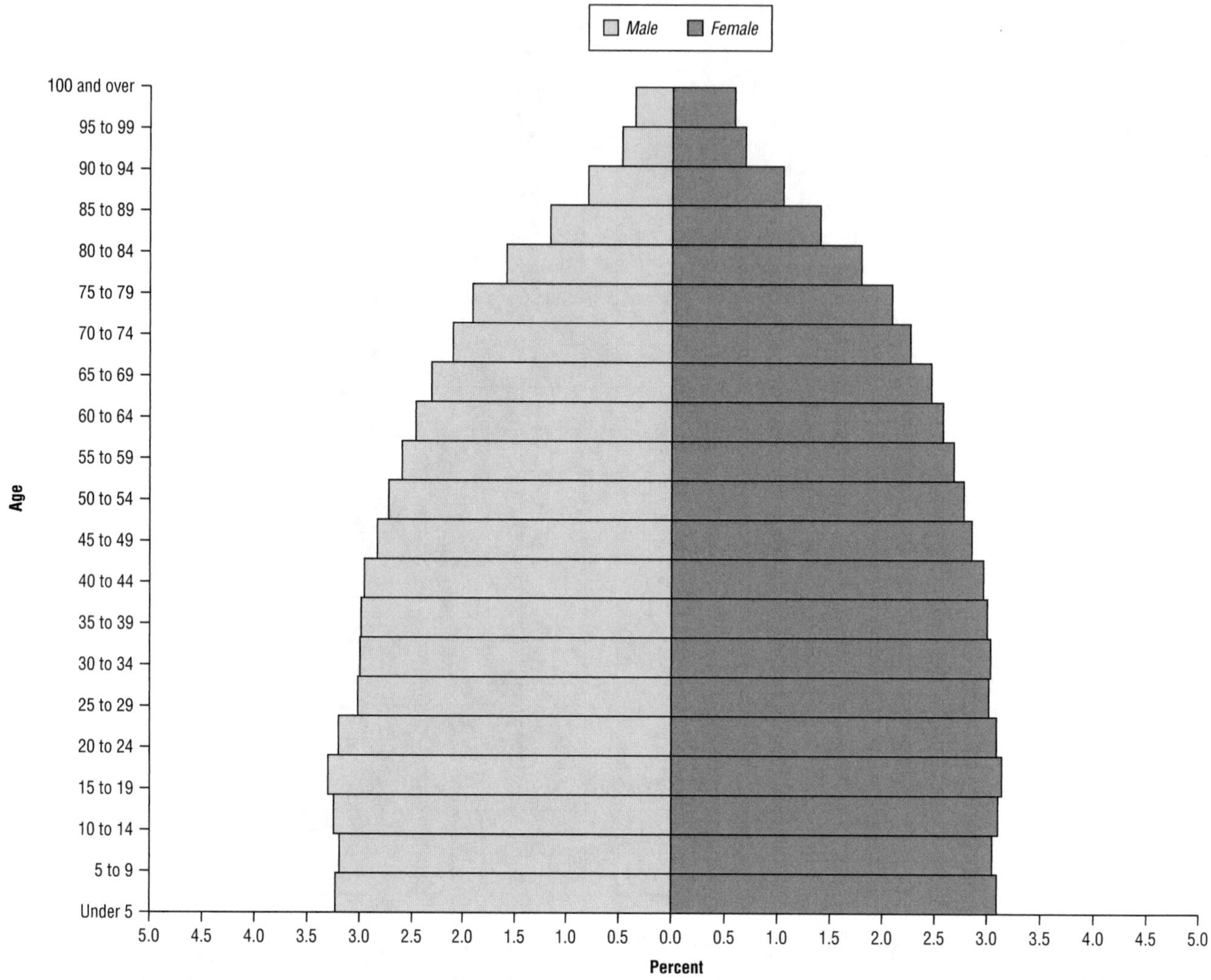

SOURCE: "(NP-P5) Projected Resident Population of the United States as of July 1, 2100, Middle Series," in *National Population Projections III. Population Pyramids: Total Resident Population of the United States by Sex, Middle Series*, U.S. Census Bureau, Population Division, Population Projections Branch, August 2002, http://www.census.gov/population/www/projections/np_p5.pdf (accessed April 15, 2009)

foreign-born population, 4 million were older adults: 1.4 million came from Latin America, 1.2 million from Europe, and 1.1 million from Asia.

WHERE OLDER AMERICANS LIVE

Greenberg reports that in 2007, adults aged 65 and older accounted for 14% or more of the population in 10 states. The proportion of the population aged 65 and older varied by state. In Florida the older adult population was 18.5%, followed by Pennsylvania and Rhode Island with 15.8% each, West Virginia with 15.1%, Iowa with 15%, Connecticut and North Dakota with 14.4% each, Arkansas and South Dakota with 14.3% each, and Massachusetts with 14.1%. (See Figure 1.10.) In 10 states—Alaska (49.6%), Nevada (48.3%), Arizona (36.2%), Utah (30.0%), New Mexico (29.7%), Idaho (27.8%), Georgia (27.7%), South Carolina (26.3%), Colorado (25.2%), and Delaware (24.7%)—the 65 and older population grew by 20% or more between 1997 and 2007. (See Figure 1.11.)

In 2010, 17.8% of Florida's population will be older adults, and by 2030 that percentage is projected to rise to 27.1%. Five other states in which the older population is predicted to exceed 25% by 2030 are Maine and Wyoming (26.5% each), New Mexico (26.4%), Montana (25.8%), and North Dakota (25.1%). (See Table 1.7.) In 2030 the states in which older adults will constitute the lowest percentage of the population are Utah (13.2%), Alaska (14.7%), Texas (15.6%), and Georgia (15.9%).

FIGURE 1.8

Population aged 65 and over, by race and Hispanic origin, 2006 and projected 2050

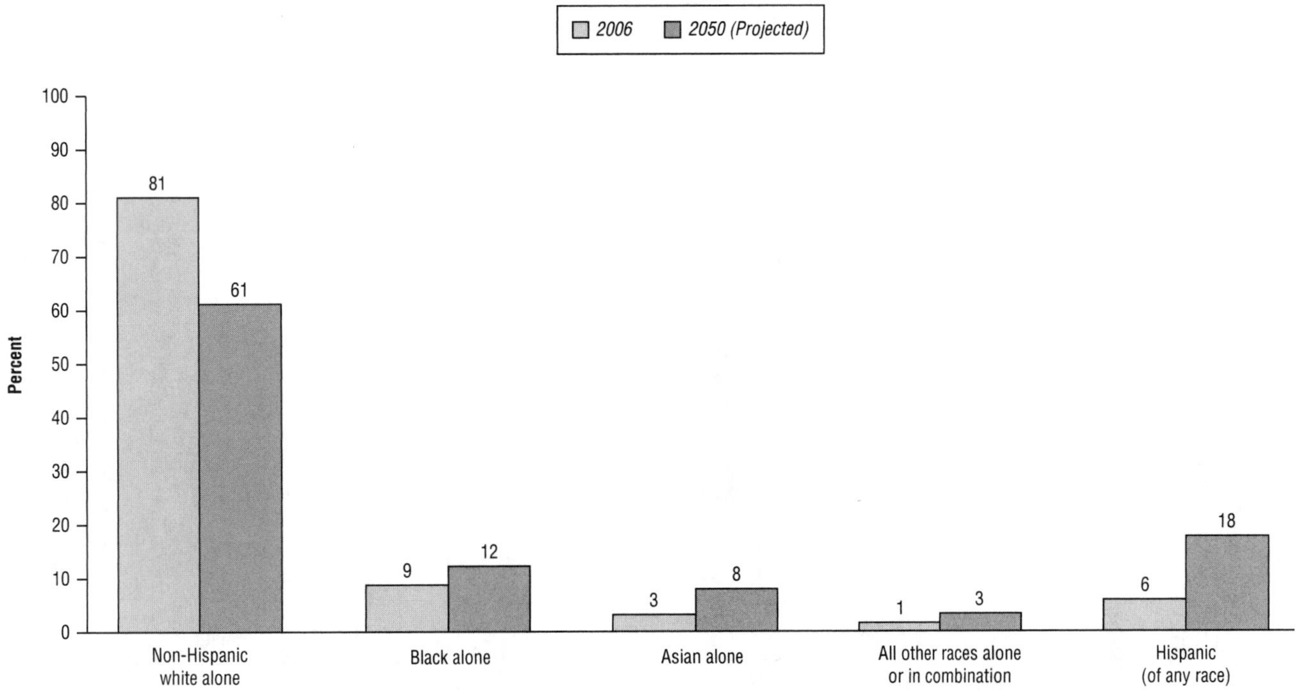

Note: The term "non-Hispanic white alone" is used to refer to people who reported being white and no other race and who are not Hispanic. The term "black alone" is used to refer to people who reported being black or African American and no other race, and the term "Asian alone" is used to refer to people who reported only Asian as their race. The use of single-race population in this report does not imply that this is the preferred method of presenting or analyzing data. The U.S. Census Bureau uses a variety of approaches. The race group "All other races alone or in combination" includes American Indian and Alaska Native, alone; Native Hawaiian and Other Pacific Islander, alone; and all people who reported two or more races.
Reference population: These data refer to the resident population.

SOURCE: "Population Age 65 and over, by Race and Hispanic Origin, 2006 and Projected 2050," in *Older Americans 2008: Key Indicators of Well-Being*, Federal Interagency Forum on Aging-Related Statistics, March 2008, http://www.agingstats.gov/agingstatsdotnet/Main_Site/Data/2008_Documents/OA_2008.pdf (accessed April 20, 2009)

TABLE 1.5

Population aged 65 and over, by race and Hispanic origin, 2006 and projected 2050

	2006 estimates		2050 projections	
Race and Hispanic origin	**Number**	**Percent**	**Number**	**Percent**
Total older population	**37,260,352**	**100.0**	**86,705,637**	**100.0**
Non-Hispanic white alone	30,187,588	80.8	53,159,961	61.3
Black alone	3,167,986	8.4	10,401,575	12.0
Asian alone	1,176,599	3.2	6,776,033	7.8
All other races alone or in combination	413,355	1.1	2,328,390	2.7
Hispanic (of any race)	2,399,320	6.4	15,178,025	17.5

Note: The term "non-Hispanic white alone" is used to refer to people who reported being white and no other race and who are not Hispanic. The term "black alone" is used to refer to people who reported being black or African American and no other race, and the term "Asian alone" is used to refer to people who reported only Asian as their race. The use of single-race populations in this report does not imply that this is the preferred method of presenting or analyzing data. The U.S. Census Bureau uses a variety of approaches. The race group "All other races alone or in combination" includes American Indian and Alaska Native, alone; Native Hawaiian and Other Pacific Islander, alone; and all people who reported two or more races.
Reference population: These data refer to the resident population.

SOURCE: "Table 2. Population Age 65 and over, by Race and Hispanic Origin, 2006 and Projected 2050," in *Older Americans 2008: Key Indicators of Well-Being*, Federal Interagency Forum on Aging-Related Statistics, March 2008, http://www.agingstats.gov/agingstatsdotnet/ Main_Site/Data/2008_Documents/OA_2008. pdf (accessed April 20, 2009)

Greenberg indicates that in 2007, 80.5% of older adults lived in metropolitan areas. Nearly two-thirds (63.3%) of these lived outside of cities and more than one-third (36.7%) were city dwellers. Almost 20% of older adults lived in nonmetropolitan areas. Greenberg also observes that older adults relocate less often than any other

FIGURE 1.9

Marital status of persons aged 65 and older, by age group and sex, 2007

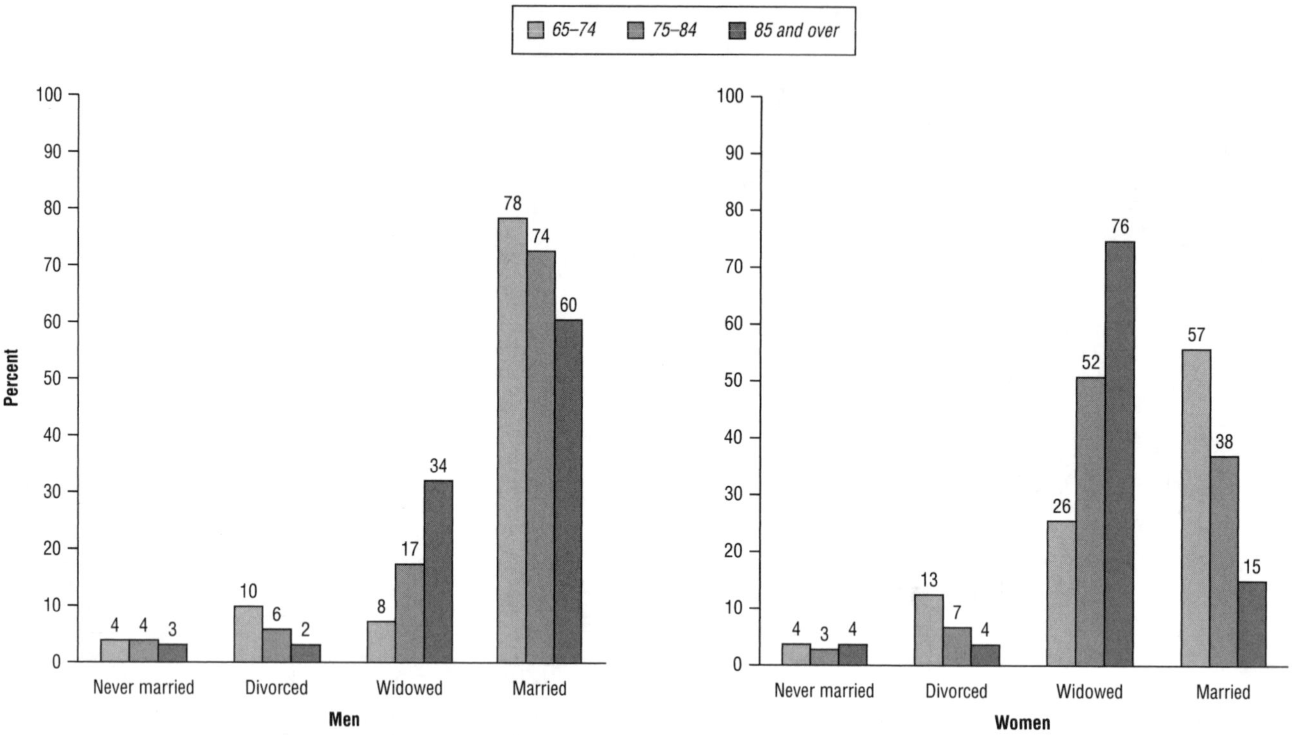

Note: Married includes married, spouse present; married, spouse absent; and separated.
Reference population: These data refer to the civilian noninstitutionalized population.

SOURCE: "Marital Status of the Population Age 65 and over, by Age Group and Sex, 2007," in *Older Americans 2008: Key Indicators of Well-Being*, Federal Interagency Forum on Aging-Related Statistics, March 2008, http://www.agingstats.gov/agingstatsdotnet/Main_Site/Data/2008_Documents/OA_2008.pdf (accessed April 20, 2009)

age group. Of the scant 4.2% of older adults who changed residence from 2006 to 2007, just 21.1% moved out of state; the majority (78.9%) remained in the same state and more than half (57.9%) stayed in the same county.

Older Americans Are More Religious

In "The Social Connectedness of Older Adults: A National Profile" (*American Sociological Review*, vol. 73, April 2008), Benjamin Cornwell, Edward O. Laumann, and L. Philip Schumm of the University of Chicago report the results of an analysis of data from the National Social Life, Health, and Aging Project, a population-based study of noninstitutionalized older Americans aged 57 to 85 that was conducted between 2005 and 2006. One of their findings is that age was positively related to religious participation. About half of adults in their 70s and 80s attended religious services weekly, compared with 40% of people in their 50s and 60s. Older adults in their 70s were twice as likely to attend religious services weekly as people in their late 50s, and those in their 80s were nearly 50% more likely to attend religious services than middle-aged adults. The researchers observe that older adults were more frequently involved with religious activities than people of other ages, that increased religious participation may be one way older adults compensate for social losses, and that religious participation has been linked to improved health of older adults.

Frank Newport of the Gallup Organization states in *Belief in God Far Lower in Western U.S.* (July 28, 2008, http://www.gallup.com/poll/109108/Belief-God-Far-Lower-Western-US.aspx), "It is well-known that older Americans are the most religious." Consistent with this observation is the fact that older adults are also more likely to say they believe in God. Newport notes that in May 2008, 88% of older adults said they had a belief in God, compared with 74% of adults aged 30 to 49 and 77% of people aged 50 to 64. (See Figure 1.12.)

ENJOYMENT OF OLDER AGE

The average person can get younger in the sense that he or she can have even more years to live as time goes on.

—Warren Sanderson, quoted by "Forty May Be the New 30 as Scientists Redefine Age" (Reuters, June 8, 2005)

TABLE 1.6

Foreign-born population by selected characteristics and region of origin, 2007

[In thousands (37,279 represents 37,279,000). As of March. The term foreign-born refers to anyone who is not a U.S. citizen at birth. This includes naturalized U.S. citizens, legal permanent residents (immigrants), temporary migrants (such as foreign students), humanitarian migrants (such as refugees), and persons illegally present in the United States. Based on Current Population Survey, Annual Social and Economic Supplement.]

Characteristic	Total foreign-born	Europe	Asia	Latin America				Other areas
				Total	Caribbean	Central America[a]	South America	
Total	**37,279**	**4,635**	**9,746**	**20,267**	**3,378**	**14,383**	**2,506**	**2,632**
Under 5 years old	359	39	103	191	21	158	12	27
5 to 14 years old	1,857	167	452	1,072	147	814	111	166
15 to 24 years old	4,459	434	885	2,809	330	2,133	345	331
25 to 34 years old	8,176	558	2,009	5,120	477	4,132	511	489
35 to 44 years old	8,380	801	2,178	4,791	796	3,431	563	611
45 to 54 years old	6,170	730	1,801	3,187	701	2,038	449	452
55 to 64 years old	3,853	712	1,213	1,652	419	954	279	275
65 to 74 years old	2,281	577	640	883	265	464	154	181
75 to 84 years old	1,314	459	365	411	167	178	65	80
85 years old and over	430	159	98	151	54	82	16	22
Educational attainment								
Persons 25 years old and over	**30,604**	**3,995**	**8,305**	**16,195**	**2,879**	**11,279**	**2,037**	**2,109**
Less than ninth grade	6,100	392	643	4,881	365	4,321	194	184
9th to 12th grade (no diploma)	3,656	209	448	2,883	371	2,343	170	116
High school graduate	7,577	1,088	1,649	4,334	982	2,730	622	505
Some college or associate's degree	4,722	813	1,245	2,177	582	1,141	454	486
Bachelor's degree	5,343	862	2,542	1,457	431	595	431	482
Advanced degree	3,206	630	1,778	462	148	148	166	336
High school graduate or more	20,848	3,394	7,214	8,431	2,144	4,615	1,673	1,809
Bachelor's degree or more	8,549	1,493	4,319	1,919	579	744	596	818
Income in 2006								
Total family households	**11,895**	**1,446**	**3,152**	**6,381**	**1,200**	**4,429**	**752**	**917**
Under $15,000	1,073	69	209	726	163	498	65	69
$15,000 to $24,999	1,451	126	206	1,043	142	839	63	76
$25,000 to $34,999	1,517	173	247	1,003	154	763	85	95
$35,000 to $49,999	1,987	208	355	1,295	234	919	141	129
$50,000 to $74,999	2,163	274	574	1,143	203	788	151	172
$75,000 and over	3,705	596	1,561	1,171	303	621	247	376
Median income (dol.)	44,706	61,811	74,297	39,169	41,762	36,249	52,464	60,538

[a]Includes Mexico.

SOURCE: "Table 42. Foreign-born Population—Selected Characteristics by Region of Origin: 2007," in *Statistical Abstract of the United States: 2009*, 128th ed., U.S. Census Bureau, 2008, http://www.census.gov/compendia/statab/tables/09s0042.pdf (accessed April 20, 2009)

In view of the myriad difficulties and challenges facing older adults, including ill health, inadequate financial resources, and the loss of friends and loved ones, it seems natural to assume that advancing age will be associated with less overall happiness and more worry. However, several studies refute this premise. Researchers find less worry among older adults than anticipated and a remarkable ability of older adults to adapt to their changing life conditions.

In "Hope I Die before I Get Old: Mispredicting Happiness across the Adult Lifespan" (*Journal of Happiness Studies*, June 2006), Heather P. Lacey, Dylan M. Smith, and Peter A. Ubel of the Center for Behavioral and Decision Sciences in Medicine in Ann Arbor, Michigan, indicate that even though both young adults and older adults express the belief that happiness declines with advancing age, self-reports refute this belief.

Lacey, Smith, and Ubel asked more than 500 study participants who were either between the ages of 21 and 40 and older than 60 to rate their own happiness at their current age and predict their happiness at age 30 and 70. The study participants were also asked to assess how happy they believe most people are at ages 30 and 70.

Both younger and older adults said they thought that for the average person, happiness declines with age. Similarly, both age groups felt that older adults were less happy, and older adults themselves opined that they and others were happier when they were younger. However, only the older adults felt that their own personal happiness would decline with age. The younger adults felt that they themselves would be as happy at age 70, but that others their age would likely see their happiness decline. Despite these beliefs, this study and others find that most people tend to become happier over time, based on their self-reports.

David G. Blanchflower and Andrew J. Oswald assert in "Is Well-Being U-shaped over the Life Cycle?" (*Social Science and Medicine*, vol. 66, no. 8, April 2008) that

FIGURE 1.10

Persons aged 65 and older as a percent of total population, 2007

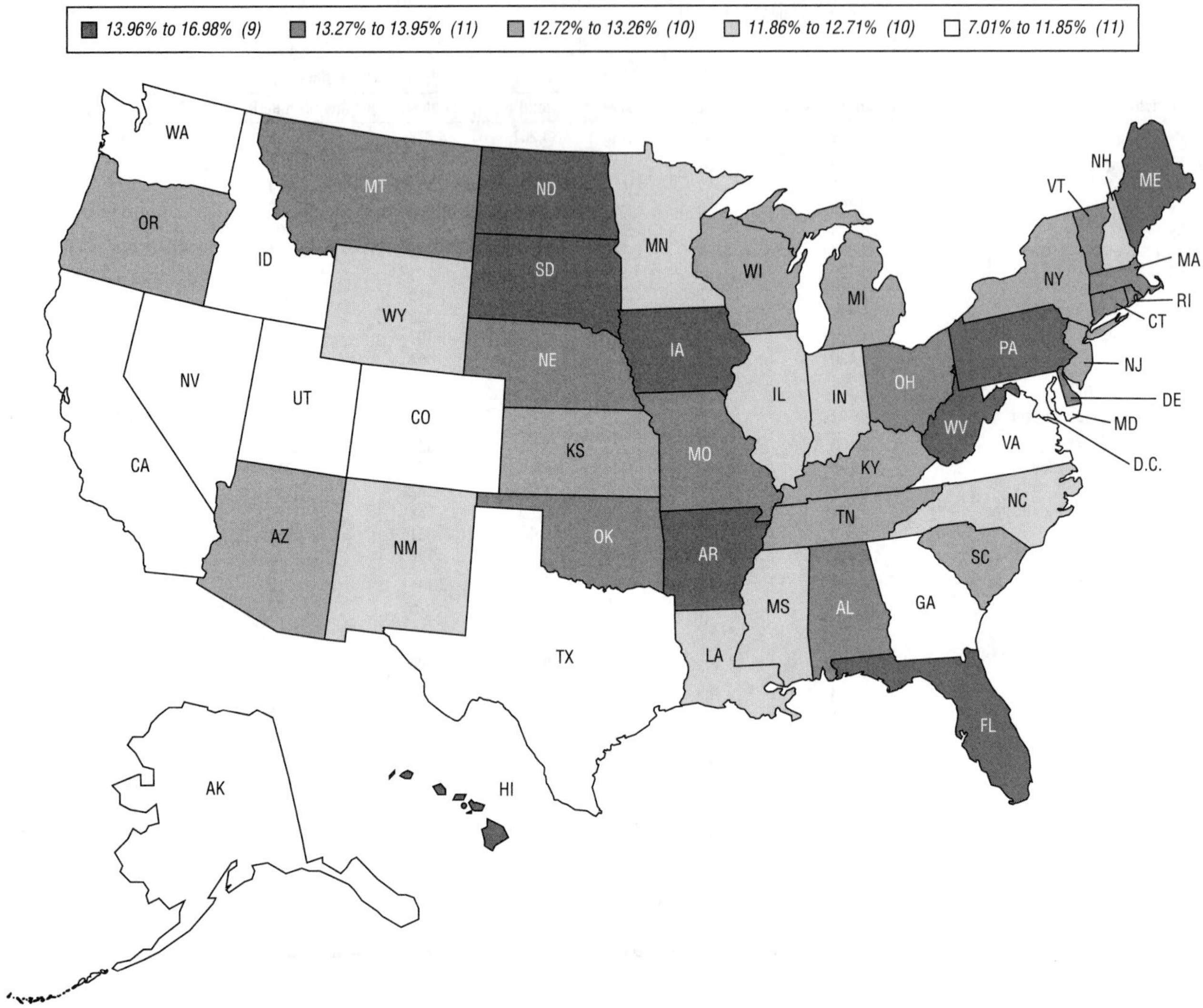

SOURCE: Saadia Greenberg, "Figure 4. Persons 65+ as a Percentage of Total Population, 2007," in *A Profile of Older Americans: 2008*, U.S. Department of Health and Human Services, Administration on Aging, 2009, http://www.mowaa.org/Document.Doc?id=69 (accessed April 20, 2009)

psychological well-being is U-shaped through life. After analyzing several data sets including data from 500,000 Americans and Europeans, the researchers conclude that happiness typically declines as people age, reaching its lowest point during middle age but then rising again throughout later life. Their finding supports other studies that have found higher levels of happiness and life satisfaction among older adults than middle-aged people.

Positive Perceptions of Aging Influence Longevity and Happiness

In a landmark study, Becca R. Levy et al. report in "Longevity Increased by Positive Self-Perceptions of Aging" (*Journal of Personality and Social Psychology*, vol. 83, no. 2, August 2002) that older people with more positive self-perceptions of aging lived 7.5 years longer than those with less positive self-perceptions of aging, even after taking into account other factors, including age, gender, socioeconomic status, loneliness, and overall health. Analyzing data from the 660 participants aged 50 and older in the Ohio Longitudinal Study of Aging and Retirement, Levy et al. compared mortality rates with responses made 23 years earlier by the participants (338 men and 322 women). The responses included agreeing or disagreeing with statements such as "As you get older, you are less useful."

Levy et al. assert that "the effect of more positive self-perceptions of aging on survival is greater than the physiological measures of low systolic blood pressure and cholesterol, each of which is associated with a longer life span of 4 years or less.... [It] is also greater than the independent contribution of lower body mass index, no

FIGURE 1.11

Percentage increase in population aged 65 and older, 1997–2007

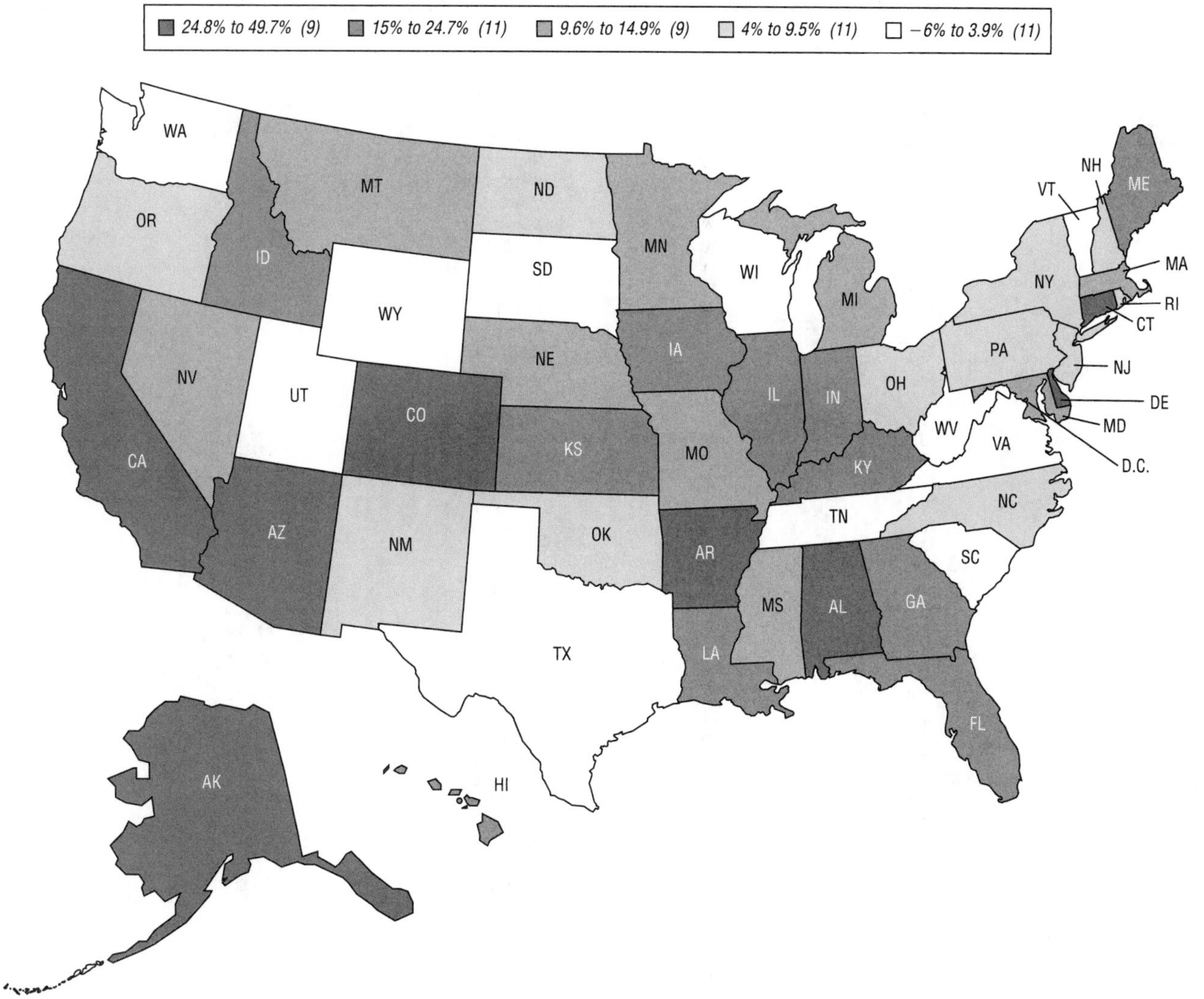

SOURCE: Saadia Greenberg, "Figure 5. Percentage Increase in Population Age 65+, 1997 to 2007," in *A Profile of Older Americans: 2008*, U.S. Department of Health and Human Services, Administration on Aging, 2009, http://www.mowaa.org/Document.Doc?id=69 (accessed April 20, 2009)

history of smoking, and a tendency to exercise; each of these factors has been found to contribute between 1 and 3 years of added life." They conclude that negative self-perceptions can diminish life expectancy, whereas positive self-perceptions can prolong it.

In "Building Blocks of Successful Aging: A Focus Group Study of Older Adults' Perceived Contributors to Successful Aging" (*American Journal of Geriatric Psychiatry*, vol. 15, no. 3, March 2007), Jennifer Reichstadt et al. find that older adults themselves believe that a positive attitude about life and aging and having the ability to adapt to change are associated with successful aging and a long, happy life. The researchers interviewed 72 older adults living in the community (as opposed to people living in institutions) and identified the factors older adults feel contribute to successful aging. The interviewees named psychosocial factors such as a sense of engagement, pursuit of continued stimulation, learning, feeling a sense of purpose in life, and being useful to others and to society as more important for successful aging than factors such as freedom from illness and disability.

ATTITUDES ABOUT AGING

People of all ages hold beliefs and attitudes about aging and older adults. Even young children can distinguish age differences, and they display attitudes that appear to be characteristic of their generation. Because attitudes strongly influence behavior and because more Americans reach older ages than ever before, interaction with older people and deeply held beliefs about growing

TABLE 1.7

Ranking of states by projected percent of population aged 65 and older, 2010 and 2030

2010 state	2010 percent	2010 rank	2030 state	2030 percent	2030 rank
United States	13.0	(x)	**United States**	19.7	(x)
Florida	17.8	1	Florida	27.1	1
West Virginia	16.0	2	Maine	26.5	2
Maine	15.6	3	Wyoming	26.5	3
Pennsylvania	15.5	4	New Mexico	26.4	4
North Dakota	15.3	5	Montana	25.8	5
Montana	15.0	6	North Dakota	25.1	6
Iowa	14.9	7	West Virginia	24.8	7
South Dakota	14.6	8	Vermont	24.4	8
Connecticut	14.4	9	Delaware	23.5	9
Arkansas	14.3	10	South Dakota	23.1	10
Vermont	14.3	11	Pennsylvania	22.6	11
Hawaii	14.3	12	Iowa	22.4	12
Delaware	14.1	13	Hawaii	22.3	13
Alabama	14.1	14	Arizona	22.1	14
Rhode Island	14.1	15	South Carolina	22.0	15
New Mexico	14.1	16	Connecticut	21.5	16
Wyoming	14.0	17	New Hampshire	21.4	17
Arizona	13.9	18	Rhode Island	21.4	18
Missouri	13.9	19	Wisconsin	21.3	19
Oklahoma	13.8	20	Alabama	21.3	20
Nebraska	13.8	21	Massachusetts	20.9	21
Ohio	13.7	22	Nebraska	20.6	22
Massachusetts	13.7	23	Mississippi	20.5	23
New Jersey	13.7	24	Ohio	20.4	24
New York	13.6	25	Arkansas	20.3	25
South Carolina	13.6	26	Missouri	20.2	26
Wisconsin	13.5	27	Kansas	20.2	27
Kansas	13.4	28	New York	20.1	28
Tennessee	13.3	29	New Jersey	20.0	29
Kentucky	13.1	30	Kentucky	19.8	30
Oregon	13.0	31	Louisiana	19.7	31
Michigan	12.8	32	Michigan	19.5	32
Mississippi	12.8	33	Oklahoma	19.4	33
Indiana	12.7	34	Tennessee	19.2	34
Louisiana	12.6	35	Minnesota	18.9	35
New Hampshire	12.6	36	Virginia	18.8	36
North Carolina	12.4	37	Nevada	18.6	37
Virginia	12.4	38	Idaho	18.3	38
Illinois	12.4	39	Oregon	18.2	39
Minnesota	12.4	40	Washington	18.1	40
Nevada	12.3	41	Indiana	18.1	41
Washington	12.2	42	Illinois	18.0	42
Maryland	12.2	43	California	17.8	43
Idaho	12.0	44	North Carolina	17.8	44
California	11.5	45	Maryland	17.6	45
District of Columbia	11.5	46	Colorado	16.5	46
Colorado	10.7	47	Georgia	15.9	47
Texas	10.5	48	Texas	15.6	48
Georgia	10.2	49	Alaska	14.7	49
Utah	9.0	50	District of Columbia	13.4	50
Alaska	8.1	51	Utah	13.2	51

SOURCE: Adapted from "Table 3. Ranking of States by Projected Percent of Population Age 65 and Older: 2000, 2010, and 2030," in *State Interim Population Projections by Age and Sex: 2004–2030*, U.S. Census Bureau, Population Division, April 21, 2005, http://www.census.gov/population/www/projections/projectionsagesex.html (accessed April 20, 2009)

old are likely influenced by cultural and societal attitudes about aging and older adults. The availability, accessibility, adequacy, and acceptability of health care and other services intended to meet the needs of older people are similarly influenced by the attitudes of younger people. The prevailing attitudes and opinions of political leaders, decision makers, health and human services personnel, and taxpayers are particularly important in shaping policies, programs, services, and public sentiment.

In nonindustrialized countries older people are often held in high esteem. Older adults are respected because they often have endured and persevered in harsh living conditions and because they have accumulated wisdom and knowledge that younger generations need to survive and carry on the traditions of their culture. In many industrialized societies, including the United States, a person's worth may be measured in terms of income (the flow of money earned through employment, interest on invest-

FIGURE 1.12

Percent of Americans who believe in God, by age, May 2008

WHICH OF THE FOLLOWING STATEMENTS COMES CLOSEST TO YOUR BELIEF ABOUT GOD?

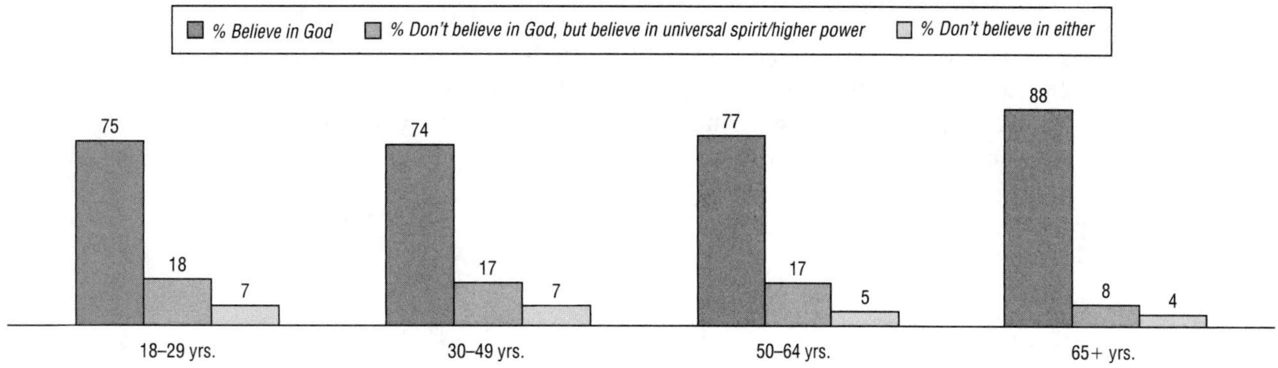

SOURCE: Frank Newport, "Which of the Following Statements Comes Closest to Your Belief about God? By Age," in *Belief in God Far Lower in Western U.S.*, The Gallup Organization, July 28, 2008, http://www.gallup.com/poll/109108/Belief-God-Far-Lower-Western-US.aspx (accessed April 20, 2009). Copyright © 2008 by The Gallup Organization. Reproduced by permission of The Gallup Organization.

ments, and other sources) and the amount of wealth accumulated. When older adults retire from full-time employment, they may lose status because they are no longer working, earning money, or "contributing" to society. When an individual's sense of self-worth and identity is closely bound to employment or occupation, retirement from the workforce can make him or her feel worthless.

Stereotypes Fuel Worries of Older Adults

Even though people of all ages worry about the future, for older adults aging may signify a future threat to their health and well-being, diminished social status, a loss of power, and the possibility of a loss of control over their life. Researchers posit that social stereotypes, such as media portrayals of older adults as weak and helpless and of old age as a time of hardship, loss, and pain, have a powerful influence on attitudes and may be another source of worry for older adults. They contend that the image of a tragic old age can create worries about having a tragic old age. Worse still, the negative image of old age can become a self-fulfilling prophecy, thereby confirming negative stereotypes and promoting ageism (discrimination or unfair treatment based on age).

For example, in "Expectations about Memory Change across the Life Span Are Impacted by Aging Stereotypes" (*Psychology and Aging*, vol. 24, no. 1, March 2009), Tara T. Lineweaver, Andrea K. Berger, and Christopher Hertzog interviewed 373 people, in three different age groups, to find out what they thought about memory throughout the adult lifespan. They were asked to rate the memory of different older adults, who were described as having positive or negative personality traits. Consistent with previous research, the study subjects believed that memory declines with advancing age. Furthermore, they rated adults described as having positive personality traits with having better memory ability and less age-related memory loss than those described as having negative personality traits. Another important finding was that the older subjects were more strongly influenced by the personality descriptions than younger subjects.

Gabriel A. Radvansky, Nicholas A. Lynchard, and William von Hippel confirm in "Aging and Stereotype Suppression" (*Aging, Neuropsychology, and Cognition*, vol. 16, no. 1, January 2009) that older adults are more likely than younger adults to believe and use stereotypic information, even when they do not intend to judge people based on stereotypes. Furthermore, older adults have trouble changing or modifying their interpretation of a situation, even when it becomes apparent that their initial interpretation was incorrect. The researchers aver that even though older adults may be more susceptible to the influence of stereotypes, this effect can be prevented, or minimized, by providing them with clear information that contradicts stereotypical information.

Baby Boomers Challenge Stereotypes

Since their inception, baby boomers have left their mark on every U.S. institution. As teenagers and young adults, they created and championed a unique blend of music, pop culture, and political activism. They have witnessed remarkable technological and medical advancements in their lifetime and have come to expect, and even loudly demand, solutions to health and social problems.

As the baby boomers begin to join the ranks of older Americans, they are fomenting a cultural revolution. The almost 80 million boomers approaching age 65 are not content to be regarded as "old." Accustomed to freedom and independence, they want to be recognized and treated as individuals rather than as stereotypes. The aging boomers are healthier, better educated, and wealthier than any other older adult cohort in history. They are redefining old age by reinventing retirement, continuing to pursue health, and challenging the public's perception of what it is to be old.

In "Aging America and the Boomer Wars" (*The Gerontologist*, vol. 48, no 6, December 2008), Harry Moody, the director of the Office of Academic Affairs for the AARP, describes the polarizing stereotypes of the baby boomers. On one side are people who characterize boomers as selfish, materialistic, whining, and greedy—people who will consume all available resources with no thought to future generations. On the other side are those who view boomers as idealistic advocates of social activism and community service. Moody cautions that these opposing stereotypes should be avoided to prevent "oversimplified polarities and to appreciate the power that public discourse and media images can have in shaping our thinking about generational change in an aging society."

CHAPTER 2
THE ECONOMICS OF GROWING OLD IN THE UNITED STATES

Security was attained in the earlier days through the interdependence of members of families upon each other and of the families within a small community upon each other. The complexities of great communities and of organized industry make less real these simple means of security. Therefore, we are compelled to employ the active interest of the Nation as a whole through government in order to encourage a greater security for each individual who composes it. . . . This seeking for a greater measure of welfare and happiness does not indicate a change in values. It is rather a return to values lost in the course of our economic development and expansion.

—Franklin D. Roosevelt, Message of the President to Congress, June 8, 1934

The economic status of older Americans is more varied than that of any other age group. Even though a few older adults are well off, most have limited resources. Historically, as a whole the older U.S. population has a lower economic status than the overall adult population. During retirement most people rely in some part on Social Security and are supplemented by pensions and assets. Some must also depend on Supplemental Security Income (SSI), a federal assistance program administered by the Social Security Administration (SSA) that guarantees a minimum level of income for needy older adults, blind, or disabled individuals. It acts as a safety net for individuals who have little or no Social Security or other income and limited resources.

With fixed incomes and sharply limited potential to improve their incomes through employment, many older people become vulnerable to circumstances such as the loss of a spouse, prolonged illness, or even economic variations such as inflation or recession that further compromise their financial well-being, sometimes plunging them into poverty. One common scenario is a couple that has planned well for retirement but then runs through all their assets to pay the health care costs of a long-term illness. When the ill partner dies, the surviving spouse is impoverished. Another example are retirees who discover, as many people did in 2009, that their retirement accounts have lost more than half of their value.

The economic downturn that began in late 2007 and intensified throughout 2008 and 2009 has had far-reaching effects for older adults. In the fact sheet "How Is the Financial Crisis Affecting Retirement Savings?" (May 2009, http://www.urban.org/uploadedpdf/411880_retirement_savings.pdf), Mauricio Soto of the Urban Institute reports that on September 30, 2007, retirement accounts contained assets totaling $8.8 trillion and that approximately 70% of these assets were invested in stocks. Between September 2007 and May 2009 retirement accounts had lost 31% of their value—a staggering $2.7 trillion. Soto observes that retirees and those nearing retirement were harder hit than workers with many years until retirement, who presumably have time to recover. Older adults have little time to recover the value of their homes, 401(k) plans, and individual retirement accounts—the key elements of financially secure retirement. Soto suggests that the diminished value of retirement assets, declining home prices, and a weak economy could prompt older adults to postpone retirement and force some retirees to return to work.

Even though some older adults may want to return to work, their prospects may be bleak. Widespread layoffs and economic uncertainty have produced increasing rates of unemployment across all age groups. Richard W. Johnson and Corina Mommaerts of the Urban Institute note in the fact sheet "Unemployment Rate Hits All-Time High for Adults Age 65 and Older" (March 2009, http://www.urban.org/UploadedPDF/411846_recessionandolderworkersfactsheetmarch2009.pdf) that the unemployment rate for workers aged 65 and older was 6.8% in February 2009, the highest reported since 1948, when the federal government began tallying unemployment data.

THE ECONOMIC WELL-BEING OF OLDER ADULTS

There are two important measures of an individual's or household's economic well-being. One is income—the flow of money earned through employment, interest on investments, and other sources. The other is asset accumulation or wealth—the economic resources (property or other material possessions) owned by an individual or household.

Income Distribution

According to the Federal Interagency Forum on Aging-Related Statistics, in *Older Americans 2008: Key Indicators of Well-Being* (March 2008, http://www.agingstats.gov/agingstatsdotnet/Main_Site/Data/2008_Documents/OA_2008.pdf), the trend in median (the middle value—half are higher and half are lower) household income of the older population has been positive, and fewer older adults are living in poverty. From 1974 to 2006 the proportion of older adults living in poverty declined. Figure 2.1 shows that since the late 1970s poverty rates have been comparable among people aged 18 to 64 and 65 and older.

In 2006 about 9% of the older population lived below the poverty threshold, compared with about 14% in 1974. (See Figure 2.1.) The proportion of the older population in the low-income bracket also fell, from 50% in 1974 to 37% in 2006. (See Figure 2.2.)

According to Saadia Greenberg of the U.S. Administration on Aging, in *A Profile of Older Americans: 2008* (2008, http://www.mowaa.org/Document.Doc?id=69), the median reported income for all older adults in 2007 was $17,424—$24,323 for males and $14,021 for females. Figure 2.3 shows the distribution of income among older adults. Households headed by people aged 65 and older had a median income of $41,851 in 2007, whereas individual median income for older adults that year was $17,424. More than half (59.5%) of households headed by an older adult had incomes of $35,000 or more, and 7.4% had incomes less than $15,000. Median household income was highest among Asian-Americans ($47,135), followed by non-Hispanic whites ($43,654), African-Americans ($32,025), and Hispanics ($31,544).

Sources of Income

Unlike younger adults, who derive most of their income from employment, older adults rely on a variety of sources of income to meet their expenses. Since the 1960s Social Security has provided the largest share of income for older Americans. In 2006 Social Security benefits were a major source of income—providing at least 50% of total income—reported for nearly two-thirds (64%) of older adult beneficiaries. (See Figure 2.4.) For 41% of unmarried Americans and 20% of couples over the age of 65 in 2006, Social Security accounted for 90% of total income.

Greenberg states that most older adults' income comes from four sources. In 2006 Social Security accounted for an average of 37%, earnings provided 28%, pensions contributed 18%, and asset income accounted for 15% of the older population's income. (See Figure 2.5.)

For older Americans in the lowest fifth of the income distribution in 2006, Social Security accounted for 83% of aggregate income (total income from all sources) and public assistance for another 8%. (See Figure 2.6.) High-

FIGURE 2.1

Poverty rate by age group, 1959–2006

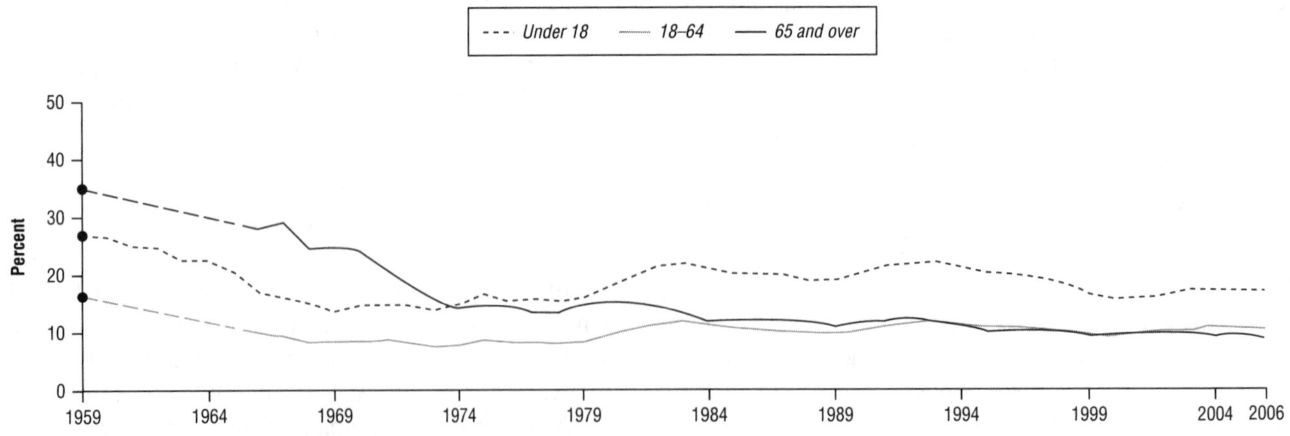

Data are not available from 1960–1965 for the 18–64 and 65 and over age groups.
Reference population: These data refer to the civilian noninstitutionalized population.

SOURCE: "Poverty Rate of the Population, by Age Group, 1959–2006," in *Older Americans 2008: Key Indicators of Well-Being*, Federal Interagency Forum on Aging-Related Statistics, March 2008, http://www.agingstats.gov/agingstatsdotnet/Main_Site/Data/2008_Documents/OA_2008.pdf (accessed April 20, 2009)

FIGURE 2.2

Income distribution of the population aged 65 and over, 1974–2006

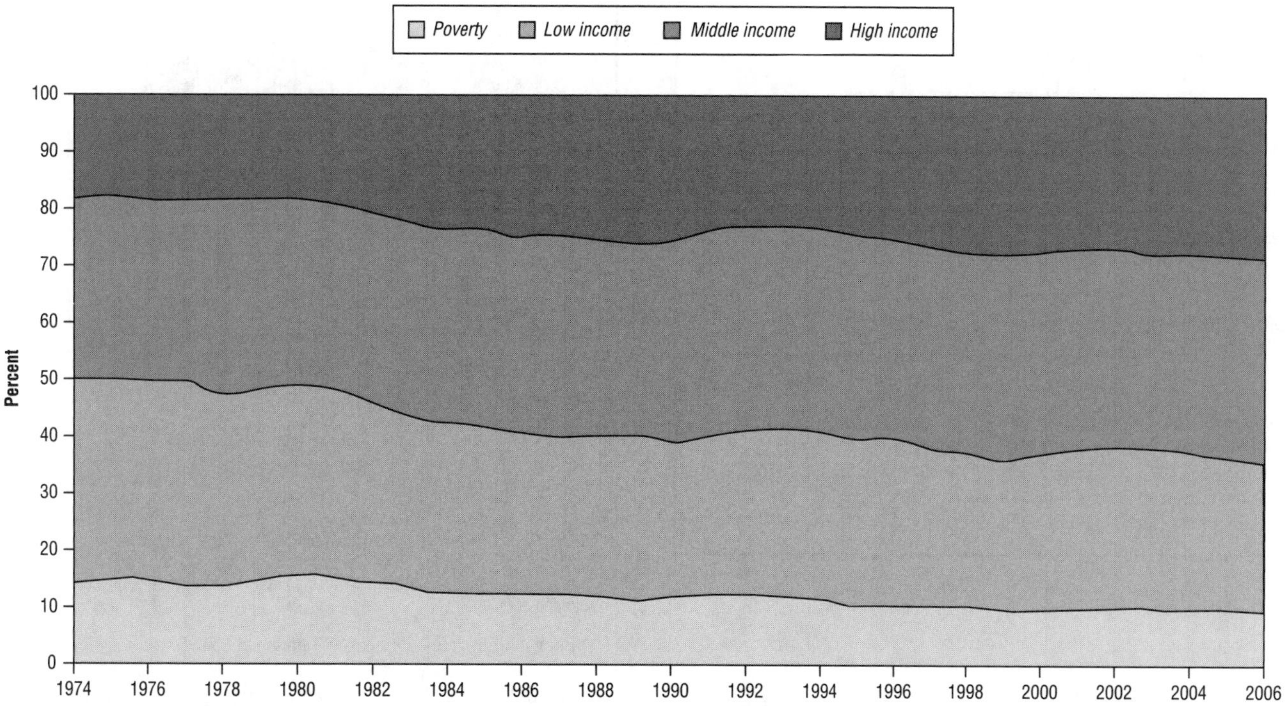

Note: The income categories are derived from the ratio of the family's income (or an unrelated individual's income) to the corresponding poverty threshold. Being in poverty is measured as income less than 100 percent of the poverty threshold. Low income is between 100 percent and 199 percent of the poverty threshold. Middle income is between 200 percent and 399 percent of the poverty threshold. High income is 400 percent or more of the poverty threshold.
Reference population: These data refer to the civilian noninstitutionalized population.

SOURCE: "Income Distribution of the Population Age 65 and over, 1974–2006," in *Older Americans 2008: Key Indicators of Well-Being*, Federal Interagency Forum on Aging-Related Statistics, March 2008, http://www.agingstats.gov/agingstatsdotnet/Main_Site/Data/2008_Documents/OA_2008.pdf (accessed April 20, 2009)

income older adults' aggregate income was about one-fifth each of pension, asset income, and Social Security, and about two-fifths were derived from earned income. Among people aged 80 and older, aggregate income largely consisted of Social Security and asset income, with earnings contributing a much smaller proportion, compared with the youngest population of older adults, those aged 65 to 69. (See Table 2.1.)

Pension Funds

Many large employers, along with most local and state governments and the federal government, offer pension plans for retirement. In the United States American Express established the first private pension plan—an employer-run retirement program—in 1875. General Motors Corporation provided the first modern plan in the 1940s.

Employers are not required to provide pensions, and pension plans do not have to include all workers; they may exclude certain jobs and/or individuals. Before 1976 pension plans could require an employee to work a lifetime for one company before becoming eligible for pension benefits. As required by the Employee Retirement Income Security Act (ERISA) of 1974, starting in 1976 an employee became eligible after 10 years of service. By 2000 most plans required five years of work before an employee became vested (eligible for benefits). In companies that offer pension plans, employees are eligible to begin receiving benefits when they retire or leave the company if they have worked for the requisite number of years and/or have reached the specified eligibility age.

DEFINED BENEFIT PLANS AND DEFINED CONTRIBUTION PLANS. There are two principal types of pension plans: defined benefit plans and defined contribution plans. Traditionally, employers offered defined benefit plans that promised employees a specified monthly benefit at retirement. A defined benefit plan may stipulate the promised benefit as an exact dollar amount, such as $100 per month at retirement. More often, however, benefits are calculated using a plan formula that considers both salary and service—for example, 1% of the average salary for the last five years of employment, for every year of service with the employer.

A defined contribution plan does not promise employees a specific amount of benefits at retirement. Instead, the

FIGURE 2.3

Persons aged 65 and over reporting income, 2007

[$17,424 median for 35.5 million persons 65+ reporting income]

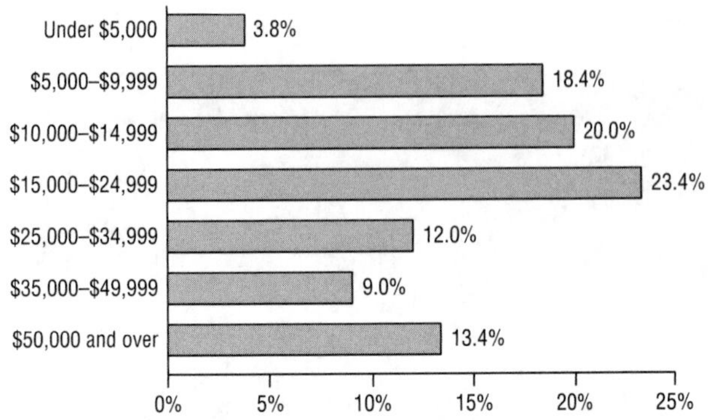

SOURCE: Saadia Greenberg, "Figure 7. Percent Distribution by Income: 2007: Persons 65+ Reporting Income," in *A Profile of Older Americans: 2008*, U.S. Department of Health and Human Services, Administration on Aging, 2009, http://www.mowaa.org/Document.Doc?id=69 (accessed April 20, 2009)

FIGURE 2.4

Percentage of older adults receiving Social Security benefits, by relative importance of benefits to total income, 2006

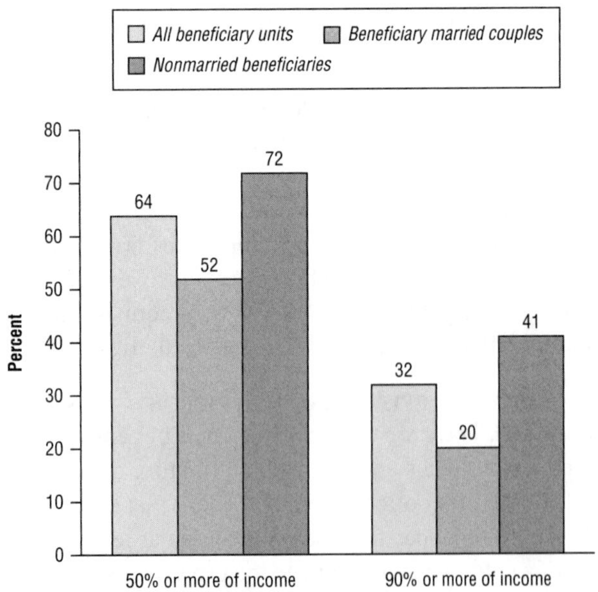

Note: An aged unit is a married couple living together or a nonmarried person, which also includes persons who are separated or married but not living together.

SOURCE: "Percentage of Aged Units Receiving Social Security Benefits, by Relative Importance of Benefits to Total Income," in *Fast Facts and Figures about Social Security, 2008*, U.S. Social Security Administration, Office of Retirement and Disability Policy, August 2008, http://www.ssa.gov/policy/docs/chartbooks/fast_facts/2008/fast_facts08.pdf (accessed April 21, 2009)

FIGURE 2.5

Aggregate income, by source, 2006

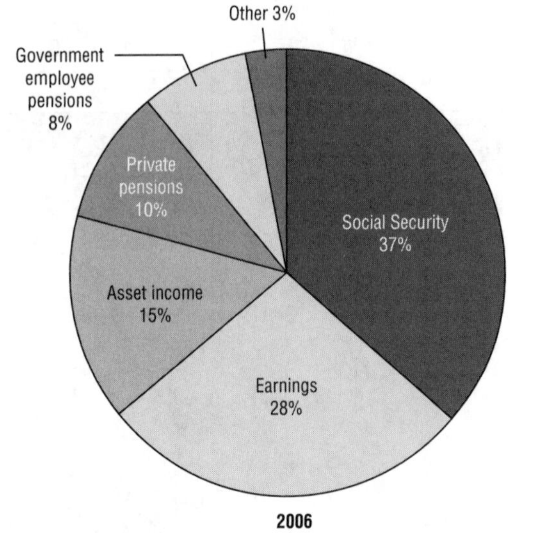

Notes: The unit of analysis is the aged unit, defined as a married couple living together or a nonmarried person, which also includes persons who are separated or married but not living together. Totals do not necessarily equal the sum of rounded components.

SOURCE: "Aggregate Income, by Source," in *Fast Facts and Figures about Social Security, 2008*, U.S. Social Security Administration, Office of Retirement and Disability Policy, August 2008, http://www.ssa.gov/policy/docs/chartbooks/fast_facts/2008/fast_facts08.pdf (accessed April 21, 2009)

employee and/or employer contribute to a plan account, sometimes at a set rate, such as 5% of earnings annually. Generally, these contributions are invested on the employee's behalf, and the amount of future benefits varies depending on investment earnings.

An example of a defined contribution plan is the 401(k) plan, which allows employees to defer receiving a portion of their salary, which is contributed on their behalf to the plan. Income taxes are deferred until the money is withdrawn at retirement. In some instances employers match employee contributions. Created in 1978, these plans were named for section 401(k) of the Internal Revenue Code.

The Urban Institute (2009, http://www.urban.org/retirement_policy/pensions.cfm) reports that about half of U.S. workers are covered by an employer pension plan that provides a defined benefit or more commonly a defined contribution plan that grows in response to employer and worker contributions. Figure 2.7 shows that among all workers, participation in defined benefit plans has declined, whereas participation in defined contribution plans has increased, with more than twice as many workers participating in defined contribution plans in 2007. Since the mid-1990s many employers have converted their defined benefit plans to hybrid plans that incorporate elements of both defined benefit and defined contribution plans. For

FIGURE 2.6

Sources of income for population aged 65 and over, by income quintile, 2006

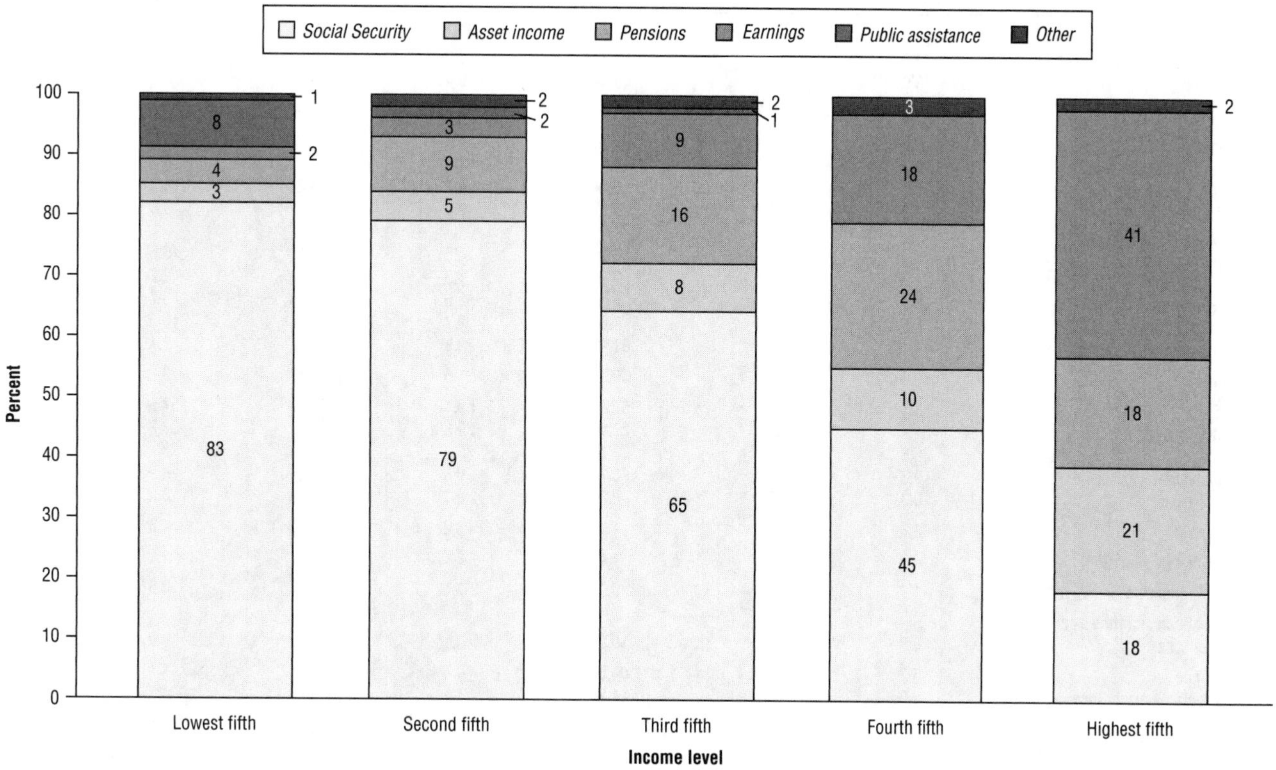

Note: A married couple is age 65 and over if the husband is age 65 and over or the husband is younger than age 55 and the wife is age 65 and over. The definition of "other" includes, but is not limited to, unemployment compensation, worker's compensation, alimony, child support, and personal contributions. Quintile limits are $11,519 for the lowest quintile, $18,622 for the second quintile, $28,911 for the third quintile, $50,064 for the fourth quintile, and open-ended for the highest quintile.
Reference population: These data refer to the civilian noninstitutionalized population.

SOURCE: "Sources of Income for Married Couples and Nonmarried People Who Are Age 65 and over, by Income Quintile, 2006," in *Older Americans 2008: Key Indicators of Well-Being*, Federal Interagency Forum on Aging-Related Statistics, March 2008, http://www.agingstats.gov/agingstatsdotnet/Main_Site/Data/2008_Documents/OA_2008.pdf (accessed April 20, 2009)

example, cash balance plans are based on defined contributions of pay credits—based on an employee's compensation rate—and interest credits deposited annually by the employer into an account, the balance of which serves as the defined benefit.

PRIVATE AND PUBLIC PENSIONS. The SSA reports in *Fast Facts and Figures about Social Security, 2008* (August 2008, http://www.ssa.gov/policy/docs/chartbooks/fast_facts/2008/fast_facts08.pdf) that the proportion of older adults' income from pensions grew rapidly during the 1960s, with private pensions more than tripling by 2006. (See Figure 2.8.) During the same period, the proportion of people receiving government pensions increased by 50%. The proportion of older adults with income from assets—the second most common source of income after Social Security—in 2006 (55%) was comparable to 1962 (54%). In contrast, the proportion of older adults with earned income declined from 36% in 1962 to 25% in 2006.

Unlike Social Security and many public plans, most private pension plans do not provide automatic cost-of-living adjustments. Without these adjustments many retirees' incomes and purchasing power erode. Military, government, and Railroad Retirement pensioners were more likely to receive cost-of-living increases than were pensioners in the private sector.

FEDERAL PENSION LAWS. Pension plan funds are often invested in stocks and bonds, much as banks invest their depositors' money. When the investment choice is a good one, the company makes a profit on the money in the fund; bad investments result in losses. During the early 1970s several major plans were terminated before they accumulated sufficient assets to pay employees and their beneficiaries retirement benefits. These asset-poor plans were unable to make good on their promises, leaving retirees without benefits despite their years of service.

To protect retirement plan participants and their beneficiaries from these catastrophic losses, ERISA was passed in 1974. ERISA established a new set of rules for participation, added mandatory and quicker vesting schedules, fixed minimum funding standards, and set standards of

TABLE 2.1

Percentage of family income from specified sources, by age group, 2006

Source of family income	55–61	62–64	Total	65–69	70–74	75–79	80 and over
Earnings	85.6	69.9	36.2	53.1	39.2	29.1	20.3
Wages and salaries	81.6	65.7	32.7	48.2	35.5	25.5	18.4
Self-employment	13.9	10.7	6.4	9.4	6.5	6	3.2
Retirement benefits	33.8	65.7	92.6	88	93.4	94.8	95.2
Social Security	21.5	55.4	89.9	84.6	91.3	92.4	92.7
Benefits other than Social Security	20.2	35.9	44.7	41	47.1	46.5	45.4
Other public pensions	9.1	14.6	15.6	14.8	15.2	16.2	16.3
Railroad retirement	0.3	0.7	0.5	0.4	0.4	0.6	0.8
Government employee pensions	8.9	14	15.1	14.5	14.8	15.6	15.7
Military	1.7	2.3	2.2	1.8	2.4	2.7	2.1
Federal	2	3	4	3.6	4	3.7	4.8
State or local	5.5	9.4	9.6	9.7	9.2	10	9.5
Private pensions or annuities	12	23.1	31.9	29.1	34.6	33.1	31.6
Income from assets	60.6	60.8	60.1	61.6	60.5	59.8	58.3
Interest	58.3	58.3	57.6	59.1	57.9	57.5	55.9
Other income from assets	31	30.5	27.5	29.8	27.9	27.2	24.7
Dividends	26.8	26.2	23.1	25	23.4	23	20.6
Rent or royalties	9.3	9.1	8.7	9.6	8.6	8.9	7.6
Estates or trusts	0.3	0.2	0.3	0.3	0.3	0.2	0.3
Veterans' benefits	3.7	3.4	4.2	3.2	3.9	4.3	5.5
Unemployment compensation	4.9	3.3	1.4	2.1	1.7	1.1	0.8
Workers' compensation	1.6	1.3	0.7	1.1	0.6	0.5	0.4
Combined public assistance and noncash benefits	8.8	10.1	10.2	9.1	10.5	9.9	11.6
Public assistance	5.2	5.8	4.5	4.5	4.7	4.4	4.4
Supplemental Security income	4.6	5.5	4.2	4.1	4.4	4.2	4.1
Other cash benefits	0.8	0.3	0.4	0.6	0.4	0.3	0.4
Noncash benefits	5.7	6.5	7.7	6.6	7.8	7.5	9.2
Food	3.9	4.1	3.4	3.7	3.5	3.4	3.1
Energy	1.5	1.6	2.3	1.9	2.5	2.1	2.6
Housing	2	3	4	3.1	3.8	4.1	5.2
Personal contributions	2.1	1.7	1.2	1.3	1.1	0.8	1.4
Number (thousands)	24,314	7,877	36,035	10,629	8,369	7,567	9,471

Reference population: These data refer to the civilian noninstitutionalized population.

SOURCE: "Table 9c. Percentage of People Age 55 and over with Family Income from Specified Sources, by Age Group, 2006," in *Older Americans 2008: Key Indicators of Well-Being*, Federal Interagency Forum on Aging-Related Statistics, March 2008, http://www.agingstats.gov/agingstatsdotnet/Main_Site/Data/2008_Documents/OA_2008.pdf (accessed April 20, 2009)

conduct for administering plans and handling plan assets. It also required disclosure of plan information, established a system for insuring the payment of pension benefits, and created the Pension Benefit Guaranty Corporation, a federal corporation, to provide uninterrupted benefit payments when pension plans are terminated.

The Retirement Equity Act of 1984 requires pension plans to pay a survivor's benefit to the spouse of a deceased vested plan participant. Before 1984 some spouses received no benefits unless the employee was near retirement age at the time of death. Under the 1984 law, pension vesting begins at age 21, or after five years on the job, and employees who have a break in employment for reasons such as maternity leave do not lose any time already accumulated.

PENSION FUNDS DECLINE. Because both private and public pension funds are invested in the stock market, many suffered serious losses in response to the stock market decline during 2008 and 2009. According to John W. Ehrhardt and Paul C. Morgan, in *Milliman 2009 Pension Funding Study* (March 2009, http://www.milliman.com/expertise/employee-benefits/products-tools/pension-funding-study/pdfs/2009-pension-funding-study-03-01-09.pdf), the 100 largest corporate (defined benefit) pension plans suffered a record $300 billion loss of funded status in 2008. Five years of pension gains were lost in 2008 and losses continued in early 2009.

The losses in funding sustained during 2008, along with the new funding requirements by the Pension Protection Act of 2006, which provides significant tax incentives to enhance and protect retirement savings for millions of Americans, have combined to create a growing pension fund deficit. The act will increase contributions to more than $50 billion. Many companies expected to defer some of the 2009 increased contribution requirement to 2010, increasing contributions to what may be record levels during that year.

FIGURE 2.7

Participation in defined contribution and defined benefit retirement plans, selected years 1992–2007

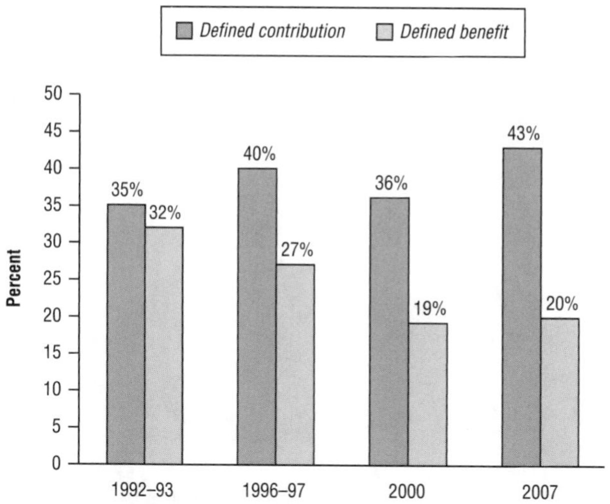

SOURCE: "Participation in Defined Contribution and Defined Benefit Retirement Plans," in *Older Workers*, U.S. Bureau of Labor Statistics, July 2008, http://www.bls.gov/spotlight/2008/older_workers/pdf/older_workers_bls_spotlight.pdf (accessed April 29, 2009)

Jim Doyle reports in "UC Pension Fund Lost Third of Its Value in 2008" (*San Francisco Chronicle*, April 16, 2009) that the California Public Employees' Retirement System—the nation's largest public pension fund—lost 27% of its value in 2008, plummeting from $253 billion to $183 billion. Dallas Salisbury, the president of the Employee Benefit Research Institute, opined that the precipitous decline in pension funds was to be expected and that "if the markets recover and everyone is patient, then what was lost will be re-earned. If the markets do not fully recover, additional contributions will be required."

Personal Savings

One of the most effective ways to prepare for retirement is to save for it. In the issue brief *The 2009 Retirement Confidence Survey: Economy Drives Confidence to Record Lows; Many Looking to Work Longer* (April 2009, http://www.ebri.org/pdf/briefspdf/EBRI_IB_4-2009_RCS1.pdf), Ruth Helman et al. report on the results of the 2009 Retirement Confidence Survey (RCS) that was cosponsored by the Employee Benefit Research Institute and Matthew Greenwald & Associates. Helman et al. report that a record-low number of Americans—just 13%, down from the previous low of 16% in 2008—said they are confident of having enough money to live comfortably in retirement. Even though this loss of confidence is largely attributable to universal issues such as economic uncertainty, inflation, and cost-of-living expenses, surveyed workers also cited job losses, pay cuts, loss of retirement savings, and increased debt as factors contributing to their concerns about their prospects in retirement.

The 2009 RCS found that American workers have saved very little for retirement. Helman et al. indicate that in 2009 more than half (53%) of workers reported having total savings and investments, excluding the value of their homes, of less than $25,000. Because this level of savings will render them woefully unprepared for retirement, 72% of workers are planning to supplement their income by working longer—either delaying retirement or working for pay in retirement. Workers also said they are taking steps to improve their financial situation such as by saving more money (25%), seeking help from financial professionals (25%), working more hours or obtaining a second job (38%), and reducing expenses (81%).

One popular way to save for retirement is to contribute to individual retirement plans. Individuals fund these retirement plans themselves. The money that they contribute can be tax deductible, the plans' earnings are not taxed, and contributors determine how the money is invested. Since 1974 one of the major types of individual retirement plans has been the individual retirement account (IRA). IRAs fall into several different categories, but the two most common types are traditional IRAs (deductible and nondeductible) and Roth IRAs; a variety of factors determine which kind of IRA best serves an individual's needs. Profit-sharing plans for the self-employed (formerly called Keogh plans) are another type of individual retirement plan.

Sixty-three percent of workers surveyed in the 2009 RCS said the major source of their retirement income will come from an IRA, 70% will primarily rely on personal savings and investments, 75% said their retirement income will come from an employer-sponsored retirement plan, 81% felt Social Security will be their major source of retirement income.

NET WORTH

Because the economic well-being of households depends on both income and wealth, assessment of income alone is not the best measure of older adults' financial health. To draw a more complete economic profile of the older population, it is necessary to evaluate older households in terms of measures of wealth, such as home equity, savings, and other assets and liabilities. For example, a household may be in the top one-fifth of the income distribution but be saddled with a large amount of debt.

Net worth is a measure of economic valuation and an indicator of financial security that is obtained by subtracting total liabilities from total assets. Greater net worth enables individuals and households to weather financial challenges such as illness, disability, job loss, divorce, widowhood, or general economic downturns.

FIGURE 2.8

Percentage of older adults receiving income, by source, 1962 and 2006

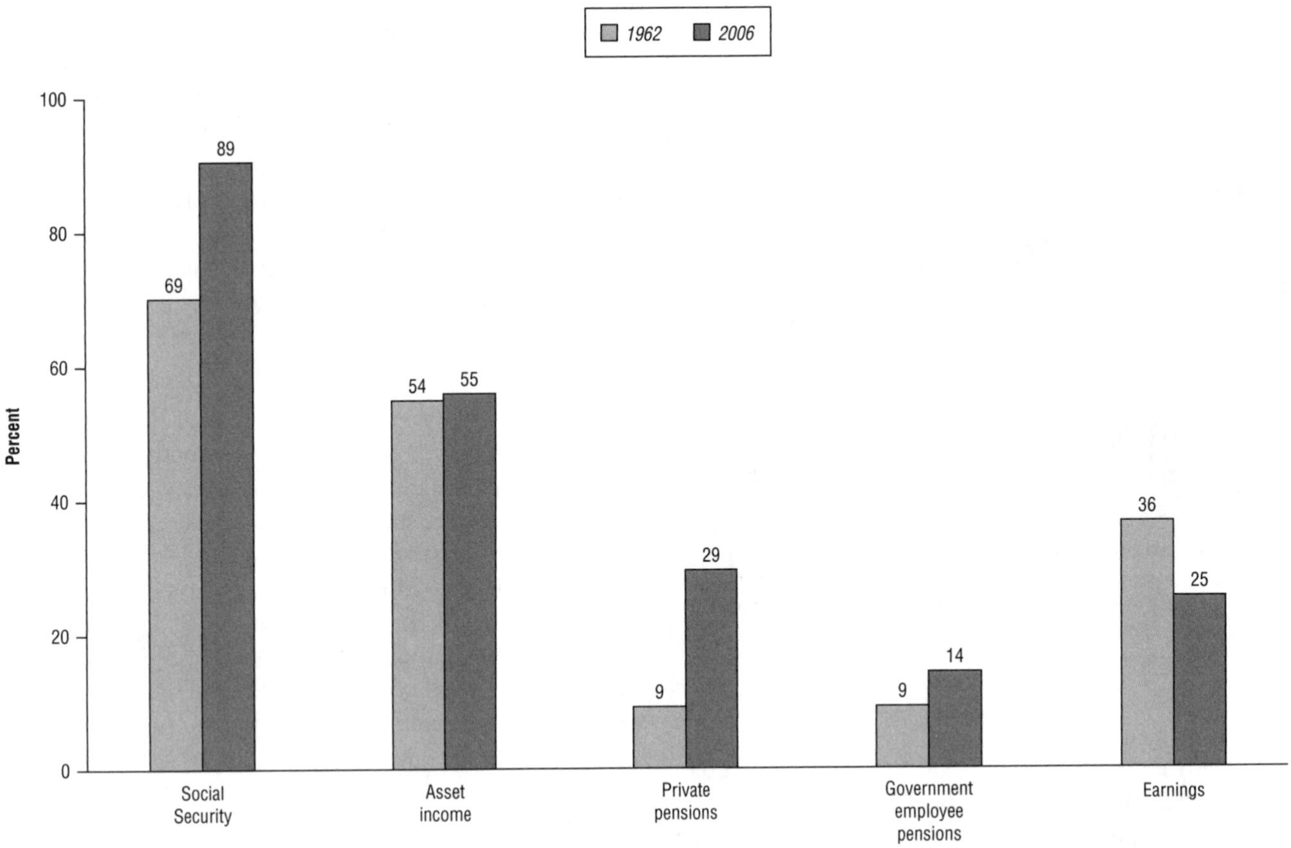

Note: An aged unit is a married couple living together or a nonmarried person, which also includes persons who are separated or married but not living together.

SOURCE: "Percentage of Aged Units Receiving Income, by Source," in *Fast Facts and Figures about Social Security, 2008*, U.S. Social Security Administration, Office of Retirement and Disability Policy, August 2008, http://www.ssa.gov/policy/docs/chartbooks/fast_facts/2008/fast_facts08.pdf (accessed April 21, 2009)

In *Older Americans 2008*, the Federal Interagency Forum on Aging-Related Statistics states that older adults' median net worth increased by 79%, from $109,000 in 1984 to $196,000 in 2005, the most recent year for which these data were available as of mid-2009. However, this increase has been substantially greater for older white adults than for older African-American adults. (See Figure 2.9.) During this period the median net worth of households headed by older white adults increased by more than 81%, from $125,000 to $226,900, whereas the median net worth of households headed by older African-American adults grew just 34%, from $28,200 to $37,800. In 2005 the median net worth of households headed by older white adults was six times greater than that of African-American households.

The median net worth of households headed by college-educated older adults rose from $238,700 in 1984 to $412,100 in 2005, a 73% increase, whereas households headed by an older adult without a high school diploma remained relatively unchanged in terms of net worth—$60,900 in 1984 and $59,500 in 2005. (See Figure 2.10.) In 2005 the median net worth of households headed by older adults with some college or more was nearly seven times greater than that headed by older adults without high school diplomas.

It is important to observe that the net worth of many older Americans declined significantly during 2008 and 2009, at least in part because home equity, which is a primary source of wealth for older Americans, declined sharply. Older adults are at a disadvantage compared with other age groups because unlike younger workers, they do not have the time to recoup their losses.

Older Adults Are Hard Hit by the Mortgage Crisis

According to the AARP Public Policy Institute, in *A First Look at Older Americans and the Mortgage Crisis* (September 2008, http://assets.aarp.org/rgcenter/econ/i9_mortgage.pdf), at the close of 2007 more than 684,000 homeowners aged 50 and older were either delinquent in mortgage payments or in foreclosure, and older adults

FIGURE 2.9

Median household net worth, by race of head of household aged 65 and over, selected years 1984–2005

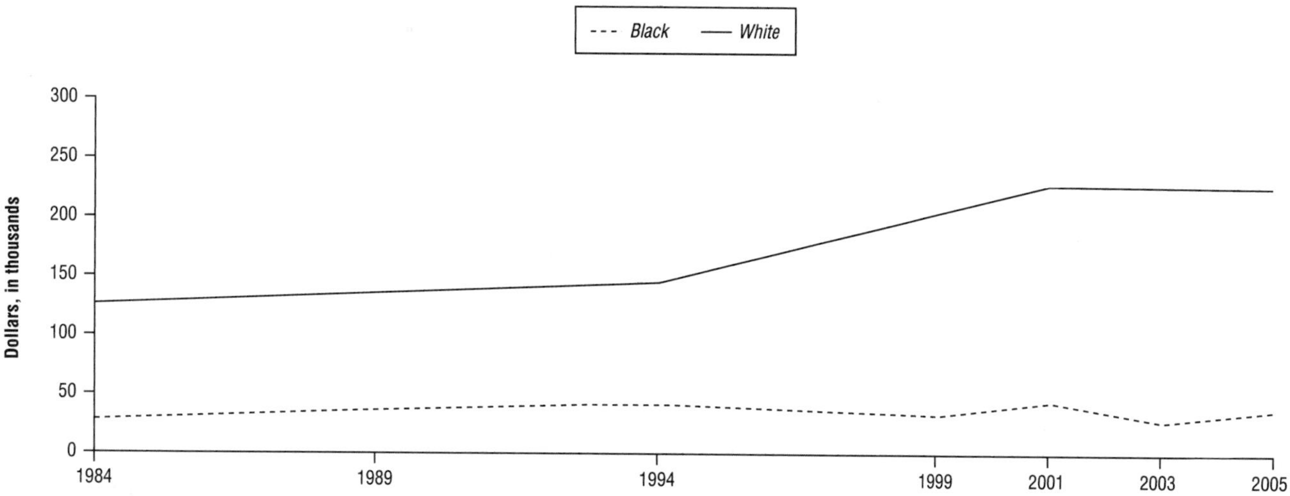

Note: Net worth data do not include pension wealth. This excludes private defined-contribution and defined-benefit plans as well as rights to Social Security wealth. Data for 1984–2003 have been inflation adjusted to 2005 dollars.
Reference population: These data refer to the civilian noninstitutionalized population.

SOURCE: "Median Household Net Worth, by Race of Head of Household Age 65 and over, in 2005 Dollars, Selected Years 1984–2005," in *Older Americans 2008: Key Indicators of Well-Being*, Federal Interagency Forum on Aging-Related Statistics, March 2008, http://www.agingstats.gov/agingstatsdotnet/Main_Site/Data/2008_Documents/OA_2008.pdf (accessed April 20, 2009),

represented 28% of all foreclosures. Older Americans with subprime first mortgages (mortgages typically made to people with poor credit for which lenders compensate by charging higher interest rates) were almost 17 times more likely to be delinquent than those with prime rate loans. The rate of foreclosures for older adults was expected to continue and even increase in 2009 as property values declined, limiting the ability of older homeowners to refinance their mortgages.

Bankruptcies Increase among Older Adults

In *Generations of Struggle* (June 2008, http://assets.aarp.org/rgcenter/consume/2008_11_debt.pdf), Deborah Thorne, Elizabeth Warren, and Teresa A. Sullivan find that in 2007 the rate of bankruptcy filings among those aged 65 and older had more than doubled since 1991 and that the average age for filing bankruptcy had increased. Americans aged 55 and older had experienced the sharpest increase in bankruptcy filings. Among older adults aged 75 to 84, the rate of filings rose by 433%.

According to Christine Dugas, in "Bankruptcy Rising among Seniors" (*USA Today*, June 20, 2008), Elizabeth Warren, a Harvard Law professor and the coauthor of the Consumer Bankruptcy Project study, explained that "in past generations, older Americans were more financially secure. Now, instead of going into retirement loaded with assets, Americans are hitting their retirement years loaded with debt."

POVERTY

Poverty rates are measures of the economic viability of populations. Poverty standards were originally based on the "economy food plan," which was developed by the U.S. Department of Agriculture (USDA) in the 1960s. The plan calculated the cost of a minimally adequate household food budget for different types of households by age of householder. Because USDA surveys showed that the average family spent one-third of its income on food, it was decided that a household with an income three times the amount needed for food was living fairly comfortably. In 1963 the poverty level was calculated by simply multiplying the cost of a minimally adequate food budget by three. Later, the U.S. Census Bureau began comparing family income before taxes with a set of poverty thresholds that vary based on family size and composition and are adjusted annually for inflation using the Consumer Price Index (CPI; a measure of the average change in consumer prices over time in a fixed market basket of goods and services).

According to Table 2.2, the poverty rate of adults aged 65 and older (9.7%) in 2007 was essentially unchanged from the previous year and represented 3.6 million older adults living in poverty. The rates recorded in 2007 for 18- to 64-year-olds (10.9%) and children under the age of 18 (18%) both exceeded that of older adults. Census Bureau data reveal that in 1959 the poverty rate for people aged 65 and older was 35%, well above the rates for the other age groups. (See Figure 2.11.) The lowest level of poverty in the older population occurred in 2006, when the rate fell to 9.4%.

FIGURE 2.10

Median household net worth, by educational attainment of head of household aged 65 and over, selected years 1984–2005

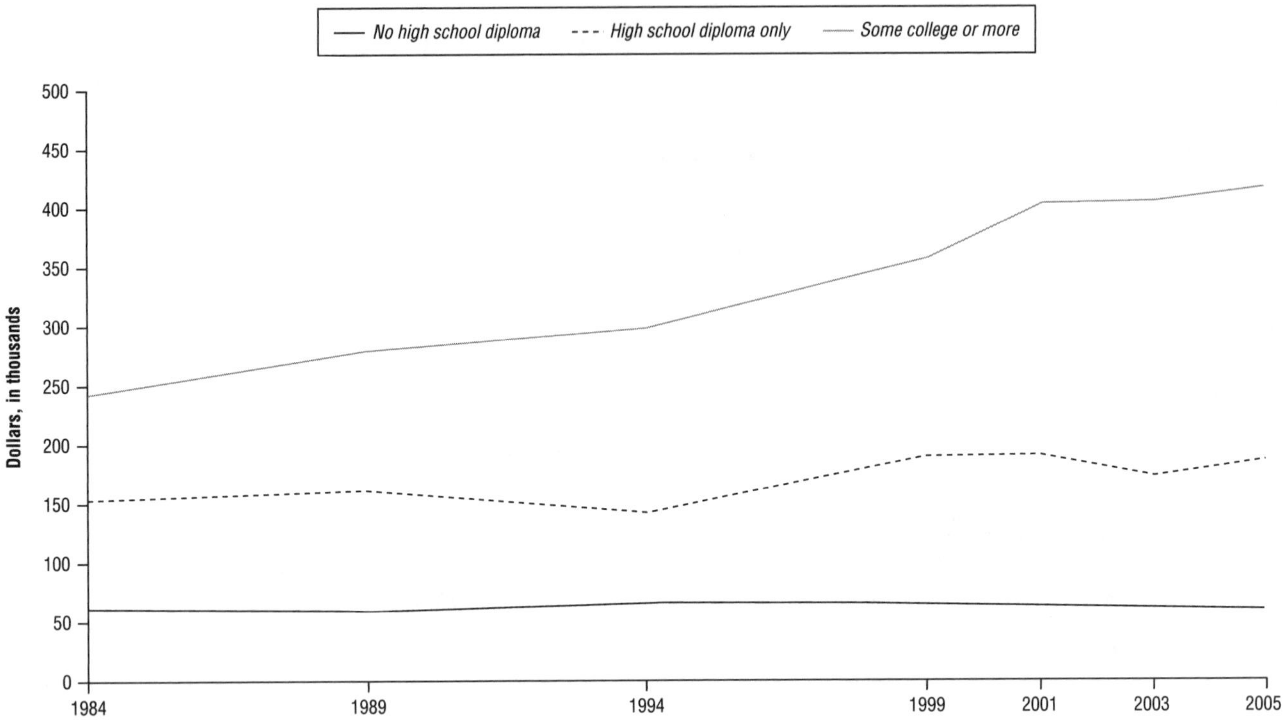

Note: Net worth data do not include pension wealth. This excludes private defined-contribution and defined-benefit plans as well as rights to Social Security wealth. Data for 1984–2003 have been inflation adjusted to 2005 dollars.
Reference population: These data refer to the civilian noninstitutionalized population.

SOURCE: "Median Household Net Worth, by Educational Attainment of Head of Household Age 65 and over, in 2005 Dollars, Selected Years, 1984–2005," in *Older Americans Update 2006: Key Indicators of Well-Being*, Federal Interagency Forum on Aging-Related Statistics, March 2008, http://www.agingstats.gov/agingstatsdotnet/Main_Site/Data/2008_Documents/OA_2008.pdf (accessed April 20, 2009)

Poverty Thresholds Are Lower for Older Adults

The Census Bureau measures need for assistance using poverty thresholds (specific dollar amounts that determine poverty status). Each individual or family is assigned one of 48 possible poverty thresholds. Thresholds vary according to family size and the ages of the members. The thresholds do not vary geographically, and they are updated annually for inflation using the CPI.

One assumption used to determine poverty thresholds is that healthy older adults have lower nutritional requirements than younger people, so they require less money for food. This assumption has resulted in different poverty thresholds for both the young and old. For example, in 2008 the poverty threshold for a single person under the age of 65 was $11,201, as opposed to $10,326 for a person aged 65 or older. (See Table 2.3.) The 2008 poverty threshold for two people including a householder under the age of 65 was $14,417, compared with $13,014 for two people including a householder aged 65 years or older.

This method of defining poverty fails to take into account the special financial and health challenges older adults may face. For example, no household costs other than food are counted, even though older adults spend a much greater percentage of their income on health care than younger people do. Also, the dollars allocated for food only consider the nutritional needs of healthy older adults; many are in poor health and may require more costly special diets or nutritional supplements.

WELL-OFF OLDER ADULTS

More older Americans live comfortably in the 21st century than at any other time in history. Those in their 70s and 80s were children of the Great Depression (1929–1941). The enforced Depression-era frugality taught them to economize and save. This generation returned from World War II (1939–1945) to inexpensive housing and GI bills (legislation that made available for veterans low-interest loans for homes or small businesses and free or inexpensive college education). During the 1940s and 1950s, their peak earning years, they enjoyed a period of unprecedented economic expansion. Since then, many have raised their children, paid off their home mortgages, invested wisely, and become eligible to receive Social Security payments that are larger than ever.

TABLE 2.2

People and families in poverty, by selected characteristics, 2006 and 2007

[Numbers in thousands]

Characteristic	2006 Total	2006 Below poverty Number	2006 Below poverty Percentage	2007 Total	2007 Below poverty Number	2007 Below poverty Percentage	Change in poverty (2007 less 2006)[a] Number	Change in poverty (2007 less 2006)[a] Percentage
People								
Total	**296,450**	**36,460**	**12.3**	**298,699**	**37,276**	**12.5**	**816**	**0.2**
Family status								
In families	245,199	25,915	10.6	245,443	26,509	10.8	594	0.2
Householder	78,454	7,668	9.8	77,908	7,623	9.8	−45	—
Related children under 18	72,609	12,299	16.9	72,792	12,802	17.6	504	0.6
Related children under 6	24,204	4,830	20.0	24,543	5,101	20.8	271	0.8
In unrelated subfamilies	1,367	567	41.5	1,516	577	38.1	9	−3.4
Reference person	567	229	40.4	609	222	36.5	−7	−3.9
Children under 18	719	323	44.9	819	332	40.5	9	−4.4
Unrelated individuals	49,884	9,977	20.0	51,740	10,189	19.7	212	−0.3
Male	24,674	4,388	17.8	25,447	4,348	17.1	−40	−0.7
Female	25,210	5,589	22.2	26,293	5,841	22.2	252	—
Race[b] and Hispanic origin								
White	237,619	24,416	10.3	239,133	25,120	10.5	704	0.2
White, not Hispanic	196,049	16,013	8.2	196,583	16,032	8.2	19	—
Black	37,306	9,048	24.3	37,665	9,237	24.5	189	0.3
Asian	13,177	1,353	10.3	13,257	1,349	10.2	−4	−0.1
Hispanic (any race)	44,784	9,243	20.6	45,933	9,890	21.5	647	0.9
Age								
Under 18 years	73,727	12,827	17.4	73,996	13,324	18.0	497	0.6
18 to 64 years	186,688	20,239	10.8	187,913	20,396	10.9	157	—
65 years and older	36,035	3,394	9.4	36,790	3,556	9.7	162	0.2
Nativity								
Native born	259,199	30,790	11.9	261,456	31,126	11.9	336	—
Foreign born	37,251	5,670	15.2	37,243	6,150	16.5	480	1.3
Naturalized citizen	14,534	1,345	9.3	15,050	1,426	9.5	81	0.2
Not a citizen	22,716	4,324	19.0	22,193	4,724	21.3	400	2.2
Region								
Northeast	54,072	6,222	11.5	53,952	6,166	11.4	−56	−0.1
Midwest	65,411	7,324	11.2	65,403	7,237	11.1	−87	−0.1
South	107,902	14,882	13.8	109,545	15,501	14.2	619	0.0
West	69,065	8,032	11.6	69,799	8,372	12.0	340	0.4
Metropolitan status								
Inside metropolitan statistical areas	249,092	29,283	11.8	251,023	29,921	11.9	638	0.2
Inside principal cities	95,138	15,336	16.1	96,731	15,983	16.5	646	0.4
Outside principal cities	153,954	13,947	9.1	154,292	13,938	9.0	−8	—
Outside metropolitan statistical areas[c]	47,357	7,177	15.2	47,676	7,355	15.4	178	0.3
Work experience								
Total, 16 years and older	231,800	24,896	10.7	233,885	25,297	10.8	401	0.1
All workers	157,352	9,181	5.8	158,468	9,089	5.7	−92	−0.1
Worked full-time, year-round	107,734	2,906	2.7	108,617	2,768	2.5	−138	−0.1
Not full-time, year-round	49,618	6,275	12.6	49,851	6,320	12.7	45	—
Did not work at least one week	74,448	15,715	21.1	75,417	16,208	21.5	493	0.4

Even though these factors have contributed to a more favorable economic status for this cohort (a group of individuals that shares a common characteristic such as birth years and is studied over time) of older adults than they would have otherwise enjoyed, most older people are not wealthy. Figure 2.12 shows that in 2007, 23.9% of households headed by older adults had total incomes of $75,000 or more and 17.4% of households headed by older adults reported incomes ranging from $50,000 to $74,999.

Much has changed since 2007. Soto explains in the fact sheet "How Is the Financial Crisis Affecting Retirement Savings?" (March 9, 2009, http://www.urban.org/UploadedPDF/411847_update-3-09-2009-pr.pdf) that between September 2007 and March 2009 the stock market lost an estimated $13 trillion. This loss devastated the retirement savings of many Americans, and even though older adults typically have fewer funds invested in stocks than younger adults, many endured substantial losses.

Older adults' responses to economic uncertainty vary. The article "Living, Working, and Saving Together in a Recessed Economy" (*AARP Bulletin Today*, April 7, 2009) opines that many older adults, having previously experienced times of economic uncertainty, are able to offer a long-range

TABLE 2.2

People and families in poverty, by selected characteristics, 2006 and 2007 [CONTINUED]

[Numbers in thousands]

	2006			2007			Change in poverty (2007 less 2006)[a]	
		Below poverty			Below poverty			
Characteristic	Total	Number	Percentage	Total	Number	Percentage	Number	Percentage
Familes								
Total	**78,454**	**7,668**	**9.8**	**77,908**	**7,623**	**9.8**	**−45**	**—**
Type of family								
Married-couple	58,964	2,910	4.9	58,395	2,849	4.9	−61	−0.1
Female householder, no husband present	14,424	4,087	28.3	14,411	4,078	28.3	−9	—
Male householder, no wife present	5,067	671	13.2	5,103	696	13.6	25	0.4

—Represents or rounds to zero.
[a]Details may not sum to totals because of rounding.
[b]Federal surveys now give respondents the option of reporting more than one race. Therefore, two basic ways of defining a race group are possible. A group such as Asian may be defined as those who reported Asian and no other race (the race-alone or single-race concept) or as those who reported Asian regardless of whether they also reported another race (the race-alone-or-in-combination concept). This table shows data using the first approach (race alone). The use of the single-race population does not imply that it is the preferred method of presenting or analyzing data. The Census Bureau uses a variety of approaches. Information on people who reported more than one race, such as white ***and*** American Indian and Alaska Native or Asian ***and*** black or African American, is available from Census 2000 through American FactFinder. About 2.6 percent of people reported more than one race in Census 2000. Data for American Indians and Alaska Natives, Native Hawaiians and Other Pacific Islanders, and those reporting two or more races are not shown separately.
[c]The "outside metropolitan statistical areas" category includes both micropolitan statistical areas and territory outside of metropolitan and micropolitan statistical areas.

SOURCE: Carmen DeNavas-Walt, Bernadette D. Proctor, and Jessica C. Smith, "Table 3. People and Families in Poverty by Selected Characteristics: 2006 and 2007," in *Income, Poverty and Health Insurance Coverage in the United States: 2007*, U.S. Census Bureau, August 2008, http://www.census.gov/hhes/www/poverty/poverty07/table3.pdf (accessed April 23, 2009)

FIGURE 2.11

Poverty rates by age, 1959–2007

Note: Data for people aged 18 to 64 and 65 and older are not available from 1960 to 1965.

SOURCE: Carmen DeNavas-Walt, Bernadette D. Proctor, and Jessica C. Smith, "Figure 4. Poverty Rates by Age, 1959 to 2007," in *Income, Poverty and Health Insurance Coverage in the United States, 2007*, U.S. Census Bureau, August 2008, http://www.census.gov/prod/2008pubs/p60-235.pdf (accessed April 23, 2009)

TABLE 2.3

Poverty thresholds, by size of family and number of related children under 18 years, 2008

Size of family unit	Related children under 18 years: None	One	Two	Three	Four	Five	Six	Seven	Eight or more
One person (unrelated individual)									
Under 65 years	11,201								
65 years and over	10,326								
Two people									
Householder under 65 years	14,417	14,840							
Householder 65 years and over	13,014	14,784							
Three people	16,841	17,330	17,346						
Four people	22,207	22,570	21,834	21,910					
Five people	26,781	27,170	26,338	25,694	25,301				
Six people	30,803	30,925	30,288	29,677	28,769	28,230			
Seven people	35,442	35,664	34,901	34,369	33,379	32,223	30,955		
Eight people	39,640	39,990	39,270	38,639	37,744	36,608	35,426	35,125	
Nine people or more	47,684	47,915	47,278	46,743	45,864	44,656	43,563	43,292	41,624

SOURCE: "Poverty Thresholds for 2008 by Size of Family and Number of Related Children under 18 Years", in *Poverty Thresholds*, U.S. Census Bureau, Housing and Household Economic Statistics Division, February 2009, http://www.census.gov/hhes/www/poverty/threshld/thresh08.html

FIGURE 2.12

Percent distribution by income of households headed by persons aged 65 and over and individuals aged 65 and over, 2007

[$41,851 median for 12.5 million family households 65+]

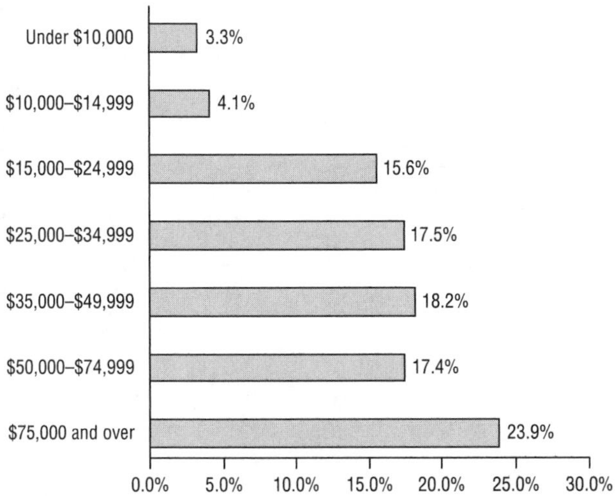

SOURCE: Saadia Greenberg, "Figure 7. Percent Distribution by Income: 2007," in *A Profile of Older Americans: 2008*, U.S. Department of Health and Human Services, Administration on Aging, 2009, http://www.mowaa.org/Document.Doc?id=69 (accessed April 20, 2009)

and measured perspective about economic upheaval and may be able to offer insight based on their experiences about how best to cope with the downturn. However, Kathleen Megan reports in "Stress Levels about the Economy Vary among Generations" (*Hartford Courant*, November 17, 2008) that some older adults, especially those who vividly remember the toll of the Great Depression, may feel panicked, fearing that the struggles and losses of those years will recur.

CONSUMER EXPENSES

On average, older households spend less than younger households because they generally have less money to spend, fewer dependents to support, and different needs and values. The U.S. Bureau of Labor Statistics reports that in 2007 the annual per capita expenditure for people aged 65 to 74 was $42,262, whereas those aged 75 and older spent just $30,414. (See Table 2.4.) Those under the age of 25 were the only group with a smaller expenditure, spending $29,457 per capita annually. The greatest amounts were spent on housing (including utilities), food, transportation, and health care. Not surprisingly, older adults spent more on health care than any other age group, both in actual dollars and as a percentage of expenditures. Older adults spent less on tobacco and smoking products, alcoholic beverages, apparel, and food away from home than other age groups.

Smaller Households Are More Expensive to Run

Most older adult households contain fewer people than younger households. Even though larger households, in general, cost more to feed, operate, and maintain, they are less expensive on a per capita basis.

Home maintenance, such as replacing a roof or major appliance, costs the same for any household, but in larger households the per capita cost is lower. Purchasing small quantities of food for one or two people may be almost as costly as buying in bulk for a larger household. Because older adults often have limited transportation and mobility, they may be forced to buy food and other necessities at small neighborhood stores that generally charge more than supermarkets and warehouse stores. Larger households may also benefit from multiple incomes.

High energy costs also cause older adults physical and financial hardship, prompting some to suffer extreme heat

TABLE 2.4

Average annual expenditures and characteristics, by age, 2007

Item	All consumer units	Under 25 years	25–34 years	35–44 years	45–54 years	55–64 years	65 years and older	65–74 years	75 years and older
Number of consumer units (in thousands)	120,171	8,150	20,499	23,416	25,245	19,462	23,400	12,011	11,390
Consumer unit characteristics:									
Income before taxes	$63,091	$31,443	$57,256	$76,540	$80,560	$71,048	$40,305	$47,708	$32,499
Age of reference person	48.8	21.5	29.6	39.6	49.4	59.2	75.2	69.1	81.5
Average number in consumer unit:									
Persons	2.5	2.0	2.8	3.2	2.7	2.1	1.7	1.8	1.5
Children under 18	.6	.4	1.1	1.3	.6	.2	.1	.1	(*)
Persons 65 and over	.3	(*)	(*)	(*)	(*)	.1	1.4	1.4	1.3
Earners	1.3	1.3	1.5	1.6	1.7	1.4	.4	.7	.2
Vehicles	1.9	1.2	1.7	2.2	2.3	2.2	1.6	1.8	1.3
Percent homeowner	67	16	47	68	75	81	79	81	77
Average annual expenditures	$49,638	$29,457	$47,510	$58,934	$58,331	$53,786	$36,530	$42,262	$30,414
Food	6,133	4,141	6,000	7,393	7,181	6,241	4,515	5,226	3,738
Food at home	3,465	2,265	3,210	4,125	4,003	3,457	2,905	3,348	2,419
Cereals and bakery products	460	274	427	548	522	456	405	459	346
Meats, poultry, fish, and eggs	777	491	692	976	907	758	634	738	520
Dairy products	387	238	368	459	442	384	332	376	284
Fruits and vegetables	600	340	529	677	684	640	557	628	479
Other food at home	1,241	922	1,194	1,465	1,447	1,219	976	1,147	789
Food away from home	2,668	1,876	2,790	3,268	3,178	2,784	1,610	1,878	1,319
Alcoholic beverages	457	461	514	469	498	533	285	346	218
Housing	16,920	9,598	17,329	20,952	19,195	17,223	12,396	13,547	11,173
Shelter	10,023	6,220	10,536	12,758	11,617	9,763	6,656	7,271	6,009
Owned dwellings	6,730	1,398	5,985	9,232	8,626	7,063	4,414	5,329	3,448
Rented dwellings	2,602	4,649	4,288	2,849	2,055	1,539	1,639	1,277	2,020
Other lodging	691	173	263	677	936	1,161	604	664	540
Utilities, fuels, and public services	3,477	1,813	3,063	3,928	4,053	3,754	3,117	3,392	2,828
Household operations	984	363	1,175	1,422	867	860	825	715	941
Housekeeping supplies	639	278	522	646	724	902	562	661	453
Household furnishings and equipment	1,797	925	2,034	2,198	1,933	1,944	1,235	1,508	943
Apparel and services	1,881	1,477	2,106	2,335	2,191	1,888	1,040	1,323	732
Transportation	8,758	5,708	9,065	10,558	9,943	9,608	5,785	7,669	3,784
Vehicle purchases (net outlay)	3,244	2,273	3,930	4,183	3,223	3,348	1,977	2,701	1,213
Gasoline and motor oil	2,384	1,760	2,446	2,870	2,846	2,504	1,461	1,862	1,039
Other vehicle expenses	2,592	1,365	2,293	2,966	3,213	2,993	1,928	2,536	1,270
Public transportation	538	310	396	540	661	763	420	569	262
Healthcare	2,853	800	1,740	2,315	2,792	3,476	4,631	4,967	4,275
Entertainment	2,698	1,448	2,462	3,551	3,163	2,730	1,966	2,636	1,255
Personal care products and services	588	337	512	662	686	632	528	599	451
Reading	118	51	72	107	137	151	143	151	136
Education	945	1,787	604	819	1,687	929	292	245	341
Tobacco products and smoking supplies	323	290	331	379	388	353	176	243	106
Miscellaneous	808	368	589	845	1,008	1,084	672	787	548
Cash contributions	1,821	549	1,027	1,569	1,972	2,746	2,282	1,923	2,661
Personal insurance and pensions	5,336	2,440	5,159	6,980	7,489	6,193	1,819	2,600	996
Life and other personal insurance	309	39	164	286	402	461	329	375	279
Pensions and Social Security	5,027	2,401	4,995	6,694	7,087	5,732	1,491	2,225	716

*Value is less than or equal to 0.05.

SOURCE: "Table 4. Age of Reference Person: Average Annual Expenditures and Characteristics, Consumer Expenditure Survey, 2007," in *Consumer Expenditures in 2007*, U.S. Department of Labor, U.S. Bureau of Labor Statistics, April 2009, http://www.bls.gov/cex/csxann07.pdf (accessed April 23, 2009)

and cold in their homes. Programs such as the Home Energy Assistance Program (HEAP; http://www.otda.state.ny.us/main/heap/), which is operated by the New York Office of Temporary and Disability Assistance, attempt to prevent older adults from suffering from a lack of heat in their home. HEAP assists eligible households to meet their home energy needs.

AGING CONSUMERS—A GROWING MARKET

Older adults have proven to be a lucrative market for many products. Packaged Facts declares in *The Mature Market: Consumer Trends and U.S. Retail Markets* (March 2007) that in 2006, 68 million consumers aged 55 and older wielded an estimated $1.6 trillion in purchasing power. It notes that on average adults over the age of 50 spend $1 trillion on products and services and $7 billion on Internet purchases. Older adults are redefining aging—only a minority of Americans expects to retire as their parents did. Older adults are now more likely to continue working, and working out, rather than retiring to the shuffleboard court or rocking chair on the front porch. As a result, they are considered an important market for an expanding array of services besides those traditionally marketed to older adults—such as health and life insurance plans and burial plots.

Baby Boomers—The Emerging "Silver" Market

The aging baby boomers (people born between 1946 and 1964) have been dubbed "zoomers" to reflect the generation's active lifestyle. Market researchers believe the sheer size of the boomer cohort and its history of self-indulgence, coupled with considerable purchasing power, ensure that this group will be the most voracious older consumers ever.

The information in this section was drawn from the Boomer Marketing Report, a quarterly survey of 1,400 consumers by the Boomer Project/Survey Sampling International that aims to determine how this generation thinks, feels, and responds to marketing and advertising messages, and from *50 Things Every Marketer Needs to Know about Boomers over 50* (2006, http://www.boomerproject.com/documents/white_papers/50_things.pdf). Included among the many insights that the Boomer Project research reveals are the following:

- Boomers at age 50 perceive themselves as 12 years younger, and they expect to live 35 more years. They consider themselves to be in early "middle age" and view 72 as the onset of old age.
- Boomers reject any and all age-related labels to describe themselves. They do not want to be called "seniors," "aged," or even "boomers," and they do not want to be compared with their parents' generation or any previous cohort of older adults.
- Boomers over the age of 50 do not want to reverse or stop the signs of aging, they simply want to postpone or slow the process. They are intent on seeking health rather than youth—feeling younger is as important as looking younger for boomers eager to age "on their own terms."
- Boomers want more time, which means that services that offer them free time to pursue work and leisure activities are likely to be in great demand. Examples of these include cleaning, home maintenance, and gardening services.
- Boomers are becoming less interested in material possessions and more interested in gaining a variety of experiences. Rather than embracing the premise that "he who has the most toys wins," boomers believe "he who chalks up the most experiences wins."
- Once dubbed the "me generation," boomers operate on the premise that they are entitled to special treatment, not because they have earned it by virtue of age, but simply because they deserve it. They want products and services that are relevant to them personally. They remain motivated to fulfill their own needs, whether these needs are for community, adventure, or a spiritual life.
- Boomers are life-long learners. Continuing education classes and opportunities to learn and enrich their lives through travel are important to this generation.
- Boomers are still interested in promoting social change. The generation known for protesting the Vietnam War (1954–1975) and questioning authority and traditional American social mores continues to support global and local humanitarian and environmental action.
- Boomers do not want to relocate to traditional retirement enclaves and communities; instead, they prefer to "age in place" in their present home or nearby. Having witnessed the institutionalization of their parents in nursing homes and other assisted living facilities, boomers are intent on remaining in their homes, and in the community, for as long as they can.

In "The Older Audience Is Looking Better Than Ever" (*New York Times*, April 19, 2009), Stuart Elliot confirms that the size of the boomer generation, its purchasing power, and the fact that boomers are more likely to try new products than past generations of older adults have made boomers an increasingly attractive demographic for marketers. Elliot asserts that the economic downturn renders them even more attractive because "older consumers who may have paid off mortgages seem a safer bet than younger ones who may get laid off in last-hired, first-fired downsizings."

Even though the boomers still represent a tremendous market for goods and services, their purchasing power was significantly diminished in 2009, following real estate and stock market declines. David Rosnick and Dean Baker of the Center for Economic and Policy Research estimate in *The Wealth of the Baby Boom Cohorts after the Collapse of the Housing Bubble* (February 2009, http://www.cepr.net/documents/publications/baby-boomer-wealth-2009-02.pdf) that younger boomers (those aged 45 to 54) lost 45% of their median net worth, from $172,400 in 2004 to $94,200 in 2009. During this same period, the net worth of older boomers (those aged 55 to 64) dropped from $315,400 to $159,800, a decrease of 50%. Because older boomers are nearing retirement age and have few working years left to make up the investment and home equity losses, Rosnick and Baker predict that many will be forced to rely on Social Security as their principal source of income in retirement.

SOCIAL SECURITY

We can never insure one hundred percent of the population against one hundred percent of the hazards and vicissitudes of life, but we have tried to frame a law which will give some measure of protection to the average citizen and to his family against the loss of a job and against poverty-ridden old age.

—President Franklin D. Roosevelt, on signing the Social Security Act, August 14, 1935

Social Security is a social insurance program funded through a dedicated payroll tax. It is also known as Old-Age, Survivors, and Disability Insurance (OASDI), which describes its three major classes of beneficiaries.

During the Great Depression poverty among the older population escalated. In 1934 more than half of older adults lacked sufficient income. Even though 30 states had some form of an old-age pension program in place, by 1935 these programs were unable to meet the growing need. Just 3% of the older population received benefits under these state plans, and the average benefit amount was about 65 cents a day.

As advocated by President Franklin D. Roosevelt (1882–1945), a Democrat, social insurance would solve the problem of economic security for older adults by creating a work-related, contributory system in which workers would provide for their own future economic security through taxes paid while employed. By the time the Social Security Act was signed into law by President Roosevelt in August 1935, 34 nations were already operating some form of a social insurance program—government-sponsored efforts to provide for the economic well-being of a nation's citizens.

According to the SSA, in "Social Security Basic Facts" (February 26, 2009, http://www.ssa.gov/pressoffice/basicfact.htm), in 2009 more than 9 out of 10 people aged 65 and older received OASDI. Retired workers and their dependents accounted for more than two-thirds (69%) of total benefits paid, whereas survivors of deceased workers accounted for 13% of the total, and disabled workers and their dependents rounded out the total with 18% of benefits paid. An estimated 94% (162 million) of the U.S. workforce was covered by Social Security.

Even though Social Security was not initially intended as a full pension, 20% of married older adults and 41% of unmarried older adults relied almost exclusively (for 90% or more of their income) on the program in 2009. In "Social Security Lifts 13 Million Seniors above the Poverty Line: A State-by-State Analysis" (February 24, 2005, http://www.cbpp.org/cms/?fa=view&id=1111), Arloc Sherman and Isaac Shapiro of the Center on Budget and Policy Priorities observe that without Social Security 46.8% of older adults would have income below the poverty line, whereas with Social Security benefits just 8.7% are below the poverty level. This capacity to lift older adults from poverty makes Social Security the country's most effective antipoverty program.

Benefits are funded through the Federal Insurance Contributions Act (FICA), which provides that a mandatory tax be withheld from workers' earnings and be matched by their employers. (Self-employed workers pay both the employer and employee shares of FICA taxes.) When covered workers retire (or are disabled), they draw benefits based on the amount they contributed to the fund. The amount of the benefit is directly related to the duration of employment and earnings—people who have worked longer and earned higher wages receive larger benefits.

Workers can retire as early as age 62 and receive reduced Social Security benefits, or they can wait until full retirement age and receive full benefits. Until 2003 the full retirement age was 65, but beginning that year it began to increase gradually, such that for people born in 1960 or later, retirement age will be 67. A special credit is given to people who delay retirement beyond their full retirement age. This credit, which is a percentage added to the Social Security benefit, varies depending on the retiree's date of birth. Workers who reached full retirement age in 2008 or later can receive a credit of 8% per year.

Table 2.5 shows the relationship between earnings and Social Security benefits. It shows average indexed monthly earnings (AIME; this is an amount that summarizes a worker's earnings) and the corresponding benefit amounts. Delaying retirement to age 70 yields the highest ration of retirement benefits to AIME.

Benefits and Beneficiaries

In "Social Security Basic Facts," the SSA notes that in 2009 the program paid benefits to 51 million people. The majority were older adults—34.9 million retired workers and their dependents, along with 6.5 million survivors of deceased workers, and 9.2 million disabled workers and their dependents. The Social Security and Medicare Boards of Trustees report in *Status of the Social Security and Medicare Programs: A Summary of the 2009 Annual Reports* (May 2009, http://www.socialsecurity.gov/OACT/TRSUM/) that in 2008, 162 million people with earnings covered by Social Security paid payroll taxes. Social Security income in 2009 was an estimated $708 billion. Table 2.6 shows the number of beneficiaries of all OASDI programs as well as the average monthly benefits paid in December 2007, the most recent month for which data were available as of mid-2009.

Social Security Amendments of 1977

Ever since 1940, the year that Americans began to receive Social Security checks, monthly retirement benefits have steadily increased, but during the 1970s they soared. Legislation enacted in 1973 provided for automatic cost-of-living adjustments (COLAs) that were intended to prevent inflation from eroding Social Security benefits. The average benefit was indexed (annually adjusted) to keep pace with inflation as reflected by the CPI. COLAs were 9.9% in 1979 and peaked at 14.3% the following year. (See Table 2.7.) These increases threatened the continued finan-

TABLE 2.5

Benefit amount for worker with maximum-taxable earnings, 2009

Retirement in Jan.	Retirement at age 62[a] AIME[d]	Retirement at age 62[a] Monthly benefits At age 62	Retirement at age 62[a] Monthly benefits In 2009	Retirement at age 65[b] AIME[d]	Retirement at age 65[b] Monthly benefits At age 65	Retirement at age 65[b] Monthly benefits In 2009	Retirement at age 70[c] AIME[d]	Retirement at age 70[c] Monthly benefits At age 70	Retirement at age 70[c] Monthly benefits In 2009
1987	$2,205	$666	$1,320	$2,009	$789	$1,562	$1,725	$1,056	$2,092
1988	2,311	691	1,313	2,139	838	1,593	1,859	1,080	2,052
1989	2,490	739	1,350	2,287	899	1,643	2,000	1,063	1,943
1990	2,648	780	1,361	2,417	975	1,701	2,154	1,085	1,893
1991	2,792	815	1,350	2,531	1,022	1,693	2,332	1,163	1,927
1992	2,978	860	1,373	2,716	1,088	1,738	2,470	1,231	1,966
1993	3,154	899	1,395	2,878	1,128	1,750	2,605	1,289	1,998
1994	3,384	954	1,442	3,024	1,147	1,733	2,758	1,358	2,052
1995	3,493	972	1,429	3,219	1,199	1,762	2,896	1,474	2,167
1996	3,657	1,006	1,442	3,402	1,248	1,789	3,012	1,501	2,151
1997	3,877	1,056	1,471	3,634	1,326	1,847	3,189	1,609	2,242
1998	4,144	1,117	1,524	3,750	1,342	1,831	3,348	1,648	2,247
1999	4,463	1,191	1,604	3,926	1,373	1,848	3,496	1,684	2,268
2000	4,775	1,248	1,639	4,161	1,435	1,885	3,707	1,752	2,302
2001	5,126	1,314	1,668	4,440	1,538	1,952	3,912	1,879	2,385
2002	5,499	1,382	1,710	4,770	1,660	2,054	4,165	1,988	2,459
2003	5,729	1,412	1,722	5,099	1,721	2,100	4,321	2,045	2,496
2004	5,892	1,422	1,700	5,457	1,784	2,133	4,532	2,111	2,523
2005	6,137	1,452	1,690	5,827	1,874	2,181	4,786	2,252	2,621
2006	6,515	1,530	1,711	6,058	1,961	2,193	5,072	2,420	2,706
2007	6,852	1,598	1,729	6,229	1,998	2,163	5,406	2,672	2,892
2008	7,260	1,682	1,779	6,479	2,030	2,148	5,733	2,794	2,956
2009	7,685	1,769	1,769	6,861	2,172	2,172	6,090	3,054	3,054

[a]Retirement at age 62 is assumed here to be at exact age 62 and 1 month. Such early retirement results in a reduced monthly benefit.
[b]Retirement at age 65 is assumed to be at exact age 65 and 0 months. For retirement in 2003 and later, the monthly benefit is reduced for early retirement. (For people born before 1938, age 65 is the normal retirement age. Normal retirement age will gradually increase to age 67.)
[c]Retirement at age 70 maximizes the effect of delayed retirement credits.
[d]AIME = Average Income Monthly Earnings
Notes: Initial monthly benefits paid at ages 65 and 70 in 2000–2001 were slightly lower than the amounts shown above because such initial benefits were partially based on a cost-of-living adjustment (COLA) for December 1999 that was originally determined as 2.4 percent based on CPIs (Consumer Price Index) published by the Bureau of Labor Statistics. Pursuant to Public Law 106-554, however, this COLA is effectively now 2.5 percent, and the above figures reflect the benefit change required by this legislation.

SOURCE: "Worker with Steady Earnings at the Maximum Level since Age 22," in *Workers with Maximum-Taxable Earnings*, U.S. Social Security Administration, Office of the Chief Actuary, October 16, 2008, http://www.socialsecurity.gov/OACT/COLA/examplemax.html (accessed April 25, 2008)

cial viability of the entire system and prompted policy makers to reconsider the COLA formula.

Some legislators felt that indexing vastly overcompensated for inflation, causing relative benefit levels to rise higher than at any previous time in the history of the program. In an attempt to prevent future Social Security benefits from rising to what many considered excessive levels, Congress passed the Social Security Amendments of 1977 to restructure the benefit plan and design more realistic formulas for benefits. Along with redefining COLAs, the 1977 amendments raised the payroll tax slightly, increased the wage base, and reduced benefits.

The 5.8% COLA increase in 2008 more than doubled from the previous year. (See Table 2.7.) Table 2.8 shows how this COLA increase translated into SSI payments that took effect in January 2009.

The Earnings Test

Legislation enacted on January 1, 2000, changed the way in which the amount that beneficiaries could earn while also receiving retirement or survivors benefits was determined. The retirement earnings test applies only to people younger than normal retirement age, which ranges from age 65 to 67 depending on year of birth. Social Security withholds benefits if annual retirement earnings exceed a certain level, called a retirement earnings test exempt amount, for people who have not yet attained normal retirement age. These exempt amounts generally increase annually with increases in the national average wage index.

Table 2.9 shows the exempt amounts from 2000 to 2009. One dollar in Social Security benefits is withheld for every $2 of earnings more than the lower exempt amount. Similarly, $1 in benefits is withheld for every $3 of earnings more than the higher exempt amount.

SUPPLEMENTAL SECURITY INCOME

SSI is designed to provide monthly cash payments to those older, blind, and disabled people who have low incomes. Even though SSI is administered by the SSA, unlike Social Security benefits, SSI benefits are not based on prior work, and the funds come from general tax revenues rather than from Social Security taxes.

In 1972 Congress passed the legislation establishing SSI to replace several state-administered programs and

TABLE 2.6

Number and average monthly benefit, by type of benefit and race, December 2007

Type of benefit	All races[a] Number	All races[a] Average monthly benefit (dollars)	White Number	White Average monthly benefit (dollars)	Black Number	Black Average monthly benefit (dollars)	Other[b] Number	Other[b] Average monthly benefit (dollars)
Total, OASDI[c]	**49,864,838**	**987.00**	**40,887,616**	**1,023.50**	**5,125,460**	**842.90**	**3,685,248**	**792.10**
OASI[d]	40,948,624	1,014.70	34,757,613	1,044.60	3,565,823	870.80	2,542,461	812.20
Retirement benefits	34,454,106	1,032.20	30,071,993	1,054.90	2,825,729	916.70	1,495,557	798.90
Retired workers	31,527,728	1,078.60	27,558,302	1,100.70	2,613,682	953.60	1,301,304	865.00
Spouses of retired workers	2,432,082	531.50	2,157,848	549.40	114,032	445.00	154,540	348.90
Children of retired workers	494,296	538.00	355,843	571.30	98,015	480.00	39,713	385.60
Survivor benefits	6,494,518	922.20	4,685,620	978.70	740,094	695.70	1,046,904	831.10
Children of deceased workers	1,891,706	704.30	1,108,777	763.90	364,422	588.90	410,109	646.10
Widowed mothers and fathers	164,665	781.80	104,463	841.90	21,039	673.60	38,525	678.90
Nondisabled widow(er)s	4,211,356	1,040.40	3,361,051	1,064.50	323,493	830.40	515,024	1,015.80
Disabled widow(er)s	224,982	645.50	110,440	653.50	30,952	560.20	82,541	668.00
Parents of deceased workers	1,809	918.00	889	943.60	188	896.10	705	893.70
DI[e]	8,916,214	859.70	6,130,003	903.60	1,559,637	779.10	1,142,787	747.50
Disabled workers	7,098,723	1,004.00	4,952,546	1,043.60	1,199,718	931.80	873,786	899.80
Spouses of disabled workers	152,802	267.00	114,610	280.10	16,519	241.90	20,859	216.30
Children of disabled workers	1,664,689	299.00	1,062,847	318.60	343,400	271.30	248,142	255.90

Note: Race and ethnic designations are collected from the form SS-5 (Application for a Social Security Card). For dependents and survivor beneficiaries, race is assumed to be the same as that shown on the SS-5 for the wage earner on whose earnings record the benefit is based.
[a]Includes 166,514 persons of unknown race. In years prior to 1993, persons of unknown race were included with white.
[b]Includes Asians and Pacific Islanders, American Indians and Alaska Natives, and a subset of the total number of beneficiaries of Hispanic origin. The distribution of beneficiaries among those three groups is not available.
[c]OASDI=Old Age Survivor Disability Insurance.
[d]OASI=Old Age Survivor Insurance.
[e]DI=Disability Insurance.

SOURCE: "Table 5.A1. Number and Average Monthly Benefit, by Type of Benefit and Race, December 2007," in *Annual Statistical Supplement, 2008*, U.S. Social Security Administration, March 2009, http://www.socialsecurity.gov/policy/docs/statcomps/supplement/2008/5a.pdf (accessed April 25, 2009)

TABLE 2.7

Social Security cost-of-living adjustments (COLA), 1975–2008

Year	COLA	Year	COLA
1975	8.0%	1992	3.0%
1976	6.4%	1993	2.6%
1977	5.9%	1994	2.8%
1978	2.6%	1995	2.6%
1979	9.9%	1996	2.9%
1980	14.3%	1997	2.1%
1981	11.2%	1998	1.3%
1982	7.4%	1999	*2.5%
1983	3.5%	2000	3.5%
1984	3.5%	2001	2.6%
1985	3.1%	2002	1.4%
1986	1.3%	2003	2.1%
1987	4.2%	2004	2.7%
1988	4.0%	2005	4.1%
1989	4.7%	2006	3.3%
1990	5.4%	2007	2.3%
1991	3.7%	2008	5.8%

*The COLA for December 1999 was originally determined as 2.4 percent based on CPIs (Consumer Price Index) published by the Bureau of Labor Statistics. Pursuant to Public Law 106–554, however, this COLA is effectively now 2.5 percent.

SOURCE: "Social Security Cost-of-Living Adjustments," in *Cost-of-Living Adjustments*, U. S. Social Security Administration, Office of the Chief Actuary, October 16, 2008, http://www.socialsecurity.gov/OACT/COLA/colaseries.html (accessed April 25, 2008)

TABLE 2.8

SSI federal payment amounts, 2008 and 2009

Recipient(s)	Unrounded annual amounts for— 2008	Unrounded annual amounts for— 2009*	Monthly amounts for 2009
Eligible individual	$7,651.53	$8,095.32	$674
Eligible couple	11,476.00	12,141.61	1,011
Essential person	3,834.53	4,056.93	338

*The unrounded amounts for 2009 equal the unrounded amounts for 2008 increased by 5.8 percent.

SOURCE: "SSI Amounts for 2009 Calculation Details," in *SSI Federal Payment Amounts*, U.S. Social Security Administration, Office of the Chief Actuary, October 16, 2008, http://www.socialsecurity.gov/OACT/COLA/SSI.html (accessed April 25, 2008)

provide a uniform federal benefit based on uniform eligibility standards. Even though SSI is a federal program, some states provide a supplement to the federal benefit.

In "SSI Monthly Statistics, March 2009" (April 2009, http://www.socialsecurity.gov/policy/docs/statcomps/ssi_monthly/2009-03/index.html), the SSA reports that of the 7.6 million people receiving SSI benefits in March 2009, over 2 million were 65 and older. Even though payments vary by age group, the average monthly benefit received by older adults in 2009 was $414.70. (See Table 2.10.)

WHAT LIES AHEAD FOR SOCIAL SECURITY?

The Social Security program faces long-range financing challenges that, if unresolved, threaten its solvency (the ability to meet financial obligations on time) in the

TABLE 2.9

Annual retirement earnings test exempt amounts, 2000–09

Year	Lower amount[a]	Higher amount[b]
2000	$10,080	$17,000
2001	10,680	25,000
2002	11,280	30,000
2003	11,520	30,720
2004	11,640	31,080
2005	12,000	31,800
2006	12,480	33,240
2007	12,960	34,440
2008	13,560	36,120
2009	14,160	37,680

[a]Applies in years before the year of attaining NRA (National Retirement Age).
[b]Applies in the year of attaining NRA (National Retirment Age), for months prior to such attainment.

SOURCE: "Annual Retirement Earnings Test Exempt Amounts," in *Exempt Amounts under the Earnings Test*, U. S. Social Security Administration, Office of the Chief Actuary, October 16, 2008, http://www.ssa.gov/OACT/COLA/rtea.html (accessed April 25, 2008)

coming decades. Since the 1980s the program has been collecting more money than it has had to pay out and will continue to do so until 2016. The surplus is not, however, cash that is set aside. Rather, it is loaned to the U.S. Treasury, which places it in the general revenue pool, and it is spent as the government sees fit.

According to the SSA, in *The 2009 Annual Report of the Board of Trustees of the Federal Old-Age and Survivors Insurance and Federal Disability Insurance Trust Funds* (May 12, 2009, http://www.socialsecurity.gov/OACT/TR/2009/tr09.pdf), without changes to the system, the amount of benefits owed will exceed taxes collected by 2016, and Social Security will have to tap into trust funds to pay benefits. The SSA estimates that the trust funds will be depleted in 2039, leaving Social Security unable to pay scheduled benefits in full to older adult retirees and its other beneficiaries. In "Status of the Social Security and Medicare Programs," the SSA urges immediate action, observing that "Social Security could be brought into actuarial balance over the next 75 years with changes equivalent to an immediate 16 percent increase in the payroll tax (from a rate of 12.4 percent to 14.4 percent) or an immediate reduction in benefits of 13 percent or some combination of the two. Ensuring that the system remains solvent on a sustainable basis beyond the next 75 years would require larger changes because increasing longevity will result in people receiving benefits for ever longer periods of retirement."

To a large extent, demographic changes precipitated this crisis. Social Security is a "pay-as-you-go" program, with the contributions of present workers paying the retirement benefits of those currently retired. The program is solvent at this time because the number of employees contributing to the system is sufficient. The earliest wave of baby boomers is still in the workforce and at its peak earning years. The large cohort of boomers is funding the smaller cohort of retirees born during the low birthrate cycle of the Great Depression. As a result, there are still fewer retirees depleting funds than there are workers contributing. The SSA notes that when monthly Social Security benefits began in 1940, a man aged 65 could expect to live an average of about 12.7 additional years; by 2010 the typical 65-year-old is likely to live on average another 17.7 years. (See Table 2.11.)

Saving Social Security

There are three basic ways to resolve Social Security's financial problems: raise taxes, cut benefits, or make Social Security taxes earn more by investing the money. It is most likely that restoring Social Security's long-term financial balance will require a combination of increased revenues and reduced expenditures. The ways to reduce expenditures include:

- Reducing initial benefits to retirees
- Raising the retirement age (already slated to rise from 65 to 67 by 2027)
- Lowering COLAs
- Limiting benefits based on beneficiaries' other income and assets

The ways to increase revenues include:

- Increasing Social Security payroll taxes
- Investing trust funds in securities with potentially higher yields than the government bonds in which they are currently invested
- Increasing income taxes on Social Security benefits

Obama Vows to Ensure the Long-Term Solvency of Social Security

During his campaign for the presidency, then-U.S. Senator Barack Obama (1961–), a Democrat, spoke out against the efforts to privatize Social Security that President George W. Bush (1946–), a Republican, championed. In view of the stock market's overall volatility and precipitous decline in late 2008, the plan to promote private retirement accounts has fallen out of favor. President Obama has expressed support for applying payroll taxes to incomes more than $250,000. However, in the spring of 2009, with the United States in the throes of an economic recession, this proposal was met with strong opposition from Republicans. For their part, Democrats staunchly oppose any reduction in benefits for those who will retire in the future. One compromise solution is a combination of both strategies—generating new revenue via tax reforms and modifying benefits for future retirees.

Even though protecting Social Security is vitally important to the nation's retirees and aging baby boomers who will soon retire, some observers believe that actions to secure it may be deferred in favor of health care and

TABLE 2.10

Average monthly SSI (Supplemental Security Income) payment, by eligibility category, age, and source of payment, March 2008–March 2009

[In dollars]

		Eligibility category		Age		
Month	Total	Aged	Blind and disabled	Under 18	18–64	65 or older
All sources						
2008						
March	476.90	390.50	493.70	567.50	492.50	393.50
April	476.40	390.70	493.00	565.40	492.00	393.70
May	477.70	391.00	494.50	571.20	492.70	394.00
June	477.00	391.10	493.50	567.70	492.00	394.10
July	475.70	391.00	492.10	562.70	491.30	393.90
August	477.40	391.20	494.00	569.90	492.30	394.20
September	476.70	391.20	493.10	566.00	491.90	394.10
October	476.80	391.50	493.20	566.30	492.20	394.30
November	477.30	391.90	493.70	567.10	492.40	394.60
December	477.80	393.50	493.90	561.30	494.00	396.00
2009						
January	504.10	411.10	521.80	603.00	519.90	414.30
February	502.80	410.60	520.30	597.90	518.80	413.90
March	503.70	411.60	521.00	599.40	519.40	414.70
Federal payments						
2008						
March	445.80	333.40	466.50	553.20	464.30	341.20
April	445.40	333.50	465.90	551.20	463.90	341.30
May	446.70	333.70	467.40	557.00	464.60	341.60
June	446.10	333.80	466.50	553.60	463.90	341.60
July	444.80	333.60	465.10	548.50	463.30	341.50
August	446.60	333.90	467.10	555.80	464.30	341.70
September	445.90	333.80	466.20	551.90	464.00	341.70
October	446.00	333.90	466.30	552.10	464.30	341.80
November	446.50	334.40	466.90	553.00	464.50	342.10
December	447.00	336.00	467.00	547.10	466.10	343.60
2009						
January	473.90	354.40	495.40	588.60	492.60	362.60
February	472.60	353.80	493.90	583.60	491.50	362.20
March	473.50	354.80	494.70	585.10	492.10	362.90
State supplementation						
2008						
March	156.30	171.50	151.10	76.40	159.60	172.20
April	156.30	171.60	150.90	76.40	159.50	172.20
May	156.40	171.70	151.10	76.60	159.60	172.30
June	156.20	171.70	150.80	76.30	159.40	172.20
July	156.10	171.70	150.70	76.30	159.20	172.20
August	156.10	171.70	150.70	76.20	159.30	172.30
September	156.00	171.80	150.60	76.10	159.10	172.20
October	156.10	171.90	150.70	76.30	159.10	172.30
November	156.00	171.90	150.50	76.00	159.10	172.40
December	156.20	172.30	150.70	76.10	159.30	172.70
2009						
January	156.00	172.20	150.40	76.00	159.00	172.50
February	155.80	172.10	150.20	75.80	158.80	172.50
March	155.90	172.30	150.20	75.80	158.80	172.60

Note: Data are for the end of the specified month and exclude retroactive payments.

SOURCE: Average Monthly Payment, by Eligibility Category, Age, and Source of Payment, March 2008–March 2009," in *SSI Monthly Statistics, March 2009*, U.S. Social Security Administration, Office of Policy, April 2009, http://www.socialsecurity.gov/policy/docs/statcomps/ssi_monthly/2009-03/table07.pdf (accessed April 25, 2008)

other economic priorities. According to the SSA, in the press release "Commissioner Astrue Praises President-Elect Obama's Call for a National Conversation on Social Security" (January 16, 2009, http://www.ssa.gov/pressoffice/pr/astrue-praises-obama-pr.html), the SSA commissioner Michael J. Astrue (1956–) said, "With all the other challenges President-elect Obama is facing, it would be understandable if he were to defer decisions on Social Security for a period of time. He is showing true leadership in starting this process earlier rather than later, and everyone at the Social Security Administration stands ready to support this effort in every way we can."

The American Recovery and Reinvestment Act

In the press release "Vice President Biden Announces $250 Recovery Payments to Go to Social Security

TABLE 2.11

Life expectancy at birth and at age 65, selected years 1940–2085[a]

Calendar year	Low cost				Intermediate				High cost			
	At birth[b]		At age 65[c]		At birth[b]		At age 65[c]		At birth[b]		At age 65[c]	
	Male	Female	Male	Female	Male	Female	Male	Female	Male	Female	Male	Female
1940	69.5	75.4	12.7	14.7	69.8	75.8	12.7	14.7	70.2	76.3	12.7	14.7
1945	71.1	76.8	13.0	15.4	71.6	77.3	13.0	15.4	72.1	78.0	13.0	15.4
1950	72.1	77.8	13.1	16.2	72.8	78.5	13.1	16.2	73.6	79.4	13.1	16.2
1955	72.6	78.2	13.1	16.7	73.5	79.2	13.1	16.7	74.6	80.3	13.1	16.7
1960	73.1	78.5	13.2	17.4	74.2	79.6	13.2	17.4	75.5	81.0	13.2	17.4
1965	73.7	78.8	13.5	18.0	75.1	80.2	13.5	18.0	76.7	81.8	13.5	18.0
1970	74.6	79.4	13.8	18.5	76.2	81.0	13.8	18.5	78.1	82.9	13.8	18.5
1975	75.2	79.9	14.2	18.7	77.2	81.7	14.2	18.7	79.3	83.9	14.2	18.7
1980	75.9	80.3	14.7	18.7	78.1	82.4	14.7	18.7	80.6	84.8	14.7	18.7
1985	76.4	80.6	15.3	18.8	78.8	83.0	15.3	18.9	81.6	85.7	15.3	18.9
1990	76.8	80.9	15.8	18.9	79.5	83.5	15.8	19.0	82.6	86.4	15.9	19.1
1995	77.2	81.2	16.2	19.0	80.1	84.0	16.3	19.2	83.5	87.2	16.5	19.4
1996	77.3	81.3	16.3	19.0	80.3	84.1	16.5	19.3	83.7	87.3	16.6	19.5
1997	77.3	81.3	16.4	19.1	80.3	84.2	16.6	19.3	83.8	87.5	16.7	19.6
1998	77.4	81.4	16.5	19.1	80.4	84.2	16.7	19.3	84.0	87.6	16.9	19.6
1999	77.4	81.4	16.6	19.1	80.6	84.3	16.8	19.4	84.1	87.7	17.0	19.7
2000	77.5	81.5	16.6	19.1	80.6	84.4	16.9	19.5	84.3	87.9	17.2	19.8
2001	77.5	81.5	16.7	19.2	80.7	84.5	17.0	19.5	84.5	88.0	17.3	19.9
2002	77.5	81.5	16.8	19.2	80.8	84.5	17.1	19.6	84.6	88.1	17.4	20.0
2003	77.6	81.6	16.8	19.2	80.9	84.6	17.2	19.6	84.7	88.2	17.5	20.1
2004	77.6	81.6	16.9	19.2	81.0	84.7	17.2	19.7	84.9	88.4	17.7	20.2
2005	77.7	81.7	16.9	19.2	81.1	84.8	17.3	19.7	85.0	88.5	17.8	20.3
2006	77.8	81.7	16.9	19.3	81.2	84.9	17.4	19.8	85.2	88.6	17.9	20.4
2007	77.8	81.7	17.0	19.3	81.3	85.0	17.5	19.8	85.4	88.8	18.0	20.5
2010	78.0	81.8	17.1	19.3	81.6	85.2	17.7	20.0	85.8	89.1	18.4	20.8
2015	78.2	82.0	17.2	19.5	82.1	85.6	18.0	20.3	86.5	89.8	19.0	21.3
2020	78.4	82.2	17.3	19.6	82.5	85.9	18.3	20.6	87.2	90.3	19.6	21.9
2025	78.6	82.4	17.4	19.7	82.9	86.3	18.6	20.9	87.8	90.9	20.1	22.4
2030	78.8	82.5	17.5	19.8	83.3	86.6	18.9	21.2	88.5	91.4	20.6	22.9
2035	79.0	82.7	17.6	19.9	83.7	86.9	19.2	21.4	89.1	91.9	21.2	23.4
2040	79.2	82.8	17.8	20.0	84.0	87.2	19.5	21.7	89.6	92.4	21.7	23.9
2045	79.4	83.0	17.9	20.1	84.4	87.5	19.8	22.0	90.2	92.9	22.2	24.3
2050	79.6	83.1	18.0	20.2	84.8	87.8	20.0	22.2	90.7	93.4	22.6	24.8
2055	79.8	83.3	18.1	20.3	85.1	88.1	20.3	22.5	91.2	93.8	23.1	25.3
2060	80.0	83.4	18.2	20.4	85.4	88.4	20.6	22.7	91.8	94.3	23.6	25.7
2065	80.2	83.5	18.3	20.5	85.7	88.7	20.8	22.9	92.2	94.7	24.0	26.1
2070	80.3	83.7	18.4	20.6	86.0	88.9	21.0	23.2	92.7	95.2	24.5	26.6
2075	80.5	83.8	18.5	20.7	86.3	89.2	21.3	23.4	93.2	95.6	24.9	27.0
2080	80.6	83.9	18.6	20.8	86.6	89.4	21.5	23.6	93.6	96.0	25.3	27.4
2085	80.8	84.0	18.7	20.9	86.9	89.7	21.7	23.8	94.1	96.4	25.8	27.8

[a]The life expectancy at a given age for a given year represents the average number of years of life remaining if a group of persons at that age were to experience the mortality rates for the series of years in which they reach each succeeding age.
[b]Life expectancy at birth for those born on January 1 of the calendar year is based on a combination of actual and estimated death rates for birth years 1940 through 2004. For birth years after 2004, these values are based solely on estimated death rates.
[c]Age 65 life expectancy for those attaining age 65 on January 1 of the calendar years before 1975 is based on actual data. For 1975 through 2004, these values are based on a combination of actual and estimated death rates. After 2004, these values are based solely on estimated death rates.

SOURCE: "Table V.A4. Cohort Life Expectancy," in *2008 OASDI Trustees Report*, U.S. Social Security Administration, Office of the Chief Actuary, March 2008, http://www.ssa.gOv/OACT/TR/TR08/V_demographic.html#203457 (accessed April 25, 2008)

and SSI Beneficiaries in May" (March 26, 2009, http://www.ssa.gov/pressoffice/pr/recovery-payments-pr.htm), the SSA notes that beginning in May 2009 the federal government would send out $250 economic recovery payments to people who receive Social Security and SSI benefits. Vice President Joseph R. Biden asserted that "these are checks that will make a big difference in the lives of older Americans and people with disabilities—many of whom have been hit especially hard by the economic crisis that has swept across the country." The one-time payment of $250 to adult Social Security beneficiaries and to SSI recipients (except those receiving Medicaid in care facilities) was expected to extend over $13 billion to more than 50 million Americans.

Older Americans Report Lower Standards of Living

In *Four in 10 Americans See Their Standard of Living Declining* (June 9, 2008, http://www.gallup.com/poll/107749/Four-Americans-See-Their-Standard-Living-Declining.aspx), Jeffrey M. Jones of the Gallup Organization indicates that in May–June 2008 a majority of Americans said their personal finances were worse than a year ago. Half of adults over the age of 50 said their standard of living had deteriorated during the past five years and just 34% said their standard of living had improved. (See Table 2.12.) In contrast, higher percentages of adults aged 18 to 29 (52%) and 30 to 49 (54%) reported improved standards of living.

TABLE 2.12

Public opinion about whether standard of living has improved or worsened over past five years, by age group, May–June 2008

WOULD YOU SAY YOUR STANDARD OF LIVING IS BETTER OR WORSE NOW THAN IT WAS FIVE YEARS AGO?

[By selected subgroup]

	Better	Worse	Same (vol.)*
Age	%	%	%
18 to 29 years	52	41	6
30 to 49 years	54	37	9
50 years and older	34	50	15
Annual household income			
Less than $30,000	28	63	9
$30,000 to <$75,000	42	47	11
$75,000 or more	61	27	11
Education level			
High school or less	38	51	11
Some college	47	43	9
College graduate only	48	36	14
Postgraduate	48	36	15

*Volunteered response

SOURCE: Jeffrey M. Jones, "Would You Say Your Standard of Living Is Better or Worse Than It Was Five Years Ago?" in *Four in 10 Americans See Their Standard of Living Declining*, The Gallup Organization, June 9, 2008, http://www.gallup.com/poll/107749/Four-Americans-See-Their-Standard-Living-Declining.aspx (accessed April 25, 2008). Copyright © 2008 by The Gallup Organization. Reproduced by permission of The Gallup Organization.

Furthermore, older adults were not optimistic about the future. When asked whether they thought their standard of living would be better or worse in five years, 53% of people aged 50 to 64 and 35% of those aged 65 and older anticipated an improved standard of living. (See Figure 2.13.) By contrast, younger adults were more confident, with 81% of 18- to 29-year-olds and 70% of 30- to 49-year-olds expressing optimism.

FIGURE 2.13

Public opinion about whether standard of living will improve or worsen over next five years, May–June 2008

FIVE YEARS FROM NOW, DO YOU THINK YOUR STANDARD OF LIVING WILL BE BETTER OR WORSE THAN IT IS NOW?

[By age group]

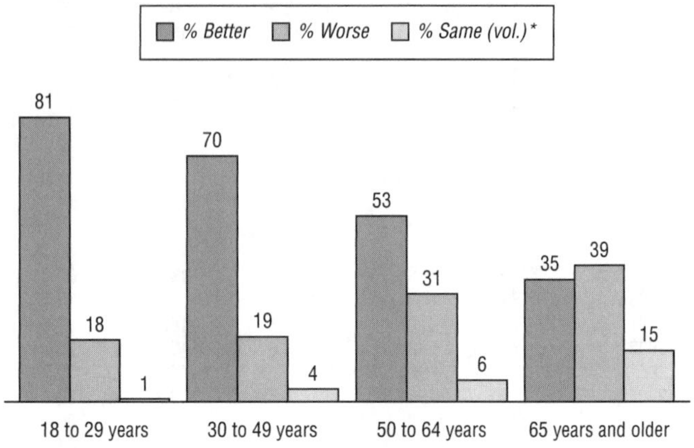

*Volunteered response

SOURCE: Jeffrey M. Jones, "Five Years from Now, Do You Think Your Standard of Living Will Be Better or Worse Than It Is Now?" in *Four in 10 Americans See Their Standard of Living Declining*, The Gallup Organization, June 9, 2008, http://www.gallup.com/poll/107749/Four-Americans-See-Their-Standard-Living-Declining.aspx (accessed April 25, 2008). Copyright © 2008 by The Gallup Organization. Reproduced by permission of The Gallup Organization.

CHAPTER 3
LIVING ARRANGEMENTS OF THE OLDER POPULATION

The vast majority of older Americans live independently in the community—they are not institutionalized in facilities such as nursing homes or retirement homes. According to data from the 2008 Current Population Survey (http://www.bls.gov/cps/) and the 2007 American Community Survey (http://www.census.gov/acs/www/), the U.S. Census Bureau estimates that less than 5% of the population aged 65 and older live in nursing homes. An additional 5% live in some type of senior housing, which frequently offers supportive services for residents. Saadia Greenberg of the U.S. Administration on Aging notes in *A Profile of Older Americans: 2008* (March 2009, http://www.mowaa.org/Document.Doc?id=69) that even though the overall numbers of older Americans living in nursing homes was small—nearly 1.6 million (4.4%) people who were 65 and older in 2007—the percentage of older adults in nursing homes increased dramatically with advancing age, from 1.3% of 65- to 74-year-olds, to 4.1% of 75- to 84-year-olds, to 15.1% of those aged 85 and older.

The living arrangements of older adults are important because they are closely associated with their health, well-being, and economic status. For example, older adults who live alone are more likely to live in poverty than those who live with their spouse or other family members. Older adults living alone may also be socially isolated, and their health may suffer because there are no family members or others nearby to serve as caregivers.

LIVING WITH A SPOUSE, OTHER RELATIVES, OR ALONE

Table 3.1 shows that 23.7 million out of 116 million households—or one out of five—were headed by a person aged 65 or older in 2007. It also shows a consistent increase in the number of households headed by people aged 75 and older, from 8.4 million in 1990 to 11.8 million in 2007.

According to Greenberg, more than half (55.3%) of community-dwelling, civilian (noninstitutionalized) older adults lived with their spouse in 2007. Significantly more older men than women—73% (11.2 million) of older men, compared with 42% (8.7 million) of older women—lived with their spouse. (See Figure 3.1.) This disparity occurs because women usually live longer than men, are generally younger than the men they marry, and are far less likely to remarry after the death of a spouse, largely because there are relatively few available older men. Among adults aged 75 and older, less than one-third (30.1%) of women were living with their spouse in 2007.

In addition, the proportion of older adults living with their spouse decreased with age. Census Bureau data reveal that in 2007, 12.2 million (64%) of adults aged 65 to 74 lived with their spouses, compared with 7.7 million (45%) of adults aged 75 and older. (See Table 3.2.)

Greenberg reports that in 2007, 10.9 million (30.2%) of community-dwelling older adults lived alone, including 7.9 million women and 2.9 million men. They represented 38.6% of older women and 19% of older men. The percentage of older adults who live alone rises with age. Half (49%) of women aged 75 and older lived alone in 2007. Table 3.3 shows that the percentage of women aged 75 and older living alone rose from 37% in 1970 to 54% in 1990 but decreased by 2007, when the figure stood at 48.8%. During the same period the percentage of older men aged 75 and older living alone remained relatively stable until 2005, and then dropped slightly to 22% in 2007.

Race and ethnicity play a role in the living arrangements of older adults. In 2007 older African-American and non-Hispanic white adults were more likely to live alone than older Hispanic and Asian-American adults—1.1 million (35%) older African-American and 9.5 million (30%) older non-Hispanic white adults, compared with 511,000 (21%) older Hispanic and 176,000 (15%) older Asian-American adults. (See Table 3.2.)

Among the racial and ethnic groups, in 2007 older Hispanic, African-American, and Asian-American women were the most likely to live with relatives other than a spouse

TABLE 3.1

Households by age of householder and size of household, selected years 1990–2007

[In millions (93.3 represents 93,300,000). As of March. Based on Current Population Survey.]

Age of householder and size of household	1990	2000	2005	2007					
				Total[a]	White[b]	Black[b]	Asian[b]	Hispanic[c]	Non-Hispanic white[c]
Total	**93.3**	**104.7**	**113.3**	**116.0**	**94.7**	**14.4**	**4.5**	**13.0**	**82.7**
Age of householder:									
15 to 24 years old	5.1	5.9	6.7	6.7	5.1	1.1	0.2	1.1	4.1
25 to 29 years old	9.4	8.5	9.2	9.7	7.6	1.4	0.5	1.7	6.0
30 to 34 years old	11.0	10.1	10.1	9.8	7.5	1.4	0.6	1.8	5.9
35 to 44 years old	20.6	24.0	23.2	22.8	18.0	3.1	1.1	3.2	15.0
45 to 54 years old	14.5	20.9	23.4	24.1	19.6	3.1	0.9	2.3	17.5
55 to 64 years old	12.5	13.6	17.5	19.3	16.2	2.1	0.6	1.5	14.8
65 to 74 years old	11.7	11.3	11.5	11.9	10.1	1.3	0.3	0.8	9.4
75 years old and over	8.4	10.4	11.6	11.8	10.5	0.9	0.3	0.5	10.0
One person	23.0	26.7	30.1	31.1	25.3	4.5	0.8	2.1	23.4
Male	9.0	11.2	12.8	13.5	11.0	1.9	0.4	1.1	10.0
Female	14.0	15.5	17.3	17.6	14.3	2.6	0.4	1.0	13.4
Two persons	30.1	34.7	37.4	38.6	32.5	4.0	1.3	2.9	29.9
Three persons	16.1	17.2	18.3	18.8	14.9	2.6	0.9	2.5	12.6
Four persons	14.5	15.3	16.4	16.2	13.1	1.8	0.9	2.7	10.6
Five persons	6.2	7.0	7.2	7.2	5.8	1.0	0.3	1.6	4.3
Six persons	2.1	2.4	2.5	2.7	2.1	0.4	0.1	1.0	1.4
Seven persons or more	1.3	1.4	1.4	1.4	1.0	0.2	0.1	0.5	0.6

[a]Includes other races, not shown separately.
[b]Beginning with the 2003 Current Population Survey (CPS), respondents could choose more than one race. 2007 data represent persons who selected this race group only and exclude persons reporting more than one race. The CPS prior to 2003 only allowed respondents to report one race group.
[c]Hispanic persons may be any race.

SOURCE: "Table 61. Households by Age of Householder and Size of Household: 1990 to 2007," in *Statistical Abstract of the United States: 2009*, 128th ed., U.S. Census Bureau, 2008, http://www.census.gov/compendia/statab/tables/09s0061.pdf (accessed April 27, 2008)

(33%, 32%, and 30%, respectively). (See Figure 3.2.) The living arrangements of older men broke down somewhat differently along racial and ethnic lines than did those of older women. Older African-American men were more than three times more likely to live alone than were older Asian-American men (29% versus 8%). Like older Hispanic women, however, older Hispanic men were the most likely of any group of older men to live with relatives other than a spouse (17%).

Multigenerational Households

The Census Bureau reports in the press release "Grandparents Day 2008: Sept. 7" (July 7, 2008, http://www.census.gov/Press-Release/www/releases/archives/facts_for_features_special_editions/012095.html) that in 2008 about 2.5 million grandparents were responsible for most of the basic needs of their grandchildren. These grandparents represented about 40% of all grandparents whose grandchildren live with them. The 2006 American Community Survey finds that 6.1 million grandparents were living in the same household with their grandchildren under the age of 18 and the 41% of these grandparents were responsible for their grandchildren. (See Table 3.4.) In "More Parents Move in with Kids" (*USA Today*, September 23, 2008), Greg Toppo and Anthony DeBarros note that the number of parents aged 65 and older moving in with adult children increased by 62% between 2000 and 2007.

Sharon Jayson reports in "Rise in Multi-generational Households Presents a Changing Family Picture" (*USA Today*, June 26, 2007) that multigenerational households tend to have bigger quarters and more income than households overall: 48% of multigenerational households have an income of $60,000 or more and 37% are in housing with four or more bedrooms.

Much of the rise in multigenerational households may be attributable to the growing older population, economic considerations, and a desire among family members to be closer to one another. However, the visibility of multigenerational families rose when 71-year-old Marian Robinson (1937–) moved into the White House with her daughter, Michelle Obama (1964–), her granddaughters, Malia (1998–) and Sasha (2001–), and her son-in-law, President Barack Obama (1961–).

HOMELESSNESS

The U.S. Department of Housing and Urban Development's Office of Community Planning and Development notes in *The Third Annual Homeless Assessment Report to Congress* (July 2008, http://www.hudhre.info/documents/3rdHomelessAssessmentReport.pdf) that between 2006 and 2007, 4% of people in homeless shelters were aged 62 and older and 20% were aged 51 to 61, compared with 55% who were aged 31 to 50 and 21% who were aged 18

FIGURE 3.1

Living arrangements of persons aged 65 and older, 2007

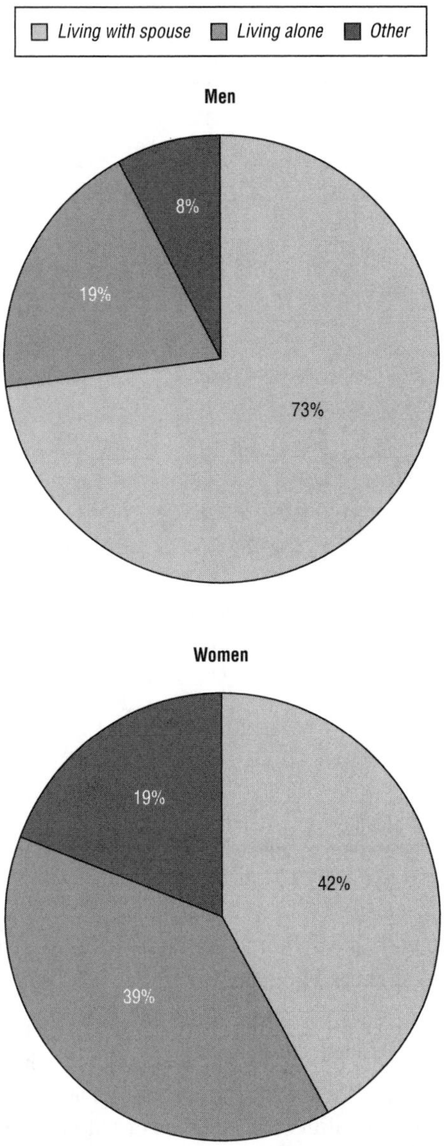

SOURCE: Saadia Greenberg, "Figure 3. Living Arrangements of Persons 65+, 2007," in *A Profile of Older Americans: 2008*, U.S. Department of Health and Human Services, Administration on Aging, 2009, http://www.mowaa.org/Document.Doc?id=69 (accessed April 20, 2009)

to 30. Figure 3.3 shows that homeless individuals were much less likely than all poor individuals to be aged 62 and older (age 62 is the federal housing program's beginning point for defining "elderly"). Older Americans may be less likely than younger ones to be homeless because social programs such as Social Security, Supplemental Security Income (SSI), Medicare, and senior housing act to prevent homelessness. Nonetheless, those older adults who become homeless spend longer periods in emergency shelters than younger homeless people. (See Table 3.5.)

Among the concerns about homelessness are the inherent health-related issues. The relationship between homelessness, health, and illness is complex. Some health problems precede homelessness and contribute to it, whereas others are consequences of homelessness; in addition, homelessness often complicates access and adherence to treatment. For example, mental illness or substance abuse (dependency on alcohol or drugs) may limit a person's ability to work, leading to poverty and homelessness. Without protection from the cold, rain, and snow, exposure to weather may result in illnesses such as bronchitis or pneumonia. Homelessness increases exposure to crime and violence, which could lead to trauma and injuries.

There are many reasons that homeless people experience difficulties gaining access to health care services and receiving needed medical care. Lacking essentials such as transportation to medical facilities, money to pay for care, and knowledge about how to qualify for health insurance and where to obtain health care services makes seeking treatment complicated and frustrating. Psychological distress or mental illness may prevent homeless people from attempting to obtain needed care, and finding food and shelter may take precedence over seeking treatment. Even when the homeless do gain access to medical care, following a treatment plan, filling prescriptions, and scheduling follow-up appointments often present insurmountable challenges to those who do not have a telephone number, address, or safe place to store medications. Furthermore, because chronic (long-term) homelessness can cause or worsen a variety of health problems, homeless people may not live to old age with the same frequency as their age peers who are not homeless.

LONG-TERM CARE, SUPPORTIVE HOUSING, AND OTHER RESIDENTIAL ALTERNATIVES

Spouses and other relatives are still the major caretakers of older, dependent members of American society. However, the number of people aged 65 and older living in long-term care facilities such as nursing homes is rising, because the older population is increasing rapidly. Even though many older adults now live longer, healthier lives, the increase in overall length of life has amplified the need for long-term care facilities and supportive housing.

Growth of the home health care industry in the early 1990s only slightly slowed the increase in the numbers of Americans entering nursing homes. Supportive housing—assisted living, congregate housing, and continuing care retirement communities—offer alternatives to nursing home care. The overarching goal of supportive housing is to enable older adults to receive needed assistance while retaining as much independence as possible.

There are three broad classes of supportive housing for older adults. The smallest and most affordable options usually house 10 or fewer older adults and are often in homes in

TABLE 3.2

Living arrangements by age and selected characteristics, 2007

[In thousands (235,848 represents 235,848,000). As of March.]

Living arrangement	Total	15 to 19 years old	20 to 24 years old	25 to 34 years old	35 to 44 years old	45 to 54 years old	55 to 64 years old	65 to 74 years old	75 years old and over
Total[a]	**235,848**	**21,152**	**20,524**	**39,830**	**42,749**	**43,430**	**32,168**	**18,978**	**17,018**
Alone	31,132	135	1,462	3,930	3,726	5,395	5,618	4,354	6,513
With spouse	121,352	214	3,011	19,908	27,856	28,527	21,928	12,172	7,734
With other persons	83,364	20,803	16,051	15,992	11,167	9,508	4,622	2,452	2,771
White	191,422	16,257	16,034	31,117	34,096	35,551	27,133	16,195	15,039
Alone	25,280	100	1,121	2,924	2,839	4,263	4,573	3,634	5,825
With spouse	103,961	193	2,662	16,837	23,200	24,207	19,117	10,757	6,989
With other persons	62,181	15,964	12,251	11,356	8,057	7,081	3,443	1,804	2,225
Black	28,117	3,310	2,895	5,229	5,306	5,088	3,210	1,833	1,248
Alone	4,467	24	264	690	671	888	828	576	527
With spouse	8,950	13	172	1,412	2,329	2,354	1,503	801	365
With other persons	14,700	3,273	2,459	3,127	2,306	1,846	879	456	356
Asian	10,679	759	921	2,332	2,348	1,888	1,249	649	533
Alone	791	2	34	232	119	133	97	75	101
With spouse	6,223	1	82	1,195	1,801	1,439	969	435	300
With other persons	3,665	756	805	905	428	316	183	139	132
Hispanic origin[b]	31,874	3,664	3,672	8,105	6,724	4,646	2,637	1,445	983
Alone	2,082	12	163	363	292	378	362	285	226
With spouse	14,764	80	828	4,156	4,123	2,797	1,564	806	411
With other persons	15,028	3,572	2,681	3,586	2,309	1,471	711	354	346
Non-Hispanic White[b]	161,775	12,875	12,644	23,610	27,840	31,168	24,685	14,852	14,103
Alone	23,383	88	979	2,610	2,569	3,911	4,242	3,380	5,604
With spouse	89,991	117	1,891	12,914	19,314	21,535	17,621	9,999	6,600
With other persons	48,401	12,670	9,774	8,086	5,957	5,722	2,822	1,473	1,899

[a]Includes other races and persons not of Hispanic origin not shown separately.
[b]Persons of Hispanic origin may be any race.

SOURCE: "Table 57. Living Arrangements of Persons 15 Years Old and over by Selected Characteristics: 2007," in *Statistical Abstract of the United States: 2009*, 128th ed., U.S. Census Bureau, 2008, http://www.census.gov/compendia/statab/tables/09s0057.pdf (accessed April 27, 2009)

TABLE 3.3

Population aged 65 and over living alone, by age group and sex, selected years 1970–2007

Year	Men		Women	
	65–74	75 and over	65–74	75 and over
		Percent		
1970	11.3	19.1	31.7	37.0
1980	11.6	21.6	35.6	49.4
1990	13.0	20.9	33.2	54.0
2000	13.8	21.4	30.6	49.5
2003	15.6	22.9	29.6	49.8
2004	15.5	23.2	29.4	49.9
2005	16.1	23.2	28.9	47.8
2006	16.9	22.7	28.5	48.0
2007	16.7	22.0	28.0	48.8

Reference population: These data refer to the civilian noninstitutionalized population.

SOURCE: "Table 5b. Population Age 65 and over Living Alone, by Age Group and Sex, Selected Years 1970–2007," in *Older Americans 2008: Key Indicators of Well-Being*, Federal Interagency Forum on Aging-Related Statistics, March 2008, http://www.agingstats.gov/agingstatsdotnet/Main_Site/Data/2008_Documents/OA_2008.pdf (accessed April 20, 2009)

residential neighborhoods. Residents share bathrooms, bedrooms, and living areas. These largely unregulated facilities are alternately known as board-and-care facilities, domiciliary care, personal care homes, adult foster care, senior group homes, and sheltered housing.

Residential care facilities, assisted living residences, and adult congregate living facilities tend to be larger, more expensive, and offer more independence and privacy than board-and-care facilities. Most offer private rooms or apartments as well as large common areas for activities and meals.

Continuing care retirement communities and life care communities are usually large complexes that offer a comprehensive range of services from independent living to skilled nursing home care. These facilities are specifically designed to provide nearly all needed care, except for hospital care, within one community. Facilities in this group tend to be the most costly.

Nursing Homes

Nursing homes fall into three broad categories: residential care facilities, intermediate care facilities, and skilled nursing facilities. Each provides a different range and intensity of services:

- A residential care facility (RCF) normally provides meals and housekeeping for its residents, plus some basic medical monitoring, such as administering medications. This

FIGURE 3.2

Living arrangements of the population aged 65 and over, by sex, race, and Hispanic origin, 2007

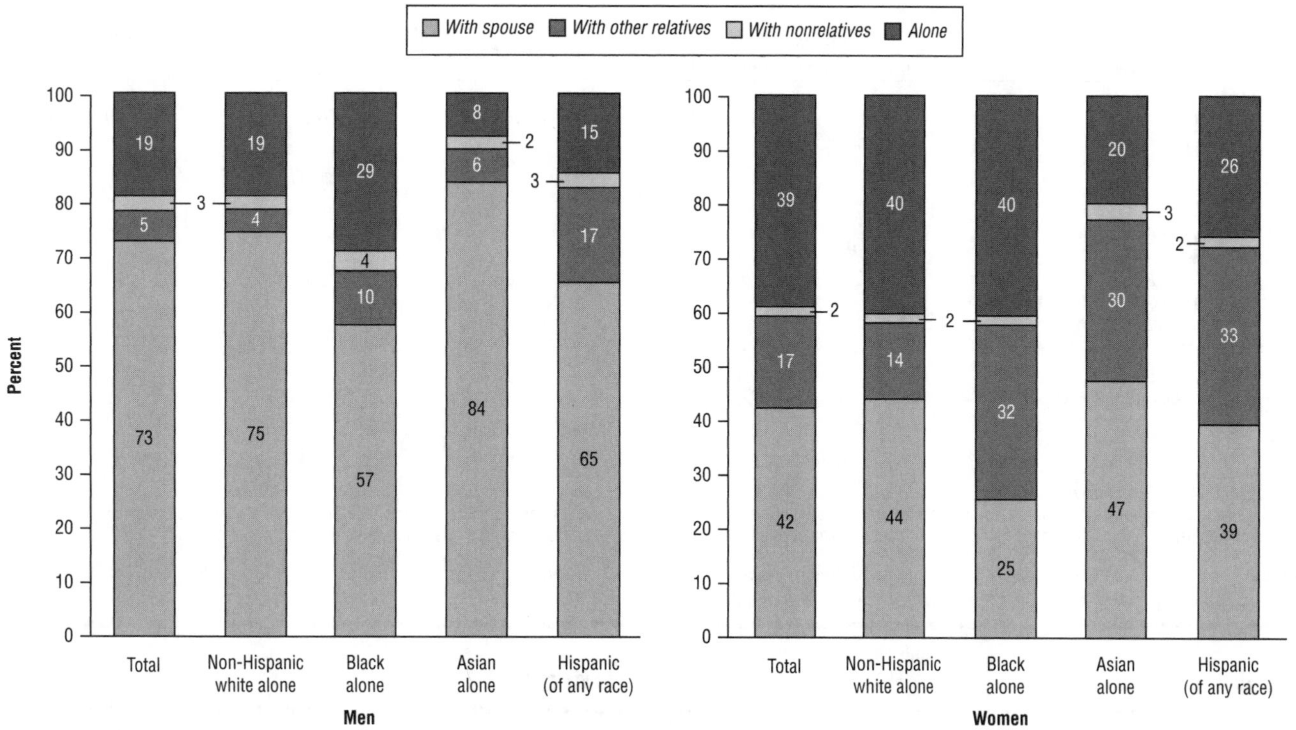

Note: Living with other relatives indicates no spouse present. Living with nonrelatives indicates no spouse or other relatives present. The term "non-Hispanic white alone" is used to refer to people who reported being white and no other race and who are not Hispanic. The term "black alone" is used to refer to people who reported being black or African American and no other race, and the term "Asian alone" is used to refer to people who reported only Asian as their race. The use of single-race populations in this report does not imply that this is the preferred method of presenting or analyzing data. The U.S. Census Bureau uses a variety of approaches.
Reference population: These data refer to the civilian noninstitutionalized population.

SOURCE: "Living Arrangements of the Population Age 65 and over, by Sex and Race and Hispanic Origin, 2007," in *Older Americans 2008: Key Indicators of Well-Being*, Federal Interagency Forum on Aging-Related Statistics, March 2008, http://www.agingstats.gov/agingstatsdotnet/Main_Site/Data/2008_Documents/OA_2008.pdf (accessed April 20, 2009)

type of home is for people who are fairly independent and do not need constant medical attention but need help with tasks such as laundry and cleaning. Many RCFs also provide social activities and recreational programs for their residents.

- An intermediate care facility (ICF) offers room and board and nursing care as necessary for people who can no longer live independently. As in the RCF, exercise and social programs are provided, and some ICFs offer physical therapy and rehabilitation programs as well.
- A skilled nursing facility (SNF) provides around-the-clock nursing care, plus on-call physician coverage. The SNF is for patients who need intensive nursing care, as well as services such as occupational therapy, physical therapy, respiratory therapy, and rehabilitation.

NURSING HOME RESIDENTS. Conducted by the National Center for Health Statistics, the National Nursing Home Survey (NNHS) is a continuing series of national sample surveys of nursing homes, their residents, and their staff. The surveys were conducted in 1973–74, 1977, 1985, 1995, 1997, and 1999. The latest survey was conducted in 2004, and its findings were published in December 2006. Even though each survey has a different focus, all of them offer some basic data about nursing home residents.

The NNHS reports that in 2004 the nation's 16,100 nursing homes had occupancy rates of 86.3% and housed nearly 1.5 million residents. In 2007 the nation's 15,825 nursing homes had occupancy rates of 83.2% and housed 1.4 million residents. (See Table 3.6.) The NNHS finds that in 2004 close to 10,000 were private facilities and 6,200 were voluntary nonprofit or government-owned facilities. More than half (54.2%) of the nursing homes were part of a chain of facilities, and the remaining were independent. The distribution of nursing homes varies by geography—the South and Midwest are home to nearly twice as many facilities as the Northeast and West. (See Table 3.6.)

DIVERSIFICATION OF NURSING HOMES. To remain competitive with home health care and the increasing array of alternative living arrangements for older adults, many nursing homes have begun to offer alternative services and

TABLE 3.4

Grandparents living with grandchildren by race and sex, 2006

[In thousands]

Race, Hispanic origin, and sex	Grandparents living with grandchildren, total	Grandparents responsible for grandchildren		
		Total	30 to 59 years old	60 years old and over
Grandparents living with own grandchildren under 18 years old (1,000)	6,062	2,455	1,663	792
Percent distribution				
Total	**100.0**	**100.0**	**100.0**	**100.0**
White alone	59.2	60.2	60.0	60.6
Black or African American alone	19.9	25.0	24.9	25.1
American Indian and Alaska Native alone	1.4	1.9	2.0	1.8
Asian alone	7.4	2.9	2.0	4.7
Native Hawaiian and other Pacific Islander alone	0.3	0.3	0.3	0.4
Some other race alone	10.4	8.1	9.1	5.9
Two or more races	1.5	1.6	1.7	1.5
Hispanic or Latino*	22.4	17.9	19.5	14.7
White alone, not Hispanic or Latino	47.6	51.0	50.4	52.3
Male	35.3	36.5	34.4	40.8
Female	64.7	63.5	65.6	59.2

*Persons of Hispanic origin may be any race.

Notes: Covers both grandparents living in own home with grandchildren present and grandparents living in grandchildren's home. The American Community Survey universe includes the household population and the population living in institutions, college dormitories, and other group quarters. Based on a sample and subject to sampling variability.

SOURCE: "Table 69. Grandparents Living with Grandchildren by Race and Sex, 2006," in *Statistical Abstract of the United States: 2009*, 128th ed., U.S. Census Bureau, 2008, http://www.census.gov/prod/2008pubs/09statab/pop.pdf (accessed April 27, 2008)

FIGURE 3.3

Age distribution of sheltered homeless individuals compared to age distribution of individuals living in poverty, 2006–07

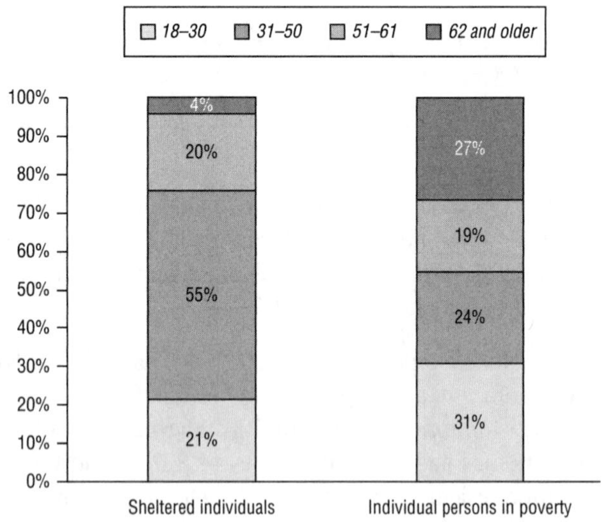

SOURCE: "Exhibit 3-5. Age Distribution of Sheltered Homeless Adult Individuals Compared to Age Distribution of Persons in Poverty Living Alone," in *The Third Annual Homeless Assessment Report to Congress*, U.S. Department of Housing and Urban Development, Office of Community Planning and Development, July 2008, http://www.hudhre.info/documents/3rdHomelessAssessmentReport.pdf (accessed April 27, 2008)

TABLE 3.5

Individuals who stayed in emergency shelters more than 180 days, by race and age group, October 2006–September 2007

Characteristics	Percentage of all sheltered homeless individuals	Percentage of individuals who are long-stayers
Race/ethnicity		
White, non-Hispanic, non-Latino	42.6	31.9
White, Hispanic/Latino	14.1	11.0
Black or African American	33.2	49.9
Other racial groups	10.2	7.3
Age[a]		
18 to 30	20.0	12.6
31 to 50	51.0	50.3
51 and older	23.0	34.9
Veteran (adults only)[b]	14.6	13.3
Disabled (adults only)[b]	40.4	40.8

[a]About 4 percent of all sheltered homeless individuals were under age 18, and less than 1 percent of individuals who are long-stayers were under age 18. Also, about 2 percent of records had missing age information.

[b]About 16 percent of records in HMIS (Homeless Management Information System) were missing information on veteran status, and 32 percent of records in HMIS were missing information on disability status.

SOURCE: "Exhibit 3-12. Individuals Who Stayed in Emergency Shelters More Than 180 Days, October 2006–September 2007," in *The Third Annual Homeless Assessment Report to Congress*, U.S. Department of Housing and Urban Development, Office of Community Planning and Development, July 2008, http://www.hudhre.info/documents/3rdHomelessAssessmentReport.pdf (accessed April 27, 2008)

programs. The NNHS finds that in 2004 more than half of all nursing homes offered specialty units or programs such as hospice (end-of-life) care, pain management, and skin wound treatment programs. About 5,100 (32%) offered units for people suffering from Alzheimer's disease or another dementia. (Alzheimer's disease is a progressive

TABLE 3.6

Nursing home beds, occupancy, and residents by geographic division and state, selected years 1995–2007

[Data are based on a census of certified nursing facilities]

Geographic division and state	Nursing homes				Beds			
	1995	2000	2006	2007	1995	2000	2006	2007
United States	16,389	16,886	15,899	15,825	1,751,302	1,795,388	1,716,102	1,711,894
New England	1,140	1,137	1,021	1,010	115,488	118,562	108,027	107,329
Connecticut	267	259	245	244	32,827	32,433	30,100	30,003
Maine	132	126	113	113	9,243	8,248	7,359	7,281
Massachusetts	550	526	453	446	54,532	56,030	50,416	50,144
New Hampshire	74	83	82	81	7,412	7,837	7,829	7,779
Rhode Island	94	99	87	86	9,612	10,271	8,889	8,780
Vermont	23	44	41	40	1,862	3,743	3,434	3,342
Middle Atlantic	1,650	1,796	1,734	1,735	244,342	267,772	261,537	260,090
New Jersey	300	361	363	362	43,967	52,195	52,126	50,991
New York	624	665	655	657	107,750	120,514	120,850	120,961
Pennsylvania	726	770	716	716	92,625	95,063	88,561	88,138
East North Central	3,171	3,301	3,090	3,084	367,879	369,657	339,079	338,747
Illinois	827	869	799	796	103,230	110,766	102,941	102,750
Indiana	556	564	511	513	59,538	56,762	56,964	57,747
Michigan	432	439	424	422	49,473	50,696	47,432	47,206
Ohio	943	1,009	958	958	106,884	105,038	93,210	93,194
Wisconsin	413	420	398	395	48,754	46,395	38,532	37,850
West North Central	2,258	2,281	2,144	2,129	200,109	193,754	180,287	178,979
Iowa	419	467	455	453	39,959	37,034	34,532	34,140
Kansas	429	392	352	350	30,016	27,067	25,908	26,081
Minnesota	432	433	399	393	43,865	42,149	35,837	34,976
Missouri	546	551	519	515	52,679	54,829	54,541	54,506
Nebraska	231	236	225	225	18,169	17,877	16,258	16,286
North Dakota	87	88	83	83	7,125	6,954	6,502	6,437
South Dakota	114	114	111	110	8,296	7,844	6,709	6,553
South Atlantic	2,215	2,418	2,345	2,345	243,069	264,147	263,950	264,674
Delaware	42	43	44	44	4,739	4,906	4,754	4,799
District of Columbia	19	20	20	20	3,206	3,078	2,988	2,982
Florida	627	732	682	681	72,656	83,365	82,319	82,498
Georgia	352	363	359	362	38,097	39,817	39,920	40,189
Maryland	218	255	233	234	28,394	31,495	29,020	29,173
North Carolina	391	410	421	422	38,322	41,376	43,768	43,929
South Carolina	166	178	176	173	16,682	18,102	18,415	18,500
Virginia	271	278	279	278	30,070	30,595	31,830	31,664
West Virginia	129	139	131	131	10,903	11,413	10,936	10,940
East South Central	1,014	1,071	1,053	1,049	99,707	106,250	108,675	108,432
Alabama	221	225	231	231	23,353	25,248	26,836	26,632
Kentucky	288	307	293	292	23,221	25,341	26,041	26,070
Mississippi	183	190	203	203	16,059	17,068	18,323	18,391
Tennessee	322	349	326	323	37,074	38,593	37,475	37,339
West South Central	2,264	2,199	2,011	1,994	224,695	224,100	216,867	216,400
Arkansas	256	255	237	236	29,952	25,715	24,684	24,566
Louisiana	337	337	293	287	37,769	39,430	37,043	36,261
Oklahoma	405	392	336	327	33,918	33,903	30,776	30,038
Texas	1,266	1,215	1,145	1,144	123,056	125,052	124,364	125,535
Mountain	800	827	773	764	70,134	75,152	73,353	72,865
Arizona	152	150	135	134	16,162	17,458	16,508	16,246
Colorado	219	225	211	209	19,912	20,240	19,982	19,836
Idaho	76	84	80	77	5,747	6,181	6,195	6,053
Montana	100	104	97	92	7,210	7,667	7,338	7,187
Nevada	42	51	47	48	3,998	5,547	5,615	5,675
New Mexico	83	80	72	72	6,969	7,289	6,939	6,912
Utah	91	93	92	93	7,101	7,651	7,724	7,904
Wyoming	37	40	39	39	3,035	3,119	3,052	3,052

form of dementia, characterized by impairment of memory and intellectual functions.)

Collaborating with other providers of health care services or on their own, many nursing homes also offer services such as adult day care and visiting nurse services for people who still live at home. Other programs include respite plans that allow caregivers who need to travel for business or vacation to leave an older relative in the nursing home temporarily.

THE PIONEER NETWORK. In response to concerns about quality of life and quality of care issues in nursing homes, leaders in nursing home reform efforts from around the

TABLE 3.6

Nursing home beds, occupancy, and residents by geographic division and state, selected years 1995–2007 [CONTINUED]

Geographic division and state	Nursing homes				Beds			
	1995	2000	2006	2007	1995	2000	2006	2007
Pacific	1,877	1,856	1,728	1,715	185,879	175,994	164,327	164,378
Alaska	15	15	15	15	814	821	725	725
California	1,382	1,369	1,283	1,274	140,203	131,762	124,416	124,745
Hawaii	34	45	46	46	2,513	4,006	4,127	4,140
Oregon	161	150	138	138	13,885	13,500	12,573	12,468
Washington	285	277	246	242	28,464	25,905	22,486	22,300

Geographic division and state	Residents				Occupancy rate[a]				Resident rate[b]			
	1995	2000	2006	2007	1995	2000	2006	2007	1995	2000	2006	2007
United States	1,479,550	1,480,076	1,433,523	1,424,824	84.5	82.4	83.5	83.2	404.5	349.1	270.6	258.5

[a]Percentage of beds occupied (number of nursing home residents per 100 nursing home beds).
[b]Number of nursing home residents (all ages) per 1,000 resident population 85 years of age and over. Resident rates for 1995–1999 are based on population estimates projected from the 1990 census. Starting with 2000 data, resident rates are based on the 2000 census and postcensal population estimates. Available from: http://www.census.gov/popest/datasets.html.
Note: Annual numbers of nursing homes, beds, and residents are based on a 15-month Online Survey Certification and Reporting Database (OSCAR) reporting cycle.

SOURCE: "Table 17. Number of Nursing Homes by Availability of Selected Special Programs and Facility Characteristics: United States, 2004," in *Nursing Home Facilities*, Centers for Disease Control and Prevention, National Center for Health Statistics, December 2006, http://www.cdc.gov/nchs/data/nnhsd/nursinghomefacilities2006.pdf#01 (accessed April 27, 2009)

United States established the Pioneer Network in 2000 as a forum for the culture change movement. The culture change in this instance was a focus on person-directed values that affirm and support each person's individuality and abilities and that apply to elders and to those who work with them. The Pioneer Network explains in "Mission, Vision and Values" (2009, http://www.pioneernetwork.net/AboutUs/Values/) that it commits to the following values:

- Know each person
- Each person can and does make a difference
- Relationship is the fundamental building block of a transformed culture
- Respond to spirit, as well as mind and body
- Risk taking is a normal part of life
- Put person before task
- All elders are entitled to self-determination wherever they live
- Community is the antidote to institutionalization
- Do unto others as you would have them do unto you
- Promote the growth and development of all
- Shape and use the potential of the environment in all its aspects: physical, organizational, psycho/social/spiritual
- Practice self-examination, searching for new creativity and opportunities for doing better
- Recognize that culture change and transformation are not destinations but a journey, always a work in progress

INNOVATION AND CULTURE CHANGE IMPROVE THE QUALITY OF LIFE FOR RESIDENTS. Even though industry observers and the media frequently decry the care provided in nursing homes, and the media publicizes instances of elder abuse and other quality of care issues, several organizations have actively sought to develop models of health service delivery that improve the clinical care and quality of life for nursing home residents.

Most nursing homes offer a broad range of activities for residents. By 2004, 12,800 (80%) nursing homes offered evening, weekend, offsite, and outdoor activities as well as pet therapy, gardening, and intergenerational activities. (See Table 3.7.) In "Culture Change in Nursing Homes: How Far Have We Come? Findings from the Commonwealth Fund 2007 National Survey of Nursing Homes" (*The Commonwealth Fund*, vol. 91, May 9, 2008), Michelle M. Doty, Mary Jane Koren, and Elizabeth L. Sturla describe the culture change movement that helps nursing homes transform from institutions to homes and the extent to which nursing homes are adopting culture change principles and practicing resident-centered care, which offers residents choices and fosters their autonomy.

Doty, Koren, and Sturla conclude that even though the survey results are mixed in terms of the extent to which nursing homes say they have adopted resident-centered practices, there is evidence of the potential for systemic, positive change within the industry. Figure 3.4 shows that in 2007, 31% of nursing homes described their facilities as fully embracing culture change and 25% said their facilities had changed in "only in a few respects or not at all" but that they were "extremely or very committed to adopting culture change." Less than half (43%) of the nursing homes described their facilities and cultures as traditional and were "not very committed to adopting culture change."

TABLE 3.7

Number of nursing homes by availability of selected special programs and facility characteristics, 2004

Facility characteristic	Total	No special programs	One or more special programs[a]	Type of program: Hospice end of life	Palliative care	Dementia care	Restorative care	Behavior problems	Pain management	Continence management	Skin wounds
All facilities	16,100	3,300	12,800	3,000	2,700	5,100	11,100	3,800	4,100	3,500	8,600
Ownership											
Proprietary	9,900	2,000	7,900	1,600	1,400	2,800	7,100	2,400	2,300	2,200	5,300
Voluntary nonprofit and other[b]	6,200	1,300	4,800	1,400	1,200	2,300	4,000	1,500	1,800	1,300	3,300
Beds											
Fewer than 50 beds	2,200	800	1,400	*	*	*	1,000	*	*400	*	800
50–99 beds	6,000	1,300	4,700	1,100	900	1,500	4,200	1,500	1,500	1,400	3,000
100 beds or more	7,800	1,100	6,700	1,700	1,500	3,200	5,800	2,000	2,200	1,900	4,800
Geographic region											
Northeast	2,800	*700	2,100	*500	*600	1,000	1,700	*600	*800	*	1,400
Midwest	5,300	1,000	4,300	800	900	2,000	3,900	1,600	1,400	1,200	2,800
South	5,400	1,000	4,400	1,300	900	1,500	3,800	1,200	1,300	1,300	3,200
West	2,600	*600	1,900	*	*	*600	1,700	*500	*600	*600	1,200
Location											
Metropolitan statistical area	10,900	2,100	8,800	2,100	1,900	3,500	7,600	2,600	2,900	2,500	6,100
Micropolitan statistical area	2,600	*600	2,000	*400	*400	900	1,700	*600	*600	*500	1,200
Other location	2,600	*600	2,000	*600	*400	700	1,800	700	600	*500	1,200
Affiliation											
Chain	8,700	1,700	7,000	1,600	1,500	2,800	6,300	2,000	2,300	2,100	4,900
Independent	7,400	1,600	5,700	1,400	1,200	2,300	4,800	1,900	1,900	1,400	3,700

*Estimate does not meet standard of reliability or precision because the sample size is less than 30. Estimates accompanied by an asterisk (*) indicate that the sample size is between 30 and 59.

[a]Includes any of the programs listed where the facility has specially trained personnel dedicated to the program. Special programs do not include special training that is provided to all personnel.

[b]Includes state and local government facilities.

Note: Numbers may not add to totals because of rounding.

SOURCE: "Table 17. Number of Nursing Homes by Availability of Selected Special Programs and Facility Characteristics: United States, 2004," in *Nursing Home Facilities*, Centers for Disease Control and Prevention, National Center for Health Statistics, December 2006, http://www.cdc.gov/nchs/data/nnhsd/nursinghomefacilities2006.pdf#01 (accessed April 27, 2009)

Facilities that identify themselves as culture change adopters and strivers are more likely than traditional facilities to provide resident-centered care. Figure 3.5 reveals that in 2007 residents determined their own daily schedules in 58% of facilities that described themselves as culture change adopters, compared with just 22% of traditional facilities.

Doty, Koren, and Sturla confirm the business benefits of culture change. Culture change adopters reported an increase in staff retention and occupancy rates and improved operating costs. In 2007, 78% of the facilities that were implementing seven or more culture change initiatives said culture change has given them a competitive advantage in their market. (See Figure 3.6.) In contrast, only 54% of traditional nursing homes that implemented three or fewer culture change initiatives reported comparable improvement in market position.

THE EDEN ALTERNATIVE. Developed in 1991 by William Thomas, the Eden Alternative is a movement that, like the Pioneer Network, seeks to transform nursing homes. The Eden Alternative strives to create nursing homes that are rich and vibrant human habitats where plants, children, and animals bring life-enriching energy to residents. The philosophy of the Eden Alternative is that providing a stimulant-rich environment will help minimize the hopelessness often felt by nursing home residents. Nursing homes based on this model are being opened across the country.

By providing gardenlike settings filled with plants and encouraging relationships with children and pets, the Eden Alternative hopes to improve the human spirit and dispel loneliness. The 10 principles (2009, http://www.edenalt.org/about/our-10-principles.html) of an Eden Alternative nursing home are:

1. The three plagues of loneliness, helplessness and boredom account for the bulk of suffering among our Elders.
2. An Elder-centered community commits to creating a Human Habitat where life revolves around close and continuing contact with plants, animals and children. It is these relationships that provide the young and old alike with a pathway to a life worth living.

FIGURE 3.4

Adoption of culture change by nursing homes, 2007

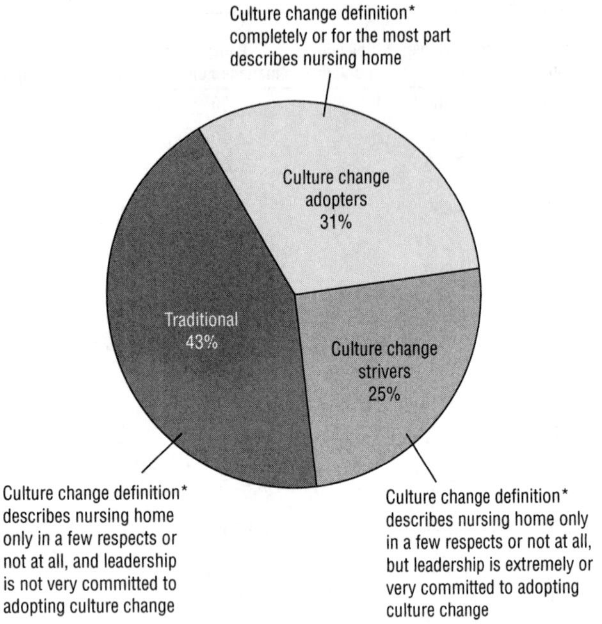

*Culture change or a resident-centered approach means an organization that has home and work environments in which care and all resident-related activities are decided by the resident; living environment is designed to be a home rather than institution; close relationships exist between residents, family members, staff, and community; work is organized to support and allow all staff to respond to residents' needs and desires; management allows collaborative and group decision making; and processes/measures are used for continuous quality improvement.

SOURCE: Michelle M. Doty, Mary Jane Koren, and Elizabeth L. Sturla, "Figure ES-1. Adoption of Culture Change by Nursing Homes, 2007," in *Culture Change in Nursing Homes: How Far Have We Come? Findings from the Commonwealth Fund 2007 National Survey of Nursing Homes*, The Commonwealth Fund, May 2008, http://www.commonwealthfund.org/Content/Publications/Fund-Reports/2008/May/Culture-Change-in-Nursing-Homes--How-Far-Have-We-Come--Findings-From-The-Commonwealth-Fund-2007-Nati.aspx (accessed April 27, 2009)

FIGURE 3.5

Resident-centered care varies between traditional nursing homes and culture change adopters, 2007

Percent of nursing homes indicating they are currently implementing resident-centered care factors:

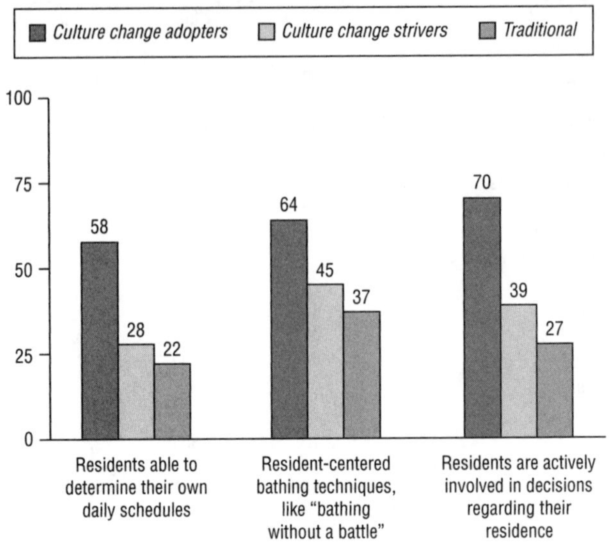

Culture Change Adopters = culture change definition completely or for most part describes nursing home. Culture Change Strivers = culture change definition describes nursing home only in a few respects or not at all but leadership is very/extermely committed to the adoption of culture change. Traditional = culture change definition describes nursing home only in a few respects or not at all AND leadership is less than very/extremely committed to the adoption of culture change.

SOURCE: Michelle M. Doty, Mary Jane Koren, and Elizabeth L. Sturla, "Figure ES-2. Residents' Ability to Determine Daily Schedules and Make Decisions Varies Widely between Culture Change Adopters and Traditional Nursing Homes," in *Culture Change in Nursing Homes: How Far Have We Come? Findings from the Commonwealth Fund 2007 National Survey of Nursing Homes*, The Commonwealth Fund, May 2008, http://www.commonwealthfund.org/Content/Publications/Fund-Reports/2008/ May/Culture-Change-in-Nursing-Homes--How-Far-Have-We-Come--Findings-From-The-Commonwealth-Fund-2007-Nati.aspx (accessed April 27, 2009)

3. Loving companionship is the antidote to loneliness. Elders deserve easy access to human and animal companionship.
4. An Elder-centered community creates opportunity to give as well as receive care. This is the antidote to helplessness.
5. An elder-centered community imbues daily life with variety and spontaneity by creating an environment in which unexpected and unpredictable interactions and happenings can take place. This is the antidote to boredom.
6. Meaningless activity corrodes the human spirit. The opportunity to do things that we find meaningful is essential to human health.
7. Medical treatment should be the servant of genuine human caring, never its master.
8. An Elder-centered community honors its Elders by de-emphasizing top-down bureaucratic authority, seeking instead to place the maximum possible decision-making authority into the hands of the Elders or into the hands of those closest to them.
9. Creating an Elder-centered community is a never-ending process. Human growth must never be separated from human life.
10. Wise leadership is the lifeblood of any struggle against the three plagues. For it, there can be no substitute.

Thomas's initiatives also include the Green House Project. This effort encompasses the design and construction of small group homes for older adults, built to a residential scale that situates necessary clinical care within a social

FIGURE 3.6

Improvements in business and operations greatest in homes with more culture change, 2007

Percent of nursing homes indicating that culture change has had the following impact: (Base: Definition of culture change describes this nursing home completely, for the most part, or in a few respects)

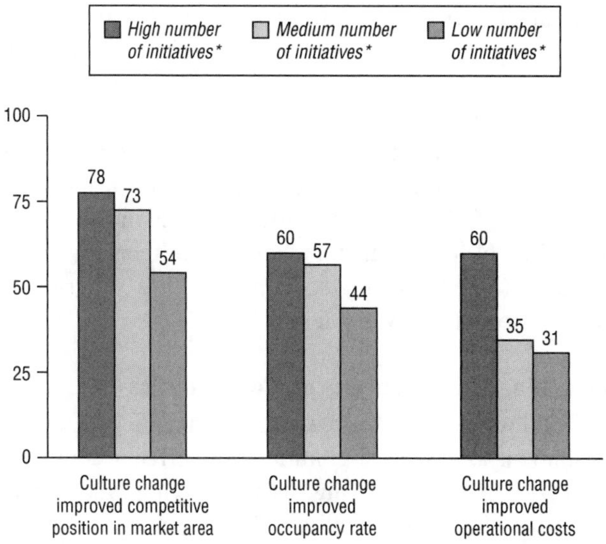

*Respondents were asked whether their home was currently implementing any of 11 different resident-centered, staff, or physical environment initiatives associated with culture change. High = 7 or more initiatives, Medium = 4 to 6 initiatives, Low = 3 or less initiatives.

SOURCE: Michelle M. Doty, Mary Jane Koren, and Elizabeth L. Sturla, "Figure ES-3. Improvements in Business and Operations Greatest in Homes with More Culture Change Initiatives under Way," in *Culture Change in Nursing Homes: How Far Have We Come? Findings from the Commonwealth Fund 2007 National Survey of Nursing Homes*, The Commonwealth Fund, May 2008, http://www.commonwealthfund.org/Content/Publications/Fund-Reports/2008/May/Culture-Change-in-Nursing-Homes--How-Far-Have-We-Come--Findings-From-The-Commonwealth-Fund-2007-Nati.aspx (accessed April 27, 2009)

model in which primacy is given to the older adults' quality of life. The goal of this social model is to provide frail older adults with an environment that promotes autonomy, dignity, privacy, and choice.

Green Houses are designed to feel more like homes than typical long-term care institutions and to blend easily into their community or surroundings. The first Green House in the nation opened in May 2003 in Tupelo, Mississippi, developed by United Methodist Senior Services of Mississippi. By June 2009 the Green House Project (http://www.ncbcapitalimpact.org/default.aspx?id=150) indicated that over 300 nursing homes across the country had been, or were being transformed in accordance with the Eden philosophy, with most featuring bright décor, gardens, pets, and on-site day care for children.

Assisted Living

Assisted living arose to bridge a gap in long-term care. It is intended to meet the needs of older adults who wish to live independently in the community but require some of the services—housekeeping, meals, transportation, and assistance with other activities of daily living—that are provided by a nursing home. (Activities of daily living are generally considered to include eating, bathing, dressing, getting to and using the bathroom, getting in or out of bed or a chair, and mobility.) Assisted living offers a flexible array of services that enable older adults to maintain as much independence as they can, for as long as possible.

Because assisted living refers to a concept and philosophy as opposed to a regulated provider of health services such as a hospital or skilled nursing facility, there is no uniform description of the services an assisted living residence must offer, and as a result there is considerable variation among assisted living facilities. These residences are regulated on a state level, and each state has its own definition of what constitutes an assisted living facility as well as its own set of rules governing them. The Agency for Healthcare Research and Quality defines in "Assisted Living Defined" (December 2006, http://www.ahrq.gov/RESEARCH/ltcscan/ltc3.htm) the term *assisted living* as "a type of residential long-term care setting known by nearly 30 different names" that includes "24-hour service and oversight, services that meet scheduled and unscheduled needs, and care/services that promote independence, with an emphasis on dignity, autonomy, choice, privacy, and home-like environment."

In "ALFA Core Principles" (May 2009, http://www.alfa.org/alfa/ALFA_Core_Principles1.asp?SnID=1057066719), the Assisted Living Federation of America, the largest national association dedicated to operating assisted living communities for older adults, explains that "the goal of assisted living is to both provide resident-centered care, and provide that care in a residential setting. The philosophy provides residents freedom of choice, independence, and the opportunity to live, aging with dignity, privacy and respect. In contrast to other long term care options, Assisted Living embraces quality of life as well as quality of care, and supports the resident's decision to live and die in the place they call home."

Assisted living residences may be located on the grounds of retirement communities or nursing homes, or they may be freestanding residential facilities. They vary in size and location as well as in services. Some are high-rise apartment complexes, whereas others are converted private homes. Most facilities contain between 25 and 120 units, which vary in size from one room to a full apartment.

The MetLife Mature Market Institute states in *The MetLife Market Survey of Nursing Home & Assisted Living Costs* (2008, http://www.metlife.com/assets/cao/mmi/publications/studies/mmi-studies-2008-nhal-costs.pdf) that "more than 900,000 Americans live in approximately 39,500 assisted living residences in the United States." A few key findings by MetLife report include:

- More than half (52%) of assisted living facilities provided care for residents with Alzheimer's disease and other dementias in 2008.
- The average age of residents was 85.
- The average length of stay was about 21 months.

Assisted living licensing regulations vary from state to state. Most states require staff certification and training and all assisted living facilities must comply with local building codes and fire safety regulations.

BOARD-AND-CARE FACILITIES. Board-and-care facilities were the earliest form of assisted living. In *Licensed Board and Care Homes: Preliminary Findings from the 1991 National Health Provider Inventory* (April 11, 1994, http://aspe.hhs.gov/daltcp/reports/licbchom.htm), Robert F. Clark et al. define the term *board-and-care homes* as "non-medical community-based facilities that provide protective oversight and/or personal care in addition to meals and lodging to one or more residents with functional or cognitive limitations." Typically, board-and-care residents have their own bedrooms and bathrooms or share them with one other person, whereas other living areas are shared.

Even though many board-and-care homes offer residents safe, homelike environments and attentive caregivers, there have been many well-publicized instances of fraud and abuse. Entirely unregulated in many states, board-and-care facilities have frequently become dumping grounds for older adults.

In an attempt to stem abuses, the federal government passed the Keys Amendment in 1978. Under the terms of this legislation, residents living in board-and-care facilities that fail to provide adequate care are subject to reduced SSI payments. This move was intended to penalize substandard board-and-care operators, but advocates for older adults contend that it actually penalizes the SSI recipients and that it has not reduced reports of abuse. With the 1992 reauthorization of the Older Americans Act of 1965, Congress provided for long-term care ombudsman programs designed to help prevent the abuse, exploitation, and neglect of residents in long-term care facilities such as board-and-care residences and nursing homes. Paid and volunteer ombudsmen monitor facilities and act as advocates for the residents.

COSTS OF ASSISTED LIVING. The cost of assisted living varies based on geography, unit size, and the services needed. According to the MetLife Mature Market Institute, in *MetLife Market Survey of Nursing Home & Assisted Living Costs*, the median (the middle value—half are higher and half are lower) monthly amount in 2008 was $2,900. Most assisted living facilities charge monthly rates and some require long-term lease arrangements.

The MetLife Mature Market Institute report considers cost for assisted living communities based on the number of services included in their base rates. Communities that included five or fewer services were "basic" and had an average monthly cost of $2,873, those providing six to nine services were "standard" and had an average monthly cost of $2,985, and those providing 10 or more services in their base rates were "inclusive" and had an average monthly cost of $3,354.

Residents or their families generally pay for assisted living using their own financial resources. Some health insurance programs or long-term care insurance policies reimburse for specific health-related care provided by assisted living facilities, and some state and local governments offer subsidies for rent or services for low-income older adults. Others may provide subsidies in the form of an additional payment for those who receive SSI or Medicaid (a federal and state health care program for people below the poverty level).

Continuing Care Retirement Communities

Continuing care retirement communities (CCRCs), also known as life care communities, offer a continuum of care—independent living, assisted living, and nursing home care—in a single facility or on common grounds. The goal of CCRCs is to enable residents to age in place (remaining in their own home rather than relocating to assisted living facilities or other supportive housing). When residents become ill or disabled, for example, they do not have to relocate to a nursing home, because health care services are available on the CCRC campus.

Like assisted living facilities, CCRCs vary in location, design, and amenities. They range from urban high rises to semirural campuses and from 100 to over 1,000 residents. Most include common dining rooms, activity and exercise areas, indoor and outdoor recreation areas, and swimming pools.

Typically, residents are required to pay an entrance fee and a fixed monthly fee in return for housing, meals, personal care, recreation, and nursing services. Many CCRCs offer other payment options, including both entrance fee and fee-for-service (paid for each visit, procedure, or treatment delivered) arrangements. In the past entrance fees were nonrefundable; however, by 2009 most newer CCRCs had instituted refundable or partially refundable entrance fees.

CCRCs may be operated by private, not-for-profit, and/or religious organizations. Entrance fees in these communities vary substantially, from $20,000 to $500,000, and monthly maintenance fees range from $600 to $2,000, depending on the size of the facility and the extent of services. With few exceptions, none of the costs of CCRCs are covered by government or private insurance.

Cohousing and Shared Housing

Older adults may share living quarters to reduce expenses, share household and home maintenance responsibilities, and gain companionship. Many choose to share the same homes in which they raised their families, because these houses are often large enough to accommodate more than one or two people. Shared housing is often called cohousing, but the terms are not exactly the same. Cohousing usually refers to planned or intentional communities of private dwellings with shared common areas that include dining rooms, meeting rooms, recreation facilities, and lounges. Cohousing and shared housing are cost-effective alternatives for those who wish to remain in their own home and for older adults who cannot afford private assisted living or continuing care retirement communities.

The cohousing concept originated in Denmark in the 1960s and spread to North America in the 1980s. According to the Cohousing Association of the United States (2009, http://www.cohousing.org/directory), in 2009 there were over 225 cohousing communities in various stages of development in North America. Cohousing participants are involved in planning the community and maintaining it, and most cohousing groups make their decisions by consensus.

In contrast, most shared housing consists of a single homeowner taking a roommate to share living space and expenses. Shared housing can also include households with three or more roommates and family-like cooperatives in which large groups of people live together.

Intergenerational cohousing or shared housing may also meet the needs of younger as well as older people. Along with the benefits of cost-sharing and companionship, home sharers and cohousing residents may exchange services—for example, help with household maintenance in exchange for babysitting.

Matt Thornhill of the Boomer Project anticipates in "Cohabiting to Cohousing" (*Jumpin' Jack Flash Newsletter*, June 2005) that aging baby boomers (people born between 1946 and 1964) will embrace cohousing. The concept of a community with shared values, care, meals, transportation, and shared homes will likely appeal to many boomers, who enjoyed communes and group-living situations in the 1960s and 1970s. Thornhill predicts that cohousing communities will even be retrofitted from existing neighborhoods, enabling boomers to age in place.

Elder Cottage Housing Opportunity Units

Elder cottage housing opportunity (ECHO) units, or "granny flats," are small, freestanding, removable housing units that are located on the same lot as a single-family house. Another name used by local zoning authorities is accessory apartments or units. Accessory apartments are self-contained second living units built into or attached to an existing single-family dwelling. They are private, generally smaller than the primary unit, and usually contain one or two bedrooms, a bathroom, a sitting room, and a kitchen.

Generally, families construct ECHO units and accessory apartments for parents or grandparents so that the older adults can be nearby while maintaining their independence. Existing zoning laws and concerns about property values and traffic patterns are obstacles to both cohousing and construction of ECHO units, but as these alternatives become more popular, local jurisdictions may be pressured to allow multifamily housing in neighborhoods that traditionally have had only single-family homes.

Retirement Communities

Developers such as the industry leader Del Webb (a division of Pulte Homes) have created and constructed communities and even entire small "cities" exclusively for older adults. Examples include the Sun City communities in Florida, Arizona, and Texas. The Florida and Arizona locations opened in the 1960s and the Texas site in 1996.

In 2009 Del Webb (http://www.delwebb.com/Homefinder/Default.aspx) boasted communities in 21 states, which were home to more than 200,000 older adults. Homes in most of these properties were available only to those families in which at least one member was 55 or older, and no one under the age of 19 was allowed to reside permanently. Sun City communities offer clubs, golf courses, social organizations, fitness clubs, organized travel, and recreational complexes. Medical facilities are located nearby.

Housing Slump Imperils Older Adults and Limits Their Mobility

Even though many older adults and baby boomers aspire to relocate to CCRCs or purchase new homes in active retirement communities, it is likely that only those with considerable financial resources will be able to do so. The decline in residential real estate prices, which began in 2006 and continued throughout 2009, made it difficult for older adults to sell their homes. Besides losing equity in their homes as prices declined, many older adults had also seen their retirement assets erode. As a result, plans to relocate were usually postponed.

According to David Streitfeld and Jack Healy, in "Phoenix Leads the Way Down in Home Prices" (*New York Times*, April 28, 2009), housing markets across the United States have suffered declining home prices since 2006. The median price of a home in the United States, which peaked above $230,000 in 2006, had fallen to $175,200 in April 2009. Declining home prices may pose the greatest threat to older adults with fixed incomes because they depend on their home equity to help finance their spending.

In "Housing Slump Changing Options for Older Americans" (Tribune Media Service, March 9, 2009), Mark Miller indicates that Larry Minnix, the chief executive of the American Association of Homes and Services for the Aging, observes that because applications to CCRCs are declining, "some are suspending or postponing entry fees. Others are providing bridge loans or retaining real estate specialists to help people prepare and sell their homes. Everyone is trying to get creative in providing help."

OWNING AND RENTING A HOME

In the press release "Census Bureau Reports on Residential Vacancies and Homeownership" (April 27, 2009, http://www.census.gov/hhes/www/housing/hvs/qtr109/files/q109press.pdf), the Census Bureau notes that the overall home ownership rate in the first quarter of 2009 was 67.3%, down slightly from the highest rate (69.2% in 2004) since the bureau began reporting these statistics in 1965. (See Table 3.8.) In 2009, 80.4% of adults aged 65 and older owned their own home.

Older householders are more likely to spend more than one-fourth of their income on housing costs than other age groups. Greenberg reports that in 2007, 46% of older adults devoted more than 25% of their income to housing costs—39% of homeowners and 73% of renters. In 2007 the median value of homes owned by older adults was $168,654, but because the median purchase price of these homes was just $45,191, 68% of older homeowners had no mortgage debt—they owned their homes free and clear.

Renters generally pay a higher percentage of their income for housing than do homeowners. Unlike most homeowners, who pay fixed monthly mortgage payments, renters often face annual rent increases. Many older adult renters living on fixed incomes are unprepared to pay these increases. Homeowners also benefit from their home equity and can borrow against it in times of financial need. In contrast, renters do not build equity and do not get a return on their investment. Also, mortgage payments are tax deductible, whereas rent payments are not.

The Subprime Mortgage and Loan Crisis Endangers Older Adults

Subprime mortgages and loans were designed to extend credit to high-risk borrowers—people with poor credit ratings. To compensate for these risks, subprime mortgages have higher interest rates—a subprime loan is always more expensive than a conventional loan made to

TABLE 3.8

Homeownership rates, by age of householder, 2004–09

[In percent]

Year/quarter	United States	Under 35 years	35 to 44 years	45 to 54 years	55 to 64 years	65 years and over
	Homeownership rates					
2009						
First quarter	67.3	39.8	65.7	74.6	79.8	80.4
2008						
Fourth quarter	67.5	40.3	66.6	74.5	79.7	80.4
Third quarter	67.9	41.0	67.2	75.2	80.0	80.1
Second quarter	68.1	41.2	67.6	75.4	80.1	80.2
First quarter	67.8	41.3	66.7	75.0	80.4	79.9
2007						
Fourth quarter	67.8	41.0	67.2	75.1	80.4	80.3
Third quarter	68.2	42.0	68.1	75.2	81.1	79.9
Second quarter	68.2	41.9	67.6	75.5	80.6	80.5
First quarter	68.4	41.7	68.3	75.8	80.4	80.9
2006						
Fourth quarter	68.9	42.8	68.9	76.4	80.7	81.2
Third quarter	69.0	43.0	68.8	76.4	80.7	81.5
Second quarter	68.7	42.4	68.9	76.3	81.0	80.6
First quarter	68.5	42.3	68.9	75.8	81.2	80.3
2005						
Fourth quarter	69.0	43.1	69.7	76.7	80.6	80.6
Third quarter	68.8	43.0	68.6	76.7	80.9	80.6
Second quarter	68.6	42.8	68.7	76.3	81.3	80.3
First quarter	69.1	43.3	70.1	76.5	81.8	80.8
2004						
Fourth quarter	69.2	43.3	70.0	77.4	81.6	80.5
Third quarter	69.0	43.1	68.6	77.4	81.2	81.8
Second quarter	69.2	43.6	69.4	77.0	82.4	81.1
First quarter	68.6	42.3	68.8	77.0	81.7	80.7

SOURCE: Robert R. Callis and Linda B. Cavanaugh, "Table 6. Homeownership Rates by Age of Householder, 2004 to 2009," in *Census Bureau Reports on Residential Vacancies and Homeownership*, U.S. Department of Commerce, U.S. Census Bureau, Housing and Household Economic Statistics Division, April 27, 2009, http://www.census.gov/hhes/www/housing/hvs/qtr109/files/q109press.pdf (accessed April 28, 2009)

a borrower with excellent credit. Many older adults were sold subprime loans when they applied for home equity loans. Sharon Hermanson of the AARP Public Policy Institute reports in "Predatory Lending FYI: The Subprime Market: Wealth Building or Wealth Stripping for Older Person" (June 2007, http://www.aarp.org/research/frauds-scams/predatory/m_6_mortgage.html) that in 2007 one out of every five subprime mortgages ended in foreclosure and that borrowers aged 65 and older were three times more likely to hold a subprime loan than borrowers under the age of 35.

Reverse Mortgages

To supplement their retirement income or to pay for health care, many older Americans turn to reverse mortgages. Reverse mortgages allow older homeowners to convert some of their home equity into cash, making it possible for them to avoid selling their home.

With a traditional mortgage homeowners make monthly payments to the lender. In a reverse mortgage the lender pays the homeowner in monthly installments and in most cases no repayment is due until the homeowner dies, sells the house, or moves permanently. Reverse mortgages help homeowners who are house-rich (have considerable equity in their home) but cash-poor stay in their home and still meet their financial obligations.

Sale/Leaseback with Life Tenancy

Another option for older homeowners is a sale/leaseback in which the homeowner gives up ownership of a home and becomes a renter. The former homeowner frequently requests life tenancy—retaining the right to live in the house as a renter for the rest of his or her life. The buyer pays the former homeowner in monthly installments and is responsible for property taxes, insurance, maintenance, and repairs.

Renting Is Often Unaffordable

The National Low-Income Housing Coalition (NLIHC) documents in *Out of Reach 2009* (April 2009, http://www.nlihc.org/oor/oor2009/oor2009pub.pdf) income and rental housing cost data for the 50 states, the District of Columbia, and Puerto Rico. For each area, the coalition calculates the income needed to be able to afford the fair market rent (FMR) of the housing. The NLIHC also calculates the number of full-time minimum wage jobs necessary to afford the FMR, which highlights the hardships faced by many families of different sizes with varying numbers of wage earners.

The NLIHC observes that in 2008 an estimated 40% of foreclosures displaced renter households and that between 2006 and 2008 the number of renter households increased by 2.2 million, whereas the number of homeowners fell by 255,000. The national median housing wage, based on each county's housing wage for a two-bedroom unit at the FMR of $928, was $17.84 per hour in 2009. Because the median hourly wage and renters' average hourly wages are less than the national median housing wage, the NLIHC observes that even when workers are employed at prevailing wages, they will find it challenging to obtain affordable rental housing. In no state can an individual working a full-time minimum wage job afford to rent a two-bedroom apartment. The average monthly SSI payment was just $674 for adults aged 65 and older in 2009. Older adults relying solely on SSI payments cannot afford rental housing anywhere in the United States.

ADDITIONAL HOUSING CHALLENGES FOR OLDER ADULTS

Physical Hazards and Accommodations

Home characteristics considered desirable by younger householders may present challenges to older adults. For example, the staircase in a two-story house may become a formidable obstacle to an older adult suffering from arthritis, heart disease, or other disabling chronic conditions. Narrow halls and doorways cannot accommodate walkers and wheelchairs. High cabinets and shelves may be beyond the reach of an arthritis sufferer. Even though houses can be modified to meet the physical needs of older or disabled people, some older houses cannot be remodeled as easily, and retrofitting them may be quite costly. Owners of condominiums in Florida, whose young-old (aged 65 to 74) residents once prized second- and third-floor units for their breezes and golf course views, are now considering installing elevators for residents in their 80s and 90s who find climbing stairs much more difficult.

Older adults, as well as advocates on their behalf, express a strong preference for aging in place. Much research confirms that most people over the age of 55 want to remain in familiar surroundings rather than move to alternative housing. To live more comfortably, those older adults who have the means can redesign and reequip their home to accommodate the physical changes associated with aging.

Simple adaptations include replacing doorknobs with levers that can be pushed downward with a fist or elbow, requiring no gripping or twisting; replacing light switches with flat "touch" switches; placing closet rods at adjustable heights; installing stoves with front- or side-mounted controls; and marking steps with bright colors. More complex renovations include replacing a bathroom with a wet room (a tiled space that is large enough to accommodate a wheelchair and that is equipped with a showerhead, a waterproof chair, and a sloping floor for a drain), placing electrical outlets higher than usual along walls, and widening passageways and doors for walkers, wheelchairs, or scooters.

Anticipating the increase in the older population in the coming years, some real estate developers are manufacturing houses designed to meet the needs of older adults and prolong their ability to live independently. These houses feature accommodations such as nonskid flooring, walls strong enough to support the mounting of grab bars, outlets at convenient heights, levers instead of knobs on doors and plumbing fixtures, and doors and hallways wide enough to allow wheelchair access.

PUBLIC HOUSING

Congress passed the U.S. Housing Act of 1937 to create low-income public housing, but according to the Milbank Memorial Fund and the Council of Large Public Housing Authorities, in *Public Housing and Supportive Services for the Frail Elderly: A Guide for Housing Authorities and Their Collaborators* (2006, http://www.milbank.org/reports/0609publichousing/0609publichousing.pdf), by 1952 only a small percentage of available housing was occupied by older adults. After 1956, when Congress authorized the development of dedicated public housing for the elderly and specifically made low-income older adults eligible for such housing, the situation began to improve. During the 1960s and 1970s many developments, specifically for low-income older adults, were constructed. Initially, these apartments were sufficient for most residents, but they were not designed to enable residents to age in place. They lacked the flexibility and the range of housing options necessary to meet the needs of frail older adults. The residents who entered public housing as young-old aged in place and are now the older-old (aged 75 and older) and more in need of supportive and health services than they were two decades ago.

Public housing itself has also aged—much of it is more than 30 years old. Many developments are badly rundown and in desperate need of renovation. Most are unequipped to offer the range of supportive services required by increasingly frail and dependent residents. Absent supportive services, the bleak alternative may be moving older people into costly, isolated institutions. Older adults may suffer unnecessary institutionalization, and nursing home care is far more costly than community-based services.

Public housing and affordable housing development are key elements of the economic stimulus plan President Obama signed into law in February 2009. The American Recovery and Reinvestment Act of 2009 provided $4 billion for the construction and repair of public housing.

In "Innovative Affordable Housing Supports Aging in Place" (*FutureAge*, November–December 2008, http://www.aahsa.org/WorkArea/showcontent.aspx?id=6788), Michele Hayunga describes how some senior housing providers are piecing together supportive services to help older adults who cannot afford assisted living to age in place safely. Examples of these creative initiatives include partnerships with other human services and volunteer organizations that enable residents to receive adult day care and home health care services, wheelchair-accessible transportation to and from medical appointments, and shopping and housekeeping services.

CHAPTER 4
WORKING AND RETIREMENT: NEW OPTIONS FOR OLDER ADULTS

Americans head off to their jobs each day as much for daily meaning as for daily bread.

—Studs Terkel, *Working: People Talk about What They Do All Day and How They Feel about What They Do* (1974)

Historically, Americans aged 65 and older have made substantial contributions to society. Examples of accomplished older adults include:

- Benjamin Franklin (1706–1790)—writer, scientist, inventor, and statesman—helped draft the Declaration of Independence at age 70.
- Thomas Alva Edison (1847–1931) worked on inventions, including the lightbulb, the microphone, and the phonograph, until his death at the age of 84.
- Rear Admiral Grace Murray Hopper (1906–1992), one of the early computer scientists and a coauthor of the computer language COBOL, maintained an active speaking and consulting schedule until her death at age 85.
- Margaret Mead (1901–1978), the noted anthropologist, returned to New Guinea when she was 72 and exhausted a much younger television film crew as they tried to keep up with her.
- Albert Einstein (1879–1955), who formulated the theory of relativity, was working on a unifying theory of the universe when he died at age 76.
- Georgia O'Keeffe (1887–1986) created masterful paintings when she was more than 80 years of age.

Older adults continue to play vital roles in industry, government, and the arts. Notable examples include:

- Former senator John Glenn (1921–), who piloted the first manned U.S. spacecraft to orbit Earth, returned to space at age 77 as a payload specialist.
- T. Boone Pickens (1928–) is a financier and chairman of BP Capital Management; he is ranked by *Forbes* as the 117th richest person in the United States.
- U.S. Senator John McCain (1936–; R-AZ) was 68 years old when he was elected in 2004 to a fourth term as senator. He was the Republican presidential candidate in the 2008 election.
- Madeleine Albright (1937–), U.S. secretary of state from 1997 to 2001, is the president of the Truman Scholarship Foundation and chairperson for both the National Democratic Institute for International Affairs and the Council of Women World Leaders Women's Ministerial Initiative. She also serves as cochair for the Commission on Legal Empowerment of the Poor and the Pew Global Attitudes Project.
- James Hansen (1941–), heads the National Aeronautics and Space Administration Goddard Institute for Space Studies and is an adjunct professor in the Department of Earth and Environmental Sciences at Columbia University. He has increased public awareness of global warming and its effects on climate change.
- Robert Redford (1937–) is an Academy Award–winning actor, director, producer, businessman, environmentalist, philanthropist, and founder of the Sundance Film Festival.
- Nancy Pelosi (1940–; D-CA) became the Speaker of the U.S. House of Representatives in January 2007. She is the first woman to hold that position.

DEFINING AND REDEFINING RETIREMENT

Retirement in the United States is usually defined by two actions: withdrawal from the paid labor force and receipt of income from pension plans, Social Security, or other retirement plans. There are, however, many people who may be viewed as retired, even though they do not fulfill the criteria of the generally accepted definition of retirement. For example, workers who retire from the military or other federal employment, which provide pension benefits after 20 years of service, may choose to continue to work and remain in the labor force for years, collecting both a salary and a pension. Other workers retire from full-time employment but continue to work part time to supplement their pension, Social Security, or retirement benefits. As a result, not all workers collecting pensions are retired, and some workers collecting salaries are retired.

Besides expanding the definition of the term *retirement*, an increasing number of older Americans are not subscribing to the traditional timing and lifestyle of retirement. Retirement is no longer an event, it is a process, and work and retirement are no longer mutually exclusive. Even though many older adults still choose to retire from full-time employment at age 65, they remain active by exploring new careers, working part time, volunteering, and engaging in a variety of leisure activities. An increasing proportion of older adults work well beyond age 65, and some choose not to retire at all.

More older Americans than ever before are delaying plans to retire or are considering reentering the workforce in response to investment losses they suffered in 2008 and 2009. Mauricio Soto of the Urban Institute reports in the fact sheet "How Is the Financial Crisis Affecting Retirement Savings?" (December 3, 2008, http://www.urban.org/UploadedPDF/901206_retirement_savings.pdf) that between September 30, 2007, and December 2, 2008, retirement accounts lost 32% ($2.8 trillion) of their value. These losses, coupled with declining home values, leave many older adults unable to finance retirement.

In *A Year-End Look at the Economic Slowdown's Impact on Middle-Aged and Older Americans* (January 2009, http://assets.aarp.org/rgcenter/econ/economic_slowdown_09.pdf), S. Kathi Brown of the AARP reveals that in 2008, 57% of Americans aged 45 and older who lost money in their investments during the past year and who were working or looking for work planned to delay retirement, and 26% had already postponed plans to retire. Thirty-eight percent of workers aged 65 and older said they expect to work longer in an effort to recoup some of their losses.

TABLE 4.1

Birth rates by age of mother, 2006 and 2007

	2007		2006	
Age of mother	**Number of births**	**Rate**	**Number of births**	**Rate**
All races and origins[a]				
Total[b]	**4,317,119**	**69.5**	**4,265,555**	**68.5**
10–14 years	6,218	0.6	6,396	0.6
15–19 years	445,045	42.5	435,436	41.9
15–17 years	140,640	22.2	138,943	22.0
18–19 years	304,405	73.9	296,493	73.0
20–24 years	1,082,837	106.4	1,080,437	105.9
25–29 years	1,208,504	117.5	1,181,899	116.7
30–34 years	962,179	99.9	950,258	97.7
35–39 years	499,916	47.5	498,616	47.3
40–44 years	105,071	9.5	105,539	9.4
45–54 years[c]	7,349	0.6	6,974	0.6

[a]Includes origin not stated.
[b]The total number includes births to women of all ages, 10–54 years. The rate shown for all ages is the fertility rate, which is defined as the total number of births (regardless of the mother's age) per 1,000 women aged 15–44 years.
[c]The total number includes births to women aged 45–54 years. The birth rate for women aged 45–49 years is computed by relating the number of births to women aged 45–54 years to women aged 45–49 years, because most of the births in this group are to women aged 45–49 years.
Notes: Data for 2007 are based on a continuous file of records received from the states. Figures for 2007 are based on weighted data rounded to the nearest individual, so categories may not add to totals. Rates are per 1,000 women in the specified age and race and Hispanic origin group.

SOURCE: Adapted from Brady E. Hamilton, Joyce A. Martin, and Stephanie J. Ventura, "Births and Birth Rates, by Age and Race and Hispanic Origin of Mother: United States, Final 2006 and Preliminary 2007," in "Births: Preliminary Data for 2007," *National Vital Statistics Reports*, vol. 57, no. 12, March 18, 2009, http://www.cdc.gov/nchs/data/nvsr/nvsr57/nvsr57_12.pdf (accessed April 29, 2009)

RECASTING WORK AND RETIREMENT

Throughout much of human history the average length of life was relatively short. In a world where most people did not expect to live beyond age 50, it was essential that personal, educational, and professional milestones be attained by certain ages. Obtaining an education, job training, marriage, parenthood, and retirement not only were designated to particular periods of life but also were expected generally to occur only once in a lifetime.

This regimented pattern of life was maintained by tradition and, more recently, reinforced by laws and regulations. In the United States government regulations and institutional rules prescribed the ages at which education began, work-life ended, and pension and Social Security benefits commenced. This timetable was based on the assumptions that these activities were to be performed "on time" and in sequence and that most growth and development occurred in the first half of life, whereas the second half was, in general, characterized by decline and disinvestment.

Social and demographic trends (including increased longevity and improved health), technological advances, and economic realities have transformed the size and composition of the labor force as well as the nature of family and work. Examples of these changes include:

- Marriage and childbearing are often postponed in favor of pursuing education and careers. Advances in reproductive technology have enabled women to delay having children by 20 years. Table 4.1 shows that the number of women aged 40 to 44 giving birth rose to 9.5 births per 1,000 women in 2007, the highest rate since 1968, when it reached 9.6. The number of births to women aged 45 to 54 rose from 6,974 in 2006 to 7,349 in 2007.
- Formal learning was once the exclusive province of the young; however, middle-aged and older adults are increasingly returning to school. According to the U.S. Census Bureau, in the press release "Back to School: 2008–2009" (June 16, 2008, http://www.census.gov/Press-Release/www/releases/archives/cb08ff-12.pdf), 37% percent of all college students were aged 25 and older in 2006 and 55% of these students attended school part time. Distance learning programs and

classes offered online have created additional opportunities for older adults who wish to continue their education. In *Staying the Course: Online Education in the United States, 2008* (November 2008, http://www.sloanconsortium.org/publications/survey/pdf/staying_the_course.pdf), I. Elaine Allen and Jeff Seaman report that online enrollment has grown faster than traditional higher education enrollment with more than 3.9 million students taking at least one online course in 2007—12% more than in the previous year. Institutions that offer online education aimed at working adults anticipate increased growth in enrollment in response to rising unemployment rates.

- Career changes and retraining have become the norm rather than the exception. Americans once pursued a single career in their lifetime; many workers now change jobs and even careers several times. According to the American Council on Education (April 2009, http://www.acenet.edu), an increasing number of adults, from military veterans to people aged 50 and older are returning to work in second, third, or even fifth careers.
- Age-based mandatory retirement no longer exists in most private-sector industries. Historically, mandatory retirement ages were justified by the argument that some occupations were either too dangerous for older workers or required high levels of physical and mental acuity. Mandatory retirement is still compulsory for federal law enforcement, correctional officers, firefighters, air traffic controllers, and commercial airline pilots. However, mandatory retirement ages have been faulted because they are arbitrary and are not based on actual physical evaluations of individual workers. As a result, some detractors view the practice of age-based mandatory retirement as a form of age discrimination.

Even though a conventional American life generally included education, work, and recreation/retirement, in this order, the current cohort (a group of individuals that shares a common characteristic such as birth years and is studied over time) of workers and retirees have the opportunity to blend, reorder, and repeat these activities as desired. Many gerontologists (professionals who study the social, psychological, and biological aspects of aging) and other aging researchers posit that there is a "third age"—a stage of working life when older workers can actively renegotiate their relationships with the labor force. Their choices, depending on life circumstances, may include remaining in the workforce, retirement, or returning to work for periods of part-time, full-time, or part-season employment. Not all workers and retirees will choose to stray from the conventional course, but increasingly they have the option to do so.

A CHANGING ECONOMY AND CHANGING ROLES

From Agricultural...

When the U.S. economy was predominantly agricultural, children were put to work as soon as they were able to contribute to the family upkeep. Similarly, workers who lived beyond age 65 did not retire; they worked as long as they were physically able. When older adults were no longer able to work, younger family members cared for them. Older people were valued and respected for their accumulated knowledge and experience and were integral members of the interconnected family and labor systems.

...to Industrial...

The Industrial Revolution shifted workers from the farm to manufacturing jobs. The work was physically demanding, the hours long, and the tasks rigidly structured. Women labored in factories and at home caring for the family. Older people found themselves displaced—their skills and experience were not relevant to new technologies and they could not physically compete with the large number of young workers eager to exploit new economic opportunities.

As industrial workers matured, some were promoted to positions as supervisors and managers. For older workers who had been with the same company for many years, labor unions provided a measure of job security through the seniority system ("first hired, last fired"). However, in an increasingly youth-oriented society older workers were often rejected in favor of younger laborers. Frequent reports of age discrimination prompted Congress to pass the Age Discrimination in Employment Act (ADEA). Enacted in 1967 to protect workers aged 40 to 65, ADEA made it illegal for employers or unions to discharge, refuse to hire, or otherwise discriminate on the basis of age. Victims are eligible for lost wages—the amount is doubled in the most blatant cases—and workers wrongfully terminated may also seek reinstatement. The ADEA Amendments of 1978 made 70 the upper age limit and prohibited mandatory retirement for most workers in the private sector and in the federal government. In 1986 Congress again amended the act to eliminate the upper age limit.

...to Service and Information

The U.S. economy continued its dramatic shift away from smokestack industries such as mining and manufacturing to an economy in which service occupations and the production and dissemination of information predominate. As such, the demand for highly educated workers has grown, and the demand for workers who perform physical labor has slackened. Many information age careers and service jobs, such as those in the fields of health, law, information technology, and communications, are ideally suited for older workers because they do not require physical labor, and employers benefit from the cumulative experience of older workers.

THE AGING LABOR FORCE

As the baby boom generation (people born between 1946 and 1964) approaches retirement age, the proportion of the U.S. population aged 65 and older will increase significantly between 2010 and 2035. However, the U.S. labor force is already undergoing a shift toward a greater number of older workers and a relative scarcity of new entrants.

Victor W. Marshall of the UNC Institute on Aging observes in *Health Age and Labor Force Disruption of Older Workers* (April 8, 2009, http://www.aging.unc.edu/infocenter/slides/MarshallV2009OlderWorkers.ppt) that the median (the middle value—half are higher and half are lower) age of the U.S. labor force is increasing from 35.4 years in 1986, to 40.8 years in 2006, to a projected 42.1 years in 2016.

Older Adults in the Labor Force

The U.S. Bureau of Labor Statistics (BLS; February 2009, http://www.bls.gov/cps/cpsaat3.pdf) reports that in 2008 older workers accounted for 4.2% of the entire U.S. labor force. From 1948 to 2007 the labor force participation of men aged 65 and older generally declined until the late 1990s, when rates leveled off or even rose slightly. (See Figure 4.1.) The observed decline in older adults' participation in the labor force during the 1970s and into the 1980s has been attributed to widespread mandatory retirement practices in many industries that forced workers to retire at age 65. In addition, the eligibility age for Social Security benefits was reduced from 65 to 62 years of age in the 1960s, enabling workers to retire earlier. The relatively stable proportion of older workers in the labor force since that time is in part because of the relaxation and elimination of mandatory retirement and the liberalization of the Social Security earnings test—the earnings limits that prompt a reduction of Social Security benefits. The labor force participation rate for older workers was at record lows during the 1980s and early 1990s but has been increasing since the late 1990s—a larger share of older workers are remaining in or returning to the labor force.

In *Older Workers* (July 2008,http://www.bls.gov/spotlight/2008/older_workers/pdf/older_workers_bls_spotlight.pdf), the BLS indicates that between 1997 and 2007 employment of workers aged 65 and older increased 101%. (See Figure 4.2.) The number of employed men over 65 increased by 75% and the number of employed women rose by 147%. Even though the overall percentage of workers aged 75 and older is small, 0.8% in 2007, it increased a staggering 172% from 1997 to 2007. This increase in older workers may reflect several factors, including economic necessity, the fact that older adults are seeking to remain vital and active into their 70s, a desire for the challenge and social interactions that work offers, or some combination of these.

Work Expectations after Age Sixty-Five

In the issue brief *The Retirement System in Transition: The 2009 Retirement Confidence Survey* (April 2009, http://www.ebri.org/files/EBRI_IB_4-2009_RCS.pdf), Ruth Helman et al. report on the results of the 2009 Retirement Confidence Survey conducted by the Employee Benefit Research Institute. The researchers indicate that in 2009, 89% of workers said their expected retirement age has increased. The struggling economy (36%) and stock market losses (28%) were the reasons most frequently cited for postponing retirement.

FIGURE 4.1

Labor force participation rate of workers aged 65 and older, 1948–2007

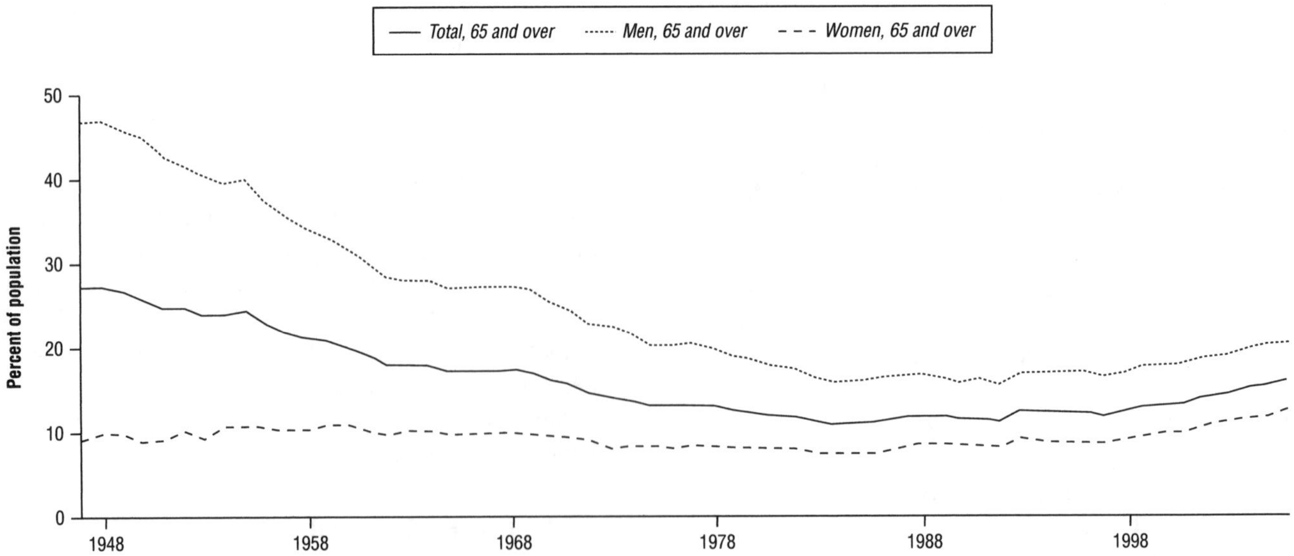

SOURCE: "Labor Force Participation Rate of Workers 65 and over, 1948–2007," in *Older Workers*, U.S. Bureau of Labor Statistics, July 2008, http://www.bls.gov/spotlight/2008/older_workers/pdf/older_workers_bls_spotlight.pdf (accessed April 29, 2009)

FIGURE 4.2

Percent increase in employment by age and sex, 1977–2007

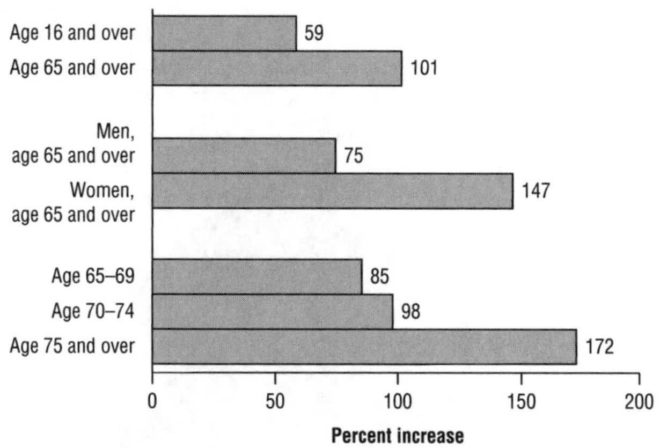

SOURCE: "Percent Increase in Employment by Age and Sex, 1977–2007," in *Older Workers*, U.S. Bureau of Labor Statistics, July 2008, http://www.bls.gov/spotlight/2008/older_workers/pdf/older_workers_bls_spotlight.pdf (accessed April 29, 2009)

According to Helman et al., 72% of workers said in 2009 they are planning to work for pay after they retire. This percentage had significantly increased from 2008, when 63% of workers said they intended to work after they retire. More workers are also taking steps to prepare for retirement. The majority (81%) reported reducing expenses and 75% reported saving for retirement, up from 68% in 2004.

Older Women Opt to Work Rather Than Retire

Between 1963 and 2005 labor force participation rates generally rose among women aged 55 and older, with the largest increase among female workers aged 55 to 61—from 44% in 1963 to 64% in 2006. (See Figure 4.3.) These increases reflect an overall increase of women in the labor force with each successive generation. During the same period the participation rate for women aged 62 to 64 rose from 29% to 43%, and among women aged 65 to 69 the rate increased from 17% to 24%. Even though the labor force participation of women aged 70 and older has remained essentially stable, in recent years participation among women in the other age groups has increased at a faster rate. These increases also serve to narrow the gap in labor force participation rates between men and women.

FIGURE 4.3

Labor force participation rates of women aged 55 and over, by age group, annual averages, 1963–2006

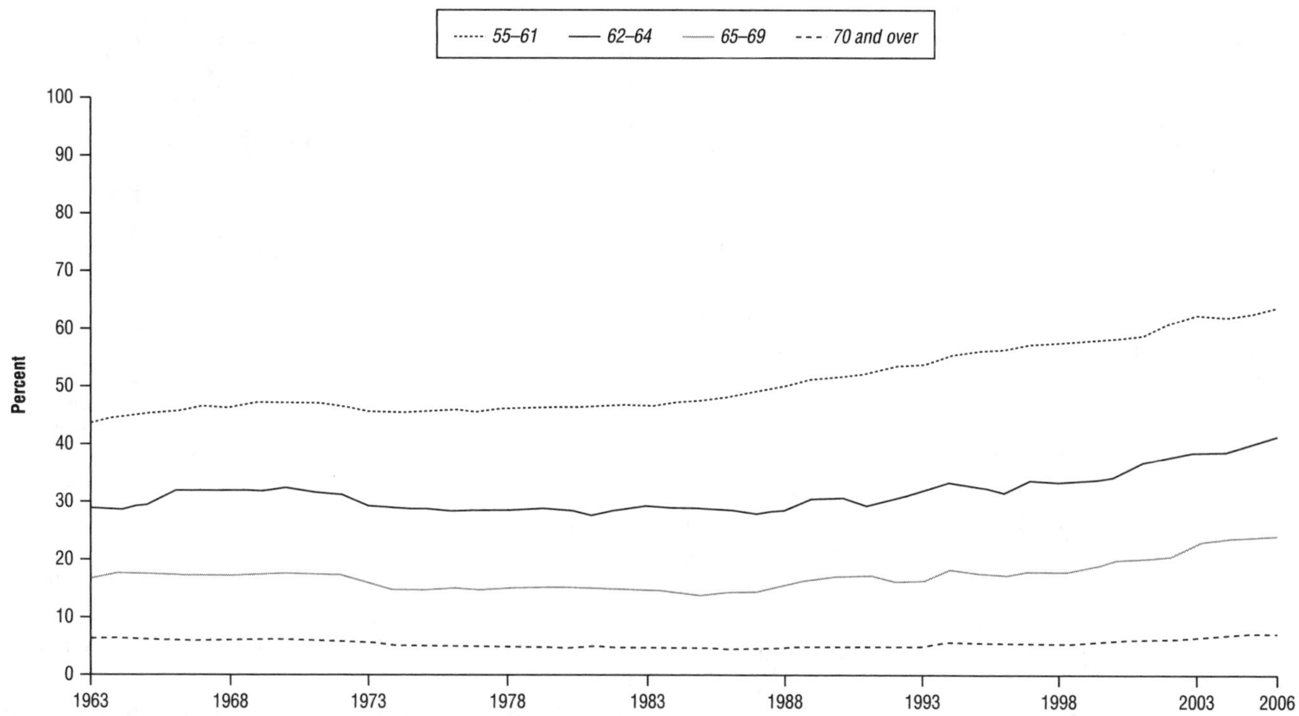

Note: Data for 1994 and later years are not strictly comparable with data for 1993 and earlier years due to a redesign of the survey and methodology of the Current Population Survey. Beginning in 2000, data incorporate population controls from Census 2000.
Reference population: These data refer to the civilian noninstitutionalized population.

SOURCE: "Labor Force Participation Rates of Women Age 55 and over, by Age Group, Annual Averages, 1963–2006," in *Older Americans 2008: Key Indicators of Well-Being*, Federal Interagency Forum on Aging-Related Statistics, March 2008, http://www.agingstats.gov/agingstatsdotnet/Main_Site/Data/2008_Documents/OA_2008.pdf (accessed April 20, 2009)

Most older women in the 21st century spent some time in the labor force when they were younger. However, the older the woman the less likely she is to have ever worked outside the home. In the United States the group of women in their late 50s and early 60s that was the first to work outside the home in large numbers is approaching retirement. Women in this cohort who are single, widowed, or divorced often continue to work to support themselves because they do not have sufficient Social Security credits to retire.

Married older women are increasingly choosing to keep working after their husbands retire, breaking with the practice of joining their husbands in retirement. In 1977 about one-third of employed women aged 65 and older were married, but by 2007 nearly half of employed women aged 65 and older were married. (See Figure 4.4.) Among the reasons cited for the growing proportion of older married women in the workforce are:

- Older women have careers they find personally satisfying as well as financially rewarding.
- They need to secure their retirement to prevent the poverty that has historically afflicted widows.
- Their income helps maintain the family standard of living and may be vital when their husband has been pressured to retire by his employer or suffers failing health.
- They enjoy the social interactions at the workplace—women value relationships with coworkers more than men, and as a result women often find retirement more isolating.

FIGURE 4.4

Percent distribution of employed women aged 65 and older, by marital status, 1997 and 2007

SOURCE: "Percentage Distribution of Employed Women Age 65 and over by Marital Status," in *Older Workers*, U.S. Bureau of Labor Statistics, July 2008, http://www.bls.gov/spotlight/2008/older_workers/pdf/older_workers_bls_spotlight.pdf (accessed April 29, 2009)

The Aging Labor Force

In *Older Workers*, the BLS documents the extent to which the U.S. workforce has aged and projects an increasing proportion of older workers in the labor force. Between 2006 and 2016 the percentage of workers aged 55 to 64 is expected to grow by 36.5%, and the number of workers aged 65 to 74 and 75 and older will rise by more than 80%. (See Figure 4.5.) By 2016 workers aged 65 and older will account for 6.1% of the total labor force.

Part-Time versus Full-Time Work

The BLS observes that the ratio of older workers choosing part-time or full-time work was relatively constant from 1977 through 1990, but between 1990 and 1995 the percentage of part-time workers rose with a corresponding decline in full-time employment. (See Figure 4.6.) After 1995 the situation reversed, with full-time employment increasing dramatically. From 1995 to 2007 the number of older workers nearly doubled, whereas the number of part-timers increased by only 19%. By 2007, 56% of older workers were full time, up 12% from 1995, when 44% of older workers were full time.

Older workers may find increasing opportunities for flexible employment and alternative work arrangements, such as working as an independent contractor rather than as an employee or as an on-call worker rather than as a daily worker. For employers, hiring part-time older workers is often an attractive alternative to hiring younger, full-time workers. Some employers value older workers' maturity, dependability, and experience. Others hire older workers to reduce payroll expenses. This reduction is achieved when part-time workers are hired as independent contractors and do not receive benefits, or when they are paid lower wages than full-time employees and not provided benefits.

FIGURE 4.5

Projected percentage change in labor force, by age, 2006–16

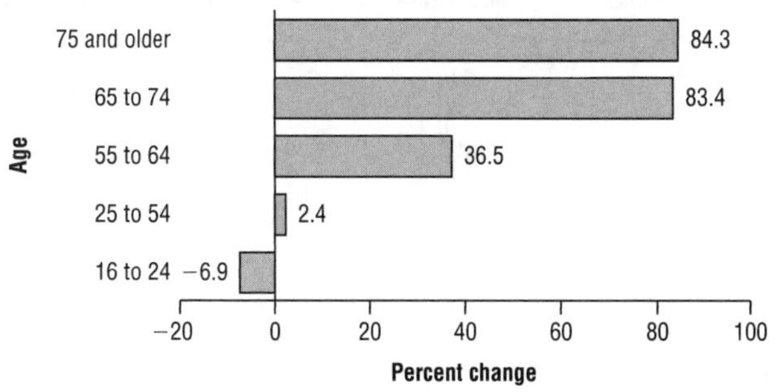

SOURCE: "Projected Percentage Change in Labor Force, by Age, 2006–2016," in *Older Workers*, U.S. Bureau of Labor Statistics, July 2008, http://www.bls.gov/spotlight/2008/older_workers/pdf/older_workers_bls_spotlight.pdf (accessed April 29, 2009)

Job Tenure

Older people tend to be stable employees who stay in the same job longer than younger employees. Job tenure is measured as the median number of years that workers have been with their current employer. According to the BLS, in January 2008 workers aged 55 to 64 had more than three times the median years of job tenure (9.9 years), compared with those aged 25 to 34 (2.7 years). (See Table 4.2.)

DISPELLING MYTHS AND STEREOTYPES ABOUT OLDER WORKERS

Older workers are often stereotyped by the mistaken belief that performance declines with age. Performance studies, however, reveal that older workers perform intellectually as well as or better than workers 30 years younger by maintaining their problem solving, communication, and creative skills. In "Myths about Older Workers" (March 2009, http://jobsearchtoolkit.pbwiki.com/f/MythsAboutOlderWorkers.pdf), the North Carolina Collaboration on Lifelong Learning and Engagement asserts that older workers have high levels of productivity, in part because their maturity, stability, and better interpersonal skills enable them to make better use of their time.

Myth: Older Workers Have Overly Increased Absenteeism

Because aging is associated with declining health, older workers are often assumed to have markedly higher rates of illnesses and absences from work. Somewhat surprisingly, the chronic (long-term) health conditions older adults may suffer tend to be manageable and do not affect attendance records. In fact, absence rates for

FIGURE 4.6

Workers aged 65 and older by work schedule, 1977– 2007

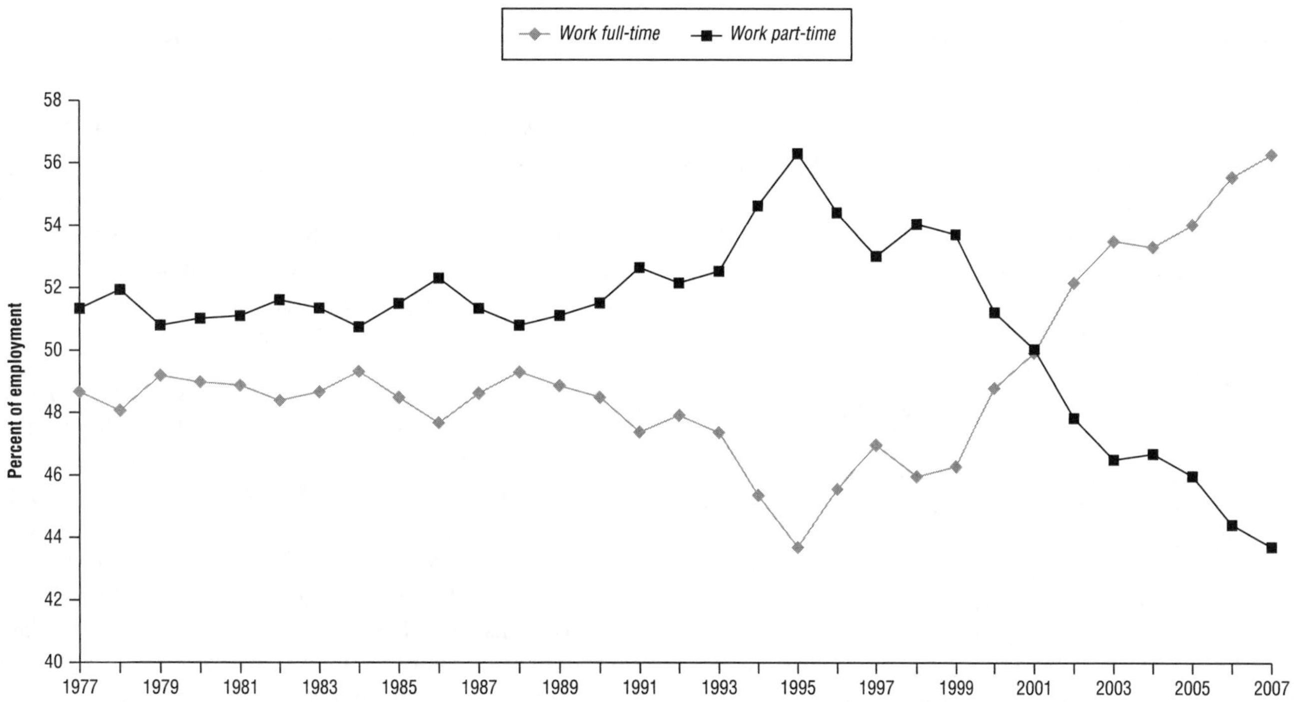

SOURCE: "Workers 65 and over by Work Schedule, 1977–2007," in *Older Workers*, U.S. Bureau of Labor Statistics, July 2008, http://www.bls.gov/spotlight/2008/older_workers/pdf/older_workers_bls_spotlight.pdf (accessed April 29, 2009)

TABLE 4.2

Median years of tenure with current employer for employed workers by age and sex, selected years 1996–2008

Age and sex	February 1996	February 1998	February 2000	January 2002	January 2004	January 2006	January 2008
Total							
16 years and over	3.8	3.6	3.5	3.7	4.0	4.0	4.1
16 to 17 years	.7	.6	.6	.7	.7	.6	.7
18 to 19 years	.7	.7	.7	.8	.8	.7	.8
20 to 24 years	1.2	1.1	1.1	1.2	1.3	1.3	1.3
25 years and over	5.0	4.7	4.7	4.7	4.9	4.9	5.1
25 to 34 years	2.8	2.7	2.6	2.7	2.9	2.9	2.7
35 to 44 years	5.3	5.0	4.8	4.6	4.9	4.9	4.9
45 to 54 years	8.3	8.1	8.2	7.6	7.7	7.3	7.6
55 to 64 years	10.2	10.1	10.0	9.9	9.6	9.3	9.9
65 years and over	8.4	7.8	9.4	8.6	9.0	8.8	10.2
Men							
16 years and over	4.0	3.8	3.8	3.9	4.1	4.1	4.2
16 to 17 years	.6	.6	.6	.8	.7	.7	.7
18 to 19 years	.7	.7	.7	.8	.8	.7	.8
20 to 24 years	1.2	1.2	1.2	1.4	1.3	1.4	1.4
25 years and over	5.3	4.9	4.9	4.9	5.1	5.0	5.2
25 to 34 years	3.0	2.8	2.7	2.8	3.0	2.9	2.8
35 to 44 years	6.1	5.5	5.3	5.0	5.2	5.1	5.2
45 to 54 years	10.1	9.4	9.5	9.1	9.6	8.1	8.2
55 to 64 years	10.5	11.2	10.2	10.2	9.8	9.5	10.1
65 years and over	8.3	7.1	9.0	8.1	8.2	8.3	10.4
Women							
16 years and over	3.5	3.4	3.3	3.4	3.8	3.9	3.9
16 to 17 years	.7	.6	.6	.7	.6	.6	.6
18 to 19 years	.7	.7	.7	.8	.8	.7	.8
20 to 24 years	1.2	1.1	1.0	1.1	1.3	1.2	1.3
25 years and over	4.7	4.4	4.4	4.4	4.7	4.8	4.9
25 to 34 years	2.7	2.5	2.5	2.5	2.8	2.8	2.6
35 to 44 years	4.8	4.5	4.3	4.2	4.5	4.6	4.7
45 to 54 years	7.0	7.2	7.3	6.5	6.4	6.7	7.0
55 to 64 years	10.0	9.6	9.9	9.6	9.2	9.2	9.8
65 years and over	8.4	8.7	9.7	9.4	9.6	9.5	9.9

Notes: Data for 1996 and 1998 are based on population controls from the 1990 census. Data beginning in 2000 reflect the introduction of Census 2000 population controls and are not strictly comparable with data for prior years. In addition, data for 2004 forward reflect updated population controls introduced annually with the release of January data.

SOURCE: "Table 1. Median Years of Tenure with Current Employer for Employed Wage and Salary Workers by Age and Sex, Selected Years, 1996–2008," in *Employee Tenure in 2008*, U.S. Department of Labor, U.S. Bureau of Labor Statistics, September 26, 2008, http://www.bls.gov/news.release/pdf/tenure.pdf (accessed April 30, 2009)

older full-time wage and salary workers differ only slightly from those of younger workers. According to the BLS, in 2008 the absence rate for workers aged 55 years and older was 3.6%, compared with 3.1% for those aged 25 to 54. (See Table 4.3.)

Myth: It Costs More to Hire Older Workers

One widely accepted myth is that hiring and training older workers is not a sound investment because they will not remain on the job long. Yet, the BLS indicates that in January 2008 workers aged 45 to 54 had an average job tenure of 9.9 years, which was more than three times longer than the 2.7 years for workers aged 25 to 34. (See Table 4.2.) Research conducted by the AARP repeatedly demonstrates that workers between the ages of 50 and 60 work for an average of 15 years. Furthermore, the Mature Workers Employment Alliance, an organization dedicated to assisting older workers in transitioning to new positions, asserts that the future work life of employees over the age of 50 generally exceeds the life of the technology for which they are trained.

In "Myths about Older Workers," the North Carolina Collaboration on Lifelong Learning and Engagement observes that older workers are less likely to change jobs frequently, which reduces the expenses associated with employee turnover. It also notes that some older workers may forgo benefits because they have insurance from previous employers or through Medicare.

The AARP observes that even though older workers' health, disability, and life insurance costs are higher than those of younger workers, they are offset by lower costs because of fewer dependents. Older workers have generally earned more vacation time and have higher pension costs, and they take fewer risks, which means they have lower accident rates. Workers over the age of 50 file fewer workers' compensation claims than younger workers—the largest numbers of claims are filed by workers between the ages of 30 and 34. Fringe benefit costs for workers of all ages are about the same overall. Finally, retaining experienced older workers actually reduces employer costs associated with recruiting, hiring, and training new, younger workers.

TABLE 4.3

Absences from work, by age and sex, 2008

Age, sex, race, and Hispanic or Latino ethnicity	2008						
	Workers in absence universe (in thousands)[a]	Absence rate[a]			Lost worktime rate[b]		
		Total	Illness or injury	Other reasons	Total	Illness or injury	Other reasons
Total, 16 years and over	102,307	3.1	2.2	0.9	1.7	1.2	0.5
16 to 19 years	1,345	2.4	1.5	.9	1.3	.7	.5
20 to 24 years	8,528	2.9	2.0	.9	1.4	.9	.6
25 years and over	92,433	3.2	2.2	.9	1.7	1.2	.5
25 to 54 years	75,837	3.1	2.1	1.0	1.7	1.1	.6
55 years and over	16,597	3.6	2.9	.7	2.0	1.7	.3
Men, 16 years and over	57,019	2.3	1.8	.5	1.2	1.0	.3
16 to 19 years	799	1.5	1.0	.5	.6	.5	.2
20 to 24 years	4,797	2.0	1.5	.4	.9	.7	.2
25 years and over	51,424	2.3	1.8	.5	1.3	1.0	.3
25 to 54 years	42,477	2.2	1.7	.5	1.2	.9	.3
55 years and over	8,946	3.0	2.5	.5	1.8	1.5	.3
Women, 16 years and over	45,288	4.1	2.7	1.4	2.3	1.4	.9
16 to 19 years	546	3.6	2.2	1.4	2.2	1.1	1.1
20 to 24 years	3,732	4.0	2.5	1.5	2.2	1.1	1.0
25 years and over	41,010	4.2	2.8	1.4	2.3	1.4	.8
25 to 54 years	33,359	4.2	2.6	1.5	2.3	1.3	.9
55 years and over	7,650	4.2	3.4	.8	2.3	1.9	.4
White	82,806	3.1	2.2	.9	1.6	1.1	.5
Black or African American	12,081	3.6	2.4	1.1	2.1	1.5	.6
Asian	5,015	2.2	1.4	.8	1.3	.7	.6
Hispanic or Latino	15,133	2.7	1.8	.9	1.4	.9	.5

[a]The absence universe includes most wage and salary workers who usually work full-time at their primary or sole job. Absences are defined as instances when persons who usually work 35 or more hours a week at their main job worked less than 35 hours during the reference week for one of the following reasons: Own illness, injury, or medical problems; child-care problems; other family or personal obligations; civic or military duty; and maternity or paternity leave. Excluded are situations in which work was missed due to vacation or personal days, holiday, labor dispute, slack work or business conditions, and the wait for a new job to begin. For multiple jobholders, absence data refer only to work missed at their main jobs. All self-employed persons are excluded, regardless of whether or not their jobs are incorporated. Conceptually, the absence rate is the ratio of workers with absences to total full-time wage and salary workers who usually work 35 hours or more on their main job.
[b]Hours absent as a percent of hours usually worked, which is derived using the number of workers in absence universe as defined in footnote 1 above, minus those who reported that their hours varied.
Note: Estimates for the above race groups (white, black or African American, and Asian) do not sum to totals because data are not presented for all races. Persons whose ethnicity is identified as Hispanic or Latino may be of any race. Updated population controls are introduced annually with the release of January data.

SOURCE: "46. Absences from Work of Employed Full-time Wage and Salary Workers by Age, Sex, Race and Hispanic or Latino Ethnicity," in *Labor Force Statistics from the Current Population Survey*, U.S. Department of Labor, U.S. Bureau of Labor Statistics, April 3, 2009, http://www.bls.gov/cps/cpsaat46.pdf (accessed April 30, 2009)

Myth: Older Workers Are Technophobes

Even though older workers may require more time to learn new technologies, their improved attitudes, study habits, and diligence often help them to surpass younger workers in training courses. There is a pervasive myth that older adults are unable to learn or use new information technology. However, the North Carolina Collaboration on Lifelong Learning and Engagement reports in "Myths about Older Workers" that in the academic year 2006–07, adults aged 50 and older accounted for 7% of students enrolled in degree programs and 24% of continuing education programs. That same academic year, over 125,000 adults aged 50 to 64 and 30,000 adults aged 65 and older were attending community college and close to 5,000 adults aged 65 and older were enrolled in a computer course.

In fact, the Randstad study *The World of Work 2007* (2007, http://www.us.randstad.com/the%20world%20of%20work%202007.pdf) firmly refutes the notion that older adults do not embrace technology. In fact, the study finds that older workers are more likely to use technology—computers, faxes, and personal digital assistants (small mobile hand-held devices that provide computing and information storage and retrieval capabilities), and mobile phones—on the job than younger workers.

Unemployment Rate for Older Workers Hits Record High in 2009

The economic slowdown that began in late 2007 and continued through 2009 substantially increased the unemployment rate for older adults. In the fact sheet "Senior Unemployment Rate Hits 31-Year High" (January 2009, http://www.urban.org/UploadedPDF/901210_senior_unemployment_rates.pdf), Richard W. Johnson of the Urban Institute notes that in December 2008 the overall U.S. unemployment rate was 7.2% and that 5.1% of workers aged 65 and older were unemployed, the highest percentage since March 1977. Johnson states that "the age-65-and-older unemployment rate has increased by 1.7 percentage points since November 2007, the last month before the current recession began." Previous economic downturns, such as the recession of 1981–82, did not have this kind of an impact on older workers—the number of unemployed older adults during that period did not increase.

Michael Luo reports in "Longer Unemployment for Those 45 and Older" (*New York Times*, April 12, 2009) that in March 2009 the unemployment rate for workers aged 45 and older was 6.4%, the highest since 1948. There were not only more unemployed older Americans but they were also more likely than younger workers to be out of work for six months or longer. Luo notes that older workers who had been laid off were out of work an average of 22.2 weeks in 2008, compared with 16.2 weeks for younger workers. When older workers find new jobs, they generally suffer a much sharper drop in salary than their younger counterparts.

AGE DISCRIMINATION

> *But more and more, America will come to believe that there is no fixed age for retirement, that work is important to individuals and to organizations, and that age itself should not disqualify anyone from being hired nor discourage anyone from seeking work.*
>
> —William Novelli, "Seizing the Human Capital in Older Workers" (November 10, 2004)

Even though the 1967 ADEA and its amendments were enacted to ban discrimination against workers based on their age, the act was also intended to promote the employment of older workers based on their abilities. Besides making it illegal for employers to discriminate based on age in hiring, discharging, and compensating employees, the act also prohibited companies from coercing older workers into accepting incentives to early retirement. In 1990 ADEA was strengthened with the passing of the Older Workers Benefit Protection Act. As well as prohibiting discrimination in employee benefits based on age, it provides that an employee's waiver of the right to sue for age discrimination, a clause sometimes included in severance packages, is invalid unless it is "voluntary and knowing."

However, age bias and discrimination persist, even though age discrimination in the workplace is against the law. More than 15,000 claims of age discrimination are filed with the Equal Employment Opportunity Commission (EEOC) every year. Most cases involve older workers who believe they were terminated unfairly, but a number of the cases involve workers who feel they have met age discrimination in hiring practices.

The number of claims received by the EEOC rose from 19,921 in fiscal year (FY) 2002 to 24,582 in FY 2008. (See Table 4.4.) The EEOC resolved 21,415 of these charges in FY 2008; however, agency data reveal that most claimants do not win. Of the claims that were resolved in FY 2008, the EEOC found "reasonable cause" that age discrimination may have occurred in just 678 cases and found "no reasonable cause" in 11,124 cases.

Pressure to Retire

There are many forms of subtle discrimination against older workers as well as ways employers can directly or indirectly exert pressure on older employees to retire or resign. This form of discrimination is "under the radar" and

TABLE 4.4

Age Discrimination in Employment Act (ADEA) charges, fiscal years 1997–2008

	Fiscal year 1997	Fiscal year 1998	Fiscal year 1999	Fiscal year 2000	Fiscal year 2001	Fiscal year 2002	Fiscal year 2003	Fiscal year 2004	Fiscal year 2005	Fiscal year 2006	Fiscal year 2007	Fiscal year 2008
Receipts	15,785	15,191	14,141	16,008	17,405	19,921	19,124	17,837	16,585	16,548	19,103	24,582
Resolutions	18,279	15,995	15,448	14,672	15,155	18,673	17,352	15,792	14,076	14,146	16,134	21,415
Resolutions by type												
Settlements	642	755	816	1,156	1,006	1,222	1,285	1,377	1,326	1,417	1,795	1,974
	3.5%	4.7%	5.3%	7.9%	6.6%	6.5%	7.4%	8.7%	9.4%	10.0%	11.1%	9.2%
Withdrawals w/benefits	762	580	578	560	551	671	710	787	764	767	958	1,252
	4.2%	3.6%	3.7%	3.8%	3.6%	3.6%	4.1%	5.0%	5.4%	5.4%	5.9%	5.8%
Administrative closures	4,986	4,175	3,601	3,232	3,963	6,254	2,824	3,550	2,537	2,639	2,754	6,387
	27.3%	26.1%	23.3%	22.0%	26.1%	33.5%	16.3%	22.5%	18.0%	18.7%	17.1%	29.8%
No reasonable cause	11,163	9,863	9,172	8,517	8,388	9,725	11,976	9,563	8,866	8,746	10,002	11,124
	61.1%	61.7%	59.4%	58.0%	55.3%	52.1%	69.0%	60.6%	63.0%	61.8%	62.0%	51.9%
Reasonable cause	726	622	1,281	1,207	1,247	801	557	515	583	612	625	678
	4.0%	3.9%	8.3%	8.2%	8.2%	4.3%	3.2%	3.3%	4.1%	4.3%	3.9%	3.2%
Successful conciliations	74	119	184	241	409	208	166	139	169	177	186	220
	0.4%	0.7%	1.2%	1.6%	2.7%	1.1%	1.0%	0.9%	1.2%	1.3%	1.2%	1.0%
Unsuccessful conciliations	652	503	1,097	966	838	593	391	376	414	435	439	458
	3.6%	3.1%	7.1%	6.6%	5.5%	3.2%	2.3%	2.4%	2.9%	3.1%	2.7%	2.1%
Merit resolutions	2,130	1,957	2,675	2,923	2,804	2,694	2,552	2,679	2,673	2,796	3,378	3,904
	11.7%	12.2%	17.3%	19.9%	18.5%	14.4%	14.7%	17.0%	19.0%	19.8%	20.9%	18.2%
Monetary benefits [Millions]*	$44.3	$34.7	$38.6	$45.2	$53.7	$55.7	$48.9	$69.0	$77.7	$51.5	$66.8	$82.8

*Does not include monetary benefits obtained through litigation.
Note: The total of individual percentages may not always sum to 100% due to rounding.

SOURCE: "Age Discrimination in Employment Act Fiscal Year 1997–FY 2008," U.S. Equal Opportunity Commission, March 11, 2009, http://www.eeoc.gov/stats/adea.html (accessed April 30, 2009)

in many instances violates the spirit, if not the letter, of ADEA.

From an employer's standpoint, age discrimination is simply the consequence of efforts to reduce payroll expenses. Employment decisions are not only based on how much an employee contributes to the company but also on the salary and benefits the company must provide the employee, relative to the cost of other employees. Because salary tends to increase with longevity on the job, older workers usually receive higher wages than younger ones. Thus, if two employees are equally productive and the older one has a higher salary, a company has an economic incentive to lay off the older worker or strongly encourage early retirement.

For many workers, early retirement is untenable. Early retirement benefits are almost always less than regular retirement benefits and may be insufficient to allow a retiree to live comfortably without working. Finding a new job is more challenging for older workers, particularly during periods of high unemployment, and they are frequently unemployed for longer periods than are younger job seekers. Furthermore, workers who refuse to accept early retirement may find themselves without jobs at all, perhaps with no pension and no severance pay.

Some labor economists contend that early retirements, whether voluntary or coerced, deprive the nation of skilled workers needed for robust growth and divest the government of the revenue that these workers would have contributed in payroll taxes.

Filing ADEA Claims—Suing the Company

> *If you're a 55-year-old male who's lost your $70,000 job, what do you do? The odds of finding any job, let alone a comparable job, are slim. So you fight.*
>
> —Howard Eglit, quoted by Robert J. Grossman in "Are You Ignoring Older Workers?" (*HR Magazine*, August 2003)

The costs involved in filing an age discrimination suit are high. Besides the financial outlay for legal representation, workers who sue their employers may be stigmatized and face further discrimination—future employers' reluctance to hire a worker who has filed a discrimination suit against a former employer. Workers caught in this scenario can suffer emotional and financial damage that may adversely affect them for the rest of their life. Nonetheless, many workers do choose to sue their employers.

Supreme Court Decisions Augment ADEA

In response to the economic downturn and continuing economic uncertainty during 2008 and 2009, many companies instituted layoffs and reductions in force in an effort to reduce costs and remain viable. Because reductions in force aim to reduce payroll, some target higher paid workers, who are often also older adults with longer tenures. ADEA is violated if an employment policy that seems neutral, such as the criteria for workers to be laid off, actually exerts a statistically significant adverse or "disparate impact" when applied to workers aged 40 and older versus younger workers.

The 2005 U.S. Supreme Court decision in *Smith v. City of Jackson* (544 U.S. 228), that workers aged 40 and older may prove discrimination under ADEA using a disparate impact theory, strengthened protections for older workers. The court stated that plaintiffs in age discrimination lawsuits do not have to prove that employers intended to discriminate, only that layoffs had a "disparate impact" on older workers. This ruling is significant because it no longer requires claimants to show that an employer deliberately targeted a single employee or group of employees. Instead, claimants can prevail if they are able to demonstrate that an employer used a neutral business practice—with no intent to discriminate—that had an adverse impact on people aged 40 and older.

In 2008 the Supreme Court ruled in *Meacham et al. v. Knolls Atomic Power Laboratory* (553 U.S. ___) that an employer defending against a disparate impact age bias claim, and not the employee making the charge, bears the burden of proving that the adverse action—in this case a reduction in workforce plan—was based on a reasonable factor other than age. The disparate impact theory is based on the principle that a policy that appears neutral may still have an adverse impact on a protected class, in this case, older workers.

In "Reductions in Force: The Supreme Court Escalates the Legal Risks" (July 15, 2008, http://www.resourcegovernment.com/articles/view.php?article_id=832), Frank Morris Jr., an attorney with Epstein Becker & Green P.C., asserts that "the court's decision unequivocally requires employers to be able to prove the reasonableness of the factors it uses to reach employment decisions that have an adverse impact on older workers.... Precisely at a time when the economy may force employers to make more [reductions in force] decisions, the Supreme Court has made defending such decisions decidedly harder for employers."

BABY BOOMERS AND RETIREES WANT TO DO GOOD WORK

> *People who were told from birth about their own significance aren't ready to stop being significant just because they've hit a career ceiling called "retirement age."*
>
> —Rosabeth Moss Kanter, "Baby Boomers Still Want to Change the World" (*Miami Herald*, August 16, 2005)

Baby Boomers Will Transform Retirement

Mark Freedman of Civic Ventures identifies in "The Boomers, Good Work, and the Next Stage of Life" (*New Face of Work Survey*, June 2005, http://www.civicventures.org/publications/surveys/new_face_of_work/new_face_of_work.pdf) 10 trends arising from analysis of the survey data:

1. The current cohort of older adults is more interested in gaining the "freedom to work" rather than the "freedom from work." Two-thirds (65%) of baby boomers intending to work in their retirement years are trailblazers, creating a new stage of life and a new stage of work.
2. Older adults want to do well by doing good—they will seek opportunities in social services, health care, and education that will enable them to generate income and improve the lives of others.
3. The timing of boomers' retirement and interest in service careers coincides with an urgent need for workers in the very sectors—health, education, and social services—they are interested in entering.
4. The coming generation of older adults may not pursue volunteer opportunities as vigorously as past generations. They are motivated to assume positions of leadership and equate paid work with being taken seriously.
5. Boomers heading into retirement may want flexible and part-time employment like opportunities currently available with retailers such as Wal-Mart and the Home Depot, but they are more interested in community service and social renewal than they are in entering the retail sector.
6. Boomers want second careers, not part-time jobs. Even though they may desire the flexibility of part-time employment, their commitment to meaningful work renders them willing to pursue education and training to prepare them for second careers that they anticipate lasting 10 to 20 years. Also, even though they may not have as many years to devote to second careers as they did to their first, they want to make comparable contributions.
7. Older adults are interested in achieving a satisfying work-life balance, but they have soundly rejected the notion that the years after age 50 represent a period of decline and disengagement.
8. The commitment to service of the current group of older adults is attributable not only to their idealism but also to their historic effort to find meaning and identity in work and the desire to work with others who share common goals.
9. Older adults are realistic about the fact that the opportunities they seek may not be readily available. There is guidance to help workers plan their financial futures, but there is no comparable "road map" to help them navigate second careers. Older adults are lacking the preparation to obtain jobs in nonprofit service organizations; likewise, this sector is similarly unprepared to accommodate the boomers poised to enter it.
10. Members of the baby boom generation are experienced at overcoming obstacles and breaking down barriers. As veterans of antiwar protests of the 1960s and the women's movement of the 1970s, boomers are used to speaking up and creating change. If the force of a social movement is required to create career opportunities for older adults, then these seasoned agitators may well be the ones to accomplish this objective.

Freedman concludes that fully realizing and benefiting from the experience, skill, and talent of older adults will be neither easy nor inevitable. However, he is confident that it will be worth the effort, asserting, "The payoff is nothing less than a society that makes sense, one that balances the joys and responsibility of engagement throughout the lifespan and across the generations. In other words, one that works better for everybody."

Volunteerism in Retirement

Volunteerism among older adults is a relatively new phenomenon. Historically, older adults were seen as the segment of society most in need of care and support. As medical technology enables people to live longer, healthier lives, and as stereotypes about aging shatter, the older population is now being recognized as a valuable resource for volunteer organizations.

Every day millions of older Americans perform volunteer work in their communities. Often having more free time as well as the wisdom and experience derived from years of living, they make ideal volunteers. Older adult volunteers are highly educated and skilled and can offer volunteer organizations many of the professional services they would otherwise have to purchase, such as legal, accounting, public relations, information systems support, and human resource management. Perhaps more important, they have empathy and compassion because they have encountered many of the same problems faced by those they seek to help.

According to the BLS, in *Volunteering in the United States, 2008* (January 23, 2009, http://www.bls.gov/news.release/pdf/volun.pdf), volunteer rates in 2008 were the lowest for people aged 65 and older (23.5% of the population) and for those aged 16 to 24 (21.9%). Volunteers aged 65 and older did, however, devote the most time—a median of 96 hours during the year—to volunteer activities. (See Table 4.5.) Older volunteers were more likely to work for religious organizations than younger volunteers. The BLS notes that 46.7% of volunteers aged 65 and older volunteered primarily for religious organizations, compared with 30.8% of volunteers aged 16 to 24.

NATIONAL SERVICE ORGANIZATIONS. Efforts to establish a national senior service during the administration of President John F. Kennedy (1917–1963), a Democrat, are described by Peter Shapiro in *A History of National Service in America* (1994). In 1963 Kennedy proposed the National Service Corps (NSC) "to provide opportunities for service for those aged persons who can assume active roles in community volunteer efforts." When the NSC was proposed, a scant 11% of the older population was involved in

TABLE 4.5

Volunteers by annual hours of volunteer activities and selected characteristics, September 2008

Characteristics in September 2008	Total volunteers (thousands)	Percent distribution of total annual hours spent volunteering at all organizations							Median annual hours[a]
		Total	1 to 14 hour(s)	15 to 49 hours	50 to 99 hours	100 to 499 hours	500 hours and over	Not reporting annual hours	
Sex									
Total, both sexes	61,803	100.0	19.8	25.5	15.5	28.9	5.4	4.7	52
Men	26,268	100.0	19.1	25.9	15.2	29.1	5.9	4.8	52
Women	35,535	100.0	20.4	25.3	15.8	28.8	5.1	4.7	52
Age									
Total, 16 years and over	61,803	100.0	19.8	25.5	15.5	28.9	5.4	4.7	52
16 to 24 years	8,239	100.0	21.9	28.2	14.7	24.1	4.9	6.1	42
16 to 19 years	4,437	100.0	22.1	31.5	16.5	21.8	4.0	4.1	40
20 to 24 years	3,802	100.0	21.8	24.5	12.6	26.8	6.0	8.4	48
25 years and over	53,564	100.0	19.5	25.1	15.7	29.7	5.5	4.5	52
25 to 34 years	9,154	100.0	25.5	27.0	13.9	24.0	4.0	5.6	40
35 to 44 years	13,016	100.0	21.6	26.7	16.5	27.0	4.1	4.1	48
45 to 54 years	13,189	100.0	18.8	25.8	16.4	29.5	5.3	4.2	52
55 to 64 years	9,456	100.0	17.8	24.9	15.9	30.8	6.4	4.3	58
65 years and over	8,749	100.0	13.1	19.9	15.0	38.5	8.6	4.9	96
Race and Hispanic or Latino ethnicity									
White	53,078	100.0	19.9	25.7	15.8	28.7	5.4	4.5	52
Black or African American	5,325	100.0	18.8	22.1	13.7	31.8	7.2	6.5	60
Asian	2,022	100.0	21.8	30.1	11.5	28.0	2.9	5.7	40
Hispanic or Latino ethnicity	4,662	100.0	23.7	26.3	14.5	23.7	5.3	6.5	40
Educational attainment[b]									
Less than a high school diploma	2,427	100.0	22.4	25.1	14.9	25.1	6.7	5.8	48
High school graduates, no college[c]	10,998	100.0	21.0	24.0	15.5	27.6	6.0	5.8	52
Some college or associate degree	15,519	100.0	20.7	25.0	15.1	29.6	5.3	4.3	52
Bachelor's degree and higher[d]	24,620	100.0	17.8	25.7	16.2	31.0	5.3	4.0	60
Marital status									
Single, never married	13,475	100.0	22.3	28.4	14.4	23.8	4.9	6.2	40
Married, spouse present	38,827	100.0	18.9	24.7	16.1	30.6	5.5	4.2	56
Other marital status[e]	9,502	100.0	20.2	24.7	15.0	29.4	5.9	4.9	52
Presence of own children under 18 years[f]									
Men									
No own children under 18 years old	17,377	100.0	18.4	26.1	14.4	29.1	6.4	5.6	52
With own children under 18 years old	8,891	100.0	20.6	25.4	16.7	29.1	4.8	3.3	52
Women									
No own children under 18 years old	22,108	100.0	19.2	24.8	15.2	29.8	5.8	5.2	52
With own children under 18 years old	13,427	100.0	22.3	26.1	16.8	27.2	3.9	3.8	48
Employment status									
Civilian labor force	44,313	100.0	21.1	26.7	15.7	27.2	4.7	4.7	48
Employed	42,131	100.0	21.2	26.5	15.9	27.3	4.5	4.7	48
Full time[g]	33,344	100.0	21.6	26.7	15.6	26.9	4.3	4.9	48
Part time[h]	8,788	100.0	19.9	25.7	16.7	28.9	5.3	3.6	52
Unemployed	2,181	100.0	19.4	29.2	12.9	25.5	8.2	4.8	48
Not in the labor force	17,491	100.0	16.6	22.7	15.1	33.2	7.4	5.0	70

[a]For those reporting annual hours.
[b]Data refer to persons 25 years and over.
[c]Includes persons with a high school diploma or equivalent.
[d]Includes persons with bachelor's, professional, and doctoral degrees.
[e]Includes divorced, separated, and widowed persons.
[f]Own children include sons, daughters, stepchildren, and adopted children. Not included are nieces, nephews, grandchildren, and other related and unrelated children.
[g]Usually work 35 hours or more a week at all jobs.
[h]Usually work less than 35 hours a week at all jobs.
Notes: Data on volunteers relate to persons who performed unpaid volunteer activities for an organization at any point from September 1, 2007, through the survey period in September 2008. Estimates for the above race groups (white, black or African American, and Asian) do not sum to totals because data are not presented for all races. Persons whose ethnicity is identified as Hispanic or Latino may be of any race.

SOURCE: "Table 2. Volunteers by Annual Hours of Volunteer Activities and Selected Characteristics, September 2008," in *Volunteering in the United States, 2008*, U.S. Department of Labor, U.S. Bureau of Labor Statistics, January 23, 2009, http://www.bls.gov/news.release/volun.t02.htm (accessed April 30, 2009)

any kind of volunteerism. The plan to engage older adults in full-time, intensive service, with a minimum one-year commitment, to combat urban and rural poverty was viewed as revolutionary. Even though the NSC proposal was championed by the Kennedy administration and widely supported in the public and private sectors, it was defeated in Congress, where reactionary lawmakers linked it to efforts aimed at promoting racial integration in the South.

Despite the defeat of the NSC, the idea of harnessing the volunteer power of older adults caught on. The Economic Opportunity Act of 1964 gave rise to the Volunteers in Service to America (VISTA) and eventually led to the launch of service programs involving low-income older adults, such as the Foster Grandparent, Senior Companion, and Senior Community Service Employment programs. The Foster Grandparent Program matched 1,000 older adults aged 60 and older with 2,500 children living in orphanages and other institutions. The older adults would spend four hours a day, five days a week, feeding, cuddling, rocking, and exercising disabled children.

The success of the Foster Grandparent Program exceeded all expectations. In 1971 the program was incorporated into the newly created ACTION agency, along with the Peace Corps, VISTA, the Service Corps of Retired Executives (SCORE), and the Active Corps of Executives. Foster Grandparents has since become part of Senior Corps, a network of programs that tap the experience, skills, and talents of older adults to meet community challenges. Through its three programs—Foster Grandparents, Senior Companions, and Retired and Senior Volunteer Program—nearly half a million Americans aged 55 and older assisted local nonprofits, public agencies, and faith-based organizations in 2008. In "Fact Sheet" (March 2009, http://www.seniorcorps.gov/pdf/factsheet_seniorcorps.pdf), the Senior Corps notes that its volunteers worked with 325,000 children and teenagers in 2008.

Another successful national volunteer program involving older adults is SCORE, the first initiative to use retired business executives as counselors and consultants to small businesses. Established by the Small Business Administration (SBA) in 1964, the program works with recipients of SBA loans and other entrepreneurs, assisting them to draft business plans, evaluate profitability, and develop marketing and sales strategies. One objective of the program is to reduce default rates on these loans. SCORE mentors business owners and provides one-to-one counseling, consultation via e-mail, and training sessions conducted on topics ranging from pricing strategies to marketing. In 2008 SCORE (http://www.score.org/media_fact_sheet.html) had 800 branches nationwide and 11,200 volunteer counselors, and conducted 196,709 face-to-face counseling sessions and 120,433 online counseling sessions.

2009 NATIONAL SERVICE BILL CALLS AMERICANS TO ACTION. In April 2009 President Barack Obama (1961–) signed into law the Edward M. Kennedy Serve America Act, a bipartisan bill that is described as the most sweeping expansion of national service in a generation. In the press release "President Obama Signs Landmark National Service Legislation" (April 21, 2009, http://www.seniorcorps.gov/about/newsroom/releases_detail.asp?tbl_pr_id=1301), the Senior Corps states that the act "reauthorizes and expands national service programs administered by the Corporation for National and Community Service, a federal agency created in 1993. The Corporation engages four million Americans in result-driven service each year, including 75,000 AmeriCorps members, 492,000 Senior Corps volunteers, 1.1 million Learn and Serve America students, and 2.2 million additional community volunteers mobilized and managed through the agency's programs."

The act is a response to a growing social need caused by the economic downturn and a desire of Americans of all ages to aide those imperiled by it. The Senior Corps reports that AmeriCorps received 17,038 online applications in March 2009, which was close to three times the 6,770 online applications received in March 2008.

ENGAGING BOOMERS IN VOLUNTEER SERVICE. The Corporation for National and Community Service is the overarching agency for national volunteering programs including Senior Corps, AmeriCorps, Learn and Serve America, and MLK Day of Service. The corporation's strategic plan for 2010 includes a national goal of gaining an additional 3 million boomer volunteers and several goals for the corporation, such as involving 500,000 boomers in corporation-sponsored national service programs and providing support from corporation-sponsored national service programs to enable 250,000 older adults to live independently. (See Table 4.6.)

TABLE 4.6

National service and volunteer targets for baby boomers, 2010

National target for 2010
Engage an additional 3 million baby boomers in volunteering, up from 25.8 million in 2005
Corporation targets for 2010
Engage 500,000 baby boomers in corporation-sponsored national service programs as participants and recruited volunteers
Ensure at least 75 percent of baby boomers in Senior Corps and AmeriCorps rate their overall service/volunteer experience as excellent
Ensure at least 75 percent of baby boomer volunteers in Senior Corps and AmeriCorps believe programs have given them a significant chance to bring about change in their community
Provide (through service and volunteering) 250,000 seniors support from corporation-sponsored national service programs to live independently
Provide 100,000 families and caregivers of seniors support from corporation-sponsored national service programs

SOURCE: "National Target for 2010, Corporation Targets for 2010," in *Corporation for National and Community Service Strategic Plan 2006–2010*, Corporation for National and Community Service, February 2006, http://www.nationalservice.gov/pdf/strategic_plan_web_04.pdf (accessed May 1, 2009)

CHAPTER 5

EDUCATION, VOTING, AND POLITICAL BEHAVIOR

EDUCATIONAL ATTAINMENT OF OLDER AMERICANS

Educational attainment influences employment and socioeconomic status, which in turn affect the quality of life of older adults. Higher levels of education are often associated with greater earning capacity, higher standards of living, and better overall health status.

As of 2007, 76% of the older population had earned high school diplomas and 19% had obtained undergraduate college degrees. (See Figure 5.1.) These figures are in contrast to those from 1965, when just 24% had earned high school diplomas and only 5% were college graduates.

Even though educational attainment has increased among older adults, significant differences remain between racial and ethnic groups. Among adults aged 65 and older in 2007, 81% of non-Hispanic whites and 72% of Asian-Americans had graduated from high school, compared with 58% of African-Americans and 42% of Hispanics. (See Figure 5.2.) Older Asian-Americans were the most likely to have graduated from college (32%), followed by older non-Hispanic whites (21%); just 10% of African-Americans and 9% of Hispanics aged 65 and older had earned bachelor's degrees.

Historically, more younger workers than older ones have obtained high school diplomas and postsecondary education (some college or a bachelor's degree or a more advanced degree). However, the educational gap between younger and older workers is narrowing. In 1997, 21.3% of older workers had less than a high school diploma, compared with 10.1% of workers aged 25 to 64. (See Figure 5.3.) By 2007 only 12.8% of older workers had less than a high school diploma, compared with 9% of younger workers.

Lifelong Learning

Live as if you were to die tomorrow. Learn as if you were to live forever.

—Mohandas Gandhi

Campuses are graying as a growing number of older people head back to school. Older adults, both working and retired, are major participants in programs once called adult education (college courses that do not lead to a formal degree). Older adults are also increasingly attending two- and four-year colleges to pursue undergraduate and graduate degrees, as well as taking personal enrichment classes and courses that are sponsored by community senior centers and parks and recreation facilities. For examples, in "Community College Facts at a Glance" (March 2009, http://www.aacc.nche.edu/AboutCC/Documents/fastfacts2009.pdf), the American Association of Community Colleges, an advocacy organization for the nation's community (two-year) colleges, indicates that as of 2009, 13% of community college students were aged 40 and older.

In 2007, 10.7% of students in all degree-granting programs were aged 40 and older. (See Table 5.1.) More than 530,000 students aged 40 and older attended full time, and an additional 1.4 million were part-time students. About 1.5 million of these older students were pursuing undergraduate degrees and over 500,000 were studying to obtain graduate degrees.

Thomas D. Snyder, Sally A. Dillow, and Charlene M. Hoffman of the National Center for Education Statistics note in *Digest of Education Statistics* (March 2009, http://nces.ed.gov/pubs2009/2009020.pdf) that in 2005 more than 2.5 million people participated in adult education programs. Older adults have the time and resources to seek learning for personal and social reasons. Some universities allow older people to audit courses (take classes without receiving credit toward a degree) for reduced or waived tuition and fees.

Older adults' motivations for returning to school have changed over time. Even though they once may have taken courses primarily for pleasure, older students in the 21st century are likely to return to school for work-related adult

FIGURE 5.1

Educational attainment of the population aged 65 and over, selected years 1965–2007

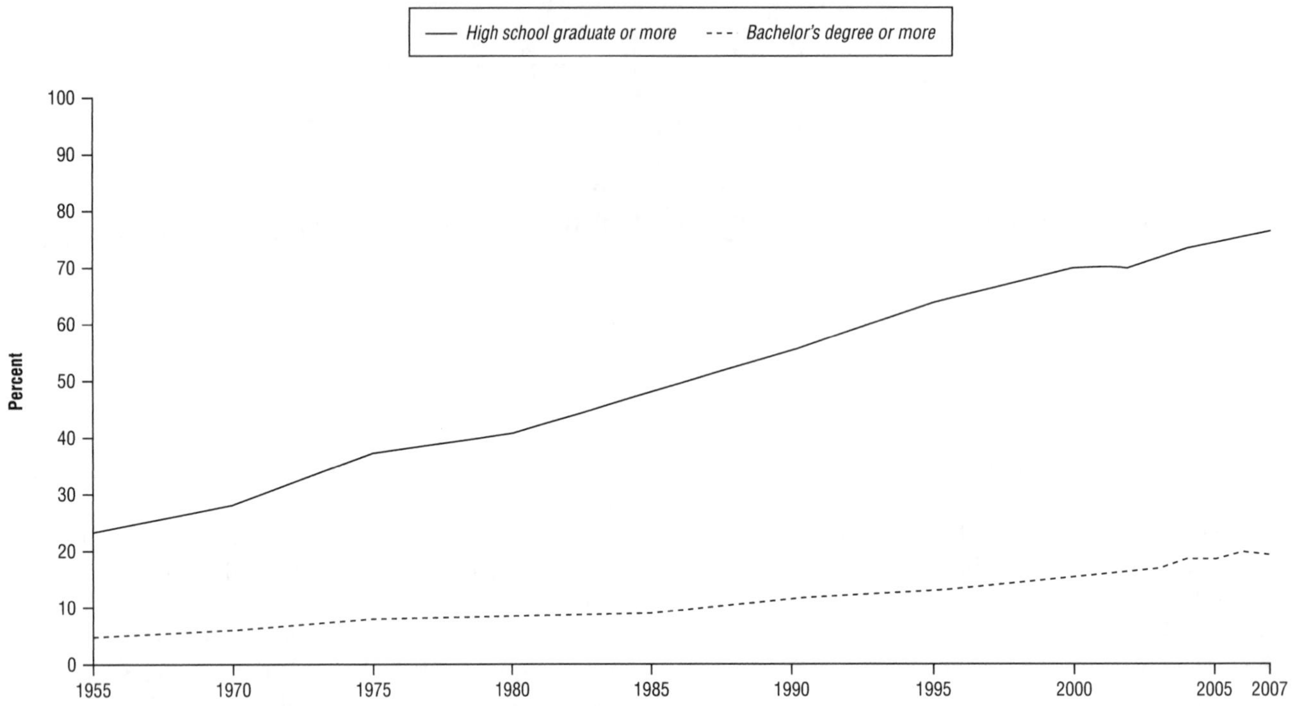

Note: A single question which asks for the highest grade or degree completed is now used to determine educational attainment. Prior to 1995, educational attainment was measured using data on years of school completed.
Reference population: These data refer to the civilian noninstitutionalized population.

SOURCE: "Educational Attainment of the Population Age 65 and over, Selected Years, 1965–2007," in *Older Americans 2008: Key Indicators of Well-Being*, Federal Interagency Forum on Aging-Related Statistics, March 2008, http://www.agingstats.gov/agingstatsdotnet/Main_Site/Data/2008_Documents/OA_2008.pdf (accessed April 20, 2009)

education. They are learning new skills, retraining for new careers, or enhancing their existing skills to remain competitive in their fields. Homemakers displaced by divorce or widowhood are often seeking education and training to enable them to reenter the workforce.

The types of education older workers pursue varies with age. Table 5.2 shows that in 2005 students aged 55 to 59 favored work-related coursework (44.7%) over personal-interest courses (18.3%), whereas those aged 65 and older were nearly as likely to be enrolled in work-related courses (21.6%) as personal interest courses (17.4%). However, the number of career or job-related courses taken per employee also declines with advancing age, from 0.9 courses for workers aged 50 to 55 to 0.3 courses per worker among employees aged 65 to 69.

ELDERHOSTELS MEET OLDER ADULTS' NEEDS FOR EDUCATION AND ADVENTURE. Founded in 1975, Elderhostel (2009, http://www.elderhostel.org/) is a nonprofit organization that provides learning adventures for people aged 55 and older. In *Annual Report, 2007* (2009, http://www.elderhostel.org/support/annualreport_mar08_nodonors.pdf), Elderhostel states that it provided educational opportunities to nearly 165,000 older adults in 2007. Approximately 8,000 Elderhostel programs a year are conducted in 90 countries. The programs are diverse and range from three- to five-day classes to field trips and cultural excursions. Traditional programs provide older adults with opportunities to study diverse cultures, explore ancient histories, study literature and art, and learn about modern peoples and issues. Some Elderhostel participants attend programs held on local college and university campuses, whereas others embark on more extensive programs that involve transcontinental travel.

Adventure programs feature outdoor sports such as walking, hiking, camping, kayaking, and biking. The programs combine adventure and learning. For example, a bicycle tour of the Netherlands also includes instruction about the country's history, art, and people. Shipboard programs explore history, art, ecology, and culture while aboard a floating classroom.

Service-learning programs involve both education and hands-on work to serve the needs of a community. Older adults conduct wildlife or marine research, tutor school children, and build affordable housing. The organization also offers a series of intergenerational programs in which older

FIGURE 5.2

Educational attainment of the population aged 65 and over, by race and Hispanic origin, 2007

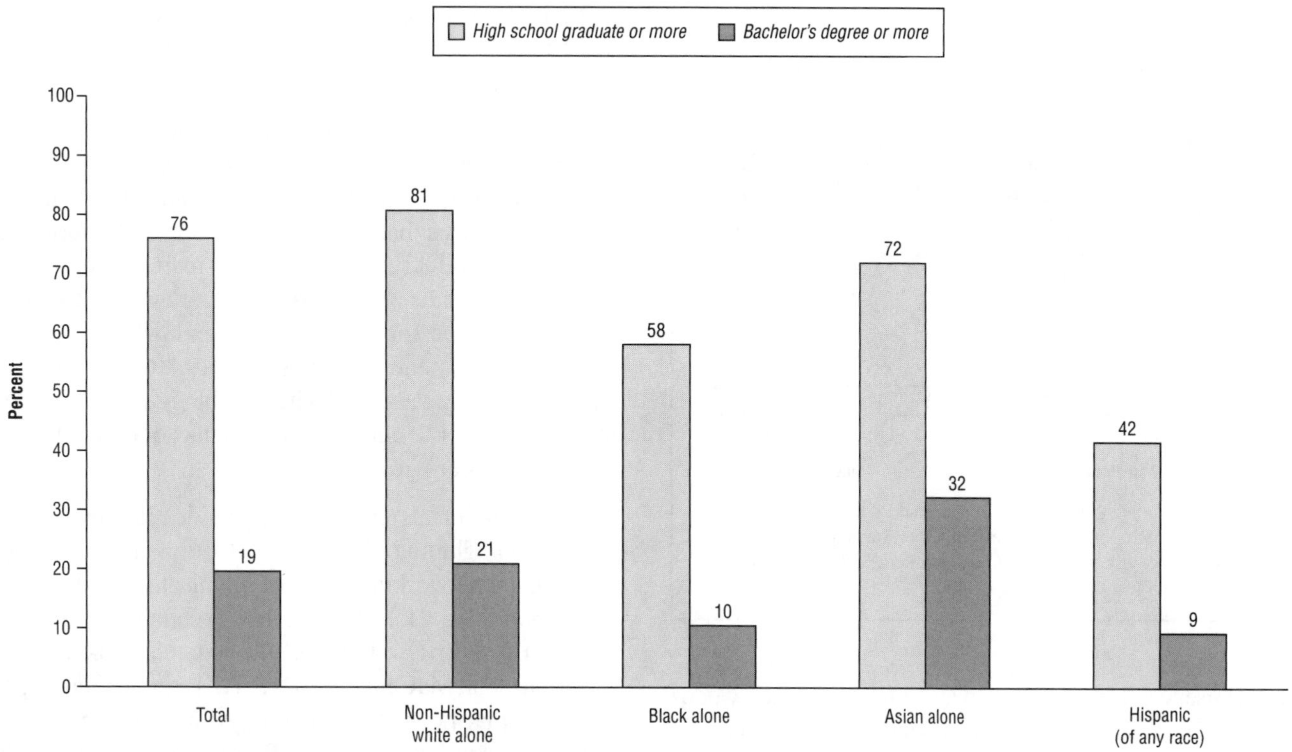

Note: The term "non-Hispanic white alone" is used to refer to people who reported being white and no other race and who are not Hispanic. The term "black alone" is used to refer to people who reported being black or African American and no other race, and the term "Asian alone" is used to refer to people who reported only Asian as their race. The use of single-race populations in this report does not imply that this is the preferred method of presenting or analyzing data. The U.S. Census Bureau uses a variety of approaches. Reference population: These data refer to the civilian noninstitutionalized population.

SOURCE: "Educational Attainment of the Population Age 65 and over, by Race and Hispanic Origin, 2007," in *Older Americans 2008: Key Indicators of Well-Being*, Federal Interagency Forum on Aging-Related Statistics, March 2008, http://www.agingstats.gov/agingstatsdotnet/Main_Site/Data/2008_Documents/OA_2008.pdf (accessed April 20, 2009)

adults and their grandchildren explore subjects that appeal to both young and old, including dinosaurs, hot-air ballooning, and space travel.

OLDER ADULTS ARE ONLINE. Rapid technological change has intensified the need for computer and information management skills and ongoing training of the workforce. The growing importance of knowledge- and information-based jobs has created a workforce that is rapidly becoming accustomed to continuous education, training, and retraining throughout one's work life.

Computer technology, especially use of the Internet, has also gained importance in Americans' lives outside of work, facilitating communication via e-mail and enabling interactions and transactions that once required travel now to occur in their homes. Examples include online banking and shopping, e-mail communication with physicians and other health care providers, and participation in online support groups.

In *Generations Online in 2009* (January 28, 2009, http://www.pewinternet.org/~/media//Files/Reports/2009/PIP_Generations_2009.pdf), Sydney Jones and Susannah Fox of the Pew Internet and American Life Project report increasing Internet use by older adults—in 2008, 78% of adults aged 50 to 64, 56% of adults aged 65 and older, 45% of adults aged 70 to 75, and 27% of adults aged 76 and older were online. The researchers observe that the biggest increase in Internet use since 2005 was among adults aged 70 to 75—26% were online in 2005 and by 2008, 45% were online.

Older adults use the Internet to conduct research, send e-mail, and purchase products, whereas younger adults use it for socializing and entertainment. According to Jones and Fox, 56% of Internet users aged 64 to 72 and 47% of users aged 64 to 72 made purchases online in 2008. More older adults are downloading videos—just 8% of adults aged 64 to 72 and 1% of adults aged 73 and older downloaded videos in 2005; by 2008, 13% of both age groups were downloading videos.

Jones and Fox explain that in 2008 younger boomers (aged 45 to 54), older boomers (aged 55 to 63), and adults aged 64 to 72 and 73 and older were more likely to seek health information online and make purchases than younger

FIGURE 5.3

Education of workers by age, 1997 and 2007

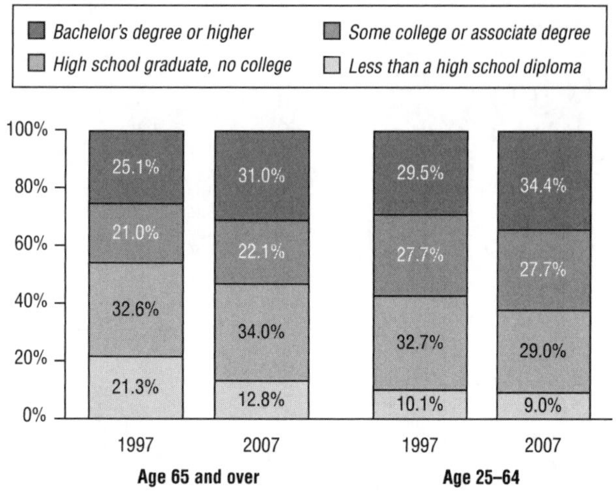

SOURCE: "Employment Distribution by Age and Education, 1997 and 2007," in *Older Workers*, U.S. Bureau of Labor Statistics, July 2008, http://www.bls.gov/spotlight/2008/older_workers/pdf/older_workers_bls_spotlight.pdf (accessed April 29, 2009)

Internet users and less likely to play games and watch videos online, send instant messages, download music, read or create blogs, or visit virtual worlds. There was much less variation by age for other online activities. Older and younger users were about the same in terms of using e-mail and search engines, researching products, obtaining news, and making travel reservations.

Even though broadband access had become more commonplace since the 2005 survey, Jones and Fox note that in 2008 older adults were less likely to have high-speed Internet access than younger adults. More than half (58%) of adults aged 55 to 59 had broadband access at home, up from 27% in 2005. Nearly half (48%) of adults aged 60 to 64, 42% of those aged 65 to 69, and 31% of adults aged 70 to 75 had broadband access, up from 23%, 13%, and 8%, respectively.

OLDER ADULTS JOIN SOCIAL NETWORKS. Jones and Fox find that even though young people were still much more likely than older adult Internet users to participate in social networking sites in 2008, 16% of adults aged 45 to 54, 9% of adults aged 55 to 64, and 5% of adults aged 65 and older had profiles at social networking sites.

In "All in the Facebook Family: Older Generations Join Social Networks" (CNN.com, April 13, 2009), John D. Sutter explains that older adults use social networks to keep up with younger family members, view photos of children and grandchildren, and communicate with peers. In April 2009 Facebook had 200 million users and was rapidly growing among women aged 55 and older, who numbered 1.5 million, a 550% increase from six months earlier. Marco R. della Cava reports in "Boomers Zero in on Social Networks" (*USA Today*, March 27, 2009) that in 2009, 16.5 million adults aged 55 and older engaged in social networking, and in the one year since AARP debuted its social networking platform, about 350,000 users had created 1,700 groups dedicated to diverse interests—from gardening to social activism.

THEY ALSO TEXT, BLOG, AND TWEET. Even though there are no reliable statistics about the numbers of older adults who use personal digital assistants (small mobile hand-held devices that provide computing and information storage and retrieval capabilities) and smart phones (mobile phone offering advanced capabilities, often with the functionality of a personal computer), and who create and maintain blogs, send text messages or "tweet" (post or enter a status update on Twitter, a blogging service that limits entries to 140 characters), the ranks of older bloggers and Twitterers are growing.

Both candidates in the 2008 presidential election had shone a spotlight on older adults' adoption of new technologies, social networking, and communication. Toby Harnden reports in "John McCain 'Technology Illiterate' Doesn't Email or Use Internet" (Telegraph.co.uk, July 18, 2008) that John McCain (1936–; R-AZ) admitted during his campaign that he was "technology illiterate," had never sent e-mail, and relied on his staffers to show him Web sites because he was just "learning to get online." Yet, in the space of a few short months, the 72-year-old senator had a Twitter account and in March 2009 conducted a full interview exclusively on Twitter with the ABC political correspondent George Stephanopoulos (1961–).

President-elect Barack Obama (1961–), a boomer and enthusiastic user of a BlackBerry (a hand-held device that serves as a cell phone, personal organizer, and wireless Internet browser), used various forms of new media and technology throughout his campaign. In "You Don't Have Mail" (Salon.com, January 27, 2009), Mike Madden describes Obama's staff as "plugged-in ... to the world of online media." He observes that at the close of the campaign, Obama's Facebook page had more than 3 million followers. Madden characterizes the Obama campaign as "one of the tech-savviest examples of how new media can boost old-school politics the country has ever seen." Since the election, President Obama, Vice President Joseph R. Biden (1942–), and their staffers continued to use the Internet and e-mail to raise awareness of issues important to them, including health care reform, stimulating the economy, and volunteerism.

OLDER ADULTS PLAY VIDEO GAMES. Video games are also popular among older adults. For some, the console game versions of their once-favorite sports help them to stay "in the game," even when an injury, disability, or illness prevents them from actually participating in tennis, bowling, or golf. Others feel that playing video games helps

TABLE 5.1

Enrollment in degree-granting institutions by sex, age, and attendance status, fall 2007

Age of student and attendance status	All levels			Undergraduate			First-professional			Graduate		
	Total	Males	Females	Total	Males	Females	Total	Males	Females	Total	Males	Females
1	2	3	4	5	6	7	8	9	10	11	12	13
All students	**18,248,128**	**7,815,914**	**10,432,214**	**15,603,771**	**6,727,600**	**8,876,171**	**350,764**	**177,988**	**172,776**	**2,293,593**	**910,326**	**1,383,267**
Under 18	668,426	277,582	390,844	668,193	277,489	390,704	18	5	13	215	88	127
18 and 19	3,963,371	1,794,001	2,169,370	3,961,149	1,793,284	2,167,865	1,291	464	827	931	253	678
20 and 21	3,642,872	1,647,492	1,995,380	3,612,195	1,635,396	1,976,799	11,926	4,454	7,472	18,751	7,642	11,109
22 to 24	3,009,713	1,381,504	1,628,209	2,474,561	1,168,612	1,305,949	133,563	61,463	72,100	401,589	151,429	250,160
25 to 29	2,550,482	1,091,510	1,458,972	1,710,195	728,331	981,864	138,825	74,285	64,540	701,462	288,894	412,568
30 to 34	1,365,912	551,208	814,704	944,123	357,944	586,179	31,764	19,067	12,697	390,025	174,197	215,828
35 to 39	980,818	368,814	612,004	709,012	251,299	457,713	13,326	7,895	5,431	258,480	109,620	148,860
40 to 49	1,266,171	423,603	842,568	935,783	304,967	630,816	12,314	6,613	5,701	318,074	112,023	206,051
50 to 64	627,603	208,067	419,536	445,568	150,103	295,465	6,197	2,902	3,295	175,838	55,062	120,776
65 and over	77,379	31,040	46,339	70,608	27,847	42,761	288	132	156	6,483	3,061	3,422
Age unknown	95,381	41,093	54,288	72,384	32,328	40,056	1,252	708	544	21,745	8,057	13,688
Full-time	11,269,892	5,029,444	6,240,448	9,840,978	4,396,868	5,444,110	316,549	159,328	157,221	1,112,365	473,248	639,117
Under 18	171,784	69,033	102,751	171,705	69,000	102,705	15	4	11	64	29	35
18 and 19	3,383,318	1,522,297	1,861,021	3,381,502	1,521,669	1,859,833	1,286	461	825	530	167	363
20 and 21	2,964,697	1,346,897	1,617,800	2,937,292	1,335,936	1,601,356	11,695	4,354	7,341	15,710	6,607	9,103
22 to 24	1,986,776	949,700	1,037,076	1,572,230	778,160	794,070	128,394	58,966	69,428	286,152	112,574	173,578
25 to 29	1,284,698	584,798	699,900	776,416	346,671	429,745	127,726	68,108	59,618	380,556	170,019	210,537
30 to 34	565,710	235,321	330,389	365,008	135,611	229,397	26,135	15,665	10,470	174,567	84,045	90,522
35 to 39	347,864	130,397	217,467	241,500	81,381	160,119	9,555	5,666	3,889	96,809	43,350	53,459
40 to 49	380,043	125,982	254,061	270,137	84,186	185,951	7,527	4,056	3,471	102,379	37,740	64,639
50 to 64	145,757	47,812	97,945	93,913	30,478	63,435	3,153	1,449	1,704	48,691	15,885	32,806
65 and over	4,868	2,260	2,608	3,185	1,471	1,714	149	68	81	1,534	721	813
Age unknown	34,377	14,947	19,430	28,090	12,305	15,785	914	531	383	5,373	2,111	3,262
Part-time	6,978,236	2,786,470	4,191,766	5,762,793	2,330,732	3,432,061	34,215	18,660	15,555	1,181,228	437,078	744,150
Under 18	496,642	208,549	288,093	496,488	208,489	287,999	3	1	2	151	59	92
18 and 19	580,053	271,704	308,349	579,647	271,615	308,032	5	3	2	401	86	315
20 and 21	678,175	300,595	377,580	674,903	299,460	375,443	231	100	131	3,041	1,035	2,006
22 to 24	1,022,937	431,804	591,133	902,331	390,452	511,879	5,169	2,497	2,672	115,437	38,855	76,582
25 to 29	1,265,784	506,712	759,072	933,779	381,660	552,119	11,099	6,177	4,922	320,906	118,875	202,031
30 to 34	800,202	315,887	484,315	579,115	222,333	356,782	5,629	3,402	2,227	215,458	90,152	125,306
35 to 39	632,954	238,417	394,537	467,512	169,918	297,594	3,771	2,229	1,542	161,671	66,270	95,401
40 to 49	886,128	297,621	588,507	665,646	220,781	444,865	4,787	2,557	2,230	215,695	74,283	141,412
50 to 64	481,846	160,255	321,591	351,655	119,625	232,030	3,044	1,453	1,591	127,147	39,177	87,970
65 and over	72,511	28,780	43,731	67,423	26,376	41,047	139	64	75	4,949	2,340	2,609
Age unknown	61,004	26,146	34,858	44,294	20,023	24,271	338	177	161	16,372	5,946	10,426
						Percentage distribution						
All students	**100.0**	**100.0**	**100.0**	**100.0**	**100.0**	**100.0**	**100.0**	**100.0**	**100.0**	**100.0**	**100.0**	**100.0**
Under 18	3.7	3.6	3.7	4.3	4.1	4.4	*	*	*	*	*	*
18 and 19	21.7	23.0	20.8	25.4	26.7	24.4	0.4	0.3	0.5	*	*	*
20 and 21	20.0	21.1	19.1	23.1	24.3	22.3	3.4	2.5	4.3	0.8	0.8	0.8
22 to 24	16.5	17.7	15.6	15.9	17.4	14.7	38.1	34.5	41.7	17.5	16.6	18.1
25 to 29	14.0	14.0	14.0	11.0	10.8	11.1	39.6	41.7	37.4	30.6	31.7	29.8
30 to 34	7.5	7.1	7.8	6.1	5.3	6.6	9.1	10.7	7.3	17.0	19.1	15.6
35 to 39	5.4	4.7	5.9	4.5	3.7	5.2	3.8	4.4	3.1	11.3	12.0	10.8
40 to 49	6.9	5.4	8.1	6.0	4.5	7.1	3.5	3.7	3.3	13.9	12.3	14.9
50 to 64	3.4	2.7	4.0	2.9	2.2	3.3	1.8	1.6	1.9	7.7	6.0	8.7
65 and over	0.4	0.4	0.4	0.5	0.4	0.5	0.1	0.1	0.1	0.3	0.3	0.2
Age unknown	0.5	0.5	0.5	0.5	0.5	0.5	0.4	0.4	0.3	0.9	0.9	1.0

them to exercise their brains, eye-hand coordination, and reflexes. Still others simply find video games as diverting and entertaining as do younger players.

According to Seth Schiesel, in "Video Games Conquer Retirees" (*New York Times*, March 30, 2007), the Norwegian Cruise Line, which caters largely to older adults, and Erickson Retirement Communities, which houses 19,000 residents on 18 campuses, have installed the Nintendo Wii game system. Game sites and publishers observe that older adults not only play video games more often than younger gamers but also spend more time playing per session. In the article "Boomers Embrace Casual Games to Keep Sharp" (Marketingvox.com, April 5, 2007), Beatrice Spaine, the marketing director of Pogo.com, a Web site that offers a variety of games, asserts that baby boomers (people born between 1946 and 1964) are its most rapidly growing group of users and opines that the site offers a virtual community for older adults that is not unlike the kind of community MySpace.com has become for teens and younger adults.

In "Can Training in a Real-Time Strategy Video Game Attenuate Cognitive Decline in Older Adults?" (*Psychology and Aging*, vol. 23, no. 4, December 2008), Chandramallika

TABLE 5.1

Enrollment in degree-granting institutions by sex, age, and attendance status, fall 2007 [CONTINUED]

Age of student and attendance status	All levels			Undergraduate			First-professional			Graduate		
	Total	Males	Females	Total	Males	Females	Total	Males	Females	Total	Males	Females
1	2	3	4	5	6	7	8	9	10	11	12	13
Full-time	100.0	100.0	100.0	100.0	100.0	100.0	100.0	100.0	100.0	100.0	100.0	100.0
Under 18	1.5	1.4	1.6	1.7	1.6	1.9	*	*	*	*	*	*
18 and 19	30.0	30.3	29.8	34.4	34.6	34.2	0.4	0.3	0.5	*	*	*
20 and 21	26.3	26.8	25.9	29.8	30.4	29.4	3.7	2.7	4.7	1.4	1.4	1.4
22 to 24	17.6	18.9	16.6	16.0	17.7	14.6	40.6	37.0	44.2	25.7	23.8	27.2
25 to 29	11.4	11.6	11.2	7.9	7.9	7.9	40.3	42.7	37.9	34.2	35.9	32.9
30 to 34	5.0	4.7	5.3	3.7	3.1	4.2	8.3	9.8	6.7	15.7	17.8	14.2
35 to 39	3.1	2.6	3.5	2.5	1.9	2.9	3.0	3.6	2.5	8.7	9.2	8.4
40 to 49	3.4	2.5	4.1	2.7	1.9	3.4	2.4	2.5	2.2	9.2	8.0	10.1
50 to 64	1.3	1.0	1.6	1.0	0.7	1.2	1.0	0.9	1.1	4.4	3.4	5.1
65 and over	*	*	*	*	*	*	*	*	0.1	0.1	0.2	0.1
Age unknown	0.3	0.3	0.3	0.3	0.3	0.3	0.3	0.3	0.2	0.5	0.4	0.5
Part-time	100.0	100.0	100.0	100.0	100.0	100.0	100.0	100.0	100.0	100.0	100.0	100.0
Under 18	7.1	7.5	6.9	8.6	8.9	8.4	*	*	*	*	*	
18 and 19	8.3	9.8	7.4	10.1	11.7	9.0	*	*	*	*	*	*
20 and 21	9.7	10.8	9.0	11.7	12.8	10.9	0.7	0.5	0.8	0.3	0.2	0.3
22 to 24	14.7	15.5	14.1	15.7	16.8	14.9	15.1	13.4	17.2	9.8	8.9	10.3
25 to 29	18.1	18.2	18.1	16.2	16.4	16.1	32.4	33.1	31.6	27.2	27.2	27.1
30 to 34	11.5	11.3	11.6	10.0	9.5	10.4	16.5	18.2	14.3	18.2	20.6	16.8
35 to 39	9.1	8.6	9.4	8.1	7.3	8.7	11.0	11.9	9.9	13.7	15.2	12.8
40 to 49	12.7	10.7	14.0	11.6	9.5	13.0	14.0	13.7	14.3	18.3	17.0	19.0
50 to 64	6.9	5.8	7.7	6.1	5.1	6.8	8.9	7.8	10.2	10.8	9.0	11.8
65 and over	1.0	1.0	1.0	1.2	1.1	1.2	0.4	0.3	0.5	0.4	0.5	0.4
Age unknown	0.9	0.9	0.8	0.8	0.9	0.7	1.0	0.9	1.0	1.4	1.4	1.4

*Rounds to zero.

Note: Degree-granting institutions grant associate's or higher degrees and participate in Title IV federal financial aid programs. Detail may not sum to totals because of rounding.

SOURCE: Thomas D. Snyder, Sally A. Dillow, and Charlene M. Hoffman, "Table 191. Total Fall Enrollment in Degree-Granting Institutions, by Level of Enrollment, Sex, Age, and Attendance Status of Student: 2007," in *Digest of Education Statistics 2008*, National Center for Education Statistics, March 2009, http://nces.ed.gov/pubs2009/2009020.pdf (accessed May 1, 2009)

Basak et al. find that older adults can improve a number of cognitive functions by playing *Rise of Nations*, a strategic video game that focuses on nation-building and territorial expansion. The researchers trained older adults in the real-time strategy video game for 23.5 hours in an attempt to improve their cognitive functions. A battery of cognitive tasks was used to assess the older adults before, during, and after video-game training. The older adults trained to play the game improved significantly more than the control participants, who had not received the training, in functions such as task switching, working memory, visual short-term memory, and reasoning.

THE POLITICS OF OLDER ADULTS

Older adults are vitally interested in politics and government, and they are especially interested in the issues that directly influence their lives, including eligibility for and reform to Social Security as well as benefits and coverage by Medicare. Historically, they are more likely to vote than adults in other age groups, and because many have retired from the workforce they have time to advocate for the policies and candidates they favor.

Older Voters Favored McCain in 2008 Presidential Election

A Gallup poll conducted just before the November 2008 presidential election found that adults aged 65 and older were more likely to support McCain (54%) than Obama (46%). (See Table 5.3.) Among adults aged 50 to 64, the situation was almost exactly the opposite—54% supported Obama and 46% favored McCain. (See Table 5.4.) Regardless, adults in both age groups were equally confident about Obama's ability to be a good president. (See Figure 5.4.)

The Pew Research poll "26%—McCain's Age Problem" (February 2007, http://pewresearch.org/databank/dailynumber/?NumberID=531) finds that in 2007 older adults were more concerned about McCain's age (he was 71 during the election and would be 72 by inauguration) than younger adults. Forty percent of adults aged 65 and older were concerned that McCain was "too old" to serve as president, compared with just 24% of voters aged 18 to 34. This finding may indicate that older adults are more aware of the limitations that often accompany advancing age and question the ability of an older person to withstand the rigors of the presidency or that they are simply more susceptible to stereotypical perceptions of older adults as being less capable.

TABLE 5.2

Participation of workers in career-related adult education, by selected characteristics, selected years 1995–2005

Characteristic of employed person	1995: Percent of adults participating in career or job-related courses	1995: Number of career or job-related courses taken, per employee	1999: Percent of adults participating in career or job-related courses	1999: Number of career or job-related courses taken, per employee	2003: Percent of adults participating in career or job-related courses*	2003: Number of career or job-related courses taken, per employee*	2005: Employed persons, in thousands	2005: Percent of adults participating: In career or job-related courses	2005: Percent of adults participating: In apprentice programs	2005: Percent of adults participating: In personal interest courses	2005: Percent of adults participating: In informal learning activities for personal interest	2005: Number of career or job-related courses taken (in thousands)	2005: Number of career or job-related courses taken, per employee
1	2	3	4	5	6	7	8	9	10	11	12	13	14
Total	**31.1**	**0.8**	**30.5**	**0.7**	**46.0**	**0.9**	**133,386**	**38.8**	**1.4**	**21.8**	**73.5**	**108,443**	**0.8**
Sex													
Male	29.0	0.7	28.3	0.6	42.7	0.8	71,754	31.7	2.0	18.5	73.4	44,512	0.6
Female	33.4	0.9	32.9	0.8	49.4	1.0	61,632	47.1	0.8	25.8	73.6	63,931	1.0
Age													
17 through 24 years	18.6	0.4	19.1	0.4	33.9	0.5	15,027	26.4	3.0	25.2	71.4	8,024	0.5
25 through 29 years	31.2	0.8	34.3	0.8	49.7	0.9	14,555	36.1	3.1	24.5	70.9	9,493	0.7
30 through 34 years	31.6	0.8	34.4	0.8	48.4	0.9	15,250	41.0	2.7	23.7	74.0	12,681	0.8
35 through 39 years	35.1	0.9	29.2	0.7	48.8	1.0	15,286	41.7	1.0	21.6	77.7	13,807	0.9
40 through 44 years	36.6	0.9	36.4	0.8	46.1	0.9	18,141	39.8	0.9	23.3	71.2	15,586	0.9
45 through 49 years	39.6	1.0	30.4	0.7	50.8	1.1	18,149	45.0	0.7	19.0	73.5	16,809	0.9
50 through 54 years	34.4	0.9	34.7	0.8	52.5	1.2	14,624	42.6	0.7	19.5	76.3	14,881	1.0
55 through 59 years	26.7	0.7	30.3	0.6	46.3	1.0	10,522	44.7	0.2	18.3	73.0	9,901	0.9
60 through 64 years	21.1	0.5	27.2	0.7	37.8	0.8	6,021	38.9	0.6	23.4	73.0	4,919	0.8
65 and over	13.7	0.4	20.3	0.4	—	—	5,812	21.6	#	17.4	74.2	2,343	0.4
65 through 69 years	—	—	—	—	33.5	0.7	3,385	19.1	#	20.9	75.4	1,102	0.3
70 years and over	—	—	—	—	22.3	0.5	2,427	25.1	#	12.6	72.6	1,241	0.5
Race/ethnicity													
White	33.2	0.8	32.8	0.6	48.5	1.0	94,881	41.3	1.2	22.2	75.3	82,511	0.9
Black	26.2	0.7	28.1	1.0	43.4	0.9	13,773	39.2	1.7	23.5	66.9	10,311	0.7
Hispanic	18.1	0.4	16.4	0.5	31.8	0.6	15,741	25.0	2.9	16.2	65.8	8,786	0.6
Asian	—	—	—	—	—	—	3,770	36.9	0.9	32.3	81.1	2,207	0.6
Pacific Islander	—	—	—	—	—	—	‡	‡	‡	‡	‡	‡	‡
Asian/Pacific Islander	25.5	0.6	32.8	0.4	50.4	0.8	†	†	†	†	†	†	†
American Indian/Alaska Native	34.0	0.9	29.5	0.7	40.0	0.7	‡	‡	‡	‡	‡	‡	‡
More than one race	—	—	—	—	—	—	3,786	39.1	1.4	22.6	77.6	3,083	0.8
Other races	—	—	—	—	—	—	‡	‡	‡	‡	‡	‡	‡
Highest level of education completed													
Less than high school completion	8.8	0.1	7.9	0.4	—	—	16,627	10.4	2.4	8.8	57.0	2,592	0.2
Eighth grade or less	—	—	—	—	9.9	0.1	5,016	2.7	4.4	3.8	46.7	197	#
9th through 12th grade, no completion	—	—	—	—	16.3	0.2	11,610	13.7	1.5	11.0	61.5	2,396	0.2
High school completion	20.9	0.4	21.4	0.8	33.2	0.6	34,121	24.7	1.3	17.1	63.4	16,640	0.5
Some vocational/technical	32.3	0.8	28.7	0.9	41.7	1.0	3,744	48.2	2.0	25.5	74.0	3,802	1.0
Some college	29.9	0.7	29.0	0.7	45.6	0.9	24,479	39.9	1.9	25.2	79.8	18,437	0.8
Associate's degree	39.2	1.0	39.7	0.9	54.5	1.1	9,943	50.4	2.3	19.1	78.4	14,224	1.4
Bachelor's degree	44.6	1.2	43.8	1.0	64.2	1.3	26,475	53.1	0.2	29.0	78.7	28,099	1.1

TABLE 5.2

Participation of workers in career-related adult education, by selected characteristics, selected years 1995–2005 [CONTINUED]

	1995		1999		2003			2005					
								Percent of adults participating					
Characteristic of employed person	Percent of adults participating in career or job-related courses	Number of career or job-related courses taken, per employee	Percent of adults participating in career or job-related courses	Number of career or job-related courses taken, per employee	Percent of adults participating in career or job-related courses*	Number of career or job-related courses taken, per employee*	Employed persons, in thousands	In career or job-related courses	In apprentice programs	In personal interest courses	In informal learning activities for personal interest	Number of career or job-related courses taken (in thousands)	Number of career or job-related courses taken, per employee
1	2	3	4	5	6	7	8	9	10	11	12	13	14
Some graduate work (or study)	50.2	1.4	46.8	1.2	71.5	1.7	17,998	61.1	1.5	28.6	88.8	24,649	1.4
No degree	44.3	1.2	54.2	1.2	68.3	1.6	2,125	53.8	‡	39.3	75.0	2,412	1.1
Master's	50.5	1.4	45.3	1.1	73.4	1.7	11,330	62.7	‡	28.2	90.5	15,394	1.4
Doctor's	40.4	1.0	34.4	0.7	58.9	1.4	1,600	49.0	‡	28.8	87.8	2,204	1.4
Professional	67.6	2.0	67.6	1.9	75.3	1.6	2,943	66.5	‡	22.1	92.9	4,639	1.6

—Not available.
*Estimates are not directly comparable to 1995, 1999, or 2005 estimates due to wording in questionnaire.
†Not applicable.
#Rounds to zero.
‡Reporting standards not met.
Note: Data do not include persons enrolled in high school or below. Race categories exclude persons of Hispanic ethnicity. Detail may not sum to totals because of rounding.

SOURCE: Adapted from Thomas D. Snyder, Sally A. Dillow, and Charlene M. Hoffman, "Table 370. Participation of Employed Persons, 17 Years Old and over, in Career-Related Adult Education during the Previous 12 Months, by Selected Characteristics of Participants, Various Years, 1995 through 2005," in *Digest of Education Statistics 2008*, National Center for Education Statistics, March 2009, http://nces.ed.gov/pubs2009/2009020.pdf (accessed May 1, 2009)

TABLE 5.3

Poll respondent groups supporting John McCain in the presidential election, October 31–November 2, 2008

Based on likely voters	Obama	McCain
	%	%
Attend church weekly	44	56
Non-Hispanic whites	44	56
65 years and older	46	54
Protestants	47	53
Men	49	51

SOURCE: Lydia Saad, "2008 Presidential Preferences: Groups Showing Modest Majority Support for John McCain," in *Blacks, Postgrads, Young Adults Help Obama Prevail*, The Gallup Organization, November 6, 2008, http://www.gallup.com/poll/111781/Blacks-Postgrads-Young-Adults-Help-Obama-Prevail.aspx (accessed May 1, 2009). Copyright © 2008 by The Gallup Organization. Reproduced by permission of The Gallup Organization.

TABLE 5.4

Poll respondent groups supporting Barack Obama in the presidential election, October 31–November 2, 2008

Based on likely voters	Obama	McCain
	%	%
Women	56	44
50 to 64 years	54	46
30 to 49 years	53	47
Catholics	53	47

SOURCE: Lydia Saad, "2008 Presidential Preferences: Groups Showing Modest Majority Support for Barack Obama," in *Blacks, Postgrads, Young Adults Help Obama Prevail*, The Gallup Organization, November 6, 2008, http://www.gallup.com/poll/111781/Blacks-Postgrads-Young-Adults-Help-Obama-Prevail.aspx (accessed May 1, 2009). Copyright © 2008 by The Gallup Organization. Reproduced by permission of The Gallup Organization.

FIGURE 5.4

Public opinion about Obama's ability to be a good president, by age, November 9–11, 2008

Confidence in Obama's ability to be a good president, by age.

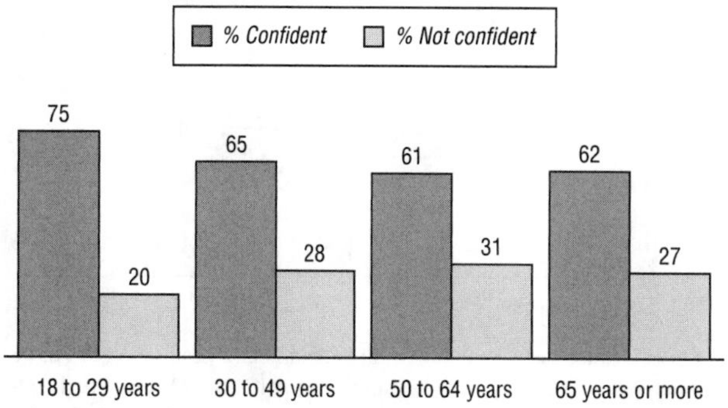

SOURCE: Lydia Saad, "Confidence in Obama's Ability to Be a Good President, by Age," in *Nearly Half of Conservatives Confident in Obama*, The Gallup Organization, November 12, 2008, http://www.gallup.com/poll/111880/Nearly-Half-Conservatives-Confident-Obama.aspx (accessed May 1, 2009). Copyright © 2008 by The Gallup Organization. Reproduced by permission of The Gallup Organization.

Older Americans Express Confidence in the New Administration

An AARP survey conducted in December 2008 characterizes Americans aged 50 and older as optimistic that Congress would address at least some of the issues of importance to them, such as financing jobs programs and reforming health care in 2009. In *AARP Bulletin Survey on Expectations for the New Administration and Congress* (http://assets.aarp.org/rgcenter/general/bulletin_congress_08.pdf), Gerard Rainville of the AARP notes that 76% of the survey respondents who named the financing of a jobs program as the top priority for Congress and the new administration felt it was at least "somewhat likely" that Congress would act to finance a jobs program in 2009. Two-thirds (67%) of the respondents who said health care reform should be the top priority for Congress and the new administration thought it was at least "somewhat likely" that Congress would act on this issue. Interestingly, more adults aged 50 and older (65%) than those aged 18 to 49 (61%) expressed confidence that Congress would address their priority issues.

As President Obama's ambitious health care reform initiative took shape in mid-2009, some older adults expressed fear that the proposed reforms would compromise their access to care. Ceci Connolly reports in "Seniors Remain Wary of Health-Care Reform" (*Washington Post*, August 9, 2009) that groups such as the 60 Plus Association, an organization that bills itself as a "conservative alternative to AARP," cautioned seniors that the reform would not only sharply limit access to care but also provided less money for treatment, including prescription drugs.

In fact, according to the article "AARP Loses Members over Health Care Stance" (*USA Today*, August 18, 2009), AARP lost 60,000 members between July 1, 2009 and mid-August 2009 in response to its stance in favor of health care reform. However, AARP spokesperson Drew Nannis explains that during the same period, AARP gained more than six times as many new members—400,000.

OLDER ADULTS RATINGS OF PAST PRESIDENTS. In February 2009 the Gallup Organization asked adults to choose the "greatest" president from among presidents historically regarded as the most revered by Americans: George Washington (1732–1799), Abraham Lincoln (1809–1865), Franklin D. Roosevelt (1882–1945), John F. Kennedy (1917–1963), and Ronald Reagan (1911–2004). (See Figure 5.5.) Roosevelt earned the highest percentage of adults aged 65 and older, presumably because they are old enough to remember him and continue to benefit from the Social Security Act he signed in 1935. In contrast, younger people were more likely to name Lincoln as the greatest president—22% of adults aged 18 to 34 choose him, compared with 23% of adults aged 35 to 64 and 20% of adults aged 65 and older.

FIGURE 5.5

Public opinion about the greatest U.S. president, by age group, February 2009

WHICH U.S. PRESIDENT IS GREATEST, BY AGE?

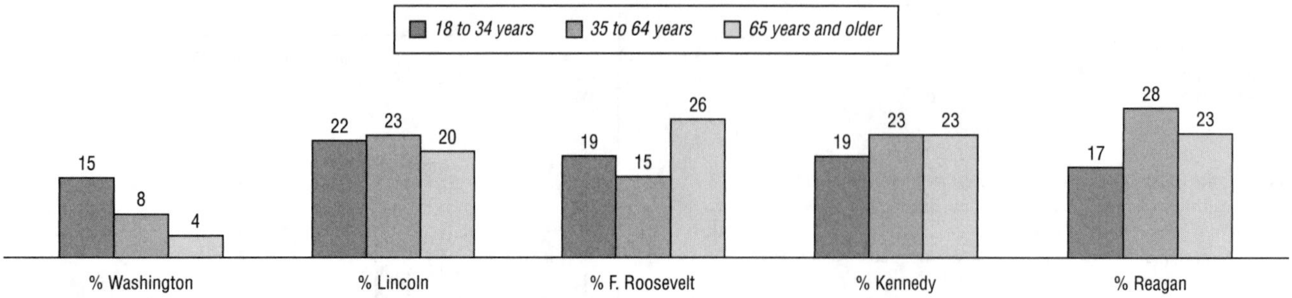

SOURCE: Lydia Saad, "Which U.S. President Is Greatest, by Age?" in *Best President? Lincoln on Par with Reagan, Kennedy*, The Gallup Organization, February 11, 2009, http://www.gallup.com/poll/114292/Best-President-Lincoln-Par-Reagan-Kennedy.aspx (accessed May 1, 2009). Copyright © 2009 by The Gallup Organization. Reproduced by permission of The Gallup Organization.

"GRAY POWER"—A POLITICAL BLOC

AARP's mission is to enhance the quality of life for all as we age, leading positive social change and delivering value to members through information, advocacy and service. We believe strongly in the principles of collective purpose, collective voice, and collective purchasing power, and these principles guide all organization efforts. AARP works tirelessly to fulfill its vision: a society in which everyone ages with dignity and purpose, and in which AARP helps people fulfill their goals and dreams. AARP speaks with one voice—united by a common motto: "To serve, not be served."

—AARP, "About AARP" (2009)

Adults aged 55 to 74 vote more than any other age group, and it is inevitable that the increasing number of Americans in this cohort will wield an enormous political impact. The AARP notes in "AARP—A Force for Social Change" (2009, http://www.aarp.org/about_aarp/aarp_overview/social_impact.html) that in 2009 it exercised considerable influence with its 36 million members in lobbying and in educating political leaders about the issues that concern older Americans.

As part of its purpose, the AARP advocates on behalf of older adults. The AARP is known as a powerful advocate on a range of legislative, consumer, and legal issues. To this end, the organization monitors issues pertinent to the lives of older Americans, assesses public opinion on such issues, and keeps policy makers apprised of these opinions. Advocacy efforts also include becoming involved in litigation when the decision could have a significant effect on the lives of older Americans. In cases regarding age discrimination, pensions, health care, economic security, and consumer issues, AARP lawyers will file amicus briefs (legal documents filed by individuals or groups that are not actual parties to a lawsuit but that are interested in influencing the outcome of the lawsuit) and support third-party lawsuits to promote the interests of older people.

Historically, the AARP has issued policy statements about topics such as age discrimination, quality of care in nursing facilities, Social Security, Medicare and other health coverage, paying for prescription drugs and long-term care, nontraditional living arrangements, and pension plan reforms. It also offers pertinent information for older adults on topics such as health, travel, employment, technology, volunteer and learning opportunities, and member discounts and benefits.

The AARP regularly responds to political and policy issues of concern to its constituency. For example, in April 2009 AARP voiced its support for S. 896, which would help homeowners facing foreclosure by granting bankruptcy judges the right to modify primary home mortgages as part of the bankruptcy process.

Silver-Haired Legislatures

The health of a democratic society may be measured by the quality of functions performed by private citizens.

—Alexis de Tocqueville

As of 2009, 31 states had "silver-haired legislatures" (activists aged 60 and older who propose and track legislation affecting older adults). Members of these legislatures are elected by their peers and try to influence bills pertaining to medical care, pension plan reform, consumer protection, and age discrimination, often by educating the real legislators and policy makers about the issues. Their ranks include former teachers, judges, doctors, business owners, and even retired legislators.

CHAPTER 6
ON THE ROAD—OLDER ADULT DRIVERS

Older adults who maintain active lifestyles and are mobile are healthier and live longer than their transportation-disadvantaged counterparts.... Public transit may provide older adults with greater mobility options, but it is generally underutilized, even if it is available.

—Rhianna JoIris Babka, Jill F. Cooper, and David R. Ragland, *Evaluation of Urban Travel Training for Older Adults* (November 15, 2008)

Readily available transportation is a vital factor in the quality of life of older adults. Transportation is essential for accessing health care, establishing and maintaining social and family relationships, obtaining food and other necessities, and preserving independence and self-esteem.

The ability to drive often determines whether an older adult is able to live independently. Driving is the primary mode of transportation in the United States, and personal vehicles remain the transportation mode of choice for almost all Americans, including older people. Surveys conducted by the AARP repeatedly confirm that people over the age of 65 make nearly all their trips in private vehicles, either as drivers or passengers. Even in urban areas where public transit is readily available, private vehicles are still used by most older people, with nondrivers relying heavily on family members or friends for transport. According to Liberty Mutual, in "On the Road" (2008, http://libertymutualmedia.com/MediaBin/PersonalMarket/Documents/Auto/Seniors/Seniors_OnTheRoad.pdf), older adult nondrivers rely on alternative forms of transportation, such as rides from family or friends, public transportation, walking, or rides in senior vans or taxicabs.

The National Highway Traffic Safety Administration states in *Older Population Traffic Safety Fact Sheet* (September 2008, http://www-nrd.nhtsa.dot.gov/Pubs/810992.PDF) that in 2006 there were 30 million drivers aged 65 and older, an 18% increase from 1996. During this same period the total number of licensed drivers grew by just 13%. Older drivers accounted for 15% of all licensed drivers in 2006, up from 14% in 1996. Federal Highway Administration data reveal that in 2007 the percentage of older drivers was comparable for men and women aged 65 to 74, but from age 75 and older somewhat more women than men were licensed drivers. (See Table 6.1.) Donald H. Camph notes in *A New Vision of America's Highways: Long-Distance Travel, Recreation, Tourism, and Rural Travel* (March 2007, http://www.transportationvision.org/docs/vision_HighwayTravel.pdf) that as the huge cohort (a group of individuals that shares a common characteristic such as birth years and is studied over time) of baby boomers (people born between 1946 and 1964) joins the ranks of older adults, the number of drivers aged 65 and older will continue to grow, exceeding 40 million by 2020.

Camph observes, however, that even though many older adults drive and many more are expected to in the future, driving is not a viable alternative for a significant number of older people. Many older adults choose to stop or limit their driving for health or safety reasons. Others do not have access to a vehicle. Camph also asserts that "more than 50 percent of nondrivers age 65 and older—or 3.6 million Americans—stay home on any given day at least partially because they lack transportation options."

Limited income also restricts many older adults' use of automobiles. According to the U.S. Bureau of Labor Statistics, car ownership costs are the second largest household expense in the United States, and the average household spends nearly as much to own and operate a car as it does on food and health care combined. Table 6.2 shows that the average costs associated with car ownership rose from $8,344 in 2005 to $8,508 in 2006, largely in response to increased spending on gas and motor oil. The cost of owning and operating an automobile, especially during periods of rising fuel prices, may be prohibitive for older adults living on fixed incomes. As a result, an ever-increasing proportion of the older population depends on alternative forms of transport in those areas where such transport is available; however, some older adults remain isolated and immobilized by the absence of accessible, affordable transportation in their communities.

TABLE 6.1

Licensed drivers, by sex and percentage in each age group and relation to population, 2007

	Male drivers			Female drivers			Total drivers		
Age	Number	Percent of total drivers	Drivers as percent of age group*	Number	Percent of total drivers	Drivers as percent of age group*	Number	Percent of total drivers	Drivers as percent of age group*
Under 16	127,069	0.1	5.8	124,493	0.1	6.0	251,562	0.1	5.9
16	682,021	0.7	30.7	670,152	0.6	31.7	1,352,173	0.7	31.2
17	1,149,836	1.1	50.8	1,107,814	1.1	51.5	2,257,650	1.1	51.1
18	1,479,844	1.4	67.8	1,393,879	1.3	67.2	2,873,723	1.4	67.5
19	1,638,371	1.6	76.0	1,546,695	1.5	75.6	3,185,066	1.5	75.8
(19 and under)	5,077,141	5.0	46.1	4,843,033	4.7	46.3	9,920,174	4.8	46.2
20	1,681,877	1.6	78.5	1,624,301	1.6	80.1	3,306,178	1.6	79.3
21	1,712,165	1.7	79.1	1,677,300	1.6	82.2	3,389,465	1.6	80.6
22	1,739,707	1.7	79.6	1,715,395	1.7	83.6	3,455,102	1.7	81.5
23	1,743,141	1.7	80.8	1,725,506	1.7	85.7	3,468,647	1.7	83.1
24	1,792,224	1.7	81.4	1,777,980	1.7	86.9	3,570,204	1.7	84.0
(20–24)	8,669,114	8.5	79.9	8,520,482	8.3	83.7	17,189,596	8.4	81.7
25–29	9,072,595	8.9	84.2	9,077,275	8.8	88.3	18,149,870	8.8	86.2
30–34	8,852,063	8.6	89.4	8,766,584	8.5	91.1	17,618,647	8.6	90.2
35–39	9,762,966	9.5	91.6	9,635,291	9.3	91.6	19,398,257	9.4	91.6
40–44	10,117,084	9.9	92.3	10,041,634	9.7	91.1	20,158,718	9.8	91.7
45–49	10,583,203	10.3	93.6	10,641,856	10.3	92.1	21,225,059	10.3	92.8
50–54	9,869,590	9.6	95.9	9,994,330	9.7	93.2	19,863,920	9.7	94.5
55–59	8,581,110	8.4	97.0	8,723,673	8.4	92.9	17,304,783	8.4	94.9
60–64	6,891,032	6.7	99.5	6,976,462	6.8	92.4	13,867,494	6.7	95.8
65–69	4,981,745	4.9	99.3	5,095,436	4.9	88.9	10,077,181	4.9	93.7
70–74	3,733,751	3.6	96.5	3,877,392	3.8	81.9	7,611,143	3.7	88.5
75–79	2,933,321	2.9	94.4	3,187,834	3.1	75.6	6,121,155	3.0	83.6
80–84	1,999,765	2.0	90.7	2,305,836	2.2	66.0	4,305,601	2.1	75.6
85 and over	1,340,456	1.3	75.4	1,589,791	1.5	42.6	2,930,247	1.4	53.2
Total	**102,464,936**	**100.0**	**87.2**	**103,276,909**	**100.0**	**83.8**	**205,741,845**	**100.0**	**85.5**

*These percentages are computed using population estimates of the Bureau of the Census. Under-16 age group is compared to 14 and 15-year-old population estimates; the other age brackets coincide with those from the Bureau of the Census.

SOURCE: "Distribution of Licensed Drivers—2007 by Sex and Percentage in Each Age Group and Relation to Population," in *Highway Statistics 2007*, U.S. Department of Transportation, Federal Highway Administration, December 2008, http://www.fhwa.dot.gov/policyinformation/statistics/2007/pdf/dl20.pdf (accessed May 6, 2009)

According to the U.S. Government Accountability Office (GAO), in *Transportation-Disadvantaged Seniors: Efforts to Enhance Senior Mobility Could Benefit from Additional Guidance and Information* (August 2004, http://www.gao.gov/new.items/d04971.pdf), in 2004 adults aged 75 and older who lived in small towns (45%) and rural areas (23%) were much less likely than residents of cities (84%) and suburbs (69%) to have access to public transportation. Rhianna JoIris Babka, Jill F. Cooper, and David R. Ragland observe in *Evaluation of Urban Travel Training for Older Adults* (November 15, 2008, http://www.tsc.berkeley.edu/news/TSCtrb2009/TrainingRhiannaJill09-2843.pdf) that even when public transportation is available, it is underutilized, at least in part because many older adults are unfamiliar with public transit and how to use it.

TRANSPORTATION INITIATIVES ADDRESS NEEDS OF OLDER ADULTS

Because ensuring access to transportation is key to older adults' independence and quality of life, several federal agencies and initiatives aim to address this need. The Federal Interagency Coordinating Council on Access and Mobility (CCAM) sponsors United We Ride, an interagency national initiative that supports states and their localities to develop coordinated human service delivery systems. The National Center on Senior Transportation (NCST) aims to assist older adults to remain active vital members of their communities by offering a range of transportation options and alternatives. The NCST-sponsored Senior Transportation program is a collaborative effort that coordinates a range of research and services intended to develop new transportation solutions, especially for rural areas. The program also champions the creative use of technology to connect with volunteers, older drivers, and older adults in need of transportation services. The NCST is overseen by the Easter Seals Inc. and receives funding via the U.S. Department of Transportation's Federal Transit Administration.

In "Tips & Facts" (2009, http://seniortransportation.easterseals.com/site/PageServer?pagename=NCST2_older_tips), the NCST reports that:

- In 2006 Americans took 10.1 billion trips on public transportation.
- Most (83%) older Americans say "public transit provides easy access to the things that they need in everyday life" and 80% believe public transportation is safer than driving alone, especially at night.

TABLE 6.2

Average annual expenditures of all consumer units, by selected types of expenditures, selected years 1990–2006

[In dollars, except as indicated (96,968 represents $96,968,000). Based on Consumer Expenditure Survey. Data are averages for the noninstitutional population. Expenditures reported here are out-of-pocket]

Type	1990	1995	2000	2002	2003	2004	2005	2006
Number of consumer units (1,000)	96,968	103,123	109,367	112,108	115,356	116,282	117,356	118,843
Expenditures, total*	**$28,381**	**$32,264**	**$38,045**	**$40,677**	**$40,817**	**$43,395**	**$46,409**	**$48,398**
Food	4,296	4,505	5,158	5,375	5,340	5,781	5,931	6,111
Food at home*	2,485	2,803	3,021	3,099	3,129	3,347	3,297	3,417
Meats, poultry, fish, and eggs	668	752	795	798	825	880	764	797
Dairy products	295	297	325	328	328	371	378	368
Fruits and vegetables	408	457	521	552	535	561	552	592
Other food at home	746	856	927	970	999	1,075	1,158	1,212
Food away from home	1,811	1,702	2,137	2,276	2,211	2,434	2,634	2,694
Alcoholic beverages	293	277	372	376	391	459	426	497
Housing*	8,703	10,458	12,319	13,283	13,432	13,918	15,167	16,366
Shelter	4,836	5,928	7,114	7,829	7,887	7,998	8,805	9,673
Utilities, fuels, and public services	1,890	2,191	2,489	2,684	2,811	2,927	3,183	3,397
Apparel and services	1,618	1,704	1,856	1,749	1,640	1,816	1,886	1,874
Transportation*	5,120	6,014	7,417	7,759	7,781	7,801	8,344	8,508
Vehicle purchases	2,129	2,638	3,418	3,665	3,732	3,397	3,544	3,421
Gasoline and motor oil	1,047	1,006	1,291	1,235	1,333	1,598	2,013	2,227
Other vehicle expenses	1,642	2,015	2,281	2,471	2,331	2,365	2,339	2,355
Health care	1,480	1,732	2,066	2,350	2,416	2,574	2,664	2,766
Entertainment	1,422	1,612	1,863	2,079	2,060	2,218	2,388	2,376
Reading	153	162	146	139	127	130	126	117
Tobacco products, smoking supplies	274	269	319	320	290	288	319	327
Personal insurance and pensions	2,592	2,964	3,365	3,899	4,055	4,823	5,204	5,270
Life and other personal insurance	345	373	399	406	397	390	381	322
Pensions and social security	2,248	2,591	2,966	3,493	3,658	4,433	4,823	4,948

*Includes expenditures not shown separately.

SOURCE: "Table 662. Average Annual Expenditures of All Consumer Units by Selected Major Types of Expenditure:1990–2006," in *Statistical Abstract of the United States: 2009*, 128th ed., U.S. Census Bureau, 2008, http://www.census.gov/compendia/statab/tables/09s0662.pdf (accessed May 6, 2009)

- Public transportation ridership increased by 30% from 1995 through 2006, growing at more than twice the rate of the U.S. population (12%) and higher than the 24% growth in highway use during the same period.

U.S. Department of Transportation's Initiatives

In his March 18, 2009, statement to the U.S. House of Representatives' Committee on Appropriations Subcommittee on Transportation, Housing and Urban Development, and Related Agencies, Ray H. LaHood (1945–; http://www.its.dot.gov/itspac/read_ahead_april2009/lahood_statement.htm), the U.S. secretary of transportation and a former Republican member of the House of Representatives from Illinois, outlined President Barack Obama's (1961–) national priorities for transportation. As part of a U.S. Department of Transportation initiative to foster livable communities and transit-oriented development, LaHood promised to "to build on innovative ways of doing business that promote mobility and enhance the unique characteristics of our neighborhoods, communities and regions" and "to enable communities to . . . better accommodate the needs of our ever-increasing older population as they give up driving."

MOTOR VEHICLE ACCIDENTS

The Insurance Institute for Highway Safety (IIHS), a nonprofit, scientific, and educational organization that is dedicated to reducing the losses from motor vehicle accidents, reports that, apart from the youngest drivers, older drivers have the highest rates of fatal crashes per mile driven. Even though older drivers tend to limit their number of miles driven as they age and they drive at the safest times—in daylight and avoiding rush-hour traffic—their rate of accidents per mile is extremely high. In *Fatality Facts 2007: Older People* (June 2009, http://www.iihs.org/research/fatality_facts_2007/olderpeople.html), the IIHS observes that among drivers involved in fatal crashes in 2007, the proportion in multiple-vehicle crashes at intersections increased with driver age, starting at ages 55 to 59. The oldest and youngest drivers have the highest fatality rates on a per-mile-driven basis, but a key difference between the two age groups is that older drivers involved in crashes are less likely than younger drivers to hurt others—older drivers pose more of a danger to themselves. Drivers under the age of 30 are responsible for far more of the injuries and deaths of others than are older adult drivers.

Table 6.3 shows that in 2005 the death rate (the number of deaths per 100,000 people) for motor vehicle–related injuries for adults aged 65 and older was 20.1%, compared with 14.9% for adults aged 45 to 64. The higher fatality rates of adults aged 75 to 84 and 85 and older who were involved in crashes—22.9% and 25.1%, respectively—are

TABLE 6.3

Death rates for motor vehicle-related injuries, by selected characteristics, selected years 1950–2005

[Data are based on death certificates]

Sex, race, Hispanic origin, and age	1950[a, b]	1960[a, b]	1970[b]	1980[b]	1990[b]	2000[c]	2004	2005
All persons				Deaths per 100,000 resident population				
All ages, age-adjusted[d]	24.6	23.1	27.6	22.3	18.5	15.4	15.2	15.2
All ages, crude	23.1	21.3	26.9	23.5	18.8	15.4	15.3	15.3
Under 1 year	8.4	8.1	9.8	7.0	4.9	4.4	3.5	3.6
1–14 years	9.8	8.6	10.5	8.2	6.0	4.3	4.0	3.6
1–4 years	11.5	10.0	11.5	9.2	6.3	4.2	4.0	3.8
5–14 years	8.8	7.9	10.2	7.9	5.9	4.3	4.1	3.6
15–24 years	34.4	38.0	47.2	44.8	34.1	26.9	26.3	25.9
15–19 years	29.6	33.9	43.6	43.0	33.1	26.0	25.2	23.6
20–24 years	38.8	42.9	51.3	46.6	35.0	28.0	27.5	28.2
25–34 years	24.6	24.3	30.9	29.1	23.6	17.3	17.6	18.0
35–44 years	20.3	19.3	24.9	20.9	16.9	15.3	15.1	15.4
45–64 years	25.2	23.0	26.5	18.0	15.7	14.3	14.7	14.9
45–54 years	22.2	21.4	25.5	18.6	15.6	14.2	15.1	15.1
55–64 years	29.0	25.1	27.9	17.4	15.9	14.4	14.1	14.7
65 years and over	43.1	34.7	36.2	22.5	23.1	21.4	20.4	20.1
65–74 years	39.1	31.4	32.8	19.2	18.6	16.5	16.1	16.7
75–84 years	52.7	41.8	43.5	28.1	29.1	25.7	24.5	22.9
85 years and over	45.1	37.9	34.2	27.6	31.2	30.4	26.1	25.1
Male								
All ages, age-adjusted[d]	38.5	35.4	41.5	33.6	26.5	21.7	21.4	21.7
All ages, crude	35.4	31.8	39.7	35.3	26.7	21.3	21.3	21.7
Under 1 year	9.1	8.6	9.3	7.3	5.0	4.6	3.8	3.5
1–14 years	12.3	10.7	13.0	10.0	7.0	4.9	4.5	4.1
1–4 years	13.0	11.5	12.9	10.2	6.9	4.7	4.2	4.2
5–14 years	11.9	10.4	13.1	9.9	7.0	5.0	4.7	4.1
15–24 years	56.7	61.2	73.2	68.4	49.5	37.4	36.4	36.5
15–19 years	46.3	51.7	64.1	62.6	45.5	33.9	32.5	30.7
20–24 years	66.7	73.2	84.4	74.3	53.3	41.2	40.4	42.3
25–34 years	40.8	40.1	49.4	46.3	35.7	25.5	25.8	26.9
35–44 years	32.5	29.9	37.7	31.7	24.7	22.0	21.9	22.2
45–64 years	37.7	33.3	38.9	26.5	21.9	20.2	21.1	21.6
45–54 years	33.6	31.6	37.2	27.6	22.0	20.4	21.9	22.2
55–64 years	43.1	35.6	40.9	25.4	21.7	19.8	19.8	20.9
65 years and over	66.6	52.1	54.4	33.9	32.1	29.5	28.2	28.5
65–74 years	59.1	45.8	47.3	27.3	24.2	21.7	21.3	23.2
75–84 years	85.0	66.0	68.2	44.3	41.2	35.6	34.7	32.4
85 years and over	78.1	62.7	63.1	56.1	64.5	57.5	44.2	44.1
Female								
All ages, age-adjusted[d]	11.5	11.7	14.9	11.8	11.0	9.5	9.3	8.9
All ages, crude	10.9	11.0	14.7	12.3	11.3	9.7	9.5	9.1
Under 1 year	7.6	7.5	10.4	6.7	4.9	4.2	3.2	3.6
1–14 years	7.2	6.3	7.9	6.3	4.9	3.7	3.5	3.1
1–4 years	10.0	8.4	10.0	8.1	5.6	3.8	3.7	3.4
5–14 years	5.7	5.4	7.2	5.7	4.7	3.6	3.4	3.0
15–24 years	12.6	15.1	21.6	20.8	17.9	15.9	15.7	14.7
15–19 years	12.9	16.0	22.7	22.8	20.0	17.5	17.5	16.2
20–24 years	12.2	14.0	20.4	18.9	16.0	14.2	13.8	13.2
25–34 years	9.3	9.2	13.0	12.2	11.5	8.8	9.1	8.8
35–44 years	8.5	9.1	12.9	10.4	9.2	8.8	8.3	8.6
45–64 years	12.6	13.1	15.3	10.3	10.1	8.7	8.6	8.5
45–54 years	10.9	11.6	14.5	10.2	9.6	8.2	8.5	8.2
55–64 years	14.9	15.2	16.2	10.5	10.8	9.5	8.8	8.9
65 years and over	21.9	20.3	23.1	15.0	17.2	15.8	14.9	14.0
65–74 years	20.6	19.0	21.6	13.0	14.1	12.3	11.7	11.2
75–84 years	25.2	23.0	27.2	18.5	21.9	19.2	17.7	16.5
85 years and over	22.1	22.0	18.0	15.2	18.3	19.3	17.9	16.4

attributable to older adults' fragility as opposed to the likelihood of being involved in an accident. Older people are more susceptible to injury, especially chest injuries, and are more likely to die as a result of those injuries. However, the IIHS indicates that relatively few deaths—less than 1%—of adults aged 70 and older are attributable to motor vehicle accidents.

The IIHS reports that in 2007, 79% of motor vehicle crash fatalities among people 70 and older involved occupants in passenger vehicles and 16% were pedestrians. The death rate per 100,000 people for pedestrians aged 70 and older in 2007 was higher than for pedestrians in all younger age groups.

In 2007, 75% of fatal crashes involving drivers aged 85 and older were multiple-vehicle accidents. Of those, nearly

TABLE 6.3

Death rates for motor vehicle-related injuries, by selected characteristics, selected years 1950–2005 [CONTINUED]

[Data are based on death certificates]

Sex, race, Hispanic origin, and age	1950[a, b]	1960[a, b]	1970[b]	1980[b]	1990[b]	2000[c]	2004	2005
White male[e]				Deaths per 100,000 resident population				
All ages, age-adjusted[d]	37.9	34.8	40.4	33.8	26.3	21.8	21.8	22.2
All ages, crude	35.1	31.5	39.1	35.9	26.7	21.6	21.9	22.3
Under 1 year	9.1	8.8	9.1	7.0	4.8	4.2	3.3	3.3
1–14 years	12.4	10.6	12.5	9.8	6.6	4.8	4.6	4.1
15–24 years	58.3	62.7	75.2	73.8	52.5	39.6	39.4	39.1
25–34 years	39.1	38.6	47.0	46.6	35.4	25.1	25.8	27.3
35–44 years	30.9	28.4	35.2	30.7	23.7	21.8	22.2	22.4
45–64 years	36.2	31.7	36.5	25.2	20.6	19.7	20.7	21.7
65 years and over	67.1	52.1	54.2	32.7	31.4	29.4	28.5	28.7

[a]Includes deaths of persons who were not residents of the 50 states and the District of Columbia.
[b]Underlying cause of death was coded according to the Sixth Revision of the International Classification of Diseases (ICD) in 1950, Seventh in 1960, Eighth Revision in 1970, and Ninth Revision in 1980–1998.
[c]Starting with the 1999 data, cause of death is coded according to ICD-10.
[d]Age-adjusted rates are calculated using the year 2000 standard population. Prior to 2003, age-adjusted rates were calculated using standard million proportions based on rounded population numbers. Starting with 2003 data, unrounded population numbers are used to calculate age-adjusted rates.
[e]The race groups, white, black, Asian or Pacific Islander, and the American Indian or Alaska Native, include persons of Hispanic and non-Hispanic origin.
Persons of Hispanic origin may be of any race. Death rates for the American Indian or Alaska Native and Asian or Pacific Islander populations are known to be underestimated.

SOURCE: Adapted from "Table 43. Death Rates for Motor Vehicle-Related Injuries, by Sex, Race, Hispanic Origin, and Age: United States, Selected Years 1950–2005," in *Health, United States, 2008. With Chartbook*, National Center for Health Statistics, 2009, http://www.cdc.gov/nchs/data/hus/hus08.pdf#listtables (accessed May 6, 2009)

half (48%) occurred at intersections. The IIHS observes that drivers over the age of 65 are more likely than younger drivers to have accidents when making left turns and attributes this to the fact that older drivers take longer to make turns, increasing the risk of a crash.

Older adults also suffer nonfatal injuries as drivers or passengers in motor vehicle crashes. In 2007 the National Center for Injury Prevention and Control recorded 230,554 nonfatal injuries in adults aged 65 and older. (See Figure 6.1; this figure shows the 172,408 injuries to occupants of vehicles and 58,146 injuries attributable to other transport.) Motor vehicle accidents (called unintentional MV-occupant) were the fourth leading cause of nonfatal injuries among adults aged 65 and older in the United States in 2007.

The data about older drivers are not all bad. According to the Centers for Disease Control and Prevention (CDC), in "Older Adult Drivers: Fact Sheet" (January 26, 2009, http://www.cdc.gov/MotorVehicleSafety/Older_Adult_Drivers/adult-drivers_factsheet.html), older adults wear seatbelts more often than any other age group except infants and preschool children, and they are less likely to drink and drive than other adult drivers. They also take fewer risks than younger drivers by limiting their driving during bad weather and at night.

AGE-RELATED CHANGES MAY IMPAIR OLDER DRIVERS' SKILLS

Most older adults retain their driving skills, but some age-related changes in vision, hearing, cognitive functions (attention, memory, and reaction times), reflexes, and flexibility of the head and neck may impair the skills that are critical for safe driving. For example, reaction time becomes slower and more variable with advancing age, and arthritis (inflammation that causes pain and loss of movement of the joints) in the neck or shoulder may limit sufferers' ability to turn their necks well enough to merge into traffic, see when backing up, and navigate intersections where the angle of intersecting roads is less than perpendicular.

Changes such as reduced muscle mass and the resultant reduction in strength, as well as decreases in the efficiency of the circulatory, cardiac, and respiratory systems are strictly related to aging. Others are attributable to the fact that certain diseases, such as arthritis and glaucoma (a disease in which fluid pressure inside the eyes slowly rises, leading to vision loss or blindness), tend to strike at later ages. The functional losses associated with these chronic (long-term) conditions are usually gradual, and many afflicted older drivers are able to adapt to them. Most older adults do not experience declines until very old age, and most learn to adjust to the limitations imposed by age-related changes. Still, a substantial proportion of older adults do stop driving in response to age-related changes. In "Realizing Dignified Transportation for Seniors" (April 14, 2009, http://media.itnamerica.org/press/ITNAmerica/__www.philanthropystories.org_30Grantsin30Days_RealizingDi.pdf), Philanthropy New York, a community of philanthropic foundations that provides more than $4 billion to thousands of nonprofit organizations around the world, reports that each

FIGURE 6.1

Ten leading causes of nonfatal injuries, ages 65–85, 2007

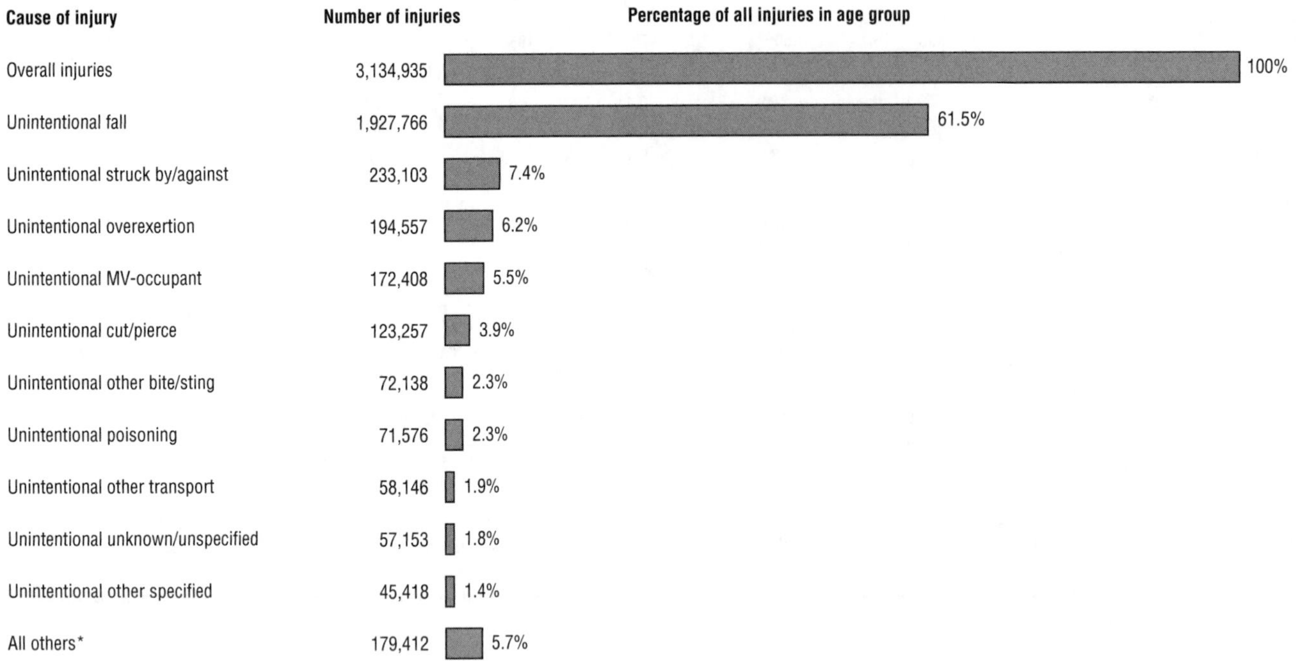

SOURCE: "10 Leading Causes of Nonfatal Injuries, United States 2007, All Races, Both Sexes, Disposition: All Cases Ages: 65–85," in *10 Leading Causes of Nonfatal Injury Reports*, National Center for Injury Prevention and Control, September 30, 2008, http://webappa.cdc.gov/sasweb/ncipc/nfilead2001.html (accessed May 6, 2009)

year more than 1 million older adults stop driving because of declines in their fitness level, vision, and ability to think clearly.

The *Physician's Guide to Assessing and Counseling Older Drivers* (May 2003, http://www.ama-assn.org/ama/pub/category/10791.html), which was copublished by the American Medical Association (AMA) and the National Highway Traffic Safety Administration (NHTSA), details medical conditions and their potential effect on driving and highlights treatment methods and counseling measures that can minimize these effects. In the preface, the AMA identifies motor vehicle injuries as the leading cause of injury-related deaths among 65- to 75-year-olds. Among adults aged 75 and older, motor vehicle–related injuries followed falls as the second leading cause of injury-related deaths. The AMA posits that significant growth in the older population and an increase in miles driven by older adults could act to triple the number of traffic fatalities in the coming years. Believing that the medical community can help stem this increase, the AMA calls on physicians to help their patients maintain or even improve their driving skills by periodically assessing them for disease- and medication-related conditions that might impair their capacity to function as safe drivers.

Acute and Chronic Medical Problems

According to the *Physician's Guide to Assessing and Counseling Older Drivers*, patients discharged from the hospital following treatment for serious illnesses may be temporarily, or even permanently, unable to drive safely. Examples of acute (short-term) medical problems that can impair driving performance include:

- Acute myocardial infarction (heart attack)
- Stroke (sudden death of a portion of the brain cells because of a lack of blood flow and oxygen) and other traumatic brain injury
- Syncope (fainting) and vertigo (dizziness)
- Seizures (sudden attacks or convulsions characterized by generalized muscle spasms and loss of consciousness)
- Surgery
- Delirium (altered mental state characterized by wild, irregular, and incoherent thoughts and actions) from any cause

The guide also notes that a variety of chronic medical conditions can also compromise driving function, such as:

- Visual disorders such as cataracts, diabetic retinopathy (damage to the blood vessels that supply the retina that can result in blindness), macular degeneration (a degenerative condition that can cause blurred vision), glaucoma, retinitis pigmentosa (an inherited condition that causes night blindness and tunnel vision), and low visual acuity (the ability to distinguish fine details) even after correction with lenses. Along with visual acuity, other visual functions decline with advancing age. For example, sensitivity to glare increases and may be exacerbated by cataracts. Because driving is largely a visual task, impaired vision can significantly compromise the ability to read signs, see lane lines, and identify pedestrians in the dark or during inclement weather.
- Cardiovascular (heart and blood vessels disorders) such as angina (chest pain from a blockage in a coronary artery that prevents oxygen-rich blood from reaching part of the heart) or syncope pose dangers to drivers because acute pain or even transient loss of consciousness increases the risk of accidents.
- Neurologic disease, including seizures, dementia, multiple sclerosis (a progressive nerve disease that can result in the loss of the ability to walk or speak), Parkinson's disease (a degenerative disease that causes tremors and slowed movement and speech), peripheral neuropathy (numbness or tingling in the hands and/or feet), and residual deficits (losses or disability) resulting from stroke all may impair the driver's ability to operate a vehicle and/or exercise sufficient caution when driving.
- Psychiatric disease, especially those mental disorders in which patients suffer hallucinations, severe anxiety, and irrational thoughts, and are unable to distinguish between reality and imagination), as well as alcohol or other substance abuse.
- Metabolic disease, such as diabetes mellitus (a condition in which there is increased sugar in the blood and urine because the body is unable to use sugar to produce energy) and hypothyroidism (decreased production of the thyroid hormone by the thyroid gland), can act to impair judgment and response time.
- Musculoskeletal disabilities, such as arthritis and injuries.
- Chronic renal (kidney) failure.

The guide notes that driving requires a range of sophisticated cognitive skills, which is why some cognitive changes can compromise driving ability. It is not unusual for memory, attention, processing speed, and executive skills—the capacity for logical analysis—to decline with advancing age. Weakening memory may make it difficult for some older drivers to process information from traffic signs and to navigate correctly. As multiple demands are made on older drivers' attention, the guide states that "drivers must possess selective attention—the ability to prioritize stimuli and focus on only the most important—in order to attend to urgent stimuli (such as traffic signs) while not being distracted by irrelevant ones (such as roadside ads)." Selective attention problems challenge older drivers to distinguish the most critical information when they are faced with many signs and signals. Drivers have to divide their attention to concentrate "on the multiple stimuli involved in most driving tasks." Processing speed affects perception-reaction time and is critical in situations where drivers must immediately choose between actions such as accelerating, braking, or steering. Executive skills enable drivers to make correct decisions after evaluating the stimuli that are related to driving, such as to stop at a red light or stop at a crosswalk when a pedestrian is crossing the street.

Medications

According to the *Physician's Guide to Assessing and Counseling Older Drivers*, many commonly used prescription and over-the-counter (nonprescription) medications can impair driving performance. In general, drugs with strong central nervous system effects, such as antidepressants, antihistamines, muscle relaxants, narcotic analgesics (painkillers), anticonvulsants (used to prevent seizures), and stimulants, have the potential to adversely affect the ability to operate a motor vehicle. The extent to which driving skills are compromised varies from person to person and between different medications used for the same purpose. The effects of prescription and over-the-counter medications may be intensified in combination with other drugs or alcohol.

The guide indicates that driving performance can be affected by medication side effects, such as "drowsiness, dizziness, blurred vision, unsteadiness, fainting, [and] slowed reaction time." Generally, these side effects are dose-dependent and lessen over time, but older adults are often more sensitive to the effects of medications and may take longer to metabolize them, prolonging their effects. Medications such as prescription sleep aids "that cause drowsiness, euphoria, and/or anterograde amnesia may also diminish insight, and the patient may experience impairment without being aware of it."

Some Fears about Older Drivers' Are Unwarranted

As the ranks of older adults swell, many states and organizations—the AMA and the NHTSA are chief among these groups—are taking action to ensure driver safety. Concern about older driver safety has intensified in recent years in response to a spate of media reports describing serious crashes involving older drivers. However, some of this concern may be unwarranted. The IIHS reports in the press release "Older Drivers' Fatal Crashes Trend Down;

Many Say That They Self-Limit Their Driving" (December 16, 2008, http://www.iihs.org/news/2008/iihs_news_121608.pdf) that "despite growing numbers on the road, fewer older drivers died in crashes and fewer were involved in fatal collisions during 1997–2006 than in years past." Even though the population of adults over the age of 70 rose by 10%, crash deaths among drivers 70 and older declined by 21%. When compared with drivers aged 35 to 54, older drivers had a decrease in being involved in fatal crashes; drivers aged 80 and older witnessed the largest decline. According to the IIHS, "Fatal crash rates fell among older drivers for most types of crashes, and the decline was dramatic for crashes at intersections," which historically have been where older drivers are overrepresented.

These findings contradict earlier research, which predicted that older drivers would make up a substantially larger proportion of drivers in fatal crashes. The precise reasons for the fatality declines have not yet been pinpointed, but the IIHS suggests that older adults increasingly self-limit driving as they age and develop physical and cognitive impairments. For example, adults aged 80 and older were more than twice as likely as those aged 65 to 69 to avoid night driving and driving in ice or snow and to make fewer trips and travel shorter distances. According to Tara Parker-Pope, in "Declining Car Risk for Older Drivers" (*New York Times*, January 12, 2009), research suggests that older drivers are in better overall health than their counterparts a decade ago, so they are less likely to make a driving mistake that can lead to an accident.

Ensuring the Safety of Older Drivers

In the *Physician's Guide to Assessing and Counseling Older Drivers*, the AMA advocates coordinated efforts among the medical and research communities, policy makers, community planners, automobile industry, and government agencies to achieve the common goal of safe transportation for the older population. The AMA calls for refined diagnostic tools to assist physicians in assessing patients' crash risk, improved access to driver assessment and rehabilitation, safer roads and vehicles, and better alternatives to driving for older adults.

Some auto insurance companies reduce payments for older adults who successfully complete driving classes such as the AARP Driver Safety Program. In "AARP Driver Safety Program History and Facts" (June 21, 2004, http://www.aarp.org/families/driver_safety/driver_sponsor/a2004-06-21-ds_history.html), the AARP notes that as of 2004 over 9 million drivers had taken the eight-hour refresher course, which offers guidance in assessing physical abilities and making adjustments accordingly. Each year approximately 34,000 courses are conducted in communities nationwide. The American Automobile Association (AAA) offers a similar program called Safe Driving for Mature Operators that strives to improve the skills of older drivers. These courses address the aging process and help drivers adjust to age-related changes that can affect driving. Both organizations also provide resources that help older drivers and their families determine whether they can safely continue driving.

As of 2009 there were no upper age limits for driving. The National Institute on Aging observes that because people age at different rates, it is not possible to choose a specific age at which to suspend driving. Setting an age limit would leave some drivers on the road too long, whereas others would be forced to stop driving prematurely. Heredity, general health, lifestyle, and surroundings all influence how people age.

Many states are acting to reduce risks for older drivers by improving roadways to make driving less hazardous. According to the GAO, in *Older Driver Safety: Knowledge Sharing Should Help States Prepare for Increase in Older Driver Population* (April 2007, http://www.gao.gov/new.items/d07413.pdf), several states have adopted Federal Highway Administration (FHWA) practices to help older drivers including:

- Wider highway lanes
- Intersections that give drivers a longer view of oncoming traffic and allow more time for left turns
- Road signs with larger, more visible letters and numbers
- Advance street name signs before intersections

Table 6.4 shows some of the FHWA practices aimed at improving older driver safety that have been widely adopted by the states.

PROVIDING ALTERNATIVE MEANS OF TRANSPORTATION

In *Transportation-Disadvantaged Seniors*, the GAO considers issues and services for "transportation-disadvantaged" older adults—those who cannot drive or have limited their driving, or those who have an income restraint, disability, or medical condition that limits their ability to travel. The GAO identifies the federal programs that address this population's mobility issues, the extent to which these programs meet their mobility needs, the program practices that enhance their mobility and the cost-effectiveness of service delivery, the obstacles to addressing mobility needs, and the strategies for overcoming these obstacles. According to the GAO, there are 15 federal programs designed to meet the transportation needs of older adults. For example, the U.S. Department of Health and Human Services funds both Community Services Block Grant Programs, which provide taxicab vouchers and bus tokens that enable low-income older adults to take general trips, and Social Services Block Grants, which provide assistance for transport to and from medical or social service appointments.

TABLE 6.4

Most widely implemented practices for improving older driver safety, 2007

Federal Highway Administration (FHWA) practice	Number of states that have implemented the practice
Advance "STOP AHEAD," "YIELD AHEAD," and "SIGNAL AHEAD" signs on approaches to intersections when existing signs or signals are not visible soon enough for drivers to respond appropriately	51
Channelizing devices such as traffic cones, tubular markers, striped panel signs, drums, or temporary barriers to separate opposing traffic in construction zones to provide conspicuous and unambiguous traffic control	48
Dashed turn path pavement markings in intersections where evidence suggests that older drivers may have difficulty negotiating turns	41
Overhead lane control signs at intersections with traffic signals where drivers may have trouble positioning themselves in the correct lane	40
Reflective devices on medians and island curbs at intersections to make them more obvious	39

Note: In our questionnaire, we asked state officials whether they had implemented 14 specific recommendations. Six of those recommendations were selected from the 136 recommendations found in FHWA's *Highway Design Handbook for Older Drivers and Pedestrians* (2001). The 8 remaining recommendations were chosen from the 35 similar recommendations cited in *FHWA's Travel Better, Travel Longer: A Pocket Guide to Improve Traffic Control and Mobility for Our Older Population* (2003).

SOURCE: "Table 1. Most Widely Implemented Practices Recommended by FHWA for Improving Older Driver Safety," in *Older Driver Safety Knowledge Sharing Should Help States Prepare for Increase in Older Driver Population*, U.S. Government Accountability Office, April 2007, http://www.gao.gov/new.items/d07413.pdf (accessed May 7, 2009)

The GAO points out that besides the programs intended to provide assistance specifically to older people, there are other programs designed to aid transportation-disadvantaged segments of the population, including older adults. For example, the Americans with Disabilities Act (ADA) of 1990 required that changes to public transportation be made to provide better accessibility for people with disabilities; about half of ADA-eligible riders are aged 65 and older. Also, the Transportation Equity Act for the 21st Century, enacted in 1998, authorized funds for several programs, including a formula grant that supported states' efforts to meet the special transportation needs of older adults and people with disabilities.

Types of Transportation for Nondrivers

Transportation for older adults can include door-to-door services such as taxis or van services, public buses that travel along fixed routes, or ride sharing in carpools. According to the U.S. Administration on Aging (AoA), in *Because We Care: A Guide for People Who Care* (2006, http://www.uwex.edu/CES/flp/families/documents/BecauseWeCare.pdf), there are three general classes of alternative transportation for older adults:

- Demand response generally requires advance reservations and provides door-to-door service from one specific location to another. Such systems offer older adults comfortable and relatively flexible transport, with the potential for adapting to the needs of individual riders. Payment of fares for demand-response transport is usually required on a per-ride basis.
- Fixed route and scheduled services follow a predetermined route, stopping at established locations at specific times to allow passengers to board and disembark. This type of service typically requires payment of fares on a per-ride basis. Older adults are often eligible for discounted rates.
- Ride sharing programs connect people who need rides with drivers who have room in their cars and are willing to take passengers. This system generally offers scheduled transportation to a particular destination, such as a place of employment, a senior center, or a medical center.

Meeting the Transportation Needs of Older Adults

In *Transportation-Disadvantaged Seniors*, the GAO cites research by the Beverly Foundation that identifies five attributes necessary for alternative transportation services for older adults:

- Availability—older adults can travel to desired locations at the times they want to go.
- Accessibility—vehicles can be accessed by those with disabilities; services can be door-to-door or door-through-door as necessary; stops are pedestrian-friendly. Door-through-door transport offers personal, hands-on assistance for older adults who may have difficulties exiting their homes, disembarking from vehicles, and/or opening doors. It is also called assisted transportation, supported (or supportive) transportation, and escorted transportation.
- Acceptability—transport is safe, clean, and easy to use.
- Affordability—financial assistance is available if necessary.
- Adaptability—multiple trips and special equipment can be accommodated.

The GAO highlights specific unmet needs: "Seniors who rely on alternative transportation have difficulty making trips for which the automobile is better suited, such as trips that involve carrying packages;... life-enhancing needs are less likely to be met than life-sustaining needs; and... mobility needs are less likely to be met in nonurban communities (especially rural communities) than in urban communities." However, the GOA notes that there are limited data available to quantify or assess the extent of the needs that go unmet. It also identifies obstacles to addressing transportation-disadvantaged older adults' mobility needs, potential strategies that federal and other government entities might take to better meet these needs, and trade-offs associated with implementing each strategy. For example, the GAO finds that older drivers are not encouraged to investigate or plan for a time when they will be unable to drive. One way to address this obstacle might be to institute educational programs that would ease older adults' transition from driver to nondriver. This strategy does, however, have the potential to increase demand for alternative transportation services and the costs associated with their provision.

To increase and improve alternative transportation services, the GAO suggests enlisting the aid of volunteer drivers; sponsoring demonstration programs, identifying best practices, and increasing cooperation among federal programs; and establishing a central clearinghouse of information that could be accessed by stakeholders in the various programs. It recommends that the AoA improve the value and consistency of information pertaining to older adults' transportation needs that is received from area agencies on aging, including providing guidance for those agencies on assessing mobility needs. The AoA is also called on to keep older adults and their caregivers better informed of alternative transportation programs and to ensure that the best methods and practices are shared among transportation and social service providers to enhance the older population's mobility.

CHAPTER 7
THE HEALTH AND MEDICAL PROBLEMS OF OLDER ADULTS

Among the fears many people have about aging is coping with losses—not only declining mental and physical abilities but also the prospect of failing health, chronic (long-term) illness, and disability. Even though aging is associated with physiological changes, the rate and extent of these changes varies widely. One person may be limited by arthritis at age 65, whereas another is vigorous and active at age 90.

Despite the increasing proportion of active healthy older adults, it is true that the incidence (the rate of new cases of a disorder over a specified period) and prevalence (the total number of cases of a disorder in a given population at a specific time) of selected diseases as well as the utilization of health care services increase with advancing age. For example, the incidence of diabetes, heart disease, breast cancer, Parkinson's disease, and Alzheimer's disease increases with age. In contrast, the incidence of other diseases, such as human immunodeficiency virus (HIV) infection, multiple sclerosis, and schizophrenia, decreases with age.

This chapter considers the epidemiology of aging—the distribution and determinants of health and illness in the population of older adults. It describes trends in aging and the health of aging Americans; distinctions among healthy aging, disease, and disability; health promotion and prevention as applied to older people; and selected diseases and conditions common in old age.

GENERAL HEALTH OF OLDER AMERICANS

The proportion of adults rating their health as fair or poor increases with advancing age. In 2006, 18.8% of people aged 55 to 64, 21.9% of those aged 65 to 74, and 28.1% of adults aged 75 and older considered themselves in fair or poor health, compared with just 5.7% of adults aged 18 to 44. (See Table 7.1.)

The Federal Interagency Forum on Aging-Related Statistics states in *Older Americans 2008: Key Indicators of Well-Being* (March 2008, http://www.agingstats.gov/agingstatsdotnet/Main_Site/Data/2008_Documents/OA_2008.pdf) that between 2004 and 2006, 80% of non-Hispanic whites aged 65 to 74 said their health was good or better than good, compared with just 67% of non-Hispanic whites aged 85 and older. (See Figure 7.1.) Older people of other races and ethnic categories followed this same pattern. Across all older age groups, non-Hispanic respondents were more likely to report good health than non-Hispanic African-American and Hispanic respondents.

The Federal Interagency Forum on Aging-Related Statistics notes that most older people have at least one chronic condition and many have several. Among the most frequently occurring conditions of older adults in 2005–06 were hypertension (52% of men and 54% of women), arthritic symptoms (43% of men and 54% of women), all types of heart disease (37% of men and 26% of women), and cancer (24% of men and 19% of women). (See Figure 7.2.)

Table 7.2 shows that rates of chronic conditions that limited activity among Americans aged 65 and older decreased from 38.7% in 1997 to 32.6% in 2006. Among adults aged 55 to 64, the conditions most likely to limit activity were arthritis or other musculoskeletal problems, heart or other circulatory disorders, diabetes, lung diseases, mental illness, and fractures or joint injury. (See Figure 7.3.) Among older people aged 65 and older, arthritis and heart disease continued to limit activity the most; however, among adults aged 75 and older, problems with vision, hearing, and senility also contributed to limiting activity. (See Figure 7.4.)

Instrumental activities of daily living (IADLs) and measures of physical, cognitive, and social functioning are ways to assess disability and often determine whether older adults can live independently in the community. IADLs include activities such as light housework, meal preparation, doing the laundry, grocery shopping, getting around outside the home, managing money, taking medications as prescribed, and using the telephone. Noninstitutionalized individuals are considered chronically disabled if they cannot perform one or more IADL for 90 days or

TABLE 7.1

Percent of adults who reported their health as fair or poor, by selected characteristics for selected years 1991–2006

[Data are based on household interviews of a sample of the civilian noninstitutionalized population]

Characteristic	1991[a]	1995[a]	1997	2000	2003	2004	2005	2006
	Percent of persons with fair or poor health							
All ages, age-adjusted[b,c]	10.4	10.6	9.2	9.0	9.2	9.3	9.2	9.2
All ages, crude[c]	10.0	10.1	8.9	8.9	9.2	9.4	9.3	9.5
Age								
Under 18 years	2.6	2.6	2.1	1.7	1.8	1.8	1.8	1.9
Under 6 years	2.7	2.7	1.9	1.5	1.4	1.5	1.6	1.9
6–17 years	2.6	2.5	2.1	1.8	2.0	2.0	1.9	1.9
18–44 years	6.1	6.6	5.3	5.1	5.6	5.7	5.5	5.7
18–24 years	4.8	4.5	3.4	3.3	3.8	3.6	3.3	3.7
25–44 years	6.4	7.2	5.9	5.7	6.3	6.4	6.3	6.3
45–54 years	13.4	13.4	11.7	11.9	12.1	12.3	11.6	12.9
55–64 years	20.7	21.4	18.2	17.9	18.9	17.9	18.3	18.8
65 years and over	29.0	28.3	26.7	26.9	25.5	26.7	26.6	24.8
65–74 years	26.0	25.6	23.1	22.5	22.3	22.4	23.4	21.9
75 years and over	33.6	32.2	31.5	32.1	29.2	31.5	30.2	28.1
Sex[b]								
Male	10.0	10.1	8.8	8.8	8.8	9.0	8.8	9.0
Female	10.8	11.1	9.7	9.3	9.5	9.6	9.5	9.5
Race[b,d]								
White only	9.6	9.7	8.3	8.2	8.5	8.6	8.6	8.6
Black or African American only	16.8	17.2	15.8	14.6	14.7	14.6	14.3	14.4
American Indian or Alaska Native only	18.3	18.7	17.3	17.2	16.3	16.5	13.2	12.1
Asian only	7.8	9.3	7.8	7.4	7.4	8.6	6.8	6.9
Native Hawaiian or other Pacific Islander only	[g]	[g]	[g]					
2 or more races	[g]	[g]	[g]	16.2	14.7	12.6	14.5	13.1
Black or African American; white	[g]	[g]	[g]	14.5	21.4	10.7	8.3	15.0
American Indian or Alaska Native; white	[g]	[g]	[g]	18.7	18.1	12.3	17.2	13.9
Hispanic origin and race[b,d]								
Hispanic or Latino	15.6	15.1	13.0	12.8	13.9	13.3	13.3	13.0
Mexican	17.0	16.7	13.1	12.8	13.7	13.4	14.3	14.1
Not Hispanic or Latino	10.0	10.1	8.9	8.7	8.7	8.9	8.7	8.8
White only	9.1	9.1	8.0	7.9	7.9	8.0	8.0	8.0
Black or African American only	16.8	17.3	15.8	14.6	14.6	14.6	14.4	14.4
Percent of poverty level[b,e]								
Below 100%	22.8	23.7	20.8	19.6	20.4	21.3	20.4	20.3
100%–less than 200%	14.7	15.5	13.9	14.1	14.4	14.4	14.4	14.4
200% or more	6.8	6.7	6.1	6.3	6.1	6.3	6.2	6.1
Hispanic origin and race and percent of poverty level[b,d,e]								
Hispanic or Latino								
Below 100%	23.6	22.7	19.9	18.7	20.6	20.2	20.2	20.6
100%–less than 200%	18.0	16.9	13.5	15.3	15.5	15.2	15.3	14.4
200% or more	9.3	8.7	8.5	8.4	9.8	8.8	9.2	8.6
Not Hispanic or Latino:								
White only:								
Below 100%	21.9	22.8	19.7	18.8	19.5	20.8	20.1	19.5
100%–less than 200%	14.0	14.8	13.3	13.4	13.9	13.8	13.8	14.2
200% or more	6.4	6.2	5.6	5.8	5.6	5.7	5.7	5.5
Black or African American only:								
Below 100%	25.8	27.7	25.3	23.8	24.4	25.7	23.3	23.0
100%–less than 200%	17.0	19.3	19.2	18.2	18.6	16.7	17.6	16.9
200% or more	10.9	9.9	9.7	9.7	9.1	9.6	9.5	9.2

longer. Measures of physical functioning, such as the ability to stoop or kneel, lift heavy objects, walk a few blocks, or reach above the head, are also used to monitor progressive disability. In 2005 older women reported more difficulties with physical functioning than older men—32% of women were unable to perform at least one physical function task, compared with 19% of men. (See Figure 7.5.)

Hospital Utilization and Physician Visits

Adults aged 65 and older have the highest rates of inpatient hospitalization and the longest average lengths of stay (ALOS). In 2006 people aged 65 and older had 3,507.9 hospital discharges per 10,000—three times the number of discharges of adults aged 45 to 64. (See Table 7.3.) The

TABLE 7.1

Percent of adults who reported their health as fair or poor, by selected characteristics for selected years 1991–2006 [CONTINUED]

[Data are based on household interviews of a sample of the civilian noninstitutionalized population]

Characteristic	1991[a]	1995[a]	1997	2000	2003	2004	2005	200
Geographic region[b]								
Northeast	8.3	9.1	8.0	7.6	8.2	7.6	7.5	8.2
Midwest	9.1	9.7	8.1	8.0	8.3	8.2	8.3	8.8
South	13.1	12.3	10.8	10.7	10.7	11.2	11.0	10.4
West	9.7	10.1	8.8	8.8	8.4	8.9	8.6	8.5
Location of residence[b]								
Within MSA[f]	9.9	10.1	8.7	8.5	8.6	8.8	8.7	8.7
Outside MSA[f]	11 9	12.6	11.1	11.1	11.5	11.5	11.2	11.7

[a]Data prior to 1997 are not strictly comparable with data for later years due to the 1997 questionnaire redesign.
[b]Estimates are age-adjusted to the year 2000 standard population using six age groups: Under 18 years, 18–44 years, 45–54 years, 55–64 years, 65–74 years, and 75 years and over.
[c]Includes all other races not shown separately.
[d]The race groups, white, black, American Indian or Alaska Native, Asian, Native Hawaiian or Other Pacific Islander, and 2 or more races, include persons of Hispanic and non-Hispanic origin. Persons of Hispanic origin may be of any race. Starting with 1999 data, race-specific estimates are tabulated according to the 1997 Revisions to the Standards for the Classification of Federal Data on Race and Ethnicity and are not strictly comparable with estimates for earlier years. The five single-race categories plus multiple-race categories shown in the table conform to the 1997 standards. Starting with 1999 data, race-specific estimates are for persons who reported only one racial group; the category 2 or more races includes persons who reported more than one racial group. Prior to 1999, data were tabulated according to the 1977 Standards with four racial groups and the Asian only category included Native Hawaiian or other Pacific Islander. Estimates for single-race categories prior to 1999 included persons who reported one race or, if they reported more than one race, identified one race as best representing their race. Starting with 2003 data, race responses of other race and unspecified multiple race were treated as missing, and then race was imputed if these were the only race responses. Almost all persons with a race response of other race were of Hispanic origin.
[e]Percent of poverty level is based on family income and family size and composition using U.S. Census Bureau poverty thresholds. Missing family income data were imputed for 16%–18% of persons in 1991 and 1995, 24%–29% of persons in 1997–1998, and 31%–34% in 1999–2006.
[f]MSA is metropolitan statistical area. Starting with 2006 data, MSA status is determined using 2000 census data and the 2000 standards for defining MSAs.
[g]Data not available.

SOURCE: "Table 60. Respondent-Assessed Health Status, by Selected Characteristics: United States, Selected Years 1991–2006," in *Health, United States, 2008. With Chartbook*, National Center for Health Statistics, 2009, http://www.cdc.gov/nchs/data/hus/hus08.pdf#listtables (accessed May 6, 2009)

highest number of discharges and longest ALOS were among adults 75 and older, 4,512.6 and 5.6 days, respectively.

The ALOS for adults aged 65 and older was 5.5 days in 2006, compared with 5 days for people aged 45 to 64. (See Table 7.3.) The ALOS among all age groups had declined since 1980, from a high of 7.5 days to 4.7 days in 2006. Among patients aged 75 and older, ALOS decreased by half, from 11.4 days in 1980 to 5.6 days in 2006.

Shorter stays are in part because of the federal government's introduction of diagnosis-related groups (DRG) in the mid-1980s. (DRGs are categories of illnesses that prescribe, and allow for, set duration of treatment.) DRG-based reimbursement encourages hospitals to discharge patients as quickly as possible by compensating hospitals for a predetermined number of days per diagnosis, regardless of the actual length of stay. Shorter lengths of stay are also attributable to the increasing use of outpatient settings as opposed to hospital admission for an expanding range of procedures such as hernia repairs, gallbladder removal, and cataract surgery.

The growing older population also uses more physician services. Visit rates increase with age among adults aged 65 and older and were more than twice as high as visit rates for children and younger adults in 2006. (See Table 7.4.) Even though women generally make more visits than men, the gender gap practically disappears among older adults.

CHRONIC DISEASES AND CONDITIONS

Chronic diseases are prolonged illnesses such as arthritis, asthma, heart disease, diabetes, and cancer that do not resolve spontaneously and are rarely cured. According to the Centers for Disease Control and Prevention (CDC), in "Chronic Disease Overview" (June 23, 2009, http://www.cdc.gov/nccdphp/index.htm), chronic illnesses account for 70% of all deaths in the United States annually. In 2005 five of the seven leading causes of death among older adults were chronic diseases: heart disease, malignant neoplasms (cancer), cerebrovascular diseases (stroke), chronic lower respiratory diseases, and diabetes mellitus (a condition in which there is increased sugar in the blood and urine because the body is unable to use sugar to produce energy). (See Table 7.5.) Even though other chronic conditions such as arthritis, asthma, and chronic bronchitis are not immediately life threatening, they compromise the quality of life of affected individuals and place an enormous financial burden on individuals, families, and the U.S. health care system.

The prevalence of some chronic conditions such as hypertension and diabetes is increasing in the general population and among older adults. In 2005–06 more than half (53.3%) of people aged 65 and older had hypertension and 18% suffered from diabetes. (See Table 7.6.) The increase in these conditions is largely attributable to increasing rates of obesity, which is implicated in the development of these and many other chronic conditions.

FIGURE 7.1

Percent of people aged 65 and over who reported having good to excellent health, by age, race, and Hispanic origin, 2004–06

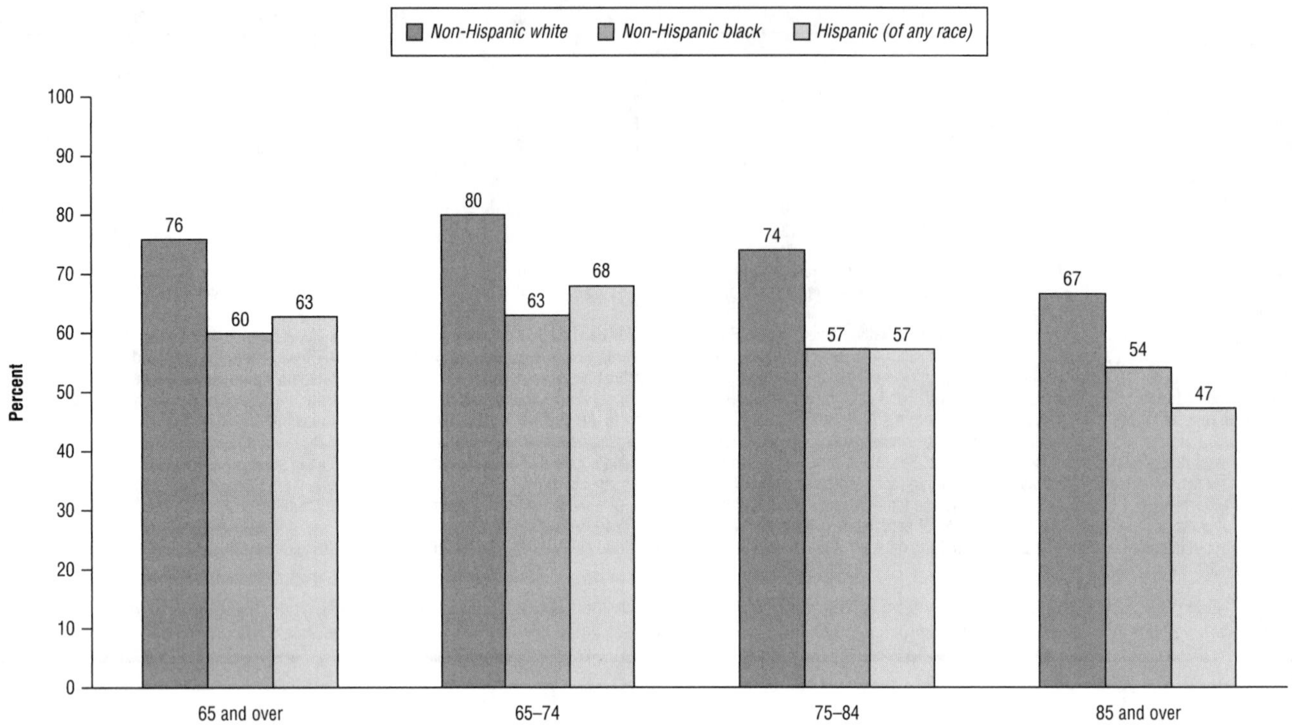

Note: Data are based on a 3-year average from 2004–2006.
Reference population: These data refer to the civilian noninstitutionalized population.

SOURCE: "Percent of People Age 65 and over Who Reported Having Good to Excellent Health, by Age Group and Race and Hispanic Origin, 2004–2006," in *Older Americans 2008: Key Indicators of Well-Being*, Federal Interagency Forum on Aging-Related Statistics, March 2008, http://www.agingstats.gov/agingstatsdotnet/Main_Site/Data/2008_Documents/OA_2008.pdf (accessed April 20, 2009)

Arthritis

The word *arthritis* literally means "joint inflammation," and it is applied to dozens of related diseases known as rheumatic diseases. When a joint (the point where two bones meet) becomes inflamed, swelling, redness, pain, and loss of motion occur. In the most serious forms of the disease, the loss of motion can be physically disabling.

More than 100 types of arthritis have been identified, but four major types affect large numbers of older Americans:

- Osteoarthritis—the most common type, generally affects people as they grow older. Sometimes called degenerative arthritis, it causes the breakdown of bones and cartilage (connective issue attached to bones) and pain and stiffness in the fingers, knees, feet, hips, and back. In the fact sheet "Osteoarthritis" (June 2006, http://www.rheumatology.org/public/factsheets/diseases_and_conditions/osteoarthritis.asp?aud=pat), the American College of Rheumatology reports that about 27 million Americans are affected by osteoarthritis. Furthermore, it estimates that 70% of people over 70 have x-ray evidence of osteoarthritis.
- Fibromyalgia—affects the muscles and connective tissues and causes widespread pain, as well as fatigue, sleep problems, and stiffness. Fibromyalgia also causes "tender points" that are more sensitive to pain than other areas of the body. In "About Fibromyalgia" (2009, http://www.fmaware.org/site/PageServer?pagename=fibromyalgia_affected), the National Fibromyalgia Association estimates that 10 million Americans suffer from this condition.
- Rheumatoid arthritis—an inflammatory form of arthritis caused by a flaw in the body's immune system. The result is inflammation and swelling in the joint lining, followed by damage to bone and cartilage in the hands, wrists, feet, knees, ankles, shoulders, or elbows. The Arthritis Foundation (2009, http://www.arthritis.org/disease-center.php?disease_id=31) indicates that rheumatoid arthritis affects about 1.3 million Americans.
- Gout—an inflammation of a joint caused by an accumulation of a natural substance, uric acid, in the joint, usually the big toe, knee, or wrist. The uric acid forms crystals in the affected joint, causing severe pain and swelling. This form affects more men than women, claiming about a million sufferers.

FIGURE 7.2

Percent of people aged 65 and over who reported having selected chronic conditions, by sex, 2005–06

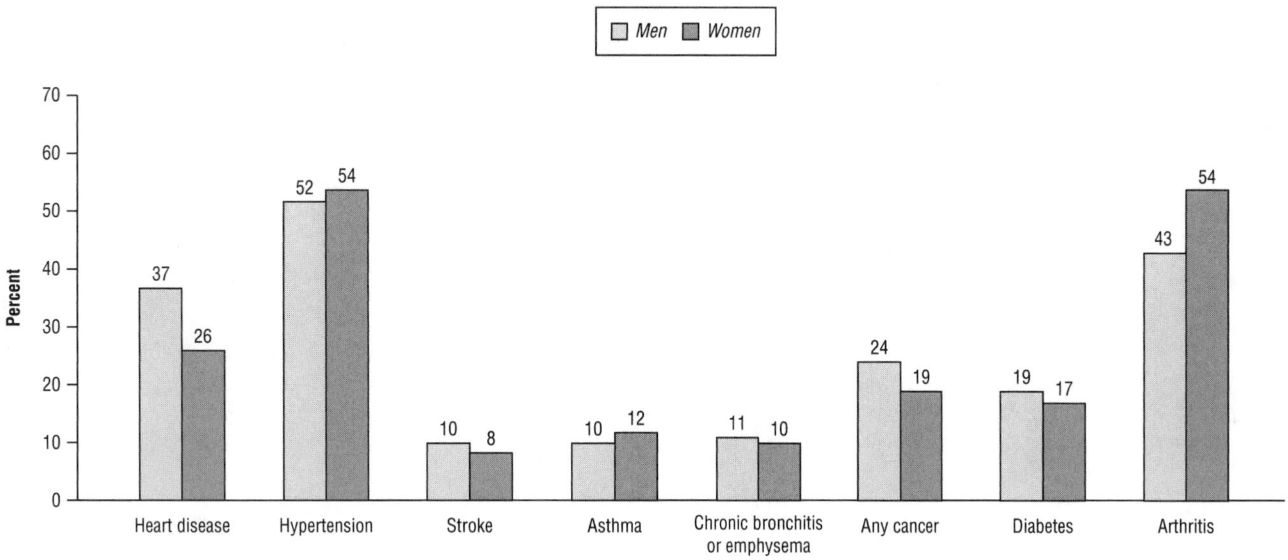

Note: Data are based on a 2-year average from 2005–2006.
Reference population: These data refer to the civilian noninstitutionalized population.

SOURCE: "Percentage of People Age 65 and over Who Reported Having Selected Chronic Conditions, by Sex, 2005–2006," in *Older Americans 2008: Key Indicators of Well-Being*, Federal Interagency Forum on Aging-Related Statistics, March 2008, http://www.agingstats.gov/agingstatsdotnet/Main_Site/Data/2008_Documents/OA_2008.pdf (accessed April 20, 2009)

PREVALENCE. Arthritis is a common problem. In "Quick Stats on Arthritis" (March 29, 2007, http://www.cdc.gov/arthritis/pressroom/index.htm), the CDC reports that in 2007, 46.4 million Americans had been diagnosed with arthritis and that nearly 19 million were disabled by the disease. The CDC predicts in "Data and Statistics" (October 8, 2008, http://www.cdc.gov/arthritis/data_statistics/national_data_nhis.htm) that the total number of people suffering from arthritis will increase to 67 million by 2030.

Arthritis is the leading cause of disability in the United States. Rheumatic and musculoskeletal disorders are the most frequently reported cause of impairment in the adult population, the leading cause of limitation of mobility, and the second leading cause of activity restriction.

Osteoporosis

Osteoporosis is a skeletal disorder characterized by compromised bone strength, which predisposes affected individuals to increased risk of fracture. The National Osteoporosis Foundation (NOF; August 11, 2008, http://www.nof.org/news/index.htm) defines osteoporosis as "about 25% bone loss compared with a healthy young adult or, on a bone density test, 2.5 standard deviations below normal." Even though some bone loss occurs naturally with advancing age, the stooped posture (kyphosis) and loss of height (greater than 1 to 2 inches [2.5 to 5.1 cm]) experienced by many older adults result from vertebral fractures caused by osteoporosis.

According to the NOF, in "Fast Facts on Osteoporosis" (March 16, 2009, http://www.nof.org/osteoporosis/diseasefacts.htm), 10 million Americans have osteoporosis and another 34 million are considered at risk of developing the condition. The NOF describes osteoporosis as "a major public health threat for an estimated 44 million Americans, or 55 percent of the people 50 years of age and older." Like other chronic conditions that disproportionately affect older adults, the prevalence of bone disease and fractures is projected to increase markedly as the population ages.

The NOF reports that one out of two women and one out of four men over the age of 50 will have an osteoporosis-related fracture in their remaining lifetime. The aging of the population and the historic lack of focus on bone health may together cause the number of fractures due to osteoporosis in the United States to exceed 3 million by 2025.

One of the goals of the treatment of osteoporosis is to maintain bone health by preventing bone loss and by building new bone. Another is to minimize the risk and impact of falls, because they can cause fractures. Figure 7.6 shows the pyramid of prevention and treatment of osteoporosis. At its base is nutrition (with adequate intake of calcium, vitamin D, and other minerals), physical exercise, and preventive measures to reduce the risk of falls. The second layer of the pyramid involves identifying and treating diseases that can cause osteoporosis, such as thyroid disease. The peak of the pyramid involves

TABLE 7.2

Limitation of activity caused by chronic conditions, by selected characteristics, selected years 1997–2006

[Data are based on household interviews of a sample of the civilian noninstitutionalized population]

Characteristic	Any activity limitation[a]			
	1997	2004	2005	2006
All ages	Percent of persons			
All ages, age-adjusted[b,c]	13.3	11.9	11.7	11.6
All ages, crude[b]	12.8	11.9	11.8	11.8
Age				
Under 18 years	6.6	7.0	7.0	7.3
Under 5 years	3.5	3.5	4.3	3.9
5–17 years	7.8	8.4	8.0	8.6
18–44 years	7.0	6.0	5.7	5.5
18–24 years	5.1	4.4	4.2	4.1
25–44 years	7.6	6.5	6.3	6.0
45–54 years	14.2	12.5	11.9	12.5
55–64 years	22.2	19.9	19.9	20.0
65 years and over	38.7	34.1	33.8	32.6
65–74 years	30.0	25.5	25.2	24.8
75 years and over	50.2	43.9	43.5	41.6
Sex[c]				
Male	13.1	11.8	11.7	11.6
Female	13.4	11.9	11.6	11.5
Race[c,d]				
White only	13.1	11.6	11.5	11.4
Black or African American only	17.1	15.3	14.1	14.1
American Indian or Alaska Native only	23.1	17.1	16.0	18.4
Asian only	7.5	6.4	6.4	6.6
Native Hawaiian or other Pacific Islander only	[g]	[h]	[h]	[h]
2 or more races	[g]	18.8	19.9	19.7
Black or African American; white	[g]	15.8[h]	10.9[h]	22.2
American Indian or Alaska Native; white	[g]	21.5	26.3	22.7
Hispanic origin and race[c,d]				
Hispanic or Latino	12.8	10.2	10.5	10.0
Mexican	12.5	10.1	11.4	9.8
Not Hispanic or Latino	13.5	12.3	11.9	11.9
White only	13.2	12.1	11.8	11.8
Black or African American only	17.0	15.3	14.2	14.1
Percent of poverty level[c,e]				
Below 100%	25.4	23.0	22.4	22.1
100%–less than 200%	17.9	16.3	16.2	16.4
200% or more	10.1	9.2	9.0	8.7
Hispanic origin and race and percent of poverty level[c,d,e]				
Hispanic or Latino:				
Below 100%	19.2	15.5	15.9	15.7
100%–less than 200%	12.7	10.5	11.0	10.6
200% or more	9.2	7.7	7.9	7.1
Not Hispanic or Latino:				
White only				
Below 100%	27.8	26.2	25.2	25.7
100%–less than 200%	19.2	18.7	18.5	18.8
200% or more	10.4	9.5	9.3	9.0
Black or African American only:				
Below 100%	28.2	27.1	25.3	22.5
100%–less than 200%	19.5	16.6	15.8	16.8
200% or more	10.7	10.3	9.5	9.0

drug therapy for osteoporosis. There are two primary types of drugs used to treat osteoporosis. Antiresorptive agents act to reduce bone loss, and anabolic agents are drugs that build bone. Antiresorptive therapies include use of bisphosphonates, estrogen, selective estrogen receptor modulators, and calcitonin. They reduce bone loss, stabilize the architecture of the bone, and decrease bone turnover.

Diabetes

Diabetes is a disease that affects the body's use of food, causing blood glucose (sugar levels in the blood) to

TABLE 7.2

Limitation of activity caused by chronic conditions, by selected characteristics, selected years 1997–2006 [CONTINUED]

[Data are based on household interviews of a sample of the civilian noninstitutionalized population]

Characteristic	Any activity limitation[a]			
	1997	2004	2005	2006
Geographic region[c]				
Northeast	13.0	11.0	10.6	11.3
Midwest	13.1	12.7	12.8	12.5
South	13.9	12.3	12.0	11.9
West	13.0	11.4	10.9	10.5
Location of residence[c]				
Within MSA[f]	12.7	11.2	11.0	11.1
Outside MSA[f]	15.5	14.9	14.5	14.2

[a]Limitation of activity is assessed by asking respondents a series of questions about limitations in their ability to perform activities usual for their age group because of a physical, mental, or emotional problem(s). The category limitation of activity includes limitations in personal care, routine needs, and other limitations due to a chronic condition.
[b]Includes all other races not shown separately.
[c]Estimates are age-adjusted to the year 2000 standard population using six age groups: Under 18 years, 18–44 years, 45–54 years, 55–64 years, 65–74 years, and 75 years and over. Age-adjusted estimates in this table may differ from other age-adjusted estimates based on the same data and presented elsewhere if different age groups are used in the adjustment procedure.
[d]The race groups, white, black, American Indian or Alaska Native, Asian, Native Hawaiian or other Pacific Islander, and 2 or more races, include persons of Hispanic and non-Hispanic origin. Persons of Hispanic origin may be of any race. Starting with 1999 data, race-specific estimates are tabulated according to the 1997 Revisions to the Standards for the Classification of Federal Data on Race and Ethnicity and are not strictly comparable with estimates for earlier years. The five single-race categories plus multiple-race categories shown in the table conform to the 1997 Standards. Starting with 1999 data, race-specific estimates are for persons who reported only one racial group; the category 2 or more races includes persons who reported more than one racial group. Prior to 1999, data were tabulated according to the 1977 Standards with four racial groups and the Asian only category included Native Hawaiian or other Pacific Islander. Estimates for single-race categories prior to 1999 included persons who reported one race or, if they reported more than one race, identified one race as best representing their race. Starting with 2003 data, race responses of other race and unspecified multiple race were treated as missing, and then race was imputed if these were the only race responses. Almost all persons with a race response of other race were of Hispanic origin.
[e]Percent of poverty level is based on family income and family size and composition using U.S. Census Bureau poverty thresholds. Missing family income data were imputed for 24% of persons in 1997 and 31%–34% in 1999–2006.
[f]MSA is metropolitan statistical area. Starting with 2006 data, MSA status is determined using 2000 census data and the 2000 standards for defining MSAs.
[g]Estimates are considered unreliable.
[h]Data not available.

SOURCE: Adapted from "Table 58. Limitation of Activity Caused by Chronic Conditions, by Selected Characteristics: United States, Selected Years 1997–2006," in *Health, United States, 2008. With Chartbook*, National Center for Health Statistics, 2009, http://www.cdc.gov/nchs/data/hus/hus08.pdf#listtables (accessed May 6, 2009)

become too high. People with diabetes can convert food to glucose, but there is a problem with insulin. In one type of diabetes (insulin-dependent diabetes, or Type 1), the pancreas does not manufacture enough insulin, and in another type (noninsulin-dependent, or Type 2), the body has insulin but cannot use the insulin effectively (this latter condition is called insulin resistance). When insulin is either absent or ineffective, glucose cannot get into the cells to be used for energy. Instead, the unused glucose builds up in the bloodstream and circulates through the kidneys. If the blood-glucose level rises high enough, the excess glucose "spills" over into the urine, causing frequent urination. This leads to an increased feeling of thirst as the body tries to compensate for the fluid lost through urination.

Type 2 diabetes is most often seen in adults and is the most common type of diabetes in the United States. In Type 2 diabetes the pancreas produces insulin, but it is not used effectively and the body resists responding to it. Heredity is a predisposing factor in the genesis of diabetes, but because the pancreas continues to produce insulin in people suffering from Type 2 diabetes, the disease is considered more of a problem of insulin resistance, in which the body is not using the hormone efficiently.

Because diabetes deprives cells of the glucose needed to function properly, several complications can develop to further threaten the lives of diabetics. The healing process of the body is slowed and there is an increased risk of infection. Complications of diabetes include higher risk and rates of heart disease; circulatory problems, especially in the legs, which are sometimes severe enough to require surgery or even amputation; diabetic retinopathy, a condition that can cause blindness; kidney disease that may require dialysis; and dental problems. Close attention to preventive health care, such as regular eye, dental, and foot examinations and control of blood sugar levels, have been shown to prevent or delay some of the consequences of diabetes.

The relatively recent rise in Type 2 diabetes in the United States is in part attributed to rising obesity among adults. Between 1997 and 2008 the percent of adults diagnosed with diabetes increased from 5% to about 8%. (See Figure 7.7.) Of all adult age groups, the highest rate of diagnosed diabetes was among adults aged 65 and older. (See Figure 7.8.) However, these rates may significantly underestimate the true prevalence of diabetes in the United States in view of National Health and Nutrition Survey findings that show sizeable numbers of adults have undiagnosed diabetes.

FIGURE 7.3

Selected chronic conditions causing limitation of activity among working-age adults, by age, 2005–06

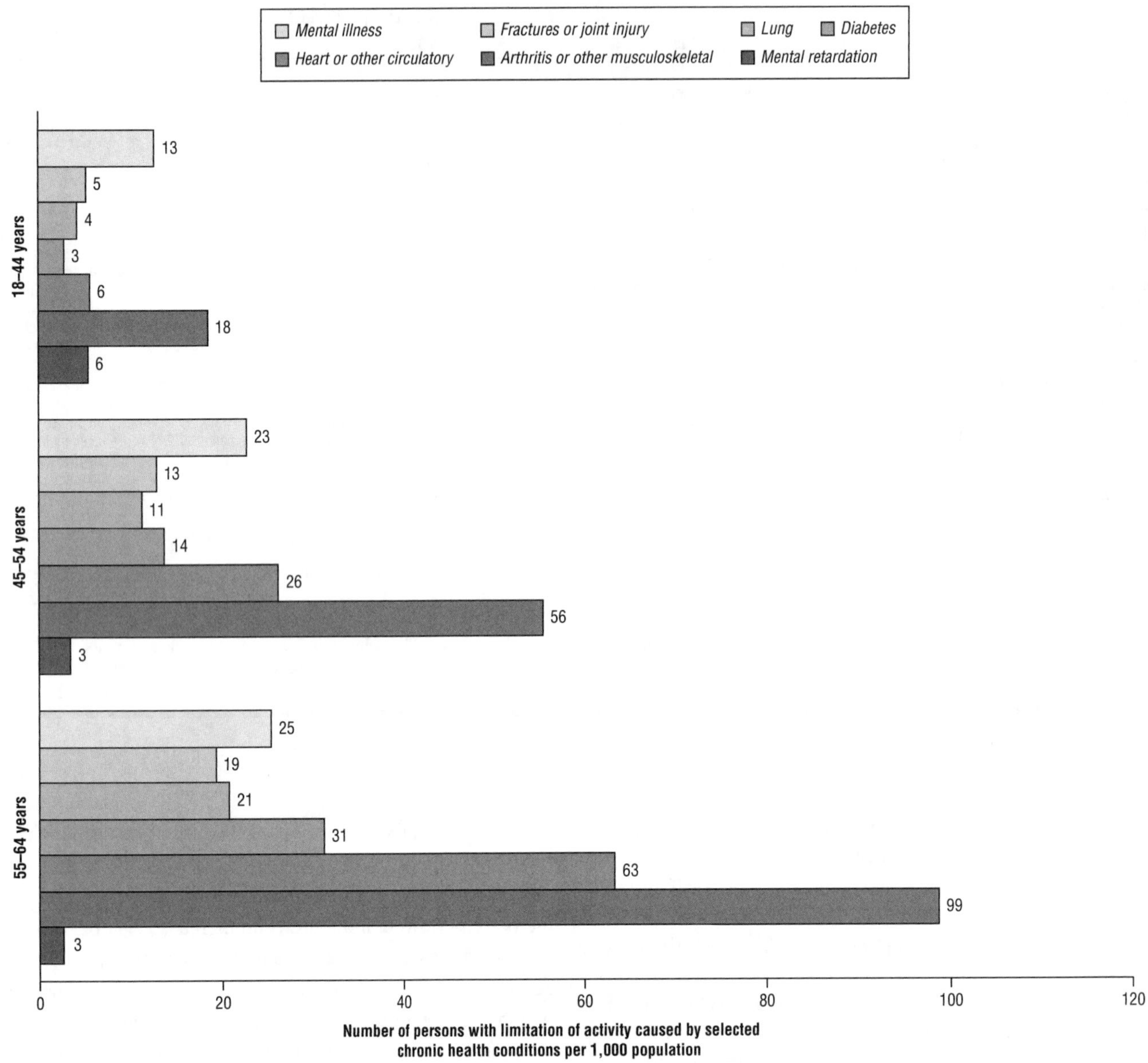

Notes: Data are for the civilian noninstitutionalized population. Adults with more than one chronic health condition causing activity limitation were counted in each category.

SOURCE: "Figure 12. Limitation of Activity Caused by Selected Chronic Health Conditions among Working-Age Adults, by Age: United States, 2004–2005," in *Health, United States, 2008. With Chartbook*, National Center for Health Statistics, 2009, http://www.cdc.gov/nchs/data/hus/hus08.pdf#listtables (accessed May 6, 2009)

Prostate Problems

Prostate problems typically occur after age 50. There are three common prostate disorders: prostatitis (inflammation of the prostate gland), benign prostatic hyperplasia (BPH; noncancerous enlargement of the prostate), and prostate cancer. Prostatitis causes painful or difficult urination and frequently occurs in younger men. BPH can also create problems with urination, but it is most common in older men. According to the National Kidney and Urological Diseases Information Clearinghouse, in *Prostate Enlargement: Benign Prostatic Hyperplasia* (June 2006, http://kidney.niddk.nih.gov/kudiseases/pubs/prostateenlargement/), 50% of men in their 60s and 90% of men in their 80s and 90s suffer from BPH.

Prostate cancer is the second most common cause of cancer death after lung cancer in American men and the sixth leading cause of death of men overall. The Amer-

FIGURE 7.4

Selected chronic conditions causing limitation of activity among older adults, by age, 2005–06

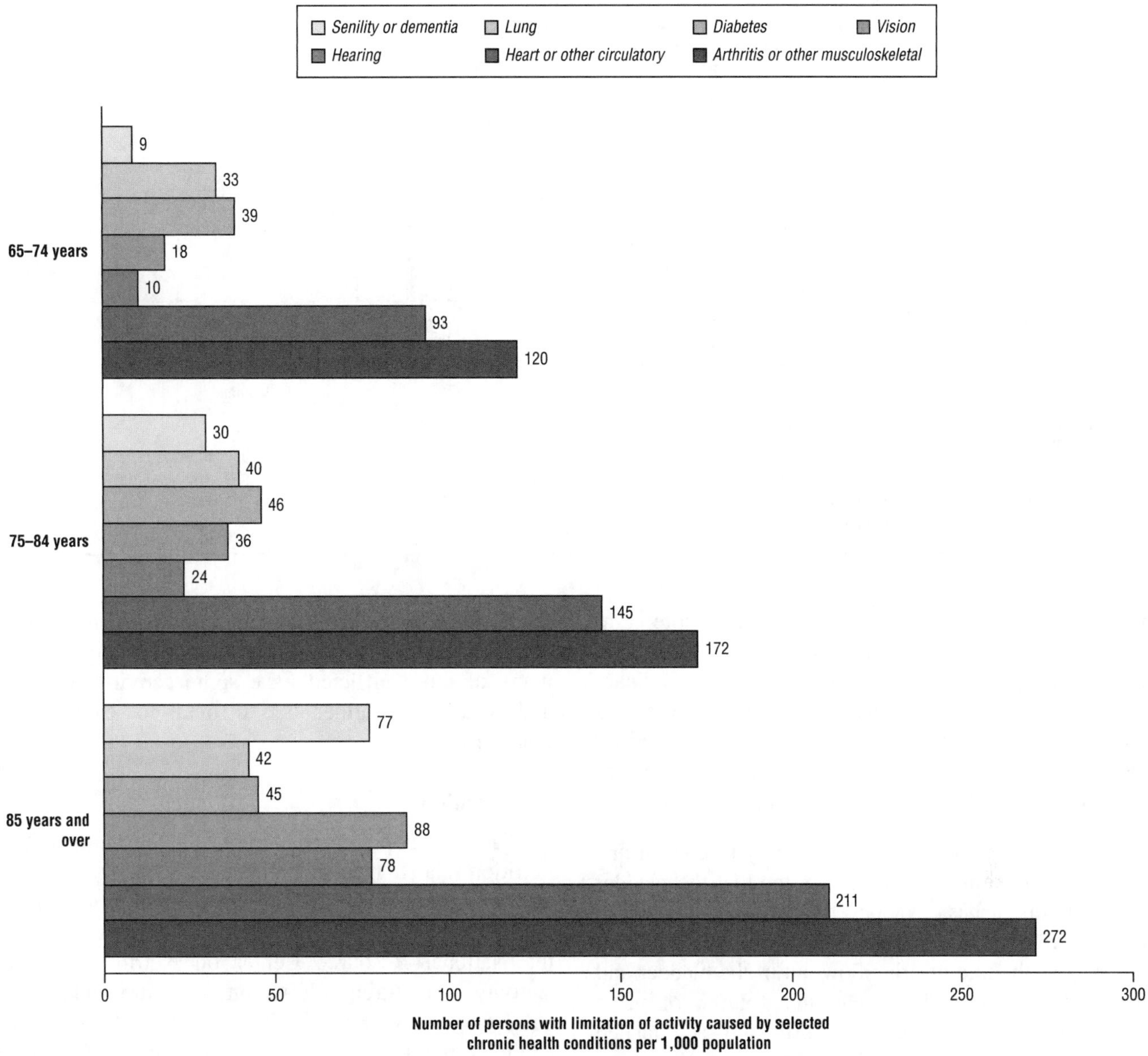

Notes: Data are for the civilian noninstitutionalized population. Adults with more than one chronic health condition causing activity limitation were counted in each category.

SOURCE: "Figure 13. Limitation of Activity Caused by Selected Chronic Health Conditions among Older Adults, by Age: United States, 2005–2006," in *Health, United States, 2008. With Chartbook*, National Center for Health Statistics, 2009, http://www.cdc.gov/nchs/data/hus/hus08.pdf#listtables (accessed May 6, 2009)

ican Cancer Society reports in *Cancer Facts and Figures, 2009* (2009, http://www.cancer.org/downloads/STT/500809web.pdf) that an estimated 192,280 men were diagnosed with prostate cancer in 2009 and 27,360 died from it. When it is diagnosed and treated early, prostate cancer is generally not life threatening, because it progresses slowly and remains localized for a long time. As a result, many men who are diagnosed late in life do not die from this disease.

Urinary Incontinence

Urinary incontinence is the uncontrollable loss of urine that is so severe that it has social or hygienic consequences. In *Urological Diseases in America* (2007, http://kidney.niddk.nih.gov/statistics/uda/Urologic_Diseases_in_America.pdf), the National Institutes of Health reports that between 15% and 50% of women of all ages suffer from incontinence ranging from mild leakage to uncontrollable wetting and that the rate tends to

FIGURE 7.5

Percent of Medicare enrollees aged 65 and older unable to perform certain physical functions, by sex, 1991 and 2005

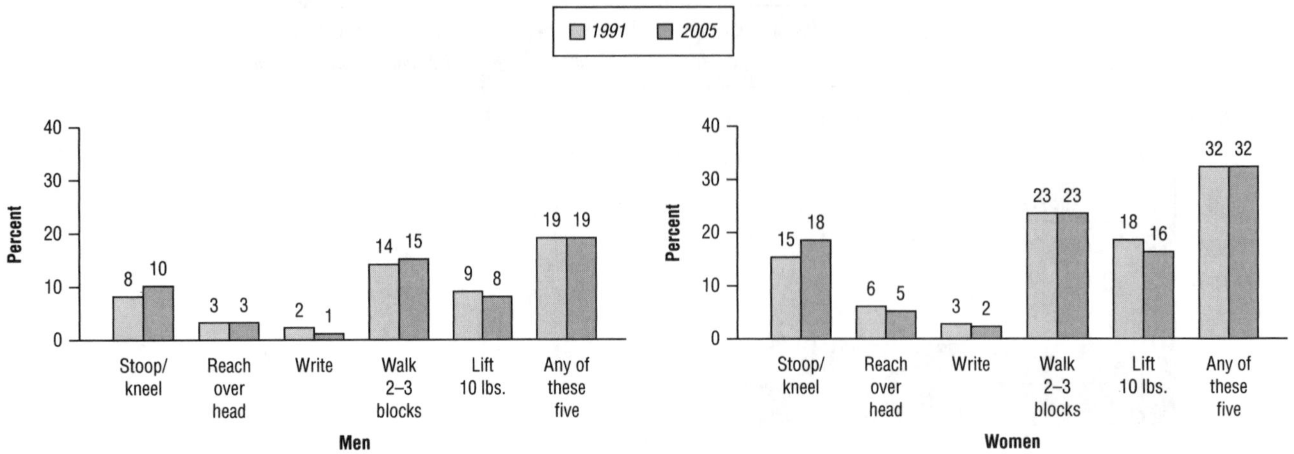

Note: Rates for 1991 are age adjusted to the 2005 population.
Reference population: These data refer to Medicare enrollees.

SOURCE: "Percentage of Medicare Enrollees Age 65 and over Who Are Unable to Perform Certain Physical Functions, by Sex, 1991 and 2005," in *Older Americans 2008: Key Indicators of Well-Being*, Federal Interagency Forum on Aging-Related Statistics, March 2008, http://www.agingstats.gov/agingstatsdotnet/Main_Site/Data/2008_Documents/OA_2008.pdf (accessed April 20, 2009)

increase with advancing age. The problem is more common in women than men, although it affects men of all ages, including 17% of men over the age of 60. Urinary incontinence can lead to many complications. For example, if untreated it increases the risk of developing serious bladder and kidney infections, skin rashes, and pressure sores, and of falls that result from rushing to use the toilet.

Age-related changes affect the ability to control urination. The maximum capacity of urine that the bladder can hold diminishes, as does the ability to postpone urination when a person feels the urge to urinate. As a person ages, the rate of urine flow out of the bladder and through the urethra slows, and the volume of urine remaining in the bladder after urination is finished increases. In women the urethra shortens and its lining becomes thinner as the level of estrogen declines during menopause, decreasing the ability of the urinary sphincter to close tightly. Among older men, the prostate gland enlarges, sometimes blocking the flow of urine through the urethra. Age-related changes increase the risk for incontinence, but it typically occurs as a symptom of an illness or other medical disorder.

Even though urinary incontinence is common, highly treatable, and frequently curable, it is underdiagnosed and often untreated because sufferers do not seek treatment. Many older adults are fearful, embarrassed, or incorrectly assume that incontinence is a normal consequence of growing old. The disorder exacts a serious emotional toll—sufferers are often homebound, isolated, or depressed and are more likely to report their health as fair to poor than their peers. In addition, urinary incontinence is often a reason for institutionalization, because many of those afflicted have some activity limitations and because incontinence is difficult for caregivers to manage.

Malnutrition

The older population is especially vulnerable to nutrition-related health problems. As people age, their energy needs decline, and it is vital for them to consume nutrient-dense foods in a lower calorie diet. According to the National Resource Center on Nutrition, Physical Activity, and Aging (2009, http://nutritionandaging.fiu.edu/aging_network/malfact2.asp), 35% to 50% of older adults in long-term care facilities and up to 65% of older adults in hospitals are at risk for malnutrition. Concerning homebound older adults, an estimated 1 million are also at risk for malnutrition.

Older adults' nutrition may be affected by many factors, including loneliness, depression, a cognitive disorder, a poor appetite, or a lack of transportation. Poor nutrition may arise in response to a major life change such as the death of a spouse. An older adult may forgo meal preparation when there is no longer someone else to cook for or eat with; and a bereaved or frail older adult may not have the stamina or motivation to shop or cook. Malnutrition may also be the result of poverty. When faced with fixed incomes and competing needs, older adults may be forced to choose between buying food or the prescription medications they need.

TABLE 7.3

Hospital discharges, days of care and average length of stay, by selected characteristics, selected years 1980–2006

[Data are based on a sample of hospital records]

Characteristic	1980[a]	1985[a]	1990	1995	2000	2004	2005	2006
				Discharges per 10,000 population				
Total, age-adjusted[b]	**1,744.5**	**1,522.3**	**1,252.4**	**1,180.2**	**1,132.8**	**1,184.3**	**1,162.4**	**1,153.1**
Total, crude	**1,676.8**	**1,484.1**	**1,222.7**	**1,157.4**	**1,128.3**	**1,192.3**	**1,174.4**	**1,168.7**
Age								
Under 18 years	756.5	614.0	463.5	423.7	402.6	430.2	411.0	393.9
Under 1 year	2,317.6	2,137.9	1,915.3	1,977.6	2,027.6	2,065.3	1,949.3	1,818.4
1–4 years	864.6	650.2	466.9	457.1	458.0	458.9	429.7	418.8
5–17 years	609.3	477.4	334.1	290.2	268.6	296.2	286.5	276.0
18–44 years	1,578.8	1,301.2	1,026.6	914.3	849.4	910.8	898.0	906.7
18–24 years	1,570.3	1,297.8	1,065.3	928.9	854.1	863.5	862.4	870.4
25–44 years	1,582.8	1,302.5	1,013.8	909.9	847.9	927.2	910.3	919.3
25–34 years	1,682.9	1,416.9	1,140.3	1,015.0	942.5	1,021.8	1,007.8	1,011.2
35–44 years	1,438.3	1,153.1	868.8	808.0	764.8	841.8	821.5	834.6
45–64 years	1,947.6	1,707.8	1,354.5	1,185.4	1,114.2	1,177.9	1,147.0	1,161.2
45–54 years	1,750.2	1,470.7	1,123.9	984.7	920.8	997.2	964.3	970.5
55–64 years	2,153.6	1,948.0	1,632.6	1,483.4	1,415.0	1,436.3	1,402.4	1,422.1
65 years and over	3,836.9	3,698.0	3,341.2	3,477.4	3,533.6	3,628.9	3,595.6	3,507.9
65–74 years	3,158.4	2,972.6	2,616.3	2,600.0	2,546.0	2,592.3	2,628.9	2,533.6
75 years and over	4,893.0	4,756.1	4,340.3	4,590.7	4,619.6	4,702.2	4,588.4	4,512.6
75–84 years	4,638.6	4,464.2	3,957.0	4,155.7	4,124.4	4,269.7	4,131.7	4,025.9
85 years and over	5,764.6	5,728.9	5,606.3	5,925.1	6,050.9	5,856.7	5,758.1	5,711.4
Sex[b]								
Male	1,543.9	1,382.5	1,130.0	1,048.5	990.8	1,025.7	1,013.0	1,000.5
Female	1,951.9	1,675.6	1,389.5	1,317.3	1,277.3	1,349.0	1,319.6	1,312.3
Sex and age								
Male, all ages	1,390.4	1,240.2	1,002.2	941.7	910.6	964.9	959.0	954.9
Under 18 years	762.6	626.4	463.1	431.3	408.6	436.4	412.2	401.5
18–44 years	950.9	776.9	579.2	507.2	450.0	464.8	471.1	476.8
45–64 years	1,953.1	1,775.6	1,402.7	1,212.0	1,127.4	1,183.6	1,148.8	1,175.7
65–74 years	3,474.1	3,255.2	2,877.6	2,762.2	2,649.1	2,685.0	2,742.6	2,584.3
75–84 years	5,093.5	5,031.8	4,417.3	4,361.1	4,294.1	4,540.5	4,388.1	4,220.3
85 years and over	6,372.3	6,406.9	6,420.9	6,387.9	6,166.6	5,838.3	5,984.1	5,983.5
Female, all ages	1,944.0	1,712.2	1,431.7	1,362.9	1,336.6	1,411.3	1,382.2	1,375.3
Under 18 years	750.2	601.0	464.1	415.7	396.2	423.7	409.8	385.9
18–44 years	2,180.2	1,808.3	1,468.0	1,318.0	1,248.1	1,361.9	1,330.9	1,343.5
45–64 years	1,942.5	1,645.9	1,309.7	1,160.5	1,101.7	1,172.5	1,145.3	1,147.3
65–74 years	2,916.6	2,754.8	2,411.2	2,469.4	2,461.0	2,514.4	2,533.1	2,490.7
75–84 years	4,370.4	4,130.4	3,678.9	4,024.1	4,013.5	4,087.4	3,957.7	3,893.0
85 years and over	5,500.3	5,458.0	5,289.6	5,743.7	6,003.3	5,865.0	5,654.4	5,584.1
Geographic region[b]								
Northeast	1,622.9	1,428.7	1,332.2	1,335.3	1,274.8	1,287.9	1,245.9	1,261.4
Midwest	1,925.2	1,584.7	1,287.5	1,132.8	1,109.2	1,143.9	1,174.9	1,168.0
South	1,814.1	1,569.4	1,325.0	1,252.4	1,209.2	1,255.5	1,202.5	1,198.8
West	1,519.7	1,469.6	1,006.6	967.4	894.0	1,011.5	1,005.9	964.1
				Days of care per 10,000 population				
Total, age-adjusted[b]	13,027.0	10,017.9	8,189.3	6,386.2	5,576.8	5,686.8	5,541.7	5,474.7
Total, crude	**12,166.8**	**9,576.6**	**7,840.5**	**6,201.7**	**5,546.5**	**5,741.2**	**5,620.9**	**5,577.8**
Age								
Under 18 years	3,415.1	2,812.3	2,263.1	1,846.7	1,789.7	1,931.8	1,918.3	1,857.6
Under 1 year	13,213.9	14,141.2	11,484.7	10,834.5	11,524.0	12,434.5	12,131.6	11,624.2
1–4 years	3,333.5	2,280.4	1,700.1	1,525.6	1,482.2	1,416.8	1,355.3	1,405.4
5–17 years	2,698.5	2,049.8	1,633.2	1,240.3	1,172.1	1,281.8	1,300.9	1,239.1
18–44 years	8,323.6	6,294.7	4,676.7	3,517.2	3,093.8	3,349.3	3,305.0	3,360.6
18–24 years	7,174.6	5,287.2	4,015.9	2,987.4	2,679.5	2,817.3	2,819.9	2,889.4
25–44 years	8,861.4	6,685.2	4,895.5	3,676.4	3,225.5	3,532.5	3,472.8	3,524.5
25–34 years	8,497.5	6,688.9	4,939.7	3,536.1	3,161.7	3,427.4	3,434.3	3,462.2
35–44 years	9,386.6	6,680.4	4,844.8	3,812.3	3,281.5	3,627.4	3,507.9	3,581.9
45–64 years	15,969.5	12,015.9	9,139.3	6,574.5	5,515.4	5,915.8	5,717.3	5,793.0
45–54 years	13,167.2	9,692.8	6,996.6	5,162.0	4,374.2	4,911.4	4,711.2	4,667.4
55–64 years	18,895.4	14,369.5	11,722.6	8,671.6	7,290.8	7,352.0	7,124.0	7,333.6
65 years and over	40,983.5	32,279.7	28,956.1	23,736.5	21,118.9	20,486.0	19,882.8	19,197.5
65–74 years	31,470.3	24,373.3	20,878.2	16,847.0	14,389.7	14,051.7	13,985.3	13,170.2
75 years and over	55,788.2	43,812.7	40,090.8	32,478.1	28,518.6	27,148.7	25,939.4	25,413.1
75–84 years	51,836.2	40,521.6	35,995.1	28,947.5	25,397.8	24,540.6	23,155.3	22,671.7
85 years and over	69,332.0	54,782.4	53,616.9	43,305.9	37,537.8	34,110.0	33,071.5	32,165.5

TABLE 7.3

Hospital discharges, days of care and average length of stay, by selected characteristics, selected years 1980–2006 [CONTINUED]

[Data are based on a sample of hospital records]

Characteristic	1980[a]	1985[a]	1990	1995	2000	2004	2005	2006
Sex[b]								
Male	12,475.8	9,792.1	8,057.8	6,239.0	5,358.8	5,411.5	5,301.3	5,208.8
Female	13,662.9	10,340.4	8,404.5	6,548.8	5,809.7	5,996.5	5,828.7	5,764.2
Sex and age								
Male, all ages	10,674.1	8,518.8	6,943.0	5,507.5	4,860.8	5,049.4	4,979.7	4,947.3
Under 18 years	3,473.1	2,942.7	2,335.7	1,998.0	1,955.7	2,015.2	2,006.2	1,968.0
18–44 years	6,102.4	4,746.6	3,517.4	2,729.7	2,175.0	2,255.6	2,282.7	2,375.6
45–64 years	15,894.9	12,290.1	9,434.2	6,822.7	5,704.4	6,123.8	5,773.5	6,004.3
65–74 years	33,697.6	26,220.5	22,515.5	17,697.4	14,897.4	14,423.4	14,502.6	13,262.1
75–84 years	54,723.3	44,087.4	38,257.8	29,642.6	26,616.7	26,458.3	25,106.9	23,972.7
85 years and over	77,013.1	58,609.5	60,347.3	45,263.6	37,765.3	34,025.9	35,179.0	32,604.0
Female, all ages	13,560.1	10,566.3	8,691.1	6,863.4	6,202.7	6,407.7	6,239.5	6,186.8
Under 18 years	3,354.5	2,675.5	2,186.8	1,687.9	1,615.1	1,844.4	1,826.1	1,741.8
18–44 years	10,450.7	7,792.0	5,820.3	4,297.9	4,010.8	4,455.4	4,341.8	4,361.5
45–64 years	16,037.1	11,765.5	8,865.1	6,341.7	5,336.4	5,718.2	5,663.9	5,592.2
65–74 years	29,764.7	22,949.2	19,592.7	16,162.0	13,971.3	13,739.5	13,549.0	13,092.4
75–84 years	50,133.3	38,424.7	34,628.3	28,502.5	24,601.0	23,249.9	21,830.1	21,782.1
85 years and over	65,990.5	53,253.6	51,000.5	42,538.6	37,444.4	34,147.9	32,103.5	31,960.3
Geographic region[b]								
Northeast	14,024.4	11,143.1	10,266.8	8,389.7	7,185.9	6,875.9	6,636.5	6,608.5
Midwest	14,871.9	10,803.6	8,306.5	5,908.8	5,005.3	4,987.1	4,954.3	4,893.5
South	12,713.5	9,642.6	8,204.1	6,659.9	5,925.1	6,141.7	5,830.4	5,844.8
West	9,635.2	8,300.7	5,755.1	4,510.6	4,082.0	4,575.1	4,690.3	4,451.6
				Average length of stay in days				
Total, age-adjusted[b]	7.5	6.6	6.5	5.4	4.9	4.8	4.8	4.7
Total, crude	**7.3**	**6.5**	**6.4**	**5.4**	**4.9**	**4.8**	**4.8**	**4.8**
Age								
Under 18 years	4.5	4.6	4.9	4.4	4.4	4.5	4.7	4.7
Under 1 year	5.7	6.6	6.0	5.5	5.7	6.0	6.2	6.4
1–4 years	3.9	3.5	3.6	3.3	3.2	3.1	3.2	3.4
5–17 years	4.4	4.3	4.9	4.3	4.4	4.3	4.5	4.5
18–44 years	5.3	4.8	4.6	3.8	3.6	3.7	3.7	3.7
18–24 years	4.6	4.1	3.8	3.2	3.1	3.3	3.3	3.3
25–44 years	5.6	5.1	4.8	4.0	3.8	3.8	3.8	3.8
25–34 years	5.0	4.7	4.3	3.5	3.4	3.4	3.4	3.4
35–44 years	6.5	5.8	5.6	4.7	4.3	4.3	4.3	4.3
45–64 years	8.2	7.0	6.7	5.5	5.0	5.0	5.0	5.0
45–54 years	7.5	6.6	6.2	5.2	4.8	4.9	4.9	4.8
55–64 years	8.8	7.4	7.2	5.8	5.2	5.1	5.1	5.2
65 years and over	10.7	8.7	8.7	6.8	6.0	5.6	5.5	5.5
65–74 years	10.0	8.2	8.0	6.5	5.7	5.4	5.3	5.2
75 years and over	11.4	9.2	9.2	7.1	6.2	5.8	5.7	5.6
75–84 years	11.2	9.1	9.1	7.0	6.2	5.7	5.6	5.6
85 years and over	12.0	9.6	9.6	7.3	6.2	5.8	5.7	5.6
Sex[b]								
Male	8.1	7.1	7.1	6.0	5.4	5.3	5.2	5.2
Female	7.0	6.2	6.0	5.0	4.5	4.4	4.4	4.4
Sex and age								
Male, all ages	7.7	6.9	6.9	5.8	5.3	5.2	5.2	5.2
Under 18 years	4.6	4.7	5.0	4.6	4.8	4.6	4.9	4.9
18–44 years	6.4	6.1	6.1	5.4	4.8	4.9	4.8	5.0
45–64 years	8.1	6.9	6.7	5.6	5.1	5.2	5.0	5.1
65–74 years	9.7	8.1	7.8	6.4	5.6	5.4	5.3	5.1
75–84 years	10.7	8.8	8.7	6.8	6.2	5.8	5.7	5.7
85 years and over	12.1	9.1	9.4	7.1	6.1	5.8	5.9	5.4
Female, all ages	7.0	6.2	6.1	5.0	4.6	4.5	4.5	4.5
Under 18 years	4.5	4.5	4.7	4.1	4.1	4.4	4.5	4.5
18–44 years	4.8	4.3	4.0	3.3	3.2	3.3	3.3	3.2
45–64 years	8.3	7.1	6.8	5.5	4.8	4.9	4.9	4.9
65–74 years	10.2	8.3	8.1	6.5	5.7	5.5	5.3	5.3
75–84 years	11.5	9.3	9.4	7.1	6.1	5.7	5.5	5.6
85 years and over	12.0	9.8	9.6	7.4	6.2	5.8	5.7	5.7

TABLE 7.3

Hospital discharges, days of care and average length of stay, by selected characteristics, selected years 1980–2006 [CONTINUED]

[Data are based on a sample of hospital records]

Characteristic	1980[a]	1985[a]	1990	1995	2000	2004	2005	2006
Geographic region[b]								
Northeast	8.6	7.8	7.7	6.3	5.6	5.3	5.3	5.2
Midwest	7.7	6.8	6.5	5.2	4.5	4.4	4.2	4.2
South	7.0	6.1	6.2	5.3	4.9	4.9	4.8	4.9
West	6.3	5.6	5.7	4.7	4.6	4.5	4.7	4.6

[a]Comparisons of data from 1980–1985 with data from subsequent years should be made with caution as estimates of change may reflect improvements in the survey design rather than true changes in hospital use.
[b]Estimates are age-adjusted to the year 2000 standard population using six age groups: under 18 years, 18–44 years, 45–54 years, 55–64 years, 65–74 years, and 75 years and over.
Notes: Excludes newborn infants. Rates are based on the civilian population as of July 1. Starting with *Health, United States, 2003,* rates for 2000 and beyond are based on the 2000 census. Rates for 1990–1999 use population estimates based on the 1990 census adjusted for net underenumeration using the 1990 National Population Adjustment Matrix from the U.S. Census Bureau. Rates for 1990–1999 are not strictly comparable with rates for 2000 and beyond because population estimates for 1990–1999 have not been revised to reflect the 2000 census.

SOURCE: "Table 102. Discharges, Days of Care, and Average Length of Stay in Nonfederal Short-Stay Hospitals, by Selected Characteristics: United States, Selected Years 1980–2006," in *Health, United States, 2008. With Chartbook,* National Center for Health Statistics, 2009, http://www.cdc.gov/nchs/data/hus/hus08.pdf#listtables (accessed May 6, 2009)

Hearing Loss

There are many causes of hearing loss, the most common being age-related changes in the ear's mechanism. Hearing loss is a common problem among older adults and can seriously compromise quality of life. People suffering from hearing loss may withdraw from social contact and are sometimes misdiagnosed as cognitively impaired or mentally ill. In 2006 nearly half (48%) of older men and one-third (35%) of older women reported having trouble hearing. (See Figure 7.9.)

Older adults are often reluctant to admit to hearing problems, and sometimes hearing loss is so gradual that even the afflicted person may not be aware of it for some time. For those who seek treatment, there is an expanding array of devices and services to mitigate the effects of hearing loss. Hearing-impaired people may benefit from high-tech hearing aids, amplifiers for doorbells and telephones, infrared amplifiers, and even companion dogs trained to respond to sounds for their owner.

Vision Changes

Almost no one escapes age-related changes in vision. Over time it becomes increasingly difficult to read small print or thread a needle at the usual distance. For many, night vision declines. This is often caused by a condition called presbyopia (tired eyes) and is a common occurrence. People who were previously nearsighted may actually realize some improvement in eyesight as they become slightly farsighted. In 2006, 16% of men and 18% of women aged 65 and older reported vision problems. (See Figure 7.9.)

Major Eye Diseases

Cataract, glaucoma, age-related macular degeneration, and diabetic retinopathy are the leading causes of vision impairment and blindness in older adults. Cataracts are the leading cause of blindness in the world. Glaucoma is a chronic disease that often requires lifelong treatment to control. Age-related macular degeneration is the most common cause of blindness and vision impairment in Americans aged 60 and older. Diabetic retinopathy is a common complication of diabetes and is considered a leading cause of blindness in the industrialized world.

CATARACTS. A cataract is an opacity, or clouding, of the naturally clear lens of the eye. The prevalence of cataracts increases dramatically with age and most develop slowly over time as they progressively cause cloudy vision and eventually almost complete blindness. Once a clouded lens develops, surgery to remove the affected lens and replace it with an artificial lens is the recommended treatment. The National Eye Institute (NEI) reports in *Vision Problems in the U.S.: Prevalence of Adult Vision Impairment and Age-Related Eye Disease in America* (2008, http://www.preventblindness.net/site/DocServer/VPUS_2008_update.pdf?docID=1561) that cataracts affect more than 22 million Americans aged 40 and older and that by age 80 half of all Americans have cataracts.

GLAUCOMA. Glaucoma is a disease that causes gradual damage to the optic nerve, which carries visual information from the eye to the brain. The loss of vision is not experienced until a significant amount of nerve damage has occurred. Because the onset is gradual and insidious (subtle), as many as half of all people with glaucoma are unaware of having the disease. In *Vision Problems in the U.S.*, the NEI reports that glaucoma affects about 2.3 million Americans aged 40 and older and that its prevalence increases with advancing age. Glaucoma is more common in African-Americans and Hispanics. Among adults aged 65 to 69, the prevalence rate for white women is 1.6%, compared with 4.6% among African-American

TABLE 7.4

Visits to physician office, hospital outpatient departments and emergency departments, by selected characteristics, 1995–2006

[Data are based on reporting by a sample of office-based physicians, hospital outpatient departments, and hospital emergency departments]

Age, sex, and race	All places[a]				Physician offices			
	1995	2000	2003	2006	1995	2000	2003	2006
				Number of visits in thousands				
Total	**860,859**	**1,014,848**	**1,114,504**	**1,123,354**	**697,082**	**823,542**	**906,023**	**901,954**
Under 18 years	194,644	212,165	223,724	231,535	150,351	163,459	169,392	181,560
18–44 years	285,184	315,774	331,015	317,502	219,065	243,011	251,853	234,063
45–64 years	188,320	255,894	301,558	310,667	159,531	216,783	257,258	256,494
45–54 years	104,891	142,233	164,431	164,692	88,266	119,474	138,634	133,402
55–64 years	83,429	113,661	137,126	145,975	71,264	97,309	118,624	123,092
65 years and over	192,712	231,014	258,206	263,649	168,135	200,289	227,520	229,837
65–74 years	102,605	116,505	120,655	124,089	90,544	102,447	106,424	108,063
75 years and over	90,106	114,510	137,552	139,560	77,591	97,842	121,096	121,774
				Number of visits per 100 persons				
Total, age-adjusted[b]	**334**	**374**	**391**	**380**	**271**	**304**	**317**	**305**
Total, crude	**329**	**370**	**390**	**382**	**266**	**300**	**317**	**307**
Under 18 years	275	293	307	315	213	226	232	247
18–44 years	264	291	301	287	203	224	229	212
45–64 years	364	422	442	418	309	358	377	345
45–54 years	339	385	406	384	286	323	343	311
55–64 years	401	481	494	465	343	412	428	392
65 years and over	612	706	753	740	534	612	664	645
65–74 years	560	656	667	665	494	577	588	579
75 years and over	683	766	850	824	588	654	748	719
Sex and age								
Male, age-adjusted[b]	290	325	338	328	232	261	273	262
Male, crude	277	314	329	322	220	251	264	256
Under 18 years	273	302	317	309	209	231	241	242
18–44 years	190	203	203	197	139	148	147	139
45–54 years	275	316	335	328	229	260	280	260
55–64 years	351	428	422	410	300	367	365	344
65–74 years	508	614	632	631	445	539	558	554
75 years and over	711	771	881	810	616	670	777	709
Female, age-adjusted[b]	377	420	442	431	309	345	360	346
Female, crude	378	424	449	440	310	348	368	355
Under 18 years	277	285	297	321	217	221	223	252
18–44 years	336	377	397	377	265	298	309	284
45–54 years	400	451	475	437	339	384	403	359
55–64 years	446	529	561	515	382	453	486	436
65–74 years	603	692	696	693	534	609	613	600
75 years and over	666	763	830	832	571	645	730	725
Race and age[c]								
White, age-adjusted[2]	339	380	399	384	282	315	332	317
White, crude	338	381	404	391	281	316	337	324
Under 18 years	295	306	330	325	237	243	260	263
18–44 years	267	301	308	292	211	239	242	225
45–54 years	334	386	409	379	286	330	352	317
55–64 years	397	480	500	465	345	416	439	402
65–74 years	557	641	653	672	496	568	582	593
75 years and over	689	764	844	820	598	658	747	721

women. Among adults aged 80 and older, glaucoma affects more than 10% of African-American men and Hispanic women.

Routine glaucoma testing is especially important for older people. There is no cure for glaucoma and no way to restore lost vision; however, medication can generally manage the condition. At later stages, laser therapy and surgery are effective in preventing further damage.

AGE-RELATED MACULAR DEGENERATION. Age-related macular degeneration (AMD) is a condition in which the macula, a specialized part of the retina responsible for sharp central and reading vision, is damaged. Symptoms include blurred vision, a dark spot in the center of the vision field, and vertical line distortion. The NEI states in *Vision Problems in the U.S.* that more than 2 million adults aged 50 and older have the advanced form of the condition.

In "Forecasting Age-Related Macular Degeneration through the Year 2050: The Potential Impact of New Treatments" (*Archives of Ophthalmology*, vol. 301, no. 20, May 27, 2009), David B. Rein et al. predict that the prevalence of early AMD will increase substantially, from 9.1 million in 2010 to 17.8 million in 2050. The researchers predict significant increases in early and advanced AMD and resulting visual impairment in the coming decades,

TABLE 7.4

Visits to physician office, hospital outpatient departments and emergency departments, by selected characteristics, 1995–2006 [CONTINUED]

[Data are based on reporting by a sample of office-based physicians, hospital outpatient departments, and hospital emergency departments]

	All placesa				Physician offices			
Age, sex, and race	1995	2000	2003	2006	1995	2000	2003	2006
Black or African American, age-adjusted	309	353	393	397	204	239	261	251
Black or African American, crude	281	324	365	379	178	214	236	235
Under 18 years	193	264	248	299	100	167	131	[d]188
18–44 years	260	257	329	331	158	149	199	180
45–54 years	387	383	445	438	281	269	315	272
55–64 years	414	495	487	515	294	373	349	347
65–74 years	553	656	761	615	429	512	602	458
75 years and over	534	745	774	744	395	568	608	569

[a]All places includes visits to physician offices and hospital outpatient and emergency departments.
[b]Estimates are age-adjusted to the year 2000 standard population using six age groups: under 18 years, 18–44 years, 45–54 years, 55–64 years, 65–74 years, and 75 years and over.
[c]Starting with 1999 data, the instruction for the race item on the Patient Record Form was changed so that more than one race could be recorded. In previous years only one race could be checked. Estimates for race in this table are for visits where only one race was recorded. Because of the small number of responses with more than one racial group checked, estimates for visits with multiple races checked are unreliable and are not presented.
[d]Estimates are considered unreliable.
Notes: Rates for 1995–2000 were computed using 1990-based postcensal estimates of the civilian noninstitutionalized population as of July 1 adjusted for net underenumeration using the 1990 National Population Adjustment Matrix from the U.S. Census Bureau. Starting with 2001 data, rates were computed using 2000-based postcensal estimates of the civilian noninstitutionalized population as of July 1. The difference between rates for 2000 computed using 1990-based postcensal estimates and 2000 census counts is minimal. Rates will be overestimated to the extent that visits by institutiontalized persons are countined in the numerator (for example, hospital emergency department visits by nursing home residents) and institutionalized persons are omitted from the denominator (the civilian noninstitutionalized population).

SOURCE: Adapted from "Table 94. Visits to Physician Offices, Hospital Outpatient Departments, and Hospital Emergency Departments, by Selected Characteristics: United States, Selected Years 1995–2006," in *Health, United States, 2008. With Chartbook*, National Center for Health Statistics, 2009, http://www.cdc.gov/nchs/data/hus/hus08.pdf#listtables (accessed May 6, 2009)

with nearly all these increases attributable to the aging of the U.S. population. However Rein et al. observe that medical therapies, such as adequate intake of zinc, vitamins A and C, and beta carotene, can reduce vision loss and blindness attributable to AMD by as much as 35%, or 565,000 fewer cases of visual impairment and blindness in 2050.

DIABETIC RETINOPATHY. Diabetic retinopathy occurs when the small blood vessels in the retina do not perform properly. Blood vessels can become blocked, break down, leak fluid that distorts vision, and sometimes release blood into the center of the eye, causing blindness. Laser treatment, called photocoagulation, can help reduce the risk of loss of vision in advanced cases of diabetic retinopathy. The disorder is a leading cause of blindness, but is less common among older adults than other types of visual impairment. In *Vision Problems in the U.S.*, the NEI reports that diabetic retinopathy affects 4.4 million Americans aged 40 and older. The prevalence of diabetic retinopathy increases with age, reflecting the higher rates of diabetes in older people.

Oral Health Problems

According to the CDC, in *Oral Health Preventing Cavities, Gum Disease, and Tooth Loss: At a Glance 2009* (2009, http://www.cdc.gov/NCCdphp/publications/aag/pdf/doh.pdf), one-fourth of adults aged 65 and older have lost all their teeth. Figure 7.9 shows that in 2006, 27% of men and 25% of women aged 65 and older had no natural teeth. For people aged 85 and older in 2006, 32% had none of their teeth. (See Table 7.7.) Older adults living in poverty were much more likely to have lost their teeth than those living above poverty, 39.4% and 25.9%, respectively.

Parkinson's Disease

According to the Parkinson's Disease Foundation, in "What Is Parkinson's Disease?" (2009, http://www. pdf.org/en/about_pd), Parkinson's disease (PD) describes a condition marked by a characteristic set of symptoms that affects about 1 million people in the United States. In "Movement Disorders" (*Medical Clinics of North America*, vol. 93, no. 2, March 2009), Meghan K. Harris et al. observe that the prevalence of PD is 1% to 2% in the population aged 65 and older, and up to 4% in individuals older than 85. PD usually begins during the 70s, but up to 10% of those affected are aged 50 or younger.

PD is caused by the death of about half a million brain cells in the basal ganglia. These cells secrete dopamine, a neurotransmitter (chemical messenger), whose function is to allow nerve impulses to move smoothly from one nerve cell to another. These nerve cells, in turn, transmit messages to the muscles of the body to begin movement. When the normal supply of dopamine is reduced, the messages are not correctly sent, and the symptoms—mild tremor (shaking), change in walking, or a decreased arm swing—of PD begin to appear.

TABLE 7.5

Leading causes of death and numbers of deaths, by age, 1980 and 2005

[Data are based on death certificates]

	1980		2005	
Age and rank order	Cause of death	Deaths	Cause of death	Deaths
25–44 years				
*	All causes	108,658	All causes	126,710
1	Unintentional injuries	26,722	Unintentional injuries	30,916
2	Malignant neoplasms	17,551	Malignant neoplasms	18,167
3	Diseases of heart	14,513	Diseases of heart	15,937
4	Homicide	10,983	Suicide	11,540
5	Suicide	9,855	Homicide	7,861
6	Chronic liver disease and cirrhosis	4,782	Human immunodeficiency virus (HIV) disease	5,681
7	Cerebrovascular diseases	3,154	Chronic liver disease and cirrhosis	2,999
8	Diabetes mellitus	1,472	Cerebrovascular dieases	2,806
9	Pneumonia and influenza	1,467	Diabetes mellitus	2,662
10	Congenital anomalies	817	Influenza and pneumonia	1,288
45–64 years				
*	All causes	425,338	All causes	458,831
1	Diseases of heart	148,322	Malignant neoplasms	149,645
2	Malignant neoplasms	135,675	Diseases of heart	103,311
3	Cerebrovascular diseases	19,909	Unintentional injuries	29,192
4	Unintentional injuries	18,140	Diabetes mellitus	16,992
5	Chronic liver disease and cirrhosis	16,089	Chronic lower respiratory diseases	16,724
6	Chronic obstructive pulmonary diseases	11,514	Cerebrovascular dieases	16,409
7	Diabetes mellitus	7,977	Chronic liver disease and cirrhosis	14,643
8	Suicide	7,079	Suicide	11,201
9	Pneumonia and influenza	5,804	Nephritis, nephrotic syndrome and nephrosis	6,169
10	Homicide	4,019	Human immunodeficiency virus (HIV) disease	6,128
65 years and over				
*	All causes	1,341,848	All causes	1,788,189
1	Diseases of heart	595,406	Diseases of heart	530,926
2	Malignant neoplasms	258,389	Malignant neoplasms	388,322
3	Cerebrovascular diseases	146,417	Cerebrovascular dieases	123,881
4	Pneumonia and influenza	45,512	Chronic lower respiratory diseases	112,716
5	Chronic obstructive pulmonary diseases	43,587	Alzheimer's disease	70,858
6	Atherosclerosis	28,081	Influenza and pneumonia	55,453
7	Diabetes mellitus	25,216	Diabetes mellitus	55,222
8	Unintentional injuries	24,844	Unintentional injuries	36,729
9	Nephritis, nephrotic syndrome, and nephrosis	12,968	Nephritis, nephrotic syndrome and nephrosis	36,416
10	Chronic liver disease and cirrhosis	9,519	Septicemia	26,243

*Category not applicable.

SOURCE: Adapted from "Table 31. Leading Causes of Death and Numbers of Deaths, by Age: United States, 1980 and 2005," in *Health, United States, 2008. With Chartbook*, National Center for Health Statistics, 2009, http://www.cdc.gov/nchs/data/hus/hus08.pdf#listtables (accessed May 6, 2009)

TABLE 7.6

Percentage of people aged 65 and over who reported having selected chronic conditions, by sex, 2005–06

	Heart disease	Hypertension	Stroke	Asthma	Chronic bronchitis or emphysema	Any cancer	Diabetes	Arthritis
	Percent							
Total	**30.9**	**53.3**	**9.3**	**10.6**	**10.0**	**21.1**	**18.0**	**49.5**
Men	36.8	52.0	10.4	9.5	10.6	23.6	19.1	43.1
Women	26.4	54.3	8.4	11.5	9.5	19.3	17.3	54.4
White, not Hispanic or Latino	32.1	51.3	8.9	10.5	10.7	23.4	16.0	50.4
Black, not Hispanic or Latino	26.2	70.4	15.6	12.3	6.0	11.5	28.8	55.1
Hispanic or Latino	22.2	53.8	6.5	9.0	6.4	12.1	25.3	39.7

Note: Data are based on a 2-year average from 2005–2006.
Reference population: These data refer to the civilian noninstitutionalized population.

SOURCE: Table 16a. Percentage of People Age 65 and over Who Reported Having Selected Chronic Conditions, by Sex, 2005–2006, in *Older Americans 2008: Key Indicators of Well-Being*, Federal Interagency Forum on Aging-Related Statistics, March 2008, http://www.agingstats.gov/agingstatsdotnet/Main_Site/Data/2008_Documents/OA_2008.pdf (accessed April 20, 2009)

FIGURE 7.6

The osteoporosis pyramid for prevention and treatment

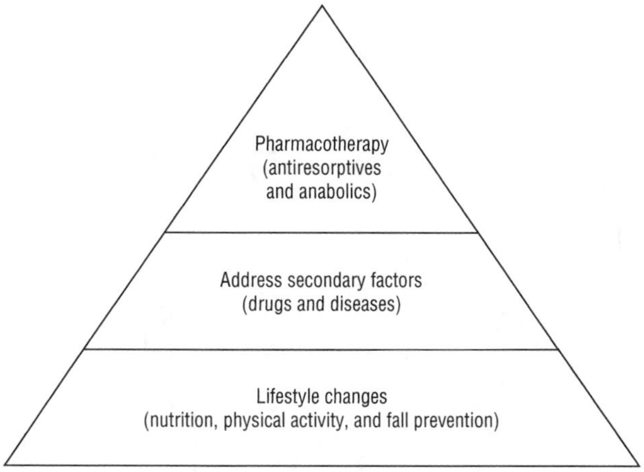

Note:
The base of the pyramid: The first step in the prevention and treatment of osteoporosis and the prevention of fractures is to build a foundation of nutrition and lifestyle measures that maximize bone health. The diet should not only be adequate in calcium and vitamin D, but should have a healthy balance of other nutrients. A weight-bearing exercise program should be developed. Cigarette smoking and excessive alcohol use must be avoided. In the older individual, at high risk for fractures, the changes in lifestyle would include a plan not only to maximize physical activity, but also to minimize the risk of falls. The use of hip protectors can be considered in some high-risk patients. Diseases that increase the risk of falls by causing visual impairment, postural hypotension (a drop in blood pressure on standing, which leads to dizziness), or poor balance should be treated. Drugs that cause bone loss or increase the risk of falls should be avoided or given at the lowest effective dose.

The second level of the pyramid: The next step is to identify and treat diseases that produce secondary osteoporosis or aggravate primary osteoporosis. These measures are the foundation upon which specific pharmacotherapy is built and should never be forgotten.

The third level of the pyramid: If there is sufficiently high risk of fracture to warrant pharmacotherapy, the patient is usually started on antiresorptives. Anabolic agents are used in individuals in whom antiresorptive therapy is not adequate to prevent bone loss or fractures.

SOURCE: Figure 9-1. The Osteoporosis Pyramid for Prevention and Treatment," in *Bone Health and Osteoporosis: A Report of the Surgeon General*, U.S. Department of Health and Human Services, Public Health Service, Office of the Surgeon General, October 14, 2004, http://www.surgeongeneral.gov/library/bonehealth/chapter_9.html#APyramidApproach (accessed May 7, 2009)

The four early warning signs of PD are tremors, muscle stiffness, unusual slowness (bradykinesia), and a stooped posture. Medications can control initial symptoms, but over time they become less effective. As the disease worsens, patients develop more severe tremors, causing them to fall or jerk uncontrollably. (The jerky body movements PD patients experience are known as dyskinesias.) At other times, rigidity sets in, rendering them unable to move. About one-third of patients also develop dementia, an impairment of cognition.

TREATMENT OF PARKINSON'S DISEASE. Management of PD is individualized and includes not only drug therapy but also daily exercise. Exercise can often lessen the rigidity of muscles, prevent weakness, and improve the ability to walk.

The main goal of drug treatment is to restore the chemical balance between dopamine and another neurotransmitter, acetylcholine. Most patients are given levodopa (L-dopa), a compound that the body converts into dopamine. Treatment with L-dopa does not, however, slow the progressive course of the disease or even delay the changes in the brain PD produces, and it may produce some unpleasant side effects such as dyskinesias.

INFECTIOUS DISEASES

Infectious (contagious) diseases are caused by microorganisms—viruses, bacteria, parasites, or fungi—that are transmitted from one person to another through casual contact, such as with the transmittal of influenza, through bodily fluids, such as with the transmittal of HIV, or from contaminated food, air, or water supplies. The CDC reports that in 2005 pneumonia and influenza remained among the top 10 causes of death for older adults, responsible for 55,453 deaths of people aged 65 and older. (See Table 7.5.) Influenza-related deaths can result from pneumonia as well as from exacerbation of chronic diseases.

Influenza

Influenza (flu) is a contagious respiratory disease caused by a virus. The virus is expelled by an infected individual in droplets into the air and may be inhaled by anyone nearby. It can also be transmitted by direct hand contact. The flu primarily affects the lungs, but the whole body experiences symptoms. Influenza is an acute (short-term) illness characterized by fever, chills, weakness, loss of appetite, and aching muscles in the head, back, arms, and legs. Influenza infection may also produce a sore throat, a dry cough, nausea, and burning eyes. The accompanying fever rises quickly—sometimes reaching 104 degrees Fahrenheit (40 degrees Celsius)—but usually subsides after two or three days. Influenza leaves the patient exhausted.

For healthy individuals, the flu is typically a moderately severe illness, with most adults back to work or school within a week. For the very old and older people who are not in good general health, however, the flu can be severe and even fatal. Complications such as secondary bacterial infections may develop, taking advantage of the body's weakened condition and lowered resistance. The most common bacterial complication is pneumonia, affecting the lungs, but sinuses, bronchi (larger air passages of the lungs), and inner ears can also become secondarily infected with bacteria. Less common but serious complications include viral pneumonia, encephalitis (inflammation of the brain), acute renal (kidney) failure, and nervous system disorders. These complications can be fatal.

Influenza can be prevented by inoculation with a current influenza vaccine, which is formulated annually

FIGURE 7.7

Prevalence of diagnosed diabetes among adults aged 18 and over, 1997–March 2008

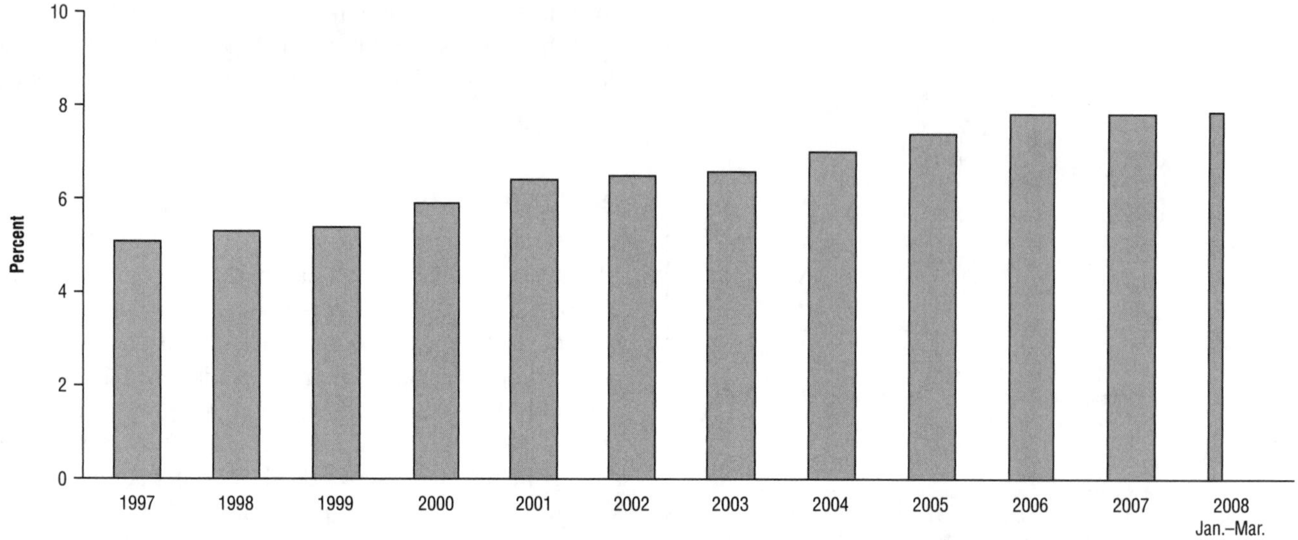

Notes: Prevalence of diagnosed diabetes is based on self-report of ever having been diagnosed with diabetes by a doctor or other health professional. Persons reporting "borderline" diabetes status and women reporting diabetes only during pregnancy were not coded as having diabetes in the analyses. The analyses excluded persons with unknown diabetes status (about 0.1% of respondents each year). Beginning with the 2003 data, the National Health Interview Survey (NHIS) transitioned to weights derived from the 2000 census. In this early release, estimates for 2000–2002 were recalculated using weights derived from the 2000 census.
Data source: Data are based on household interviews of a sample of the civilian noninstitutionalized population.

SOURCE: "Figure 14.1. Prevalence of Diagnosed Diabetes among Adults Aged 18 Years and over: United States, 1997–March 2008," in *Early Release of Selected Estimates Based on Data from the January–March 2008 National Health Interview Survey*, Centers for Disease Control and Prevention, National Center for Health Statistics, September 2008, http://www.cdc.gov/nchs/data/nhis/earlyrelease/200809_14.pdf

to contain the influenza viruses expected to cause the flu the upcoming year. Immunization produces antibodies to the influenza viruses, which become most effective after one or two months. The CDC advises that older adults get flu shots early in the fall, because peak flu activity usually occurs around the beginning of the new calendar year. In 2006, 67% of non-Hispanic white, 45% of Hispanic, and 47% of non-Hispanic African-American older adults reported receiving influenza shots within the past 12 months. (See Figure 7.10.) In "Questions & Answers: Seasonal Flu Shot" (July 16, 2008, http://www.cdc.gov/flu/about/qa/flushot.htm), the CDC reports that immunization reduces hospitalization by 30% to 70% among noninstitutionalized older adults. Among nursing home residents, the flu shot reduces the risk of hospitalization by 50% to 60% and the risk of death by 80%.

The year 2009 saw the beginning of the threat of H1N1 (sometimes called the swine flu), which was eventually classified as a pandemic influenza (a virulent human flu that causes a global outbreak of serious illness from a new strain of an influenza virus). The World Health Organization reports in "Pandemic (H1N1) 2009—Update 58" (http://www.who.int/csr/don/2009_07_06/en/index.html) that as of July 6, 2009, H1N1 had been reported in 135 countries. According to the U.S. Department of Health and Human Services, in "What Age Groups Are Most Likely to Be Affected during an Influenza Pandemic?" (April 3, 2009, http://www.pandemicflu.gov/faq/pandemicinfluenza/1080.html), the most recent pandemic influenzas in 1957 and 1968 seriously affected infants, older adults and people with underlying health problems, whereas during the 1918 pandemic influenza most deaths were of young adults. In August 2009 the CDC (http://www.cdc.gov/h1n1flu/qa.htm) reported that it began gathering data on the H1N1 outbreak in mid-April. It observed, "The information analyzed by CDC supports the conclusion that 2009 H1N1 flu has caused greater disease burden in people younger than 25 years of age than older people. At this time, there are few cases and few deaths reported in people older than 64 years old, which is unusual when compared with seasonal flu." The CDC also noted that people with "previously recognized high risk medical conditions from seasonal influenza appear to be associated with increased risk of complications from this 2009 H1N1. These underlying conditions include asthma, diabetes, suppressed immune systems, heart disease, kidney disease, [and] neurocognitive and neuromuscular disorders."

Pneumonia

Pneumonia is a serious lung infection. Symptoms of pneumonia are fever, chills, cough, shortness of breath,

FIGURE 7.8

Prevalence of diagnosed diabetes among adults aged 18 and over, by age group and sex, January–March 2008

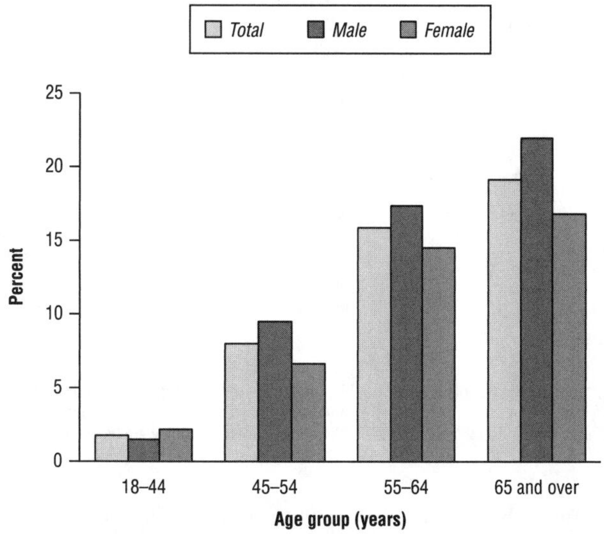

Notes: Prevalence of diagnosed diabetes is based on self-report of ever having been diagnosed with diabetes by a doctor or other health professional. Persons reporting "borderline"diabetes status and women reporting diabetes only during pregnancy were not coded as having diabetes in the analyses. The analyses excluded 6 persons (0.1%) with unknown diabetes status.
Data source: Data are based on household interviews of a sample of the civilian noninstitutionalized population.

SOURCE: "Figure 14.2. Prevalence of Diagnosed Diabetes among Adults Aged 18 Years and over, by Age Group and Sex: United States, 1997–March 2008," in *Early Release of Selected Estimates Based on Data from the January–September 2008 National Health Interview Survey*, Centers for Disease Control and Prevention, National Center for Health Statistics, September 2008, http://www.cdc.gov/nchs/data/nhis/earlyrelease/200809_14.pdf

FIGURE 7.9

Percentage of people aged 65 and over who reported having any trouble hearing, any trouble seeing, or no natural teeth, by sex, 2006

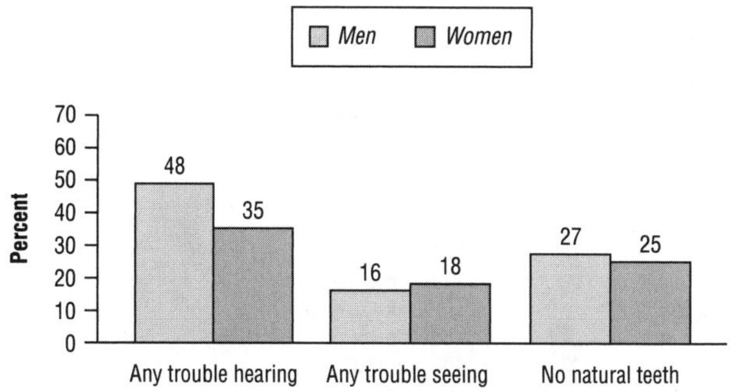

Note: Respondents were asked "Which statement best describes your hearing without a hearing aid: good, a little trouble, a lot of trouble, deaf?" For the purposes of this indicator the category "Any trouble hearing" includes "a little trouble, a lot of trouble, and deaf." Regarding their vision, respondents were asked "Do you have any trouble seeing, even when wearing glasses or contact lenses?" The category "Any trouble seeing" also includes those who in a subsequent question report themselves as blind. Lastly, respondents were asked, in one question, "Have you lost all of your upper and lower natural (permanent) teeth?"
Reference population: These data refer to the civilian noninstitutionalized population.

SOURCE: "Percentage of People Age 65 and over Who Reported Having Any Trouble Hearing, Any Trouble Seeing, or No Natural Teeth, by Sex, 2006," in *Older Americans 2008: Key Indicators of Well-Being*, Federal Interagency Forum on Aging-Related Statistics, March 2008, http://www.agingstats.gov/agingstatsdotnet/Main_Site/Data/2008_Documents/OA_2008.pdf (accessed April 20, 2009)

chest pain, and increased sputum production. Pneumonia may be caused by viruses, bacteria, or fungi; however, the pneumococcus bacterium is the most important cause of serious pneumonia.

In older adults pneumococcal pneumonia is a common cause of hospitalization and death. Joseph P. Lynch and George G. Zhanel indicate in "Streptococcus pneumoniae: Epidemiology, Risk Factors, and Strategies for Prevention" (*Seminars in Respiratory and Critical Care Medicine*, vol. 30, no. 2, April 2009) that there are 45 to 90 cases per 100,000 in adults aged 65 and older per year. About one-quarter of adults aged 65 and older who contract pneumococcal pneumonia develop bacteremia (bacteria in the blood), and as many as 30% of older adults who develop bacteremia die.

Older adults are two to three times more likely than other adults to develop pneumococcal infections. A single vaccination can prevent most cases of pneumococcal pneumonia. The CDC recommends that all people aged 65 and older receive the pneumonia vaccine, and since 1998 an increasing proportion of the older population reports having been vaccinated. (See Figure 7.10.) In 2006, 62% of non-Hispanic white, 36% of non-Hispanic African-American, and 33% of Hispanic older adults had received a pneumococcal vaccination.

MANDATORY IMMUNIZATION FOR NURSING HOME RESIDENTS. Nursing home residents are required to be immunized against influenza and pneumonia; nursing homes that fail to enforce this requirement risk losing reimbursement from the Medicare and Medicaid programs. The regulation, which was issued by the Centers for Medicare and Medicaid Services in August 2005, intends to ensure that the most vulnerable older adults receive their flu and pneumococcal vaccinations. People aged 65 and older are among the most vulnerable, especially those in the close quarters of nursing homes, where infection can spread more easily.

DISABILITY IN THE OLDER POPULATION

Americans are not only living longer but also are developing fewer chronic diseases and disabilities. The current cohort (a group of individuals that shares a common characteristic such as birth years and is studied over time) of older Americans are defying the stereotype that

TABLE 7.7

Percentage of people aged 65 and over who reported having any trouble hearing, any trouble seeing, or no natural teeth, by selected characteristics, 2006

Sex	Age and poverty status	Any trouble hearing	Any trouble seeing	No natural teeth
		Percent		
Both sexes	65 and over	40.5	17.4	25.9
	65–74	31.9	13.6	22.8
	75–84	46.3	20.0	28.5
	85 and over	61.8	26.5	32.0
	Below poverty	36.6	26.0	39.4
	Above poverty	42.1	16.4	25.9
Men	65 and over	47.7	16.1	26.8
	65–74	40.8	11.9	22.8
	75–84	54.6	19.4	32.7
	85 and over	66.3	30.7	30.6
Women	65 and over	35.1	18.4	25.1
	65–74	24.3	15.1	22.7
	75–84	40.3	20.4	25.5
	85 and over	59.8	24.6	32.6

Note: Respondents were asked "Which statement best describes your hearing without a hearing aid: good a little trouble, a lot of trouble, deaf?" For the purposes of this indicator the category "Any trouble hearing" includes "a little trouble, a lot of trouble, and deaf." Regarding their vision, respondents were asked "Do you have any trouble seeing, even when wearing glasses or contact lenses?" and the category "Any trouble seeing" includes those who in a subsequent question report themselves as blind. Lastly, respondents were asked, in one question, "Have you lost all of your upper and lower natural (permanent) teeth?"
Reference population: These data refer to the civilian noninstitutionalized population.

SOURCE: "Table 17a. Percentage of People Age 65 and over Who Reported Having Any Trouble Hearing, Any Trouble Seeing, or No Natural Teeth, by Selected Characteristics, 2006," in *Older Americans 2008: Key Indicators of Well-Being*, Federal Interagency Forum on Aging-Related Statistics, March 2008, http://www.agingstats.gov/agingstatsdotnet/Main_Site/Data/2008_Documents/OA_2008.pdf (accessed April 20, 2009)

aging is synonymous with increasing disability and dependence.

In "Recent Declines in Chronic Disability in the Elderly U.S. Population: Risk Factors and Future Dynamics" (*Annual Review of Public Health*, vol. 29, April 2008), Kenneth G. Manton of Duke University reports on data from the 1982 and 2004–05 National Long-Term Care Surveys, which surveyed approximately 20,000 Medicare enrollees. Manton notes that the proportion of Americans aged 65 and older with a chronic disability significantly declined about 2.2% per year during this period due to improved nutrition, sanitation, and education. However, he cautions that obesity may threaten the downward trend in disability. Obesity increases the risk of developing potentially disabling chronic diseases such as heart disease, Type 2 diabetes, high blood pressure, stroke, osteoarthritis, respiratory problems, and some forms of cancer.

DRUG USE AMONG OLDER ADULTS

According to the National Institute on Drug Abuse, in "Trends in Prescription Drug Abuse" (July 22, 2008, http://www.nida.nih.gov/ResearchReports/Prescription/prescription5.html), in 2008 adults aged 65 and older made up 13% of the population, yet accounted for approximately one-third of all medications prescribed in the United States. Dima M. Qato et al. find in "Use of Prescription and Over-the-Counter Medications and Dietary Supplements among Older Adults in the United States" (*Journal of the American Medical Association*, vol. 300, no. 24, December 2008) that 29% of older adults use at least five prescription drugs and about 70% of older adults who take prescription medications also use over-the-counter (nonprescription) drugs, dietary supplements, or both. The researchers explain that "several factors have likely contributed to this increase in the rate of [the use of five or more medications] among older adults over the last decade. These include intensification of therapy for common chronic medical conditions (e.g., diabetes, cardiovascular disease), increased access to medications because of policy changes (e.g., Medicare Part D and assistance programs), and growth of the generic drug market." Qato et al. conclude that older adults are not only the largest per capita consumers of prescription medications but also are at high risk for untoward medication-related interactions.

Prescription drug costs have skyrocketed since the early 1990s. In 2004 the average cost per person was $2,107. (See Figure 7.11.) Out-of-pocket costs for prescription drugs have increased, creating serious financial hardships for many older adults. Historically, Medicare did not cover most outpatient prescription drugs; however, beginning in January 2006 it started covering prescription drugs. It pays for brand-name and generic drugs and offers a choice of prescription drug plans to Medicare beneficiaries. The cost, or monthly premium, for Medicare prescription drug coverage varies depending on the plan—whether the plan has a deductible and the amount of coinsurance or co-payment for each prescription.

Older Adults Respond Differently to Drugs

Many factors influence the efficacy, safety, and success of drug therapy with older patients. These factors

FIGURE 7.10

Percentage of adults aged 65 and older who reported having been vaccinated against influenza and pneumococcal disease, by race and Hispanic origin, 1989–2006

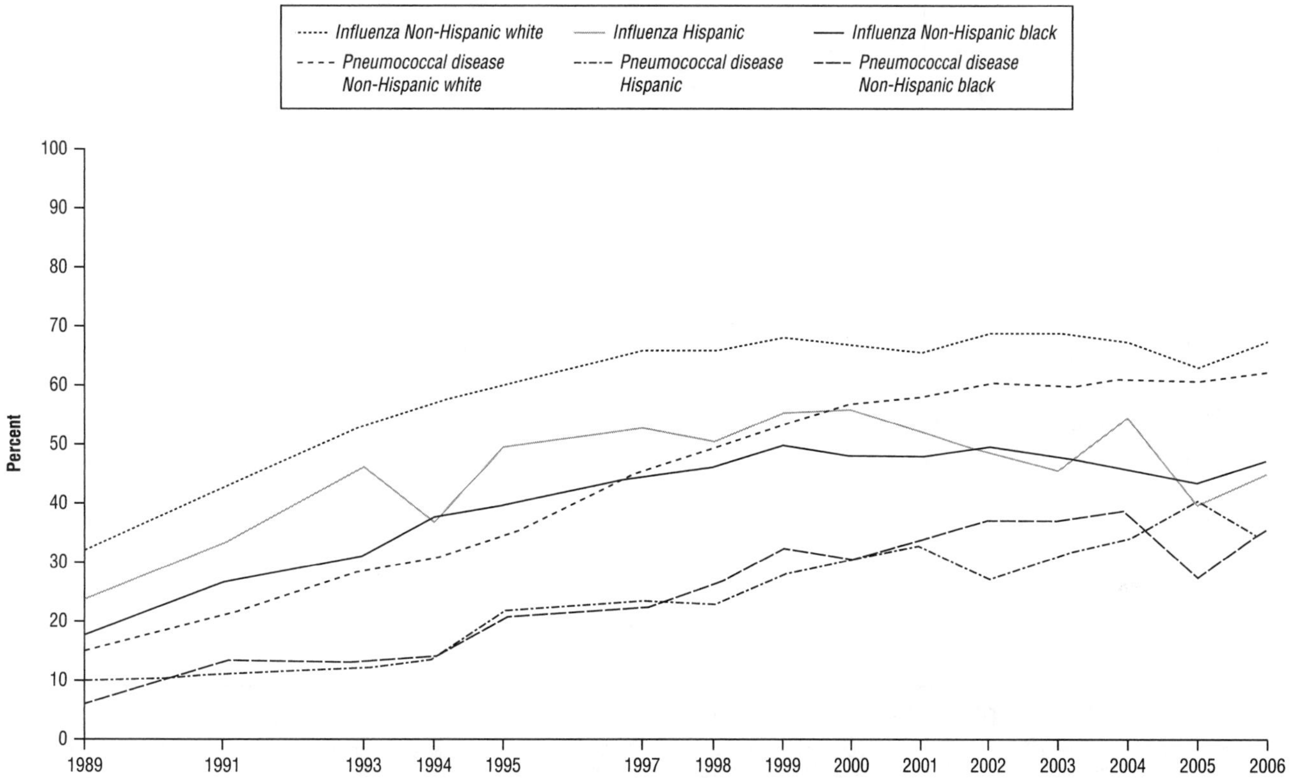

Note: For influenza, the percentage vaccinated consists of people who reported having a flu shot during the past 12 months and does not include receipt of nasal spray flu vaccinations. For pneumococcal disease, the percentage refers to people who reported ever having a pneumonia vaccination.
Reference population: These data refer to the civilian noninstitutionalized population.

SOURCE: "Percentage of People Age 65 and over Who Reported Having Been Vaccinated against Influenza and Pneumococcal Disease, by Race and Hispanic Origin, Selected Years, 1989–2006," in *Older Americans 2008: Key Indicators of Well-Being*, Federal Interagency Forum on Aging-Related Statistics, March 2008, http://www.agingstats.gov/agingstatsdotnet/Main_Site/Data/2008_Documents/OA_2008.pdf (accessed April 20, 2009)

include the effects of aging on pharmacokinetics—the absorption, distribution, metabolism, and excretion of drugs. Of the four, absorption is the least affected by aging. In older people, absorption is generally complete, just slower. The distribution of most medications is related to body weight and composition changes that occur with aging such as decreased lean muscle mass, increased fat mass, and decreased total body water.

Health professionals who care for older adults know that drug dosages must often be modified based on changing organ function and estimates of lean body mass. They coined the adage "start low and go slow" to guide prescribing drugs for older adults. For example, some initial doses of drugs should be lower because older adults have decreased total body water, which might increase the concentration of the drug. Fat-soluble drugs may also have to be administered in lower doses because they may accumulate in fatty tissues, resulting in longer durations of action. The mechanism used to clear a drug via metabolism in the liver or clearance (excretion) through the kidneys changes with aging and is affected by interactions with other medications. Pharmacodynamics (tissue sensitivity to drugs) also changes with advancing age. Among older adults, the complete elimination of a drug from body tissues, including the brain, can take weeks longer than it might in younger people because of a combination of pharmacokinetic and pharmacodynamic effects.

Adherence, Drug-Drug Interactions, and Polypharmacy

Adherence (taking prescription medications regularly and correctly) is a challenge for older people who may suffer from memory loss, impaired vision, or arthritis. Abigail Flinders et al. note in "Prescribing for Older People" (*Nursing Older People*, vol. 21, no. 2, March 2009) that about half of older adults fail to take their medications at the right times and in the right amounts. Strategies to improve adherence include weekly pill

FIGURE 7.11

Average annual prescription drug costs and sources of payment for noninstitutionalized Medicare enrollees aged 65 and older, in 2002 dollars, 1992–2004

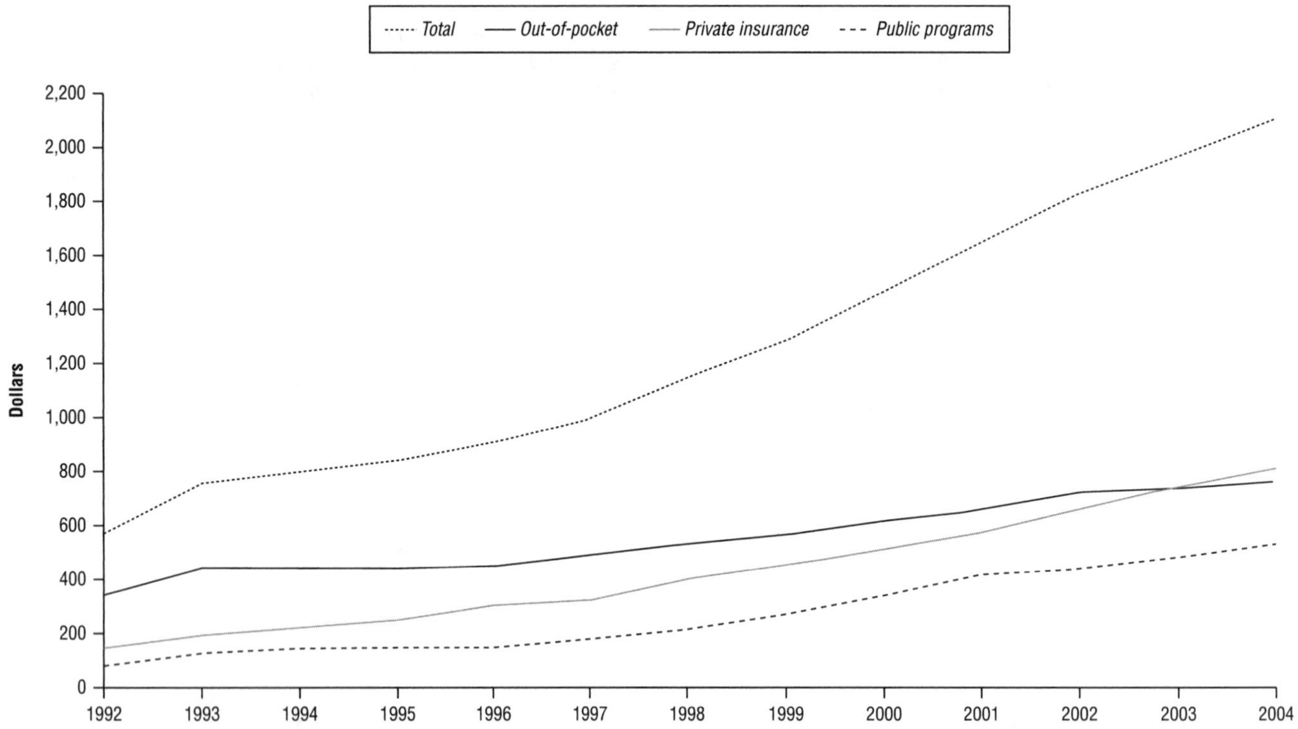

Note: Dollars have been inflation adjusted to 2004 using the Consumer Price Index (Series CPI-U-RS). Reported costs have been adjusted by a factor of 1.205 to account for underreporting of prescription drug use. Public programs include Medicare, Medicaid, Department of Veterans Affairs, and other State and Federal programs.
Reference population: These data refer to Medicare enrollees.

SOURCE: "Average Annual Prescription Drug Costs and Sources of Payment among Noninstitutionalized Medicare Enrollees Age 65 and over, 1992–2004," in *Older Americans 2008: Key Indicators of Well-Being*, Federal Interagency Forum on Aging-Related Statistics, March 2008, http://www.agingstats.gov/agingstatsdotnet/Main_Site/Data/2008_Documents/OA_2008.pdf (accessed April 20, 2009)

boxes, calendars, and easy-to-open bottles with large-print labels.

Qato et al. indicate that drug-drug interactions are more frequent among older adults because they are more likely than people of other ages to be taking multiple medications. Dangerous drug-drug interactions may occur when two or more drugs act together to either intensify or diminish one another's potency and effectiveness or when in combination they produce adverse side effects. For example, a person who takes heparin, a blood-thinning medication, should not take aspirin, which also acts to thin the blood. Similarly, antacids can interfere with the absorption of certain drugs used to treat Parkinson's disease, hypertension, and heart disease.

Polypharmacy is the use of many medications at the same time. It also refers to prescribing more medication than is needed or a medication regimen that includes at least one unnecessary medication. The major risk associated with polypharmacy is the potential for adverse drug reactions and interactions. Drug-induced adverse events may masquerade as other illnesses or precipitate confusion, falls, and incontinence, potentially prompting the physician to prescribe yet another drug. This "prescribing cascade" is easily prevented. It requires that physicians ensure that all medications prescribed are appropriate, taken correctly, safe, and effective. It may also be prevented by older adults' maintenance of accurate and complete records of all their prescription and over-the-counter drug use.

LEADING CAUSES OF DEATH

The top three leading causes of death among adults aged 65 and older—heart disease, malignant neoplasms, and cerebrovascular diseases—were unchanged from 1980 to 2005. (See Table 7.5.) In 2005 Alzheimer's disease, a degenerative disease of the brain that affects many areas of cognitive function, rose to fifth place on the list of leading causes of death and was responsible for 70,858 deaths.

Heart Disease

Even though deaths from heart disease have declined, it still kills more Americans than any other single disease.

According to the American Heart Association, in "Risk Factors and Coronary Heart Disease and Stroke" (January 30, 2008, http://www.americanheart.org/presenter.jhtml?identifier=539), 82% of people who die of heart disease are aged 65 and older.

Several factors account for the decreasing numbers of deaths from heart disease, including better control of hypertension and cholesterol levels and changes in exercise and nutrition. The increasing ranks of trained mobile emergency personnel (paramedics) and the widespread use of cardiopulmonary resuscitation and immediate treatment have also increased the likelihood of surviving an initial heart attack.

The growing use of statin drugs (drugs that reduce blood cholesterol levels) to reduce the risk of heart disease as well as procedures such as cardiac catheterization, coronary bypass surgery, pacemakers, angioplasty (a procedure to open narrowed or blocked blood vessels of the heart), and stenting (using wire scaffolds that hold arteries open) have improved the quality, and in some instances extended the lives, of people with heart disease.

Cancer

Cancer is the second leading cause of death among older adults. (See Table 7.5.) The American Cancer Society indicates in *Cancer Facts and Figures, 2009* that about 77% of all cancers are diagnosed after age 55. The likelihood of dying of cancer increases every decade after the age of 30. In 2005 among people aged 65 to 74, there were 742.7 deaths per 100,000 people; for those aged 75 to 84, this rate was 1,274.8 per 100,000 people; and for those aged 85 and older, it was 1,637.7 per 100,000 people. (See Table 7.8.)

Success in treating certain cancers, such as Hodgkin's disease and some forms of leukemia, has been offset by the rise in rates of other cancers, such as breast and lung cancers. Table 7.5 shows that the number of cancer deaths among adults aged 65 and older rose sharply from 258,389 in 1980 to 388,322 in 2005. Progress in treating cancer has largely been related to screenings, early diagnoses, and new drug therapies.

Stroke

Stroke (cerebrovascular disease or "brain attack") is the third leading cause of death and is the principal cause of disability among older adults. (See Table 7.5.) In "Risk Factors and Coronary Heart Disease and Stroke," the American Heart Association reports that "the chance of having a stroke about doubles for each decade of life after age 55."

According to the National Center for Health Statistics, in *Health, United States, 2008* (2009, http://www.cdc.gov/nchs/data/hus/hus08.pdf), and Melonie Heron et al. of the CDC, in "Deaths: Final Data for 2006" (*National Vital Statistics Reports*, vol. 57, no. 14, April 17, 2009), in 1980 strokes killed 219 people per 100,000 in the 65 to 74 age group. The death rate was reduced by more than half in 2006, with 96.3 people per 100,000 dying of strokes. There was a comparable decline for people aged 75 to 84. There were 335.1 deaths per 100,000 population for this age group in 2006, down from 786.9 in 1980. The improvement was even greater for people aged 85 and older. There were 1,039.6 deaths per 100,000 for this age group in 2006, less than half the rate of 2,283.7 per 100,000 in 1980.

HEALTHY AGING

According to the CDC, ample research demonstrates that healthy lifestyles have a greater effect than genetic factors in helping older people prevent the deterioration traditionally associated with aging. People who are physically active, eat a healthy diet, do not use tobacco, and practice other healthy behaviors reduce their risk for chronic diseases, have half the rate of disability of those who do not, and can delay disability by as many as 10 years.

Among the recommended health practices for older adults is participating in screening programs and early detection practices such as screenings for hypertension, cancer, diabetes, and depression. Screening detects diseases early in their course, when they are most treatable; however, many older adults do not obtain the recommended screenings. For example, even though immunizations reduce the risk for hospitalization and death from influenza and pneumonia, the Federal Interagency Forum on Aging-Related Statistics notes in *Older Americans 2008* that in 2006, 36% of older adults had not received flu shots and 67% of Hispanic, 64% of African-American, and 38% of white older adults had not been vaccinated against pneumonia.

Because falls are the most common cause of injuries and injury deaths in older adults, injury prevention is a vitally important way to prevent disability. The CDC reports in "Falls among Older Adults: An Overview" (January 19, 2009, http://www.cdc.gov/HomeandRecreationalSafety/Falls/adultfalls.html) that over one-third of adults aged 65 and older fall each year, and of those who fall, 20% to 30% suffer injuries that impair mobility and independence. Removing tripping hazards in the home, such as rugs, and installing grab bars in bathrooms are simple measures that can greatly reduce older Americans' risk for falls and fractures.

The current cohort of older adults is better equipped to prevent the illness, disability, and death associated with many chronic diseases than any previous generation. They are less likely to smoke, drink, or experience detrimental stress than younger people, and older adults have better eating habits than their younger counterparts. They are, however, less likely to exercise. Increasing evidence

TABLE 7.8

Death rates for malignant neoplasms, selected characteristics, selected years 1950–2005

[Data are based on death certificates]

Sex, race, Hispanic origin, and age	1950[a,b]	1960[a,b]	1970[b]	1980[b]	1990[b]	2000[c]	2004	2005
All persons				Deaths per 100,000 resident population				
All ages, age-adjusted[d]	193.9	193.9	198.6	207.9	216.0	199.6	185.8	183.8
All ages, crude	139.8	149.2	162.8	183.9	203.2	196.5	188.6	188.7
Under 1 year	8.7	7.2	4.7	3.2	2.3	2.4	1.8	1.8
1–4 years	11.7	10.9	7.5	4.5	3.5	2.7	2.5	2.3
5–14 years	6.7	6.8	6.0	4.3	3.1	2.5	2.5	2.5
15–24 years	8.6	8.3	8.3	6.3	4.9	4.4	4.1	4.1
25–34 years	20.0	19.5	16.5	13.7	12.6	9.8	9.1	9.0
35–44 years	62.7	59.7	59.5	48.6	43.3	36.6	33.4	33.2
45–54 years	175.1	177.0	182.5	180.0	158.9	127.5	119.0	118.6
55–64 years	390.7	396.8	423.0	436.1	449.6	366.7	333.4	326.9
65–74 years	698.8	713.9	754.2	817.9	872.3	816.3	755.1	742.7
75–84 years	1,153.3	1,127.4	1,169.2	1,232.3	1,348.5	1,335.6	1,280.4	1,274.8
85 years and over	1,451.0	1,450.0	1,320.7	1,594.6	1,752.9	1,819.4	1,653.3	1,637.7
Male								
All ages, age-adjusted[d]	208.1	225.1	247.6	271.2	280.4	248.9	227.7	225.1
All ages, crude	142.9	162.5	182.1	205.3	221.3	207.2	198.4	198.9
Under 1 year	9.7	7.7	4.4	3.7	2.4	2.6	1.8	2.1
1–4 years	12.5	12.4	8.3	5.2	3.7	3.0	2.6	2.6
5–14 years	7.4	7.6	6.7	4.9	3.5	2.7	2.7	2.7
15–24 years	9.7	10.2	10.4	7.8	5.7	5.1	4.8	4.8
25–34 years	17.7	18.8	16.3	13.4	12.6	9.2	8.6	8.8
35–44 years	45.6	48.9	53.0	44.0	38.5	32.7	29.1	28.9
45–54 years	156.2	170.8	183.5	188.7	162.5	130.9	124.3	121.6
55–64 years	413.1	459.9	511.8	520.8	532.9	415.8	376.7	369.5
65–74 years	791.5	890.5	1,006.8	1,093.2	1,122.2	1,001.9	907.6	899.1
75–84 years	1,332.6	1,389.4	1,588.3	1,790.5	1,914.4	1,760.6	1,662.1	1,649.7
85 years and over	1,668.3	1,741.2	1,720.8	2,369.5	2,739.9	2,710.7	2,349.5	2,319.3
Female								
All ages, age-adjusted[d]	182.3	168.7	163.2	166.7	175.7	167.6	157.4	155.6
All ages, crude	136.8	136.4	144.4	163.6	186.0	186.2	179.1	178.8
Under 1 year	7.6	6.8	5.0	2.7	2.2	2.3	1.9	1.5
1–4 years	10.8	9.3	6.7	3.7	3.2	2.5	2.4	2.0
5–14 years	6.0	6.0	5.2	3.6	2.8	2.2	2.2	2.2
15–24 years	7.6	6.5	6.2	4.8	4.1	3.6	3.4	3.3
25–34 years	22.2	20.1	16.7	14.0	12.6	10.4	9.6	9.1
35–44 years	79.3	70.0	65.6	53.1	48.1	40.4	37.7	37.5
45–54 years	194.0	183.0	181.5	171.8	155.5	124.2	113.8	115.8
55–64 years	368.2	337.7	343.2	361.7	375.2	321.3	293.2	287.4
65–74 years	612.3	560.2	557.9	607.1	677.4	663.6	627.1	610.9
75–84 years	1,000.7	924.1	891.9	903.1	1,010.3	1,058.5	1,023.5	1,020.3
85 years and over	1,299.7	1,263.9	1,096.7	1,255.7	1,372.1	1,456.4	1,340.1	1,324.6
White male[e]								
All ages, age-adjusted[d]	210.0	224.7	244.8	265.1	272.2	243.9	224.4	222.3
All ages, crude	147.2	166.1	185.1	208.7	227.7	218.1	209.9	210.6
25–34 years	17.7	18.8	16.2	13.6	12.3	9.2	8.6	8.5
35–44 years	44.5	46.3	50.1	41.1	35.8	30.9	28.2	28.4
45–54 years	150.8	164.1	172.0	175.4	149.9	123.5	117.5	115.7
55–64 years	409.4	450.9	498.1	497.4	508.2	401.9	364.9	356.5
65–74 years	798.7	887.3	997.0	1,070.7	1,090.7	984.3	896.3	889.9
75–84 years	1,367.6	1,413.7	1,592.7	1,779.7	1,883.2	1,736.0	1,652.7	1,646.2
85 years and over	1,732.7	1,791.4	1,772.2	2,375.6	2,715.1	2,693.7	2,348.9	2,322.7

suggests that behavior change, even late in life, is beneficial and can improve disease control and enhanced quality of life.

Maintaining a Healthy Weight

The United States is in the throes of an obesity epidemic. Obesity is defined as a body mass index (a number that shows body weight adjusted for height) greater than or equal to 30 kilograms per meters squared. In 2008 about 27% of adults aged 60 and older were obese, and the group of adults aged 40 to 59 that will soon join the ranks of older Americans reported the highest rate of obesity at 31%. (See Figure 7.12.) Furthermore, the percentages of older adults that are obese have increased from 1988–94, when just 24% of men and 27% of women aged 65 to 74, and 13% of men and 19% of women aged 75 and older were obese. (See Figure 7.13.) By 2005–06, 33% of men and 37% of women aged 65 to 74, and 25% of men and 24% of women aged 75 and older were obese. In "Obesity and Aging" (*Clinics in Chest Medicine*, vol. 30, no. 3,

TABLE 7.8

Death rates for malignant neoplasms, selected characteristics, selected years 1950–2005 [CONTINUED]

[Data are based on death certificates]

Sex, race, Hispanic origin, and age	1950[a,b]	1960[a,b]	1970[b]	1980[b]	1990[b]	2000[c]	2004	2005
Black or African American male[e]				Deaths per 100,000 resident population				
All ages, age-adjusted[d]	178.9	227.6	291.9	353.4	397.9	340.3	301.2	293.7
All ages, crude	106.6	136.7	171.6	205.5	221.9	188.5	176.2	175.4
25–34 years	18.0	18.4	18.8	14.1	15.7	10.1	10.0	11.9
35–44 years	55.7	72.9	81.3	73.8	64.3	48.4	38.4	36.2
45–54 years	211.7	244.7	311.2	333.0	302.6	214.2	197.0	186.1
55–64 years	490.8	579.7	689.2	812.5	859.2	626.4	569.2	568.3
65–74 years	636.5	938.5	1,168.9	1,417.2	1,613.9	1,363.8	1,209.7	1,183.8
75–84 years[f]	853.5	1,053.3	1,624.8	2,029.6	2,478.3	2,351.8	2,087.2	2,017.5
85 years and over	[g]	1,155.2	1,387.0	2,393.9	3,238.3	3,264.8	2,748.8	2,683.7

[a]Includes deaths of persons who were not residents of the 50 states and the District of Columbia.
[b]Underlying cause of death was coded according to the Sixth Revision of the International Classification of Diseases (ICD) in 1950, Seventh Revision in 1960, Eighth Revision in 1970, and Ninth Revision in 1980–1998.
[c]Starting with 1999 data, cause of death is coded according to ICD-10.
[d]Age-adjusted rates are calculated using the year 2000 standard population. Prior to 2003, age-adjusted rates were calculated using standard million proportions based on rounded population numbers. Starting with 2003 data, unrounded population numbers are used to calculate age-adjusted rates.
[e]The race groups, white, black, Asian or Pacific Islander, and American Indian or Alaska Native, include persons of Hispanic and non-Hispanic origin. Persons of Hispanic origin may be of any race. Death rates for the American Indian or Alaska Native and Asian or Pacific Islander populations are known to be underestimated.
[f]In 1950, rate is for the age group 75 years and over.
[g]Data not available.
Notes: Age groups were selected to minimize the presentation of unstable age-specific death rates based on small numbers of deaths and for consistency among comparison groups. In 2003, seven states reported multiple-race data. In 2004, 15 states reported multiple-race data. In 2005, 21 states and the District of Columbia reported multiple-race data.

SOURCE: Adapted from "Table 37. Death Rates for Malignant Neoplasms, by Sex, Race, Hispanic Origin, and Age: United States, Selected Years 1950–2005," in *Health, United States, 2008. With Chartbook*, National Center for Health Statistics, 2009, http://www.cdc.gov/nchs/data/hus/hus08.pdf#listtables (accessed May 6, 2009)

September 2009), John Harrington and Teofilo Lee-Chiong assert that the number of obese older adults will increase by 5.4% in 2010 and will rise to 18% by 2025.

The National Center for Health Statistics states that overweight and obese individuals are at an increased risk for multiple health problems, including hypertension, high cholesterol, Type 2 diabetes, coronary heart disease, congestive heart failure, stroke, arthritis, obstructive sleep apnea, and other serious conditions.

Smoking

According to the Federal Interagency Forum on Aging-Related Statistics, in *Older Americans 2008*, the per capita tobacco consumption declined in the United States in the last decades of the 20th century. By 2007 fewer people over the age of 65 (9% of men and 8% of women) smoked than all other age groups.

The U.S. surgeon general explains that even older adult smokers can realize health benefits from quitting. For example, a smoker's risk of heart disease begins to decline almost immediately after quitting, regardless of how long the person smoked.

Physical Activity

Regular physical activity comes closer to being a fountain of youth than any prescription medicine. Along with helping older adults to remain mobile and independent, exercise can lower the risk of obesity, heart disease, some cancers, stroke, and diabetes. It can also delay osteoporosis and arthritis, reduce symptoms of depression, and improve sleep quality and memory. Despite these demonstrated benefits, in 2008 just 27% of adults aged 65 to 74 and 17% of those aged 75 and older engaged in regular leisure-time physical activity. (See Figure 7.14.)

Use of Preventive Health Services

More widespread use of preventive services is a key to preserving and extending the health and quality of life of older Americans. Screening for early detection of selected cancers—such as breast, cervical, and colorectal—as well as diabetes, cardiovascular disease, and glaucoma can save lives and slow the progress of chronic disease. Because people with a regular source of medical care are more likely to receive basic medical services, such as routine checkups, which present the opportunity to receive preventive services, it is not surprising that in 2008 more than 95% of adults aged 65 and older reported having a regular source of medical care. (See Figure 7.15.) Given that Medicare covers many preventive services and screenings, it seems unlikely that cost prevents older adults from obtaining these services. In fact, the CDC notes in the 2008 National Health Interview Survey (March 2009, http://www.cdc.gov/nchs/data/nhis/earlyrelease/200903_03.pdf) that just 2.3% of respondents aged 65 and older reported that they failed to obtain needed medical care because of cost during the 12 months preceding the interview.

FIGURE 7.12

Prevalence of obesity among adults, by age group and sex, January–September 2008

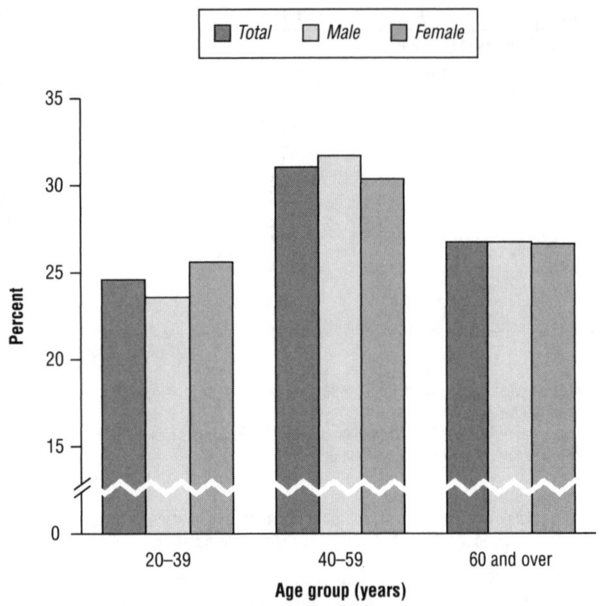

Notes: Obesity is defined as a Body Mass Index (BMI) of 30 kg/m^2 or more. The measure is based on self-reported height and weight. The analyses excluded 922 people (4.9%) with unknown height or weight. Data source: Data are based on household interviews of a sample of the civilian noninstitutionalized population.

SOURCE: "Figure 6.2. Prevalence of Obesity among Adults Aged 20 Years and over, by Age Group and Sex: United States, January–September 2008," in *Early Release of Selected Estimates Based on Data from the January–September 2008 National Health Interview Survey*, Centers for Disease Control and Prevention, National Center for Health Statistics, March 2009, http://www.cdc.gov/nchs/data/nhis/earlyrelease/200903_06.pdf (accessed May 11, 2009)

SEXUALITY IN AGING

Despite the popular belief that sexuality is exclusively for the young, sexual interest, activity, and capabilities are often lifelong. Even though the growing population of older adults will likely spur additional research, to date there are scant data about levels of sexual activity among older adults. The data that are available are often limited to community-dwelling older adults, so there is nearly no information about the sexual behavior of institutionalized older adults.

After age 50 sexual responses slow; however, very rarely does this natural and gradual diminution cause older adults to end all sexual activity. More important, in terms of curtailing older adults' sexual activity is the lack of available partners, which limits opportunities for sexual expression, especially for older women. Another issue is the greater incidence of illness and progression of chronic diseases that occurs with advancing age. Medical problems with the potential to adversely affect sexual function include diabetes, hypothyroidism (a condition in which the thyroid is underactive—producing too little thyroid hormones), neuropathy (a disease or abnormality of the nervous system), cardiovascular disease, urinary tract infections, prostate cancer, incontinence, arthritis, depression, and dementia. Many pharmacological treatments for chronic illnesses have sexual side effects ranging from diminished libido (sexual desire and drive) to erectile dysfunction. For example, some medications (e.g., antihypertensives, antidepressants, diuretics, steroids, anticonvulsants, and blockers) have high rates of sexual side effects.

One of the biggest recent changes in the sex lives of older adults is older men's use of potency drugs for erectile dysfunction (Viagra, Cialis, and Levitra) to enhance their performance. Since the 1998 debut of Viagra, these pharmaceutical solutions to erectile changes affecting older men have enjoyed tremendous popularity. Concern about the drugs' potential impact on vision arose when a suspected link between Viagra and vision loss led to lawsuits. However, Ernst R. Schwarz et al. of the Cedars-Sinai Medical Center in Los Angeles, California, find in "The Effects of Chronic Phosphodiesterase-5 Inhibitor Use on Different Organ Systems" (*International Journal of Impotence Research*, vol. 19, no. 2, March–April 2007) that occurrence of the vision disorder was similar to that of the general population.

Sexuality Transmitted Diseases

In "Sexual Activity and STDs among Seniors" (*U.S. Pharmacist*, vol. 33, no. 8, August 2008), Mary Ann. E. Zagaria of MZ Associates Inc. in Norwich, New York, observes that most adults aged 57 to 85 are engaged in spousal or other intimate relationships and regard sexuality as an important part of life. Zagaria also reports that older adults are one-sixth less likely to use condoms, which offer considerable protection from sexually transmitted diseases (STDs), than younger adults. Complicating matters, aging is associated with changes that increase the risk of any kind of infection, including STDs.

According to Mark J. Simone and Jonathan Appelbaum, in "Management of HIV/AIDS in Older Adults" (*Geriatrics*, vol. 63, no. 12, December 2008), the prevalence of HIV in older adults is increasing, and in 2005, 25% of people with HIV were aged 50 and older. Zagaria notes that HIV in older adults is being diagnosed in growing numbers when compared with previous years. She asserts that the number of older adults infected with HIV is expected to rise as baby boomers (people born between 1946 and 1964) continue to age.

There are several reasons for the rise in STDs, and particularly HIV/AIDS in older adults. Zagaria asserts that:

- Health care practitioners do not always ask about older adults' sexual activity or test them for HIV.
- Older adults may be embarrassed or reluctant to talk with health professionals about STDs.

FIGURE 7.13

Percentage of obese adults aged 65 and older, by sex and age group, selected years 1988–2006

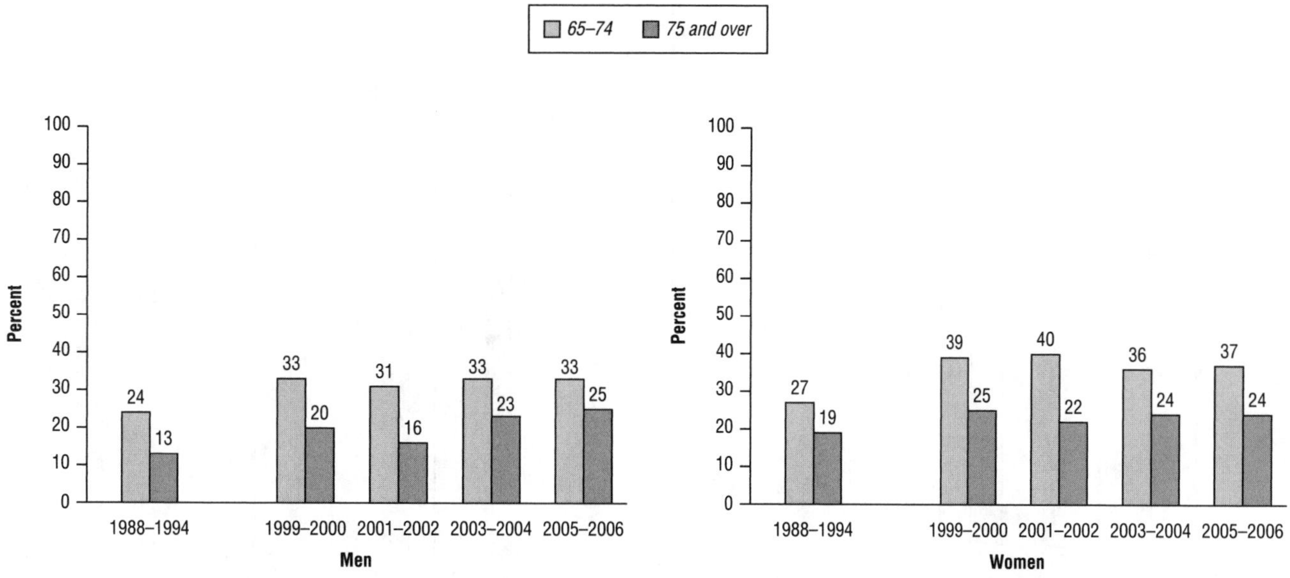

Reference population: These data refer to the civilian noninstitutionalized population.

SOURCE: "Percentage of People Age 65 and over Who Are Obese, by Sex and Age Group, Selected Years 1988–2006," in *Older Americans 2008: Key Indicators of Well-Being*, Federal Interagency Forum on Aging-Related Statistics, March 2008, http://www.agingstats.gov/agingstatsdotnet/Main_Site/Data/2008_Documents/OA_2008.pdf (accessed April 20, 2009)

- Older adults may mistake signs and symptoms of HIV/AIDS with other illness or aging.
- Delays in testing may not only result in older adults having STDs for longer periods but also, in the case of HIV infection, may delay treatment that can prevent the development of AIDS.

Data from the 2008 National Health Interview Survey reveal that adults aged 65 and older were the least likely to have ever had an HIV test of any age group. Just 15% of men and 10% of women aged 65 and older reported having had an HIV test. (See Figure 7.16.)

THE UNITED STATES LACKS SPECIALISTS IN GERIATRIC MEDICINE

In 1909 the American doctor Ignatz L. Nascher (1863–1944) coined the term *geriatrics* from the Greek *geras* (old age) and *iatrikos* (physician). Geriatricians are physicians trained in internal medicine or family practice who obtain additional training and medical board certification in the diagnosis and treatment of older adults.

The American Geriatrics Society (2008, http://www.americangeriatrics.org/news/geria_faqs.shtml) observes that as of April 2008 board-certified geriatricians numbered 7,590—1 for every 2,500 Americans aged 75 and older—fewer than half of the estimated need. Because of the growth of the older population, this ratio will decrease to 1 geriatrician for every 4,254 Americans in 2030. The shortage of specially trained physicians will intensify as the baby boom generation joins the ranks of older adults. The American Geriatrics Society contends that financial disincentives pose the greatest barrier to new physicians entering geriatrics. Geriatricians are almost entirely dependent on Medicare reimbursement, and low Medicare reimbursement, which directly influences their earning potential, dissuades some physicians from entering the field. Other prospective geriatricians may also be discouraged by having to spend at least part of their workdays in nursing homes.

FIGURE 7.14

Percent of adults aged 18 years and over who engaged in regular leisure-time physical activity, by age group and sex, January–September 2008

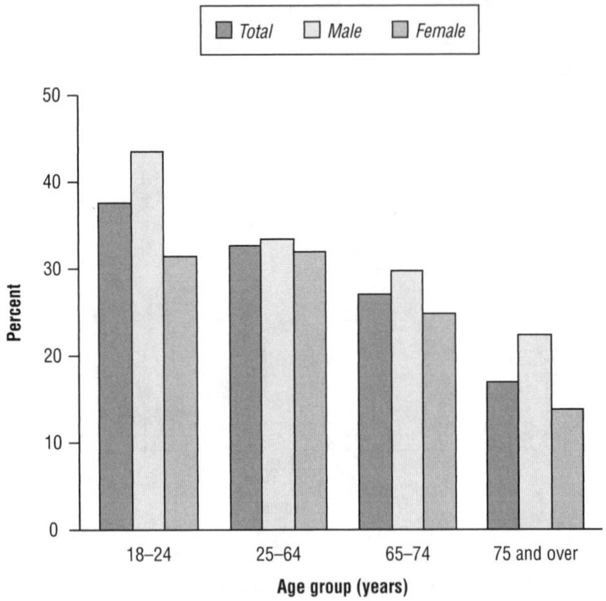

Notes: This measure reflects the definition used for the physical activity Leading Health Indicator (Healthy People 2010, (15)). Regular leisure-time physical activity is defined as engaging in light-moderate leisure-time physical activity for greater than or equal to 30 minutes at a frequency greater than or equal to five times per week or engaging in vigorous leisure-time physical activity for greater than or equal to 20 minutes at a frequency greater than or equal to three times per week.
Data source: Data are based on household interviews of a sample of the civilian noninstitutionalized population.

SOURCE: "Figure 7.2. Percentage of Adults Aged 18 Years and over Who Engaged in Regular Leisure-Time Physical Activity, by Age Group and Sex: United States, January–September 2008," in *Early Release of Selected Estimates Based on Data from the January–September 2008 National Health Interview Survey*, Centers for Disease Control and Prevention, National Center for Health Statistics, March 2009, http://www.cdc.gov/nchs/data/nhis/earlyrelease/200903_07.pdf (accessed May 11, 2009)

FIGURE 7.15

Percent of persons of all ages with a usual place to go for medical care, by age group and sex, January–September 2008

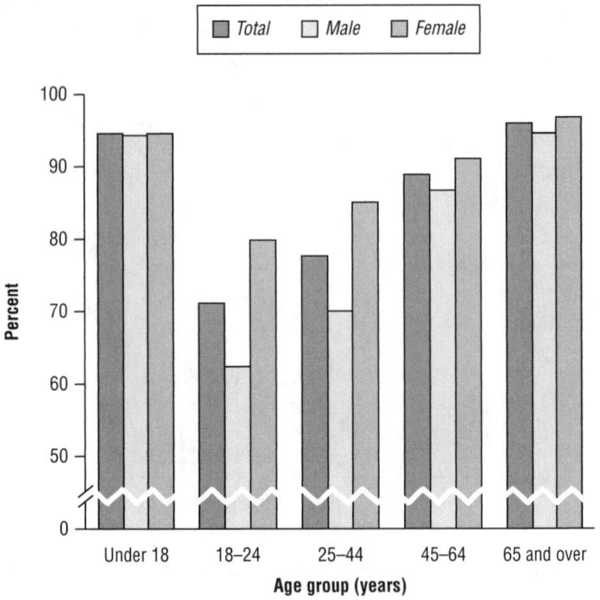

Notes: The usual place to go for medical care does not include a hospital emergency room. The analyses excluded 247 persons (1.3%) with an unknown usual place to go for medical care.
Data source: Data are based on household interviews of a sample of the civilian noninstitutionalized population.

SOURCE: "Figure 2.2. Percentage of Persons of All Ages with a Usual Place to Go for Medical Care, by Age Group and Sex: United States, January–September 2008," in *Early Release of Selected Estimates Based on Data from the January–September 2008 National Health Interview Survey*, Centers for Disease Control and Prevention, National Center for Health Statistics, March 2009, http://www.cdc.gov/nchs/data/nhis/earlyrelease/200903_02.pdf (accessed May 11, 2009)

FIGURE 7.16

Percentage of adults aged 18 years and over who had ever been tested for HIV, by age group and sex, January–September 2008

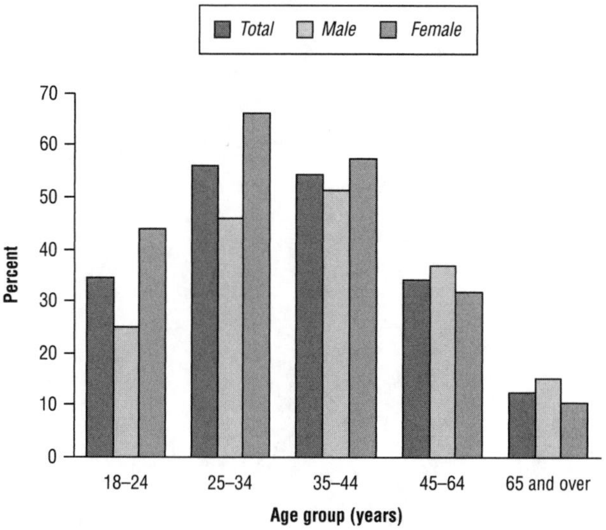

Notes: The analyses excluded 913 adults (4.8%) with unknown human immunodeficiency virus (HIV) test status. Individuals who received HIV testing solely as a result of blood donation were considered as not having been tested for HIV. Data are based on household interviews of a sample of the civilian noninstitutionalized population.

SOURCE: "Figure 10.2. Percentage of Adults Aged 18 and over Who Had Ever Been Tested for Human Immunodeficiency Virus, by Age Group and Sex: United States, January–September 2008," in *Early Release of Selected Estimates Based on Data from the January–September 2008 National Health Interview Survey*, Centers for Disease Control and Prevention, National Center for Health Statistics, March 2009, http://www.cdc.gov/nchs/data/nhis/earlyrelease/200903_10.pdf (accessed May 25, 2009)

CHAPTER 8

MENTAL HEALTH AND MENTAL ILLNESS

Changes in mental capabilities are among the most feared aspects of aging. As Mark E. Williams of the University of Virginia School of Medicine states in "Mild Cognitive Impairment: Who Is Confused?" (*Conference Report Highlights of the American Geriatrics Society 2005 Annual Meeting*, May 2005), mental health problems that impair functioning are among the most common age-related changes—their prevalence doubles every five years, increasing from an estimated 1% among those aged 60 years old, to 20% at age 80, to 50% or higher among those aged 85 and older.

The aging population has spurred interest in age-related problems in cognition—the process of thinking, learning, and remembering. Cognitive difficulties much milder than those associated with organic brain diseases, such as Alzheimer's disease or dementia, affect a significant proportion of older adults. Organic brain diseases, often referred to as organic brain syndromes, refer to physical disorders of the brain that produce mental health problems as opposed to psychiatric conditions, which may also cause mental health problems. A landmark study supported by the National Institute on Aging (NIA) and summarized by Frederick W. Unverzagt et al. in "Prevalence of Cognitive Impairment: Data from the Indianapolis Study of Health and Aging" (*Neurology*, vol. 57, November 2001) estimates that in 2001, 23.4% of community-dwelling older adults and 19.2% of nursing home residents suffered some degree of cognitive impairment, besides those who suffered from much more serious cognitive impairment. The prevalence of this mild cognitive impairment grew significantly with age, with rates increasing by about 10% for every 10 years of age after age 65. Unverzagt et al. conclude that "cognitive impairment short of dementia affects nearly one in four community-dwelling elders and is a major risk factor for later development of dementia."

Because the number of people with mental impairments such as dementia is anticipated to increase as the population ages, and older adults with mental impairment are at risk for institutionalization, the financial costs to individuals and to society are expected to escalate. As such, the mental health and illness of older adults is an increasingly important public health issue.

MENTAL HEALTH

Mental health may be measured in terms of an individual's abilities to think and communicate clearly, learn and grow emotionally, deal productively and realistically with change and stress, and form and maintain fulfilling relationships with others. Mental health is a principle component of wellness (self-esteem, resilience, and the ability to cope with adversity), which influences how people feel about themselves.

When mental health is defined and measured in terms of the absence of serious psychological distress, then older adults fare quite well compared with other age groups. The 2008 National Health Interview Survey, which was conducted by the Centers for Disease Control and Prevention (CDC), questioned whether respondents had experienced serious psychological distress within the 30 days preceding the interview. Adults aged 65 and older were the least likely to have experienced serious psychological distress (2.8%), compared with those aged 45 to 64 (3.8%) and adults aged 18 to 44 (2.9%). (See Figure 8.1.)

Experience Shapes Mental Health in Old Age

One theory of aging, called continuity theory and explained by Robert Atchley in *The Social Forces in Later Life: An Introduction to Social Gerontology* (1985), posits that people who age most successfully are those who carry forward the habits, preferences, lifestyles, and relationships from midlife into late life. This theory has gained credence from research studies that find that traits measured in midlife are strong predictors of outcomes in later life and that many psychological and social characteristics are stable across the lifespan. For most people, old age does not represent a

FIGURE 8.1

Percent of adults who experienced serious psychological distress during the past 30 days, by age group and sex, January–September 2008

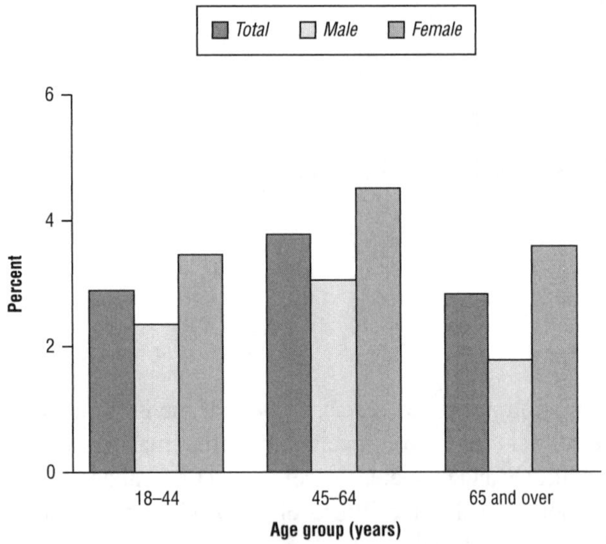

Notes: Six psychological distress questions are included in the Sample Adult Core component. These questions ask how often a respondent experienced certain symptoms of psychological distress during the past 30 days. The response codes (0–4) of the six items for each person are summed to yield a scale with a 0–24 range. A value of 13 or more for this scale is used here to define serious psychological distress (16).
Data source: Data are based on household interviews of a sample of the civilian noninstitutionalized population.

SOURCE: "Figure 13.2. Percentage of Adults Aged 18 Years and over Who Experienced Serious Psychological Distress during the Past 30 Days, by Age Group and Sex: United States, January–September 2008," in *Early Release of Selected Estimates Based on Data from the January–September 2008 National Health Interview Survey*, Centers for Disease Control and Prevention, National Center for Health Statistics, March 2009, http://www.cdc.gov/nchs/data/nhis/earlyrelease/200903_13.pdf (accessed May 11, 2009)

radical departure from the past; changes often occur gradually and sometimes unnoticeably. Most older adults adapt to the challenges and changes associated with later life using well-practiced coping skills acquired earlier in life.

Adults who have struggled with mental health problems or mental disorders throughout their life often continue to suffer these same problems in old age. Few personal problems disappear with old age, and many progress and become more acute. Marital problems, which may have been kept at bay because one or both spouses were away at work, may intensify when a couple spends more time together in retirement. Reduced income, illness, and disability in retirement can aggravate an already troubled marriage and strain even healthy interpersonal, marital, and other family relationships.

Older age can be a period of regrets, which can lead to mutual recriminations. With life expectancy rising, married couples can now expect to spend many years together in retirement. Most older couples manage the transition, but some have problems.

Coping with losses of friends, family, health, and independence may precipitate mental health problems. Hearing loss is common, and close correlations have been found between loss of hearing and depression. Visual impairment limits mobility and the ability to read and watch television. Loss of sight or hearing can cause perceptual disorientation, which in turn may lead to depression, paranoia, fear, and alienation.

A constant awareness of the imminence of death can also become a problem for older adults. Even though most older adults resolve their anxieties and concerns about death, some live in denial and fear. How well older adults accept the inevitability of death is a key determinant of satisfaction and emotional well-being in old age.

Memory

Because memory is a key component of cognitive functioning, declining memory that substantially impairs older adults' functioning is a major risk factor for institutionalization. In "Trends in the Prevalence and Mortality of Cognitive Impairment in the United States: Is There Evidence of a Compression of Cognitive Morbidity?" (*Alzheimer's and Dementia*, vol. 4, no. 2, March 2008), Kenneth M. Langa et al. compare the cognitive health of older adults in 1993 and 2002 and find that rates of cognitive impairment declined from 12.2% to 8.7%. The researchers determine that improvements in cognitive health were associated with higher levels of education and financial status. They hypothesize that improved treatment for conditions such as stroke and heart disease may account for some of this improvement. Langa et al.'s results also support the idea that the brains of more educated people may have more "cognitive reserve," so that they are better able to defend against impairment damage from Alzheimer's or other diseases that compromise memory and cognition.

According to Roni Caryn Rabin, in "For a Sharp Brain, Stimulation" (*New York Times*, May 13, 2008), Americans worry about heart health, stroke, and diabetes but "downright dread" developing Alzheimer's disease. Rabin reports that studies of older adults who maintain their sharp minds tend to be healthy and physically active and have strong connections to their family, friends, and community. They are also likely to be involved in intellectually stimulating and challenging activities. However, these findings are associations and do not prove causation. In other words, it is not yet known, for example, whether mentally alert older adults stay sharp because they perform intellectually demanding activities or whether they are engaged in these activities because they are mentally alert.

ORGANIC BRAIN DISEASES—DEMENTIAS

Dementia refers to a range of mental and behavioral changes caused by cerebrovascular or neurological diseases that permanently damage the brain, impairing the activity of brain cells. These changes can affect memory, speech, and the ability to perform the activities of daily living.

Occasional forgetfulness and memory lapses are not signs of dementia. Dementia is caused by disease and is not the inevitable result of growing older. Many disorders may cause or simulate dementia, which is not a single disorder—dementia refers to a condition caused by a variety of diseases and disorders, a small proportion of which are potentially reversible.

Furthermore, research suggests that not all people with mild cognitive impairment will progress over time to dementia. Alex J. Mitchell and Mojtaba Shiri-Feshki conducted a large meta-analysis (a review that looks at the findings of many studies) and published their findings in "Rate of Progression of Mild Cognitive Impairment to Dementia—Meta-analysis of 41 Robust Inception Cohort Studies" (*Acta Psychiatrica Scandinavica*, vol. 119, no. 4, April 2009). The researchers show that only a minority (20% to 40%) of people developed dementia even after long-term follow-up and that the risk appeared to decrease slightly with time. The analysis also suggests that mild cognitive impairment is not necessarily a transitional state between normal age-related changes and dementia. Mitchell and Shiri-Feshki find that some patients do not progress and others actually improve.

Multi-infarct Dementia

The NIA indicates in "Multi-infarct Dementia Fact Sheet" (February 5, 2009, http://www.nia.nih.gov/Alzheimers/Publications/dementia.htm) that multi-infarct dementia is the most common form of vascular dementia and accounts for 10% to 20% of all cases of progressive dementia. It usually affects people between the ages of 60 and 75 and is more likely to occur in men than in women. Multi-infarct dementia is caused by a series of small strokes that disrupt blood flow and damage or destroy brain tissue. Sometimes these small strokes are "silent"—meaning that they produce no obvious symptoms and are detected only on imaging studies, such as computed tomography or magnetic resonance imaging scans of the brain. An older adult may have a number of small strokes before experiencing noticeable changes in memory, reasoning, or other signs of multi-infarct dementia.

Because strokes occur suddenly, the loss of cognitive skills and memory present quickly, although some affected individuals may appear to improve for short periods of time, then decline again after having more strokes. Establishing the diagnosis of multi-infarct dementia is challenging because its symptoms are difficult to distinguish from those of Alzheimer's disease. Treatment cannot reverse the damage already done to the brain. Instead, it focuses on preventing further damage by reducing the risk of additional strokes. This entails treating the underlying causes of stroke, such as hypertension, diabetes, high cholesterol, and heart disease. Surgical procedures to improve blood flow to the brain, such as carotid endarterectomy, angioplasty (a procedure to open narrowed or blocked blood vessels of the heart), or stenting (using wire scaffolds that hold arteries open), as well as medications to reduce the risk of stroke are also used to treat this condition.

PEOPLE WITH DIABETES MAY BE AT INCREASED RISK. Rachel A. Whitmer et al. reveal in "Hypoglycemic Episodes and Risk of Dementia in Older Patients with Type 2 Diabetes Mellitus" (*Journal of the American Medical Association*, vol. 301, no. 15, April 15, 2009) that people with Type 2 diabetes may be at an increased risk for developing dementia. The researchers find that just two episodes of dangerously low blood sugar, called hypoglycemia, which is caused by excess insulin, increased the risk by 80%, and people who had three or more episodes had a 94% increase in risk—meaning they had nearly twice the risk of developing dementia as people with normal blood sugar levels.

Alzheimer's Disease

Alzheimer's disease (AD) is the most common form of dementia among older adults. It is characterized by severely compromised thinking, reasoning, behavior, and memory, and it may be among the most fearsome of age-related disorders because it challenges older adults' ability to live independently. The disease was named after Alois Alzheimer (1864–1915), the German neurologist who first described the anatomical changes in the brain—the plaques and tangles that are the characteristic markers of this progressive, degenerative disease.

According to the Alzheimer's Association, in *2009 Alzheimer's Disease Facts and Figures* (2009, http://www.alz.org/national/documents/report_alzfactsfigures2009.pdf), an estimated 5.3 million Americans were afflicted with AD in 2009. The overwhelming majority of AD sufferers (5.1 million) were aged 65 and older. Women have a higher lifetime risk of developing the disease because, on average, they live longer than men.

The Alzheimer's Association projects that the number of people aged 65 and older with AD will reach 7.7 million in 2030 and that new AD cases per year will likely increase from 454,000 in 2010, to 615,000 in 2029, to 959,000 in 2050. The association asserts that if a cure or preventive measure is not found by 2050, then the number of Americans aged 65 and older with AD will range from 11 million to 16 million and more than 60% of people with AD will be aged 85 and older.

SYMPTOMS AND STAGES. In general, AD has a slow onset, with symptoms such as mild memory lapses and disorientation that may not be identified as problematical beginning between the ages of 55 and 80. As the disease progresses, memory loss increases and mood swings are frequent, accompanied by confusion, irritability, restlessness, and problems communicating. AD patients may experience trouble finding words, impaired judgment, difficulty performing familiar tasks, and changes in behavior and personality.

In "Stages of Alzheimer's" (2009, http://www.alz.org/alzheimers_disease_stages_of_alzheimers.asp), the Alzheimer's Association describes the seven stages of how AD progresses. The stages range from the first and second, in which there is no and then little apparent cognitive decline, to stage 3, which is marked by mild lapses and is often discernable to family, friends, and coworkers. Stage 4 is called mild or early stage AD, and during this stage moderate cognitive decline is observed. For example, AD patients may have diminished recall of recent activities or current events and compromised ability to perform tasks such as paying bills or shopping for groceries. In stages 5 and 6 memory impairment continues along with personality changes, sleep disturbances, and, if left unsupervised, a dangerous tendency to wander off and become lost.

Ultimately, the disease progresses to stage 7, when patients are entirely unable to care for themselves. In their terminal stages, AD victims require round-the-clock care and supervision. They no longer recognize family members, other caregivers, or themselves, and they require assistance with daily activities such as eating, dressing, bathing, and using the toilet. Eventually, they may become incontinent, blind, completely unable to communicate, and have difficulty swallowing.

Melonie Heron et al. of the CDC report in "Deaths: Final Data for 2006" (*National Vital Statistics Reports*, vol. 57, no. 14, April 2009) that in 2006 AD was the seventh leading cause of death in adults of all ages. According to the Alzheimer's Association, in *2009 Alzheimer's Disease Facts and Figures*, in 2006 AD claimed 72,914 lives and was the fifth leading cause of death among adults aged 65 and older.

GENETIC ORIGINS OF AD. AD is not a normal consequence of growing older. It is a disease of the brain that develops in response to genetic predisposition and nongenetic causative factors. Scientists have identified some genetic components of the disease and have observed the different patterns of inheritance, ages of onset, genes, chromosomes, and proteins linked to the development of AD.

In "The *mec*-4 Gene Is a Member of a Family of *Caenorhabditis elegans* Genes That Can Mutate to Induce Neuronal Degeneration" (*Nature*, February 14, 1991), Monica Driscoll and Martin Chalfie of Columbia University report their discovery that a mutation in a single gene could cause AD. The defect was in the gene that directs cells to produce a substance called amyloid protein. The researchers also find that low levels of acetylcholine, a neurotransmitter involved in learning and memory, contribute to the formation of hard deposits of amyloid protein that accumulate in the brains of AD patients. In healthy people, the protein fragments are broken down and excreted by the body.

In 1995 three more genes linked to AD were identified. Two genes appear to be involved with forms of early onset AD, which can begin as early as age 30. The third gene, known as apolipoprotein E (apoE), is involved in important physiological functions throughout the body. It regulates lipid metabolism and helps redistribute cholesterol. In the brain, apoE participates in repairing nerve tissue that has been injured. According to the NIA, in "Cortex Area Thinner in Youth with Alzheimer's-Related Gene" (*Science Daily*, April 24, 2007), 40% of late-onset AD patients have at least one apoE-4 gene, whereas only 10% to 25% of the general population has an apoE-4 gene. The NIA notes in "Alzheimer's Disease Genetics Fact Sheet" (November 2008, http://www.nia.nih.gov/) that several studies have confirmed that the apoE-4 gene increases the risk of developing AD, but it is not yet known how it acts to increase this risk. The NIA points out that inheriting the apoE-4 gene does not necessarily mean that a person will develop AD and that the absence of the gene does not ensure that an individual will not develop AD. The NIA also suggests that additional genes related to AD risk may be identified by a genome-wide association study, which rapidly scans markers across the genomes (complete sets of deoxyribonucleic acid) of many people to detect genetic variations associated with a particular disease.

As of 2009 there were two NIA initiatives that were under way: the Alzheimer's Disease Genetics Study and the Alzheimer's Disease Genetics Consortium. These initiatives collect and analyze blood samples and other information from thousands of families around the world with members who do and do not have late-onset AD. The NIA also supports the National Cell Repository for Alzheimer's Disease, a national repository of clinical information and DNA that is available to researchers.

DIAGNOSTIC TESTING. Historically, the only sure way to diagnose AD was to examine brain tissue under a microscope, during an autopsy. Examining the brain of a patient who has died of AD reveals a characteristic pattern that is the hallmark of the disease: tangles of fibers (neurofibrillary tangles) and clusters of degenerated nerve endings (neuritic plaques) in areas of the brain that are crucial for memory and intellect.

Even though it does not provide as definitive a diagnosis as an examination of the brain, a complete physical, psychiatric, and neurological history and examination can usually produce an accurate diagnosis of AD. Diagnostic tests for AD may also include analysis of blood and spinal fluid as well as the use of brain scans (computed tomography and magnetic resonance imaging) to detect strokes or tumors and to measure the volume of brain tissue in areas of the brain used for memory and cognition. Such brain scans assist to accurately identify people with AD and to predict who may develop AD in the future.

The NIA explains in "Alzheimer's Disease Genetics Fact Sheet" that apoE testing is used as a research tool to identify research subjects who may have an increased risk of developing AD. Investigators are then able to look for early brain changes in research subjects and compare the effectiveness of treatments for people with different apoE profiles. Because the apoE test does not accurately predict who will or will not develop AD, it is useful for studying AD risk in populations but not for determining any one individual's specific risk.

In "Cerebrospinal Fluid Biomarker Signature in Alzheimer's Disease Neuroimaging Initiative Subjects" (*Annals of Neurology*, vol. 65, no. 4, April 2009), Leslie M. Shaw et al. describe a new test that can accurately detect AD in its earliest stages, before dementia symptoms begin. The test measures the concentration of specific biomarkers, in this case proteins (tau protein and amyloid beta42 polypeptide) in spinal fluid that can indicate AD. Shaw et al. note that subjects with low concentrations of amyloid beta42 and high levels of tau in their spinal fluid were more likely to develop AD. The test had an 87% accuracy rate when predicting which subjects with early memory problems and other symptoms of cognitive impairment would ultimately be diagnosed with AD.

A simple and accurate test, such as the cerebrospinal fluid biomarkers, that distinguishes people with AD from those with cognitive problems or dementias arising from other causes will prove useful for scientists, physicians, and other clinical researchers. An accurate test would not only identify those at risk of developing AD and allow the detection of AD early enough for the use of experimental medications to slow the progress of the disease but also monitor the progress of treatments aimed at preventing AD or slowing its progression. However, the availability of tests to predict who may develop AD raises ethical and practical questions: Do people really want to know their risks of developing AD? Is it helpful to predict a condition that is not yet considered preventable or curable?

TREATMENT. There is still no cure or prevention for AD, and treatment focuses on managing symptoms. Medication may slow the appearance of some symptoms and can lessen others, such as agitation, anxiety, unpredictable behavior, and depression. Physical exercise and good nutrition are important, as is a calm and highly structured environment. The object is to help the AD patient maintain as much comfort, normalcy, and dignity for as long as possible.

In 2009 there were five prescription drugs for the treatment of AD that had been approved by the U.S. Food and Drug Administration (FDA), and National Institutes of Health (NIH) affiliates and pharmaceutical companies were involved in clinical trials of new drugs to treat AD. All the drugs being tested were intended to improve the symptoms of AD and slow its progression, but none was expected to cure AD. The investigational drugs aim to address three aspects of AD: to improve cognitive function in people with early AD, to slow or postpone the progression of the disease, and to control behavioral problems such as wandering, aggression, and agitation of patients with AD.

There is also some evidence that a combination of vitamin E and anti-inflammatory drugs play a role in slowing the progress of AD. According to Megan Rauscher, in "Vitamin E May Slow Alzheimer's Disease" (Reuters, May 4, 2009), the findings of an NIH-funded study conducted at the Massachusetts General Hospital Memory Disorders Unit, the VA Bedford Medical Center, and Harvard Medical School were presented at the annual meeting of the American Geriatrics Society in May 2009. The investigators followed a total of 540 AD patients who received traditional treatment as well as either vitamin E but no anti-inflammatory drug, an anti-inflammatory drug but no vitamin E, both vitamin E and an anti-inflammatory drug, or neither. Subjects who took both vitamin E and the anti-inflammatory drug appeared to have a slower decline of mental and physical function over the course of three years of follow-up.

CARING FOR THE AD PATIENT. AD affects members of the patient's family. Even though medication may suppress some symptoms and occasionally slow the progression of the disease, eventually most AD patients require constant care and supervision. Until recently, nursing homes and residential care facilities were not equipped to provide this kind of care, and if they accepted AD patients at all, they admitted only those in the earliest stages of the disease. Since 2000 a growing number of nursing homes have welcomed AD patients, even though they are more difficult and costly to care for than older adults without AD. This change is primarily financially motivated, because nursing home occupancy rates have been dropping in response to the growth of alternative housing for older adults. According to Genworth Financial, in *Genworth 2009 Cost of Care Survey: Home Care Providers, Adult Day Health Care Facilities, Assisted Living Facilities, and Nursing Homes* (April 2009, http://www.genworth.com/content/etc/medialib/genworth_v2/pdf/ltc_cost_of_care.Par.8024.File.dat/cost_of_care.pdf), these nursing homes offer families with ample financial resources—annual costs range from $50,594 to $125,925, depending on the location of the facility in the United States and the intensity of services—an alternative to caring for the AD patient at home.

Many children and other relatives of AD patients care for the affected family member at home as long as possible because they cannot afford institutional care or they feel a moral obligation to do so. No matter how willing and devoted the caregiver, the time, patience, and resources required to provide care over a long period are immense, and the task is often overwhelming. As the patient's condition progresses, caregivers often find themselves socially isolated. Caregiving has been linked to increased rates of depression, compromised immune function, and a greater use of medication and psychotropic drugs (medications used to improve mood and relieve symptoms of mental distress).

Caregivers who participate in support groups and make use of home health aids, adult day care, and respite care (facilities where patients stay for a limited number of days) not only feel healthier but also are better able to care for AD patients and maintain them at home longer than those who do not.

MENTAL ILLNESS

Older people with mental illnesses were once considered senile—that is, mentally debilitated as a result of old age. Serious forgetfulness, emotional disturbances, and other behavioral changes do not, however, occur as a normal part of aging. They may be caused by chronic illnesses such as heart disease, thyroid disorders, or anemia; infections, poor diet, or lack of sleep; or prescription drugs, such as narcotic painkillers, sedatives, and antihistamines. Social isolation, loneliness, boredom, or depression may also cause memory lapses. When accurately diagnosed and treated, these types of problems can frequently be reversed.

Mental illness refers to all identifiable mental health disorders and mental health problems. In the landmark study *Mental Health: A Report of the Surgeon General, 1999* (1999, http://www.surgeongeneral.gov/library/mentalhealth/home.html), the U.S. Surgeon General defines mental disorders as "health conditions that are characterized by alterations in thinking, mood, or behavior (or some combination thereof) associated with distress and/or impaired functioning." The surgeon general distinguishes mental health disorders from mental health problems, describing the signs and symptoms of mental health problems as less intense and of shorter duration than those of mental health disorders, but it acknowledges that both mental health disorders and problems may be distressing and disabling.

The surgeon general observes that nearly 20% of people aged 55 and older experience mental disorders that are not part of normal aging. The most common disorders, in order of estimated prevalence rates, are anxiety (11.4%), severe cognitive impairment (6.6%), and mood disorders (4.4%) such as depression. The surgeon general also points out that mental disorders in older adults are frequently unrecognized, underreported, and undertreated.

Diagnosing mental disorders in older adults is challenging, because their symptoms and presentation may be different from that of other adults. For example, many older adults complain about physical as opposed to emotional or psychological problems, and they present symptoms that are not typical of depression or anxiety disorders. Accurate identification, detection, and diagnosis of mental disorders in older adults are also complicated by the following:

- Mental disorders often coexist with other medical problems.
- The symptoms of some chronic diseases may imitate or conceal psychological disorders.
- Older adults are more likely to report physical symptoms than psychological ones, because there is less stigma associated with physical health or medical problems than with mental health problems.

Serious Psychological Distress

The Substance Abuse and Mental Health Services Administration reports in *Serious Psychological Distress among Adults Aged 50 or Older: 2005 and 2006* (June 26, 2008, http://www.oas.samhsa.gov/2k8/SPDolder/SPDolderadults.pdf) that about 7% of adults aged 50 and older experience serious psychological distress (SPD) each year—8.8% of adults aged 50 to 64 and 4.5% of those age 65 and older. Examples of SPD include prolonged or intense anxiety, depression, or other emotional stress. Of those aged 50 and older who reported SPD during the past year, 53.7% received mental health treatment, 6.2% did not receive treatment even though they felt they needed it, and 40.1% did not think they needed treatment and did not receive it.

Adults aged 50 to 64 with SPD were more likely than those aged 65 and older to have received mental health treatment—57.8% and 41.8%, respectively. (See Figure 8.2.) Adults aged 50 to 64 were also more likely than those aged 65 and older to have not received treatment even though they recognized a need for it—7.9% and 1.3%, respectively. However, adults aged 65 and older were more likely than those aged 50 to 64 to have not received treatment and not recognize a need for it—56.8% and 34.2%, respectively.

Depression

Symptoms of depression are an important indicator of physical and mental health in older adults, because people who experience many symptoms of depression are also more likely to report higher rates of physical illness, disability, and health service utilization.

The prevalence of clinically relevant depressive symptoms (as distinguished from brief periods of sadness or depressed mood) increases with advancing age. According to the Federal Interagency Forum on Aging-Related Statistics, in *Older Americans 2008: Key Indicators of Well-Being* (March 2008, http://www.agingstats.gov/agingstatsdotnet/Main_Site/Data/2008_Documents/OA_2008.pdf), in 2004, 19% of adults aged 85 and older experienced these symptoms, compared with 13% of those aged 65 to 74. (See Figure 8.3.) Older women from 65 to 84 reported depressive symptoms more than older men did. Sixteen percent of women aged 65 to 74 reported depressive symptoms, compared with 10% of men the same age.

FIGURE 8.2

Percentages of people aged 50 and older with serious psychological distress who reported past year mental health treatment and perceived need for treatment, by age group, 2005 and 2006

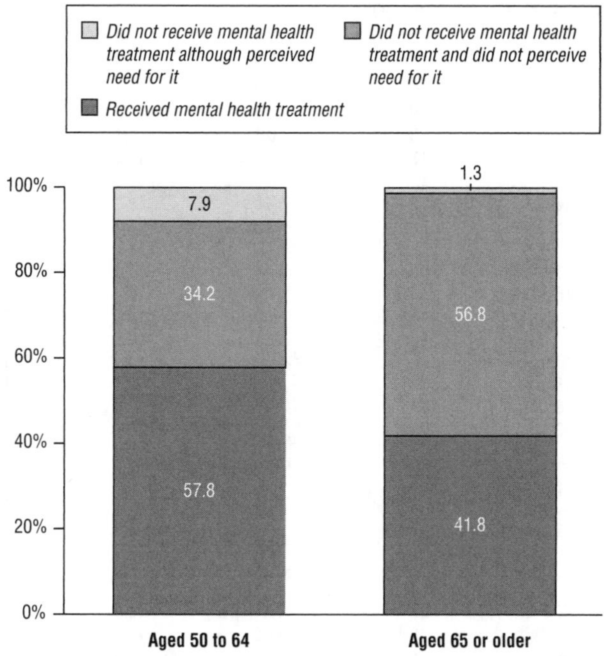

SOURCE: "Figure 1. Percentages of Persons Aged 50 or Older with Past Year Serious Psychological Distress (SPD) Who Reported Past Year Mental Health Treatment and Perceived Need for Treatment, by Age Group: 2005 and 2006," in *The NSDUH Report—Serious Psychological Distress among Adults Aged 50 or Older: 2005 and 2006*, Substance Abuse and Mental Health Services Administration, Office of Applied Studies, June 26, 2008, http://www.oas.samhsa.gov/2k8/SPDolder/SPDolderadults.pdf (accessed May 11, 2009)

Often, illness itself can trigger depression in older adults by altering the chemicals in the brain. Examples of illnesses that can touch off depression are diabetes, hypothyroidism, kidney or liver dysfunction, heart disease, and infection. In patients with these ailments, treating the underlying disease usually eliminates the depression. David M Clarke and Kay C. Currie find in "Depression, Anxiety, and Their Relationship with Chronic Diseases: A Review of the Epidemiology, Risk, and Treatment Evidence" (*Medical Journal of Australia*, vol. 190, no. 7, April 6, 2009) not only strong evidence for the association of physical illness, depression, and anxiety but also their effects on outcomes—how well patients fare. Clarke and Currie indicate that people with disabling chronic illnesses such as arthritis, stroke, and pulmonary diseases are likely to become depressed. Furthermore, they note that some prescription medications, as well as over-the-counter (nonprescription) drugs, may also cause depression.

Depression causes some older adults to deliberately neglect or disregard their medical needs by eating poorly and failing to take prescribed medication or taking it incorrectly. These may be covert acts of suicide. Actual suicide, which is frequently a consequence of serious depression, is highest among older adults relative to all other age groups. In 2005 the death rate for suicide among people aged 75 to 84 and adults age 85 and older was 16.9%. (See Table 8.1.) Older men had the highest rates—35.8% for those aged 75 to 84 and 45% for those aged 85 and older. Heron et al. indicate that in 2006 the death rate for suicide among people aged 75 to 84 and adults age 85 and older was 15.9%.

TREATMENT OF DEPRESSION. According to the surgeon general, in *Mental Health*, despite the availability of effective treatments for depression, a substantial fraction of

FIGURE 8.3

Percentage of people aged 65 and over with clinically relevant depressive symptoms, by age group and sex, 2004

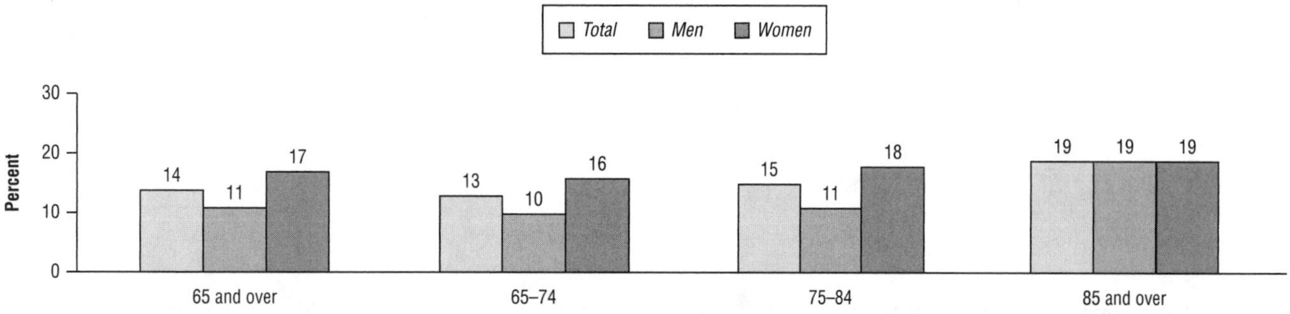

Note: The definition of "clinically relevant depressive symptoms" is four or more symptoms out of a list of eight depressive symptoms from an abbreviated version of the Center for Epidemiological Studies Depression Scale (CES-D) adapted by the Health and Retirement Study. The CES-D scale is a measure of depressive symptoms and is not to be used as a diagnosis of clinical depression.
Reference population: These data refer to the civilian noninstitutionalized population.

SOURCE: "Percentage of People Age 65 and over with Clinically Relevant Depressive Symptoms, by Age Group and Sex, 2004," in *Older Americans 2008: Key Indicators of Well-Being*, Federal Interagency Forum on Aging-Related Statistics, March 2008, http://www.agingstats.gov/agingstatsdotnet/Main_Site/Data/2008_Documents/OA_2008.pdf (accessed April 20, 2009)

TABLE 8.1

Death rates for suicide, by selected characteristics, selected years 1950–2005

[Data are based on death certificates]

Sex, race, Hispanic origin, and age	1950[a,b]	1960[a,b]	1970[b]	1980[b]	1990[b]	2000[c]	2004	2005
All persons				Deaths per 100,000 resident population				
All ages, age-adjusted[d]	13.2	12.5	13.1	12.2	12.5	10.4	10.9	10.9
All ages, crude	11.4	10.6	11.6	11.9	12.4	10.4	11.0	11.0
Under 1 year	f	f	f	f	f	f	g	g
1–4 years	f	f	f	f	f	f	g	g
5–14 years	0.2	0.3	0.3	0.4	0.8	0.7	0.7	0.7
15–24 years	4.5	5.2	8.8	12.3	13.2	10.2	10.3	10.0
15–19 years	2.7	3.6	5.9	8.5	11.1	8.0	8.2	7.7
20–24 years	6.2	7.1	12.2	16.1	15.1	12.5	12.5	12.4
25–44 years	11.6	12.2	15.4	15.6	15.2	13.4	13.9	13.7
25–34 years	9.1	10.0	14.1	16.0	15.2	12.0	12.7	12.4
35–44 years	14.3	14.2	16.9	15.4	15.3	14.5	15.0	14.9
45–64 years	23.5	22.0	20.6	15.9	15.3	13.5	15.4	15.4
45–54 years	20.9	20.7	20.0	15.9	14.8	14.4	16.6	16.5
55–64 years	26.8	23.7	21.4	15.9	16.0	12.1	13.8	13.9
65 years and over	30.0	24.5	20.8	17.6	20.5	15.2	14.3	14.7
65–74 years	29.6	23.0	20.8	16.9	17.9	12.5	12.3	12.6
75–84 years	31.1	27.9	21.2	19.1	24.9	17.6	16.3	16.9
85 years and over	28.8	26.0	19.0	19.2	22.2	19.6	16.4	16.9
Male								
All ages, age-adjusted[d]	21.2	20.0	19.8	19.9	21.5	17.7	18.0	18.0
All ages, crude	17.8	16.5	16.8	18.6	20.4	17.1	17.7	17.7
Under 1 year	f	f	f	f	f	f	g	g
1–4 years	f	f	f	f	f	f	g	g
5–14 years	0.3	0.4	0.5	0.6	1.1	1.2	0.9	1.0
15–24 years	6.5	8.2	13.5	20.2	22.0	17.1	16.8	16.2
15–19 years	3.5	5.6	8.8	13.8	18.1	13.0	12.6	12.1
20–24 years	9.3	11.5	19.3	26.8	25.7	21.4	20.8	20.2
25–44 years	17.2	17.9	20.9	24.0	24.4	21.3	21.7	21.6
25–34 years	13.4	14.7	19.8	25.0	24.8	19.6	20.4	19.9
35–44 years	21.3	21.0	22.1	22.5	23.9	22.8	23.0	23.1
45–64 years	37.1	34.4	30.0	23.7	24.3	21.3	23.7	24.0
45–54 years	32.0	31.6	27.9	22.9	23.2	22.4	24.8	25.2
55–64 years	43.6	38.1	32.7	24.5	25.7	19.4	22.1	22.2
65 years and over	52.8	44.0	38.4	35.0	41.6	31.1	29.0	29.5
65–74 years	50.5	39.6	36.0	30.4	32.2	22.7	22.6	22.7
75–84 years	58.3	52.5	42.8	42.3	56.1	38.6	34.8	35.8
85 years and over	58.3	57.4	42.4	50.6	65.9	57.5	45.0	45.0
Female								
All ages, age-adjusted[d]	5.6	5.6	7.4	5.7	4.8	4.0	4.5	4.4
All ages, crude	5.1	4.9	6.6	5.5	4.8	4.0	4.6	4.5
Under 1 year	f	f	f	f	f	f	g	g
1–4 years	f	f	f	f	f	f	g	g
5–14 years	0.1	0.1	0.2	0.2	0.4	0.3	0.5	0.3
15–24 years	2.6	2.2	4.2	4.3	3.9	3.0	3.6	3.5
15–19 years	1.8	1.6	2.9	3.0	3.7	2.7	3.5	3.0
20–24 years	3.3	2.9	5.7	5.5	4.1	3.2	3.6	4.0
25–44 years	6.2	6.6	10.2	7.7	6.2	5.4	6.0	5.8
25–34 years	4.9	5.5	8.6	7.1	5.6	4.3	4.7	4.7
35–44 years	7.5	7.7	11.9	8.5	6.8	6.4	7.1	6.8
45–64 years	9.9	10.2	12.0	8.9	7.1	6.2	7.6	7.2
45–54 years	9.9	10.2	12.6	9.4	6.9	6.7	8.6	8.0
55–64 years	9.9	10.2	11.4	8.4	7.3	5.4	6.1	6.1
65 years and over	9.4	8.4	8.1	6.1	6.4	4.0	3.8	4.0
65–74 years	10.1	8.4	9.0	6.5	6.7	4.0	3.8	4.0
75–84 years	8.1	8.9	7.0	5.5	6.3	4.0	3.9	4.0
85 years and over	8.2	6.0	5.9	5.5	5.4	4.2	3.6	4.0

affected older adults do not receive treatment, largely because they either do not seek it or because their depression is not identified, accurately diagnosed, or effectively treated. For example, even though older patients respond well to antidepressant medications, some physicians do not prescribe them to older patients already taking many drugs for chronic medical conditions because they do not want to risk drug-drug interactions or add another drug to an already complicated regimen. As a result, only a minority of older adults diagnosed with depression receives the appropriate drug dose and duration of treatment for depression.

Common treatments for depression include psychotherapy, with or without the use of antidepressant medica-

TABLE 8.1

Death rates for suicide, by selected characteristics, selected years 1950–2005 [CONTINUED]

[Data are based on death certificates]

Sex, race, Hispanic origin, and age	1950[a,b]	1960[a,b]	1970[b]	1980[b]	1990[b]	2000[c]	2004	2005
White male[e]				Deaths per 100,000 resident population				
All ages, age-adjusted[d]	22.3	21.1	20.8	20.9	22.8	19.1	19.6	19.6
All ages, crude	19.0	17.6	18.0	19.9	22.0	18.8	19.6	19.7
15–24 years	6.6	8.6	13.9	21.4	23.2	17.9	17.9	17.3
25–44 years	17.9	18.5	21.5	24.6	25.4	22.9	23.8	23.5
45–64 years	39.3	36.5	31.9	25.0	26.0	23.2	26.1	26.6
65 years and over	55.8	46.7	41.1	37.2	44.2	33.3	31.2	32.1
65–74 years	53.2	42.0	38.7	32.5	34.2	24.3	24.2	24.9
75–84 years	61.9	55.7	45.5	45.5	60.2	41.1	37.1	38.4
85 years and over	61.9	61.3	45.8	52.8	70.3	61.6	48.4	48.2

[a]Includes deaths of persons who were not residents of the 50 states and the District of Columbia.
[b]Underlying cause of death was coded according to the Sixth Revision of the International Classification of Diseases (ICD) in 1950, Seventh Revision in 1960, Eighth Revision in 1970, and Ninth Revision in 1980–1998.
[c]Starting with 1999 data, cause of death is coded according to ICD–10.
[d]Age-adjusted rates are calculated using the year 2000 standard population. Prior to 2003, age-adjusted rates were calculated using standard million proportions based on rounded population numbers. Starting with 2003 data, unrounded population numbers are used to calculate age-adjusted rates.
[e]The race groups, white, black, Asian or Pacific Islander, and American Indian or Alaska Native, include persons of Hispanic and non-Hispanic origin. Persons of Hispanic origin may be of any race. Death rates for the American Indian or Alaska Native and Asian or Pacific Islander populations are known to be underestimated.
[f]Data not available.
[g]Rates based on fewer than 20 deaths are considered unreliable and are not shown.
Note: Age groups were selected to minimize the presentation of unstable age-specific death rates based on small numbers of deaths and for consistency among comparison groups.

SOURCE: Adapted from "Table 45. Death Rates for Suicide, by Sex, Race, Hispanic Origin, and Age: United States, Selected Years 1950–2005," in *Health, United States, 2008. With Chartbook*, National Center for Health Statistics, 2009, http://www.cdc.gov/nchs/data/hus/hus08.pdf#listtables (accessed May 6, 2009)

tions, and electroconvulsive therapy (ECT). Psychotherapy is most often used to treat mild to moderate depression and is prescribed for a limited, defined period, generally ranging from 10 to 20 weeks. ECT is used for life-threatening depression that does not respond to treatment with antidepressant drugs.

In "The Effect of a Primary Care Practice-Based Depression Intervention on Mortality in Older Adults: A Randomized Trial" (*Annals of Internal Medicine*, vol. 146, no. 10, May 15, 2007), a five-year study of 1,226 older patients, Joseph J. Gallo et al. not only find that depression is independently associated with mortality risk in older adults but also confirm that treatment for depression reduces this risk. Of the total number of subjects, about 600 were determined to be suffering from major or minor depression. During the five-year follow-up, 223 subjects had died. Subjects who received treatment for depression were 33% less likely to die than those who were not treated.

Anxiety Disorders

Anxiety disorders (extreme nervousness and apprehension or sudden attacks of anxiety without apparent external causes) can be debilitating and destructive. Symptoms may include fear, a "knot" in the stomach, sweating, or elevated blood pressure. If the anxiety is severe and long lasting, more serious problems may develop. People suffering from anxiety over an extended period may have headaches, ulcers, irritable bowel syndrome, insomnia, or depression. Because anxiety tends to create various other emotional and physical symptoms, a cascade effect can occur in which these new or additional problems produce even more anxiety.

Unrelenting anxiety that appears unrelated to specific environments or situations is called generalized anxiety disorder. People suffering from this disorder worry excessively about the events of daily life and the future. They are also more likely to experience physical symptoms such as shortness of breath, dizziness, rapid heart rate, nausea, stomach pains, and muscle tension than people afflicted with other panic disorders, social phobias, or agoraphobia (fear of being in an open space or a place where escape is difficult).

The surgeon general estimates in *Mental Health* the prevalence of anxiety disorder as about 11.4% in adults aged 55 years and older. Phobic anxiety disorders such as social phobia, which causes extreme discomfort in social settings, are among the most common mental disturbances in late life. In contrast, the prevalence of panic disorder (0.5%) and obsessive-compulsive disorder (1.5%) is low in older adults. Generalized anxiety disorder, rather than specific anxiety syndromes, may be more prevalent in older people.

Effective treatment for anxiety involves medication, primarily benzodiazepines, such as Valium, Librium, and Xanax, as well as psychotherapy. Like other medications, the effects of benzodiazepines may last longer in older adults, and their side effects may include drowsiness, fatigue, physical impairment, memory or other cognitive impairment, confusion, depression, respiratory problems, abuse or dependence problems, and withdrawal reactions.

Nondrug treatment may also be effective for older adults suffering from debilitating anxiety. Melinda A. Stanley et al. compared cognitive behavioral therapy (CBT; goal-oriented treatment that focuses on changing thoughts to solve psychological problems) to enhanced usual care (treatment that consists of biweekly telephone calls to ensure patient safety and provide minimal support) for treatment of generalized anxiety disorder in older adults and reported their findings in "Cognitive Behavior Therapy for Generalized Anxiety Disorder among Older Adults in Primary Care: A Randomized Clinical Trial" (*Journal of the American Medical Association*, vol. 301, no. 14, April 8, 2009). The researchers find that the CBT, which consisted of education and awareness, motivational interviewing, relaxation training, cognitive therapy, problem-solving skills training, and behavioral sleep management, resulted in greater relief from worry and depressive symptoms and improved general mental health for older patients with general anxiety disorder than the enhanced usual care.

Schizophrenia

Schizophrenia is an extremely disabling form of mental illness. Its symptoms include hallucinations, paranoia, delusions, and social isolation. People suffering from schizophrenia "hear voices," and over time the voices take over in the schizophrenic's mind, obliterating reality and directing all kinds of erratic behaviors. Suicide attempts and violent attacks are common in the lives of schizophrenics. In an attempt to escape the torment inflicted by their brains, many schizophrenics turn to drugs. The National Institute of Mental Health indicates in *Schizophrenia* (2009, http://www.nimh.nih.gov/health/publications/schizophrenia/schizophrenia-booket-2009.pdf) that most symptoms of schizophrenia emerge early in life—the late teens or 20s and rarely begin after age 45.

In *Mental Health*, the surgeon general notes that the prevalence of schizophrenia among adults aged 65 years and older is estimated as 0.6%, less than half of the 1.3% that is estimated for the population aged 18 to 54. However, the economic burden of late-life schizophrenia is high. Even though the use of nursing homes and state hospitals for patients with all mental disorders has declined over the past two decades, this decline is small for older patients with schizophrenia.

Drug treatment of schizophrenia in older adults is complicated. The medications used to treat schizophrenia, such as Haldol, effectively reduce symptoms (e.g., delusions and hallucinations) of many older patients, but they also have a high risk of disabling side effects, such as tardive dyskinesias (involuntary, rhythmic movements of the face, jaw, mouth, tongue, and trunk). Even newer atypical antipsychotic medication used to treat the symptoms of schizophrenia such as Abilify can produce troubling side effects including tremors, restlessness, shakes, muscle stiffness, or other involuntary movements.

MISUSE OF ALCOHOL AND PRESCRIPTION DRUGS

The surgeon general observes in *Mental Health* that older adults are more likely to misuse, as opposed to abuse, alcohol and prescription drugs. The surgeon general estimates that the prevalence of heavy drinking (12 to 21 drinks per week) in the cohort (a group of individuals that shares a common characteristic such as birth years and is studied over time) of older adults is 3% to 9%. The prevalence rates are expected to rise as the baby boomer (people born between 1946 and 1964) cohort, with its history of alcohol and illegal drug use, joins the ranks of older adults. In "Substance Use Disorder among Older Adults in the United States in 2020" (*Addiction*, vol. 104, no. 1, January 2009) Beth Han et al. forecast that the number of adults aged 50 and older with substance use disorder (alcohol/illicit drug dependence or abuse) is projected to double from an average of 2.8 million per year in 2006 to 5.7 million in 2020. The current group of older adults is more likely to suffer substance misuse problems, such as drug dependence, arising from underuse, overuse, or erratic use of prescription and over-the-counter medications.

Figure 8.4 shows that in 2008 adults aged 65 and older had the lowest rate of excessive alcohol consumption—just 5%—of all age groups. Older men (9%) were much more likely than older women (2%) to have met the National Health Interview Survey criteria for excessive

FIGURE 8.4

Prevalence of types of drinkers

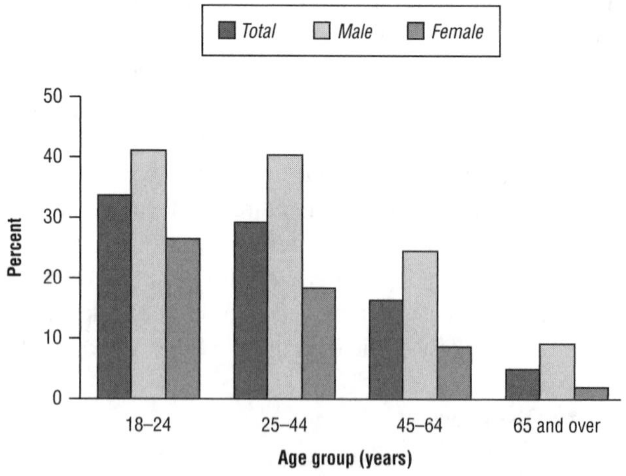

Notes: The analyses excluded 315 adults (1.6%) with unknown alcohol consumption. Data are based on household interviews of a sample of the civilian noninstitutionalized population.

SOURCE: "Figure 3. Prevalence of Types of Drinkers," in *Module 10C: Older Adults and Alcohol Problems, NIAA: Social Work Education for the Prevention and Treatment of Alcohol Use Disorders*, National Institute on Alcohol Abuse and Alcoholism, March 2005, http://pubs.niaaa.nih.gov/publications/Social/Module10COlderAdults/Module10C.html (accessed May 12, 2009)

alcohol consumption (five or more drinks in one day at least once in the past year).

Prevalence of Types of Older Problem Drinkers

In *Module 10C: Older Adults and Alcohol Problems* (March 2005, http://pubs.niaaa.nih.gov/publications/Social/Module10COlderAdults/Module10C.html), the National Institute on Alcohol Abuse and Alcoholism (NIAAA) describes the prevalence of three types of problem drinkers: at-risk drinkers, problem drinkers, and alcohol-dependent drinkers.

- At-risk drinking is alcohol use that increases the risk of developing alcohol-related problems and complications. People over the age of 65 who drink more than seven drinks per week (one per day) are considered at-risk of developing health, social, or emotional problems caused by alcohol.
- Problem drinkers have already suffered medical, psychological, family, financial/economic, self-care, legal, or social consequences of alcohol abuse.
- Alcohol-dependent drinkers suffer from a medical disorder characterized by loss of control over consumption, preoccupation with alcohol, and continued use despite adverse health, social, legal, and financial consequences.

Figure 8.5 shows the estimated prevalence rates of these different types of drinkers as well as the majority (65%) of older adults that abstains from alcohol consumption.

FIGURE 8.5

Prevalence of types of drinkers

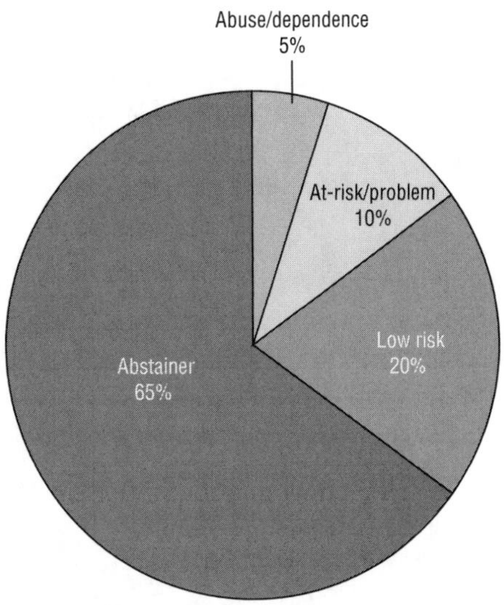

SOURCE: "Figure 3. Prevalence of Types of Drinkers," in *Module 10C: Older Adults and Alcohol Problems, NIAA: Social Work Education for the Prevention and Treatment of Alcohol Use Disorders*, National Institute on Alcohol Abuse and Alcoholism, March 2005, http://pubs.niaaa.nih.gov/publications/Social/Module10COlderAdults/Module10C.html (accessed May 12, 2009)

Types of Older Problem Drinkers

Another way to characterize older problem drinkers is by the duration and the patterns of their drinking histories. The first group consists of those over the age of 60 who have been drinking most of their lives. The members of this group are called survivors or early onset problem drinkers. They have beaten the statistical odds by living to old age despite heavy drinking. These are the people most likely to suffer medical problems such as cirrhosis of the liver (a chronic degenerative disease of the liver marked by scarring of liver tissue and eventually liver failure) and mental health disorders such as depression.

The second group, intermittents, has historically engaged in binges or bout drinking interspersed with periods of relative sobriety. These drinkers are at risk for alcohol abuse because they are more likely than others to self-medicate with alcohol to relieve physical pain and emotional distress or to assuage loneliness and social isolation.

Reactors or late-onset problem drinkers make up the third group. The stresses of later life, particularly the loss of work or a spouse, may precipitate heavy drinking. These people show few of the physical consequences of prolonged drinking and fewer disruptions of their lives.

Alcohol-Related Issues Unique to Older Adults

Older adults generally have a decreased tolerance to alcohol. Consumption of a given amount of alcohol by older adults usually produces higher blood-alcohol levels than it would in a younger population. Chronic medical problems such as cirrhosis may be present, but older adults are less likely to require detoxification and treatment of alcohol-withdrawal problems. One possible explanation is that few lifelong alcohol abusers survive to old age.

Because older adults usually take more medication than people in other age groups, they are more susceptible to drug-alcohol interactions. Alcohol reduces the safety and efficacy of many medications and, in combination with some drugs, may produce coma or death. Adverse consequences of alcohol consumption in older adults are not limited to problem drinkers. Older adults with medical problems, including diabetes, heart disease, liver disease, and central nervous system degeneration, may also suffer adverse reactions from alcohol consumption.

SCREENING, DIAGNOSIS, AND TREATMENT. The NIAAA advocates screening to identify at-risk drinkers, problem drinkers, and dependent drinkers to determine the need for further diagnostic evaluation and treatment. Furthermore, in *Module 10C* it provides a screening protocol that recommends that:

- All adults aged 60 and older should be screened for alcohol and prescription drug use/abuse as part of any medical examination or application for health or social services.

- Annual rescreening should be performed if certain physical symptoms emerge or if the individual is undergoing major life changes, stresses, or transitions.
- These screening criteria apply to any health, social, work, or recreation setting that serves older adults and are not limited to medical care and substance treatment settings.

Diagnosis of problem drinking in the older population is complicated by the fact that many psychological, behavioral, and physical symptoms of problem drinking also occur in people who do not have drinking problems. For example, brain damage, heart disease, and gastrointestinal disorders often develop in older adults independent of alcohol use, but may also occur with drinking. In addition, mood disorders, depression, and changes in employment, economic, or marital status often accompany aging but can also be symptoms of alcoholism. Alcohol-induced organic brain syndrome is characterized by cognitive impairment—memory lapses, confusion, and disorientation. As a result, some older alcoholics may be incorrectly diagnosed as suffering from dementia or other mental illness.

Older problem drinkers make up a relatively small proportion of the total number of clients seen by most agencies for treatment of alcohol abuse. There is little data about the effectiveness of intervention and treatment, which usually consists of some combination of counseling and education, in the older population. Nonetheless, the chances for recovery among older drinkers are considered good, because older clients tend to complete the full course of therapy more often than younger clients.

Simon Coulton et al. assert in "The Effectiveness and Cost-Effectiveness of Opportunistic Screening and Stepped Care Interventions for Older Hazardous Alcohol Users in Primary Care (AESOPS): A Randomised Control Trial Protocol" (*BMC Health Services Research*, vol. 8, no. 129, June 2008) that even though the prevalence of harmful alcohol consumption in adults aged 55 years and older is generally lower than the general population, because it is associated with a wide range of physical, psychological, and social problems, it merits attention and effective treatment. Coulton et al. note that there is an association between increased alcohol consumption and increased risk of falls, heart disease, hypertension, stroke, alcohol-related liver disease, and many cancers. Alcohol consumption can contribute to the development of dementia and other age-related cognitive deficits as well as psychological problems including depression, anxiety, and suicide.

CHAPTER 9
CARING FOR OLDER ADULTS—CAREGIVERS

In the United States most long-term care of older adults continues to be provided by families as opposed to nursing homes, assisted living facilities, social service agencies, or government programs. This continuing commitment to family care of older adults in the community is remarkable in view of relatively recent changes in the fabric of American society. American family life has undergone significant changes in the past three decades. Most households require two incomes, and greater numbers of women have entered the workforce. Delayed marriage and childbearing has produced a so-called sandwich generation of family caregivers that is simultaneously caring for two generations: their children and their parents. For the first time in history, adults may spend more years caring for a parent than for a child. Increased geographic separation of families further compounds the difficulties of family caregiving.

Another challenge is that the supply of caregivers is not keeping pace with the growth in the older population. The number of older adults for every 100 adults of working age (from 20 to 64) is called the dependency ratio. Laura B. Shrestha of the Congressional Research Service notes in *Age Dependency and Social Security Solvency* (October 27, 2008, http://aging.senate.gov/crs/ss4.pdf) that by 2010 there will be an estimated 20.9 older adults for every 100 working-age adults. (See Table 9.1.) When the youngest members of the baby boomer generation (those born between 1946 and 1964) begin approaching retirement age in 2025, there will be 31.2 older adults for every 100 people of working age.

In *Retooling for an Aging America: Building the Health Care Workforce* (2008, http://www.nap.edu/openbook.php?record_id=12089&page=R1), the Institute of Medicine's Committee on the Future Health Care Workforce for Older Americans reports that an increasing number of Americans are hiring caregivers to assist with older relatives. About 3 million workers were employed in direct caregiving for older adults in 2006, and the need for these caregivers is expected to outpace supply, largely because of the aging population but also because the number of women aged 26 to 54, the group that typically provides home care and personal care services, is not expected to grow.

Furthermore, the Committee on the Future Health Care Workforce for Older Americans observes that about 80% of older adults rely exclusively on unpaid help from family and friends for assistance at home, and less than 10% receive all their care from paid workers. An estimated 29 million to 52 million Americans—as many as 31% of all U.S. adults—provide some kind of unpaid help or care.

FAMILY CAREGIVERS

According to the Family Caregiver Alliance, in "2009 National Policy Statement" (2009, http://www. caregiver .org/caregiver/jsp/content_node.jsp?nodeid=22 79), 78% of adults who received long-term care at home in 2009 relied exclusively on informal caregivers—family and friends. Every year, about 44.4 million Americans devote 37.1 billion hours providing this care, which includes help with tasks such as bathing, meal preparation, and managing medications, for adult family members.

The Family Caregiver Alliance also reports that in 2009, 70% of people with Alzheimer's disease were cared for at home, where family members provided at least 75% of their care.

Caregiving in the United States

In the fact sheet "Selected Caregiver Statistics" (2005, http://www.caregiver.org/caregiver/jsp/content_no de.jsp?nodeid=439), the Family Caregiver Alliance describes the average caregiver as a middle-aged (35 to 64 years old) working woman who spends an average of 4.3 years caring for a parent who lives about 20 minutes away. One-fifth of caregivers provide 40 hours of care per week and more than 40% of caregivers have provided care for 5 years or longer and 20% for more than 10 years. Older

TABLE 9.1

Age dependency ratios, 2010–30

Year	Population (in thousands)				Dependency ratio (number of dependents per 100 persons of working age)		
	Total	Children (0–19)	Working age (20–64)	Older persons (65–65+)	All dependents	Children (0–19)	Older persons (65–65+)
2010	314,740	84,895	190,083	39,762	65.6	44.7	20.9
2011	317,226	84,959	191,627	40,640	65.5	44.3	21.2
2012	319,718	85,087	192,733	41,898	65.9	44.1	21.7
2013	322,215	85,283	193,681	43,251	66.4	44.0	22.3
2014	324,710	85,525	194,629	44,556	66.8	43.9	22.9
2015	327,202	85,796	195,496	45,910	67.4	43.9	23.5
2016	329,662	86,106	196,245	47,311	68.0	43.9	24.1
2017	332,086	86,466	196,874	48,746	68.7	43.9	24.8
2018	334,497	86,859	197,405	50,233	69.4	44.0	25.4
2019	336,892	87,247	197,826	51,819	70.3	44.1	26.2
2020	339,270	87,547	198,213	53,510	71.2	44.2	27.0
2021	341,626	87,736	198,642	55,248	72.0	44.2	27.8
2022	343,958	87,883	199,059	57,016	72.8	44.1	28.6
2023	346,255	88,003	199,475	58,777	73.6	44.1	29.5
2024	348,514	88,233	199,736	60,545	74.5	44.2	30.3
2025	350,729	88,597	199,789	62,343	75.5	44.3	31.2
2026	352,871	88,942	199,847	64,082	76.6	44.5	32.1
2027	354,936	89,266	199,965	65,705	77.5	44.6	32.9
2028	356,946	89,574	200,139	67,233	78.3	44.8	33.6
2029	358,898	89,863	200,347	68,688	79.1	44.9	34.3
2030	360,794	90,133	200,644	70,017	79.8	44.9	34.9

SOURCE: Adapted from Laura B. Shrestha, "Appendix Table 1. Age Dependency Ratios, United States,1950–2080," in *Age Dependency Ratios and Social Security Solvency*, Congressional Research Service, The Library of Congress, October 27, 2006, http://aging.senate.gov/crs/ss4.pdf (accessed May 12, 2009)

caregivers (aged 50 and older) are more likely than younger ones to have been caregiving for more than 10 years.

Caregiving can take a toll on physical and mental health and well-being. Research reveals that caregivers may suffer a range of health problems including:

- Elevated blood pressure and insulin levels, which in turn increase the risk of developing cardiovascular disease.
- High levels of physical and emotional stress and impaired immune function, which renders them less able to defend against illness.
- Depression, anxiety, anger, and other emotional problems.

The Economics of Caregiving

Most of the costs and responsibility for long-term care for older adults rest with family caregivers in the community. The shift toward increasing reliance on this informal system of care was spurred by changes in the health care delivery financing system that resulted in shorter hospital stays, rising costs of nursing home care, older adults preferring home care over institutional care, and a shortage of workers in all long-term care settings. Taken together, these factors continue to increase the likelihood that frail, disabled, and ill older adults will be cared for by relatives in the community.

During the next few decades, as the number of older people needing assistance to remain independent increases dramatically, the burden and cost of providing care to an ill or disabled relative will affect almost every U.S. household. UnitedHealthcare and the National Alliance for Caregiving observe in *Evercare Survey of the Economic Downturn and its Impact on Family Caregiving* (April 28, 2009, http://www.caregiving.org/data/EVC_Caregivers_Economy_Report%20FINAL_4-28-09.pdf) that if the services of family caregivers for older adults were replaced by paid home health care staff, the cost would be $375 billion per year, more than the combined costs of home health care and nursing home care.

The Economic Downturn Affects Informal Caregiving

To assess the impact of the economic downturn on caregivers and the people they care for, UnitedHealthcare and the National Alliance for Caregiving (NAC) surveyed more than 1,000 family caregivers between February and March 2009 and reported the findings in *Evercare Survey of the Economic Downturn and its Impact on Family Caregiving*. The survey finds that the economic downturn has placed additional pressure on caregivers, forcing many to change their living situations, use savings, or take on additional debt to pay for expenses associated with caregiving. Among the survey's key findings are:

- Forty-three percent reported the economic downturn has resulted in a pay cut or reduction in their work hours, and 15% said they have been laid off.
- Close to 6 out of 10 (59%) working caregivers said they are less comfortable taking time off from work to provide care, and one-third (35%) reported working additional hours or taking an additional job.

- Half (51%) of caregivers said the economic downturn has increased their stress about their ability to continue to provide caregiving services.
- During the 12 months before the survey, 21% of caregivers had moved in with the person for whom they provide care. Caregivers with household incomes of less than $50,000 (27%) were twice as likely as those with higher incomes (14%) to have made such a move.
- Two-thirds (63%) of caregivers said they are saving less for retirement.
- Nearly a quarter (24%) of caregivers said they have cut back on spending associated with caregiving, and 13% said the economy has caused them to spend more on expenses associated with caregiving.

Furthermore, 65% of the caregivers who are spending more on the people they care for in response to the economic downturn said this additional spending is a hardship, causing them difficulties in paying for their own basic necessities and bills. Other financial consequences of the downturn include being unable to sell a home or place a relative in a facility as planned and increased credit card debt.

The caregivers surveyed also reported emotional consequences of the economic downturn. More caregivers under the age of 65 said they feel additional stress than their older counterparts, 54% and 31%, respectively. One out of seven (14%) caregivers said the economy has forced them to spend less time caregiving, and one out of four (27%) reported that outside assistance from government agencies and nonprofit organizations has been cut back. Nineteen percent of caregivers said the quality of care their relative is receiving has declined as a result of the economy. Caregivers with the lowest household income (less than $25,000) were more likely to report a negative effect on the quality of care (27%) than those with higher incomes (14%).

Paid Caregivers Are Also Affected

In the press release "Escalating Energy Costs Threaten Health Care for Critically Ill and Homebound Seniors: Home Care Nurses, Aides, and Therapists Drive 4.8 Billion Miles per Year to Reach Shut-in Patients" (June 25, 2008, http://www.nahc.org/media/mediaPR _06 2508.html), the National Association for Home Care and Hospice (NAHC) reports that the home care workers who provide services for older adults and people with disabilities drive 4.8 billion miles (7.7 billion km) each year and that rising gasoline prices threaten their ability to travel to patients, particularly those who live in rural communities. The NAHC notes that home health agencies located in rural areas have higher costs in general and are especially hard hit by high fuel costs. Furthermore, in 2007 many rural home care agencies were operating at break-even, whereas 44% lost money.

THE CONTINUUM OF FORMAL SERVICES

As the older population increases, the segment of the population available to provide unpaid care, generally consisting of family members, has decreased. Because the availability of caregivers has diminished, increasing numbers of older adults in need of assistance will have to rely on a combination of family caregiving and paid professional services or on professional services alone.

Home Health Care

Home health care agencies provide a wide variety of services. Services range from helping with activities of daily living, such as bathing, light housekeeping, and meals, to skilled nursing care. Home health agencies employ registered nurses, licensed practical nurses, and nursing or home health aides to deliver the bulk of home care services. Other personnel involved in home health care include physical therapists, social workers, and speech-language pathologists.

Home health care grew faster in the early 1990s than any other segment of health services. Its growth may be attributable to the observation that in many cases caring for patients at home is preferable to and more cost effective than care provided in a hospital, nursing home, or some other residential facility.

Before 2000 Medicare coverage for home health care was limited to patients immediately following discharge from the hospital. By 2000 Medicare covered beneficiaries' home health care services with no requirement for prior hospitalization. There were also no limits to the number of professional visits or to the length of coverage. As long as the patient's condition warranted it, the following services were provided:

- Part-time or intermittent skilled nursing and home health aide services
- Speech-language pathology services
- Physical and occupational therapy
- Medical social services
- Medical supplies
- Durable medical equipment (with a 20% co-payment)

Since 2000 the population receiving home care services has changed. As of 2009, much of home health care was associated with rehabilitation from critical illnesses, and fewer users were long-term patients with chronic (long-term) conditions. This changing pattern of use reflects a shift from longer-term care for chronic conditions to short-term postacute care. Compared with postacute care users, the long-term patients are older, more functionally disabled, more likely to be incontinent, and more expensive to serve.

According to the NAHC, in *Basic Statistics about Home Care* (2008, http://www.nahc.org/facts/08HC_Stats.pdf), approximately 7.6 million people received home care services from 83,000 providers of home care services, and annual expenditures for home health care services were an estimated $57.6 billion in 2007.

Respite Care and Adult Day Care

Respite care enables caregivers to take much-needed breaks from the demands of caregiving. It offers relief for families who may be overwhelmed and exhausted by the demands of caregiving and may be neglecting their own needs for rest and relaxation.

Respite care takes many forms. In some cases the respite worker comes to the home to take care of the older adult so that the caregiver can take a few hours off for personal needs, relaxation, or rest. Inpatient respite care, which is offered by some nursing homes and board-and-care facilities, provides an alternative to in-home care. Respite care is also available for longer periods, so that caregivers can recuperate from their own illnesses or even take vacations.

Adult day care programs, freestanding or based in hospitals, provide structured daytime programs where older adults may receive the social, health, and recreational services they need to restore or maintain optimal functioning. Even though they are not specifically intended to provide respite for caregivers, adult day care programs temporarily relieve families of the physical and emotional stress of caregiving.

Community Services

Besides home health care services, many communities offer a variety of services to help older adults and their caregivers:

- Home care aides to assist with chores such as housecleaning, grocery shopping, or laundry, as well as to help with the activities of daily living.
- Repair services to help with basic home maintenance, as well as minor changes to make homes secure and safe, such as the installation of grab bars in bathrooms, special seats in the shower, or ramps for wheelchairs.
- Home-delivered meal programs offering nutritious meals to those who can no longer cook or shop for groceries.
- Companion and telephone reassurance services to keep in touch with older adults living alone (volunteers make regular visits or phone calls to check on and maintain contact with isolated older adults).
- Trained postal or utility workers to spot signs of trouble at the homes of the older people.
- Personal Emergency Response Systems devices that allow older adults to summon help in emergencies (when the user pushes the button on the wearable device, it sends a message to a response center or police station).
- Senior centers offering recreation programs, social activities, educational programs, health screenings, and meals.
- Communities providing transportation to help older adults run errands, attend medical appointments, and make related trips (such services are often subsidized or free of charge).
- Adult day care centers providing care for older adults who need supervised assistance (services may include health care, recreation, meals, rehabilitative therapy, and respite care).

Home and Community-Based Services

Home and community-based services refer to the entire array of supportive services that help older people live independently in their homes and communities. In 1981 federal law implemented the Medicaid Home and Community-Based Services (HCBS) waiver program. Before the passage of this legislation, Medicaid long-term care benefits were primarily limited to nursing homes. The HCBS legislation provided a vehicle for states to offer services not otherwise available through their Medicaid programs to serve people in their own homes and communities, thereby preserving their independence and ties to family and friends at a cost no higher than that of institutional care. States have the flexibility to design HCBS waiver programs to meet the specific needs of defined groups.

Seven specific services may be provided under HCBS waivers: case management services, homemaker services, home health aide services, personal care services, adult day care/health care services, respite care services, and rehabilitation services. Other services may be provided at the request of the state if approved by the federal government. Services must be cost effective and necessary for the prevention of institutionalization. Services may be provided to older adults and people with disabilities, people with developmental disabilities or mental retardation, and people with physical or mental illness. States have flexibility in designing their waiver programs; this allows them to tailor their programs to the specific needs of the populations they want to serve.

The HCBS waiver program has experienced tremendous growth since its enactment in 1981. According to the Centers for Medicare and Medicaid Services (CMS, June 8, 2009, http://www.cms.hhs.gov/MedicaidStWaivProgDemoPGI/05_HCBSWaivers-Section1915(c).asp), 48 states and the District of Columbia offered about 287 such programs in 2009.

The National Aging Network

The National Aging Network (February 11, 2009, http://www.aoa.gov/AoARoot/AoA_Programs/OAA/Aging_Network/Index.aspx), which is funded by the Older Americans

Act (OAA), provides funds for supportive home and community-based services to 56 State Units on Aging, 244 tribal organizations, and 2 native Hawaiian organizations. It also awards funds for disease prevention/health promotion services, elder rights programs, the National Family Caregiver Support Program, and the Native American Caregiver Support Program. All older Americans may receive services through the OAA, but it specifically targets vulnerable older populations—those older adults disadvantaged by social or health disparities.

Eldercare Locator

The U.S. Administration on Aging sponsors the Eldercare Locator Directory, a nationwide toll-free service that helps older adults and their caregivers find local services. The service is also available online (http://www.eldercare.gov/Eldercare.NET/Public/Home.aspx) so that consumers can easily link to information and referral services. The Eldercare Locator program connects those who contact it to an information specialist who access to a database of more than 4,800 entries.

BenefitsCheckUp

The National Council on Aging offers the online BenefitsCheckUp program (http://www.benefitscheckup.org), which examines a database of more than 1,700 programs to determine older adults' eligibility for federal, state, and local private and public benefits and programs. Users respond to a few confidential questions, and the database tells them which federal, state, and local programs they might be eligible for and how to apply. It is the first Internet-based service designed to help older Americans, their families, caregivers, and community organizations determine quickly and easily which benefits they qualify for and how to claim them.

In each state, there are about 70 programs available to individuals. Among the programs included are those that help older adults find income support, prescription drug savings, government health programs, energy assistance, property tax relief, nutrition programs, in-home services, veteran's programs, and volunteer, educational, and training programs. As of July 2009, the BenefitsCheckUp program had helped over 2.3 million people find benefits worth $7.3 billion to which they were entitled.

Geriatric Care Managers Help Older Adults Age in Place

The increasing complexity of arranging care for older adults, especially when families live at a distance from the older adults in need of care, has given rise to a relatively new service profession: geriatric care management. Geriatric care managers have varied educational backgrounds and professional credentials. They may be gerontologists, nurses, social workers, or psychologists who specialize in issues related to aging and services for older adults. Care managers generally work with a formal or informal network of social workers, nurses, psychologists, elder law attorneys, advocates, and agencies that serve older adults.

Geriatric care managers work with families and increasingly with corporations wishing to assist employees to create flexible plans of care to meet the needs of older adults. They oversee home health staffing needs, monitor the quality of in-home services and equipment, and serve as liaisons for families at a distance from their older relatives. In "Geriatric Assessment and Care Managers" (2008, http://www.helpguide.org/elder/geriatric_assessment.htm), Helpguide.com indicates that fees range from $50 to $300 for an initial evaluation to $50 to $200 per hour for follow-up, monitoring, and communicating with the family.

Hired homemakers/caregivers, transportation services, home modifications, and other services are also available. The total monthly cost of aging in place (older people remaining in their own home rather than relocating to assisted living facilities or other supportive housing) varies. An older adult who needs light housekeeping or companionship for three hours twice a week might spend around $300 a month, whereas one who needs 24-hour-a-day supervision might pay $5,000 per month or more—much more if care from a certified home health aide or licensed vocational nurse is required.

To determine public awareness of the geriatric manager profession, the degree of concern about selected aspects of aging, and the current involvement in caregiving, the National Association of Professional Geriatric Care Managers had Harris Interactive survey 2,075 U.S. adults, and the results were reported in "National Association of Professional Geriatric Care Managers Elder Care and Aging Issues Survey—Results" (2008, http://www.caremanager.org/displaycommon.cfm?an=1&subarticlenbr=137). The association states that just 32% of survey respondents were familiar with the profession. Older respondents and those with higher levels of educational attainment and higher incomes were more likely to be familiar with geriatric case managers, possibly because they had personal experience with a geriatric case manager or the ability to hire one.

CHAPTER 10
HEALTH CARE USE, EXPENDITURES, AND FINANCING

Health care use and expenditures tend to be concentrated among older adults. Because older adults often suffer multiple chronic conditions, they are hospitalized more frequently, use the most prescription and over-the-counter (nonprescription) drugs, make the highest number of physician visits, and require care from more physician-specialists and other health care providers—such as podiatrists and physical therapists—than any other age group.

Nearly all older Americans have health insurance through Medicare, which covers inpatient hospitalization, outpatient care, physician services, home health care, short-term skilled nursing facility care, hospice (end-of-life care) services, and prescription drugs. Historically, older adults' use of health care services has changed in response to physician practice patterns, advances in medical technology, and Medicare reimbursement for services. For example, advances in medical technology and physician practice patterns have shifted many medical procedures once performed in hospitals to outpatient settings such as ambulatory surgery centers.

Another example of changes in utilization occurred during the 1980s, when the average lengths of stay (ALOS) in hospitals for Medicare patients declined in response to the introduction of prospective payment and diagnostic-related groups—methods that are used to reimburse various providers for services performed. Even though the ALOS decreased, between 1992 and 2005 the hospitalization rate increased from 306 to 350 hospital stays per 1,000 Medicare enrollees. (See Figure 10.1.)

Older adults are responsible for disproportionate health care expenditures. The Centers for Medicare and Medicaid Services (CMS) projects that the national health expenditure will grow to $4.4 trillion by 2018. (See Table 10.1; note that because these numbers are projections, they differ from numbers presented in other tables and figures.) Medicare is projected to reach $932 billion by 2018, accounting for more than 21% of all health care expenditures.

FINANCING HEALTH CARE FOR OLDER ADULTS

The United States is the only industrialized nation that does not have a national health care program. In nearly all other developed countries, government national medical care programs cover almost all health-related costs, from birth to long-term care.

In the United States the major government health care entitlement programs are Medicare and Medicaid. They provide financial assistance for people aged 65 and older, the poor, and people with disabilities. Before the existence of these programs, many older Americans could not afford adequate medical care. For older adults who are beneficiaries, the Medicare program provides reimbursement for hospital and physician care, whereas Medicaid pays for the cost of nursing home care.

MEDICARE

The spirit in which this law is written draws deeply upon the ancient dreams of all mankind. In Leviticus, it is written, "Thou shall rise up before the hoary head, and honor the face of an old man."

—Senator Russell B. Long (D-LA) at the original vote for Medicare in 1965

The Medicare program, which was enacted under Title XVIII ("Health Insurance for the Aged") of the Social Security Act, was signed into law by President Lyndon B. Johnson (1908–1973), a Democrat, and went into effect on July 1, 1966. That year 19 million older adults entered the program. Michelle M. Megellas of Novartis Pharmaceuticals forecasts in "Medicare Modernization: The New Prescription Drug Benefit and Redesigned Part B and Part C" (*Proceedings Baylor University Medical Center*, vol. 19, no. 1, January 2006) that by 2030 the number of Americans insured by Medicare will exceed 78 million.

The establishment of the Medicare program in 1966 served to improve equity in health care. Before the creation of Medicare about half of the older population was uninsured,

FIGURE 10.1

Medicare-covered hospital and skilled nursing facility stays per 1,000 Medicare enrollees aged 65 and over in fee-for-service, 1992–2005

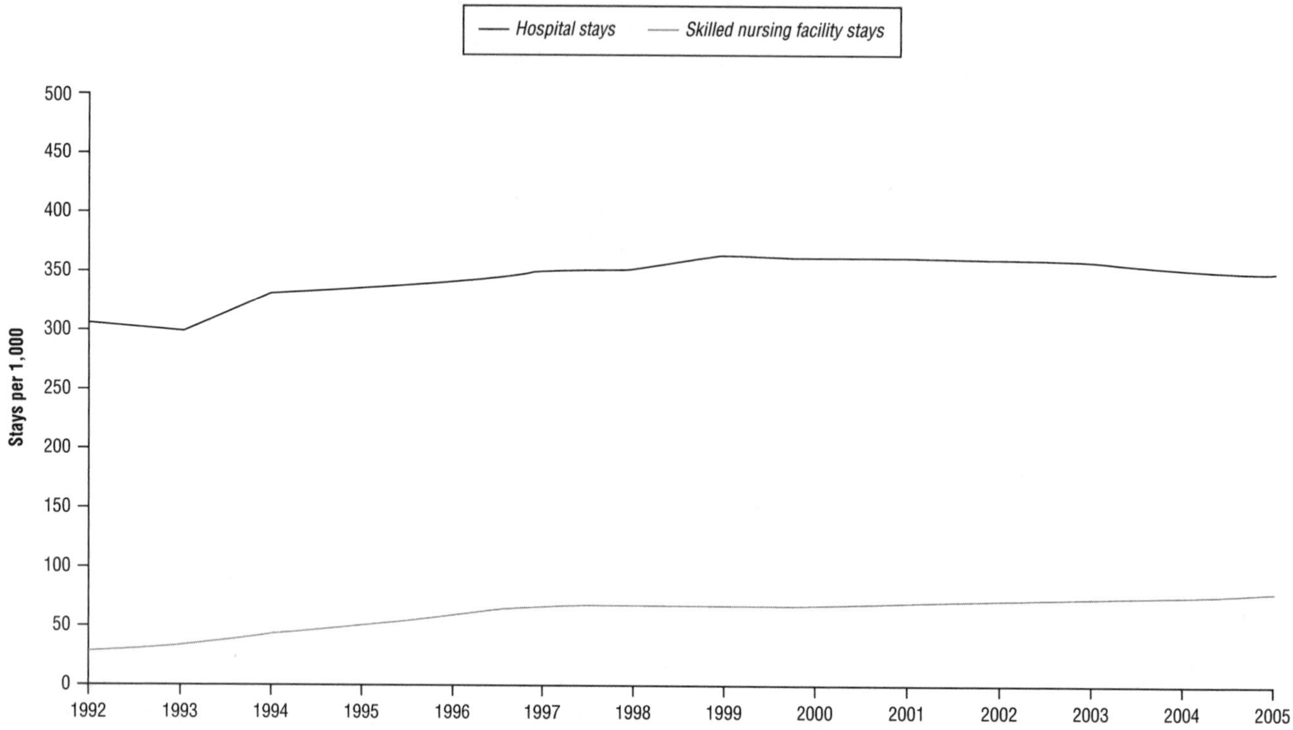

Note: Beginning in 1994, managed care enrollees were excluded from the denominator of all utilization rates because utilization data are not available for them. Prior to 1994, managed care enrollees were included in the denominators; they comprised 7 percent or less of the Medicare population.
Reference population: These data refer to Medicare enrollees in fee-for-service.

SOURCE: "Medicare-Covered Hospital and Skilled Nursing Facility Stays per 1,000 Medicare Enrollees Age 65 and over in Fee-for-Service, 1992–2005," in *Older Americans 2008: Key Indicators of Well-Being*, Federal Interagency Forum on Aging-Related Statistics, March 2008, http://www.agingstats.gov/agingstatsdotnet/Main_Site/Data/2008_Documents/OA_2008.pdf (accessed April 20, 2009)

and the insured population was often limited to benefits of just $10 per day. Furthermore, because poverty rates among older adults hovered at about 30%, the older population could not be expected to pay for private health insurance. The Medicare program extended health care coverage to a population with growing health needs and little income.

In 2004, nearly 50 years after its inception, the Medicare program covered 53% of the health care costs of older Americans. (See Figure 10.2.) Medicaid covered 9% and other payers, primarily private health insurers, covered 19%. Older adults paid 19% of their health care costs out of pocket. Historically, Medicare has focused almost exclusively on acute (short-term) care services such as hospitals, physicians, and short-term rehabilitation and home health care, but in 2006 Medicare offered its first prescription drug benefits. Other public and private payers finance long-term care.

The Medicare program is composed of several parts:

- Part A provides hospital insurance. Coverage includes physicians' fees, nursing services, meals, semiprivate rooms, special care units, operating room costs, laboratory tests, and some drugs and supplies. Part A also covers rehabilitation services, limited posthospital skilled nursing facility care, home health care, and hospice care for the terminally ill.
- Part B (Supplemental Medical Insurance) is elective medical insurance; enrollees must pay premiums to get coverage. It covers private physicians' services, diagnostic tests, outpatient hospital services, outpatient physical therapy, speech pathology services, home health services, and medical equipment and supplies.
- A newer, third part of Medicare, sometimes known as Part C, is the Medicare Advantage program, which was established by the Balanced Budget Act of 1997 to expand beneficiaries' options and allow them to participate in private-sector health plans.
- Part D, the Medicare prescription drug benefit, was enacted after Congress passed the Prescription Drug, Improvement, and Modernization Act of 2003.

According to the CMS, in *2009 Annual Report of the Boards of Trustees of the Federal Hospital Insurance and*

TABLE 10.1

National health expenditures by source of funds, selected years, 2003–18

			Third-party payments							
						Public				
Year	Total	Out-of-pocket payments	Total	Private health insurance	Other private funds	Total	Federal[a]	State and local[a]	Medicare[b]	Medicaid[c]
					Amount in billions					
Historical estimates										
2003	$1,734.9	$224.6	$1,510.3	$603.7	$127.6	$779.0	$552.3	$226.7	$282.7	$270.3
2004	1,854.8	234.9	1,620.0	645.9	134.2	839.9	599.5	240.4	311.2	290.5
2005	1,980.6	247.0	1,733.6	690.0	144.6	899.0	640.3	258.7	339.4	311.5
2006	2,112.7	255.0	1,857.7	731.3	153.4	973.0	707.6	265.4	402.3	309.4
2007	2,241.2	268.6	1,972.6	775.0	162.0	1,035.7	754.4	281.3	431.2	329.4
Projected										
2008	2,378.6	278.8	2,099.8	817.4	173.8	1,108.6	810.6	298.0	466.0	352.1
2009	2,509.5	282.7	2,226.7	854.4	181.8	1,190.5	873.2	317.3	503.1	386.0
2010	2,624.4	290.7	2,333.7	891.6	191.6	1,250.5	912.4	338.2	515.5	419.1
2011	2,770.3	301.5	2,468.8	933.9	202.4	1,332.4	972.2	360.2	547.4	452.0
2012	2,930.7	313.6	2,617.0	978.7	214.5	1,423.9	1,040.1	383.7	584.9	487.5
2013	3,110.9	327.5	2,783.5	1,028.8	227.3	1,527.4	1,117.6	409.7	627.9	527.4
2014	3,313.0	344.5	2,968.4	1,087.0	241.1	1,640.3	1,202.0	438.3	674.4	571.8
2015	3,541.3	363.2	3,178.1	1,151.9	257.8	1,768.4	1,298.3	470.1	729.1	621.3
2016	3,790.2	383.1	3,407.1	1,221.7	276.4	1,908.9	1,403.9	505.0	789.4	675.6
2017	4,061.7	404.5	3,657.2	1,296.9	296.0	2,064.3	1,521.3	542.9	857.7	735.2
2018	4,353.2	427.4	3,925.8	1,376.4	316.4	2,233.0	1,648.9	584.2	931.9	800.7
					Per capita amount					
Historical estimates										
2003	$5,967	$773	$5,195	$2,076	$439	$2,679	$1,900	$780	d	d
2004	6,319	800	5,519	2,200	457	2,861	2,043	819	d	d
2005	6,687	834	5,853	2,330	488	3,035	2,162	873	d	d
2006	7,062	852	6,210	2,444	513	3,252	2,365	887	d	d
2007	7,421	889	6,532	2,566	536	3,429	2,498	931	d	d
Projected										
2008	7,804	915	6,890	2,682	570	3,637	2,660	978	d	d
2009	8,160	919	7,241	2,778	591	3,871	2,839	1,032	d	d
2010	8,458	937	7,522	2,874	617	4,031	2,941	1,090	d	d
2011	8,851	963	7,887	2,984	647	4,257	3,106	1,151	d	d
2012	9,282	993	8,288	3,100	679	4,509	3,294	1,215	d	d
2013	9,767	1,028	8,739	3,230	713	4,795	3,509	1,286	d	d
2014	10,312	1,072	9,240	3,384	750	5,106	3,741	1,364	d	d
2015	10,929	1,121	9,808	3,555	796	5,457	4,007	1,451	d	d
2016	11,598	1,172	10,426	3,739	846	5,841	4,296	1,545	d	d
2017	12,325	1,227	11,097	3,935	898	6,264	4,616	1,647	d	d
2018	13,100	1,286	11,814	4,142	952	6,720	4,962	1,758	d	d
					Percent distribution					
Historical estimates										
2003	100.0	12.9	87.1	34.8	7.4	44.9	31.8	13.1	16.3	15.6
2004	100.0	12.7	87.3	34.8	7.2	45.3	32.3	13.0	16.8	15.7
2005	100.0	12.5	87.5	34.8	7.3	45.4	32.3	13.1	17.1	15.7
2006	100.0	12.1	87.9	34.6	7.3	46.1	33.5	12.6	19.0	14.6
2007	100.0	12.0	88.0	34.6	7.2	46.2	33.7	12.6	19.2	14.7
Projected										
2008	100.0	11.7	88.3	34.4	7.3	46.6	34.1	12.5	19.6	14.8
2009	100.0	11.3	88.7	34.0	7.2	47.4	34.8	12.6	20.0	15.4
2010	100.0	11.1	88.9	34.0	7.3	47.7	34.8	12.9	19.6	16.0
2011	100.0	10.9	89.1	33.7	7.3	48.1	35.1	13.0	19.8	16.3
2012	100.0	10.7	89.3	33.4	7.3	48.6	35.5	13.1	20.0	16.6
2013	100.0	10.5	89.5	33.1	7.3	49.1	35.9	13.2	20.2	17.0
2014	100.0	10.4	89.6	32.8	7.3	49.5	36.3	13.2	20.4	17.3
2015	100.0	10.3	89.7	32.5	7.3	49.9	36.7	13.3	20.6	17.5
2016	100.0	10.1	89.9	32.2	7.3	50.4	37.0	13.3	20.8	17.8
2017	100.0	10.0	90.0	31.9	7.3	50.8	37.5	13.4	21.1	18.1
2018	100.0	9.8	90.2	31.6	7.3	51.3	37.9	13.4	21.4	18.4

Federal Supplementary Medical Insurance Trust Funds (May 12, 2009, http://www.cms.hhs.gov/ReportsTrustFunds/downloads/tr2009.pdf), in 2008 over $468 million was spent to provide coverage for the 45.2 million people who were enrolled in Medicare. The majority (37.8 million or 84%) of Medicare recipients were aged 65 and older and 7.4 million were people with disabilities. The CMS estimates that 91.4 million people will be eligible for Medicare by 2050.

Reimbursement under Medicare

Historically, Medicare reimbursed physicians on a fee-for-service basis (paid for each visit, procedure, or treatment

TABLE 10.1

National health expenditures by source of funds, selected years, 2003–18 [CONTINUED]

			Third-party payments							
						Public				
Year	Total	Out-of-pocket payments	Total	Private health insurance	Other private funds	Total	Federal[a]	State and local[a]	Medicare[b]	Medicaid[c]
Historical estimates				Annual percent change from previous year shown						
2003	—	—	—	—	—	—	—	—	—	—
2004	6.9	4.6	7.3	7.0	5.1	7.8	8.6	6.0	10.1	7.5
2005	6.8	5.2	7.0	6.8	7.8	7.0	6.8	7.6	9.1	7.2
2006	6.7	3.3	7.2	6.0	6.1	8.2	10.5	2.6	18.5	−0.7
2007	6.1	5.3	6.2	6.0	5.6	6.4	6.6	6.0	7.2	6.4
Projected										
2008	6.1	3.8	6.4	5.5	7.3	7.0	7.5	5.9	8.1	6.9
2009	5.5	1.4	6.0	4.5	4.6	7.4	7.7	6.5	8.0	9.6
2010	4.6	2.8	4.8	4.3	5.3	5.0	4.5	6.6	2.5	8.6
2011	5.6	3.7	5.8	4.8	5.7	6.5	6.6	6.5	6.2	7.8
2012	5.8	4.0	6.0	4.8	5.9	6.9	7.0	6.5	6.9	7.8
2013	6.2	4.4	6.4	5.1	6.0	7.3	7.5	6.8	7.3	8.2
2014	6.5	5.2	6.6	5.7	6.1	7.4	7.5	7.0	7.4	8.4
2015	6.9	5.4	7.1	6.0	6.9	7.8	8.0	7.3	8.1	8.7
2016	7.0	5.5	7.2	6.1	7.2	7.9	8.1	7.4	8.3	8.7
2017	7.2	5.6	7.3	6.2	7.1	8.1	8.4	7.5	8.7	8.8
2018	7.2	5.7	7.3	6.1	6.9	8.2	8.4	7.6	8.6	8.9

[a]Includes Medicaid SCHIP (State Children's Health Insurance Program) Expansion and SCHIP.
[b]Subset of federal funds.
[c]Subset of federal and state and local funds.
[d]Calculation of per capita estimates is inappropriate.
Notes: Per capita amounts based on July 1 census resident based population estimates. Numbers and percents may not add to totals because of rounding. The health spending projections were based on the 2007 version of the National Health Expenditures (NHE) released in January 2009.

SOURCE: "Table 3. National Health Expenditures; Aggregate and per Capita Amounts, Percent Distribution and Annual Percent Change by Source of Funds: Calendar Years 2003–2018," in *National Health Expenditures Projections 2008–2018*, Centers for Medicare and Medicaid Services, Office of the Actuary, February 23, 2009, http://www.cms.hhs.gov/NationalHealthExpendData/downloads/proj2008.pdf (accessed May 19, 2009)

delivered), as opposed to per capita (per head) or per member per month (PMPM). In response to the increasing administrative burden of paperwork, reduced compensation, and delays in reimbursements, some physicians opt out of Medicare participation—they do not provide services under the Medicare program and choose not to accept Medicare patients into their practice. Others continue to provide services to Medicare beneficiaries, but they do not "accept assignment"—that is, their patients must pay out of pocket for services and then seek reimbursement from Medicare.

The Tax Equity and Fiscal Responsibility Act of 1982 authorized a "risk managed care" option for Medicare, based on agreed-on prepayments. Beginning in 1985, CMS could contract to pay health care providers, such as health maintenance organizations (HMOs) or other prepaid plans, to serve Medicare and Medicaid patients. These groups were paid a predetermined amount per enrollee for their services. These became known as Medicare-risk HMOs.

During the 1980s and 1990s the federal government, employers that provided health coverage for retiring employees, and many states sought to control costs by encouraging Medicare and Medicaid beneficiaries to enroll in Medicare-risk HMOs. Medicare-risk HMOs kept costs down because, essentially, the federal government paid the health plans that operated them with fixed fees—a predetermined dollar amount PMPM. For this fixed fee, Medicare recipients were to receive a fairly comprehensive, preset array of benefits. The PMPM payment provided a financial incentive for Medicare-risk HMO physicians to control costs, unlike physicians who were reimbursed on a fee-for-service basis.

Even though Medicare recipients were generally satisfied with these HMOs (even when enrolling meant they had to change physicians and thereby end long-standing relationships with their family doctors), many of the health plans did not fare as well. The health plans suffered for a variety of reasons: some plans had underestimated the service utilization rates of older adults, and some were unable to provide the stipulated range of services as effectively as they were intended. For other plans, the PMPM payment was simply not sufficient to enable them to cover all the clinical services and administrative overhead.

Regardless, the health plans providing these "senior HMOs" competed fiercely to market to and enroll older adults. Some health plans feared that closing their Medicare-risk programs would be viewed negatively by employer groups, which, when faced with the choice of plans that offered coverage for both younger workers and retirees or one that only covered the younger workers, would choose the

FIGURE 10.2

Sources of payment for health care services for Medicare enrollees aged 65 and over, by type of service, 2004

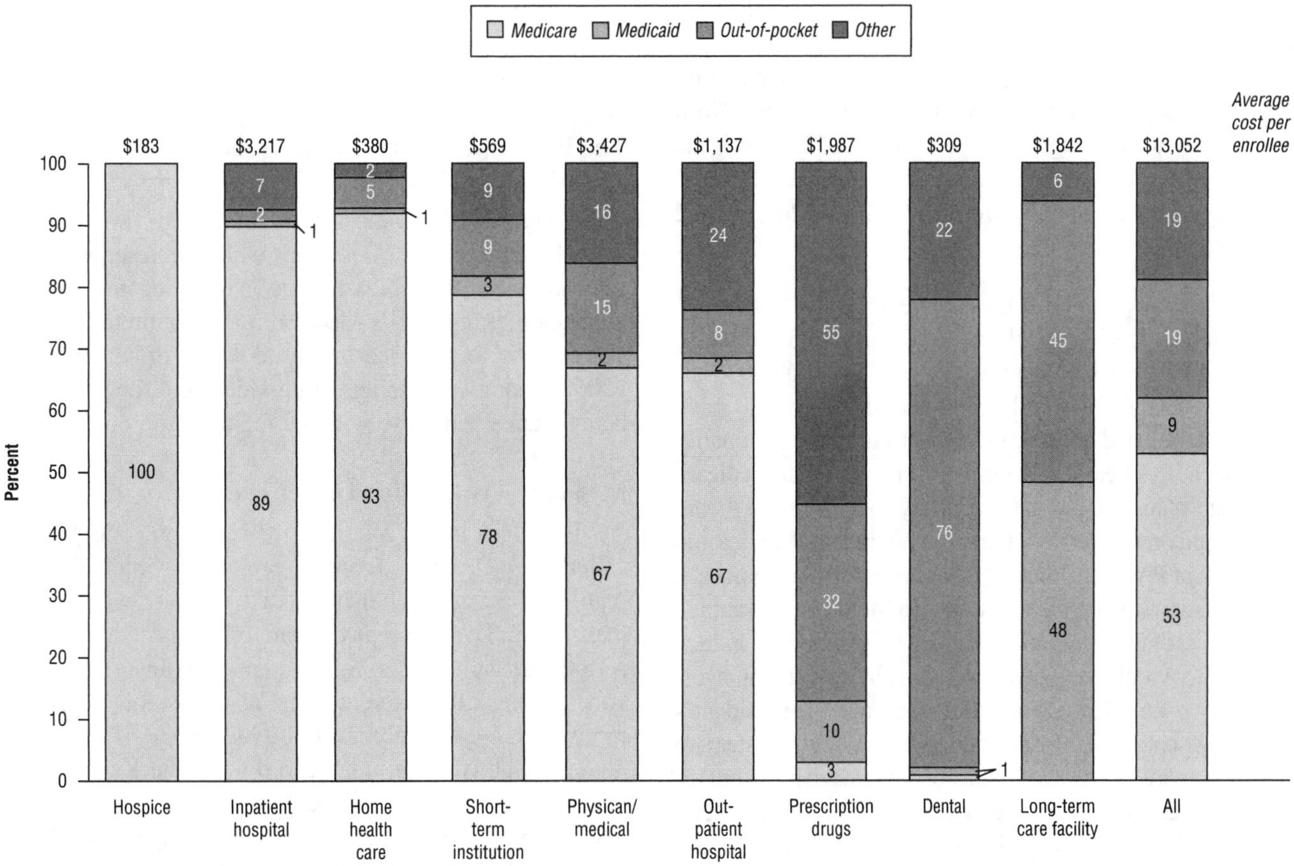

Note: "Other" refers to private insurance, Department of Veterans Affairs, and other public programs.
Reference population: These data refer to Medicare enrollees.

SOURCE: "Sources of Payment for Health Care Services for Medicare Enrollees Age 65 and over, by Type of Service, 2004," in *Older Americans 2008: Key Indicators of Well-Being*, Federal Interagency Forum on Aging-Related Statistics, March 2008, http://www.agingstats.gov/agingstatsdotnet/Main_Site/Data/2008_Documents/OA_2008.pdf (accessed April 20, 2009)

plans that covered both. Despite losing money, most health plans maintained their Medicare-risk programs to avoid alienating the employers they depended on to enroll workers who were younger, healthier, and less expensive to serve than the older adults.

About 10 years into operations, some Medicare-risk programs faced a challenge that proved unbeatable. Their enrollees had aged and required even more health care services than they had previously. For example, a senior HMO member who had joined as a healthy 65-year-old could now be a frail 75-year-old with multiple chronic health conditions requiring many costly health care services. The PMPM had increased over the years, but for some health plans it was simply insufficient to cover their costs. Many health plans, especially the smaller ones, were forced to end their Medicare-risk programs abruptly, leaving thousands of older adults scrambling to join other health plans. Others have endured, offering older adults comprehensive care and generating substantial cost savings for employers and the federal government.

Medicare Advantage

The Balanced Budget Act of 1997 replaced the Medicare-risk plans with Medicare+Choice, which later became known as Medicare Advantage. These plans offer Medicare beneficiaries a wider range of managed care plan options than just HMOs—older adults can join preferred provider organizations and provider-sponsored organizations that generally offer greater freedom of choice of providers (physicians and hospitals) than is available through HMO membership.

When older adults join Medicare Advantage plans that have entered into contracts with the CMS, the plans are paid a fixed amount PMPM, which represents Medicare's share of the cost of the services. The attraction of these plans is that members no longer have to pay the regular

Medicare deductibles and co-payments for Medicare-covered services. Some plans charge modest monthly premiums, and/or nominal co-payments as services are used, but there are no other charges by the plan for physician visits, hospitalization, or use of other covered services. However, members of Medicare Advantage plans must continue to pay the Medicare Part B monthly premium. According to the Kaiser Family Foundation, in the fact sheet "Medicare Advantage" (April 2009, http://www.kff.org/medicare/up load/2052-12.pdf), the number of Medicare beneficiaries enrolled in the Medicare Advantage plans has doubled from 5.3 million in 2003 to 10.2 million in 2009.

In "Medicare and HMOs—The Search for Accountability" (*New England Journal of Medicine*, vol. 360, no. 20, May 14, 2009), Richard Kronick of the University of California, San Diego, asserts that, in general, these plans have failed to make good on their promises to improve the quality and efficiency of health care delivery. He notes that Medicare Advantage plans are paid substantially more than Medicare would spend on similar beneficiaries under fee for service and observes that President Barack Obama (1961–), a Democrat, has called for reducing payment rates to Medicare Advantage plans. According to Kronick, the CMS planned to reduce payments to Medicare Advantage plans in 2010 by an average of 4% to 4.5% lower than 2009 rates, and the president's budget advocated the use a competitive bidding system to determine payment rates to Medicare Advantage plans beginning in 2012. Kronick suggests that leveling the financial playing field is a necessary first step to improve quality and efficiency, but he also believes the CMS must hold the plans accountable for their performance by creating "rewards and sanctions to encourage plans to perform well."

Insurance to Supplement Medicare Benefits

In 2006, 11.9 million (34.1%) older adults had private insurance obtained through the workplace to supplement their Medicare coverage. (See Table 10.2.) The most popular private insurance is supplemental insurance known as Medigap insurance. Federal regulations mandate that all Medigap policies sold offer a standard minimum set of benefits, but there are 10 standard variations that offer additional coverage and benefits. As Table 10.2 shows, the percentage of older adults with Medigap insurance has declined from 32.5% in 1995 to 23.5% in 2006, and the percentage with only Medicare or another public plan has risen from 10.5% in 1995 to 13.9% in 2006.

Besides Medigap policies, older adults may also purchase Medicare supplement health insurance called Medicare SELECT, which offers essentially the same coverage as Medigap policies, but it requires use of preferred providers—specific hospitals and in some cases plan physicians—to receive full benefits. Even though Medicare SELECT policies restrict older adults' choices, they are generally less expensive than Medigap policies.

A less popular option is hospital indemnity coverage—insurance that pays a fixed cash amount for each day of hospitalization up to a designated number of days. Some coverage may have added benefits such as surgical benefits or skilled nursing home benefits. Most policies have a maximum annual number of days or a lifetime maximum payment amount.

The Prescription Drug, Improvement, and Modernization Act

Congress passed the Prescription Drug, Improvement, and Modernization Act of 2003, which represents the largest expansion of Medicare since its creation in 1965. The legislation established a Medicare prescription drug benefit. The benefit was phased in and took full effect in January 2006. Among other things, it provides help for low-income beneficiaries and those with the highest drug costs.

Medicare Prescription Drug Coverage

Enrollees in the Medicare prescription drug program, called Part D, pay a monthly premium, which varies by plan, and a yearly deductible that in 2009 was no more than $295. They also pay a part of the cost of their prescriptions, including a co-payment or coinsurance. Costs vary among the different drug plans—some plans offer more coverage and access to a wider range of drugs for a higher monthly premium. According to the Kaiser Family Foundation (2009, http://healthplantracker.kff.org/topic results.jsp?i=33&rt=1), in 2009 the average monthly premium was $45.26. Older adults with limited incomes may not have to pay premiums or deductibles for the drug coverage.

The CMS estimates that as of February 2009, 41 million Medicare beneficiaries had prescription drug coverage. (See Table 10.3.) Nearly 27 million (65%) were enrolled in Part D, 6 million (15%) had coverage through an employer or union, and another 8 million (20%) had coverage from another source.

Medicare Drug Benefit Earns Mixed Reviews

The new Medicare drug benefit does not appear to have completely solved the problem of improving older adults' access to prescription medications. In "Access to Prescription Drugs for Medicare Beneficiaries" (*Tracking Report No. 23*, March 2009), James D. Reschovsky and Laurie E. Felland of the Center for Studying Health System Change observe that even though the Medicare drug benefit began in January 2006, the same proportion—about 8% of older adult Medicare beneficiaries in 2003 and 2007—chose not to fill at least one prescription drug because of cost concerns. By contrast, the percentage of working-age adults who chose not to fill at least one prescription because of cost concerns increased during this same period. Presumably, there should have been a comparable increase observed among Medicare beneficiaries. Because the same percentage of Medicare beneficiaries

TABLE 10.2

Health insurance coverage for persons aged 65 and over, according to type of coverage and selected characteristics, selected years 1992–2006

[Data are based on household interviews of a sample of the civilian noninstitutionalized population]

	Medicare Health Maintenance Organization[a]					Medicaid[b]				
Characteristic	**1992**	**1995**	**2000**	**2005**	**2006**	**1992**	**1995**	**2000**	**2005**	**2006**
Age					Number in millions					
65 years and over	1.1	2.6	5.9	4.6	6.7	2.7	2.8	2.7	3.2	3.3
					Percent of population					
65 years and over	3.9	8.9	19.3	14.5	19.2	9.4	9.6	9.0	10.1	9.4
65–74 years	4.2	9.5	20.6	13.9	19.1	7.9	8.8	8.5	9.9	9.2
75–84 years	3.7	8.3	18.5	15.3	19.7	10.6	9.6	8.9	9.9	9.1
85 years and over	g	7.3	16.3	13.9	17.7	16.6	13.6	11.2	11.9	10.9
Sex										
Male	4.6	9.2	19.3	13.5	18.6	6.3	6.2	6.3	7.2	6.7
Female	3.4	8.6	19.3	15.2	19.6	11.6	12.0	10.9	12.3	11.5
Race and Hispanic origin										
White, not Hispanic or Latino	3.6	8.4	18.4	13.2	17.2	5.6	5.4	5.1	6.1	5.9
Black, not Hispanic or Latino	g	7.9	20.7	17.1	24.1	28.5	30.3	23.6	23.6	21.8
Hispanic	g	15.5	27.5	27.2	37.0	39.0	40.5	28.7	29.2	23.4
Percent of poverty level[c]										
Below 100%	3.6	7.7	18.4	—	—	22.3	17.2	15.9	—	—
100%–less than 200%	3.7	9.5	23.4	—	—	6.7	6.3	8.4	—	—
200% or more	4.2	10.1	18.0	—	—	*	*	*	—	—
Marital status										
Married	4.6	9.5	18.7	13.8	18.9	4.0	4.3	4.3	5.4	4.5
Widowed	2.3	7.7	19.4	15.0	17.9	14.9	15.0	13.6	14.9	14.4
Divorced	g	9.7	24.4	17.1	23.5	23.4	24.5	20.2	20.0	17.7
Never married	g	g	15.8	13.9	21.4	19.2	19.0	17.0	21.3	21.6

	Employer-sponsored plan[d]					Medigap[e]				
Characteristic	**1992**	**1995**	**2000**	**2005**	**2006**	**1992**	**1995**	**2000**	**2005**	**2006**
Age					Number in millions					
65 years and over	12.5	11.3	10.7	11.6	11.9	9.9	9.5	7.6	8.2	8.2
					Percent of population					
65 years and over	42.8	38.6	35.2	36.4	34.1	33.9	32.5	25.0	25.7	23.5
65–74 years	46.9	41.1	36.6	38.1	35.6	31.4	29.9	21.7	23.2	21.3
75–84 years	38.2	37.1	35.0	35.5	33.3	37.5	35.2	27.8	27.3	24.8
85 years and over	31.6	30.2	29.4	31.8	30.0	38.3	37.6	31.1	30.8	28.9
Sex										
Male	46.3	42.1	37.7	39.4	36.8	30.6	30.0	23.4	23.8	21.9
Female	40.4	36.0	33.4	34.2	31.9	36.2	34.4	26.2	27.1	24.8
Race and Hispanic origin										
White, not Hispanic or Latino	45.9	41.3	38.6	39.5	37.1	37.2	36.2	28.3	29.1	26.7
Black, not Hispanic or Latino	25.9	26.7	22.0	27.9	23.7	13.6	10.2	7.5	9.5	8.8
Hispanic	20.7	16.9	15.8	18.6	17.1	15.8	10.1	11.3	11.1	8.9
Percent of poverty level[c]										
Below 100%	29.0	32.1	28.1	—	—	30.8	29.8	22.6	—	—
100%–less than 200%	37.5	32.0	27.0	—	—	39.3	39.1	28.4	—	—
200% or more	58.4	52.8	49.0	—	—	32.8	32.2	26.2	—	—
Marital status										
Married	49.9	44.6	41.0	41.7	39.7	33.0	32.6	25.6	27.0	24.0
Widowed	34.1	30.3	28.7	30.4	28.4	37.5	35.2	26.7	26.2	25.1
Divorced	27.3	26.6	22.4	25.1	22.8	27.9	24.1	16.9	19.8	18.1
Never married	38.0	35.1	28.5	29.1	25.8	29.1	26.2	21.9	15.4	17.1

chose not to fill at least one prescription drug because of cost concerns in 2003 and 2007, it may be that the new Medicare drug benefit prevented or slowed a comparable decline in access to prescription drugs for older adults.

A significant difference between older adults covered by Medicare and working-age adults with prescription drug coverage is that the Medicare drug benefit has a coverage gap known as the "doughnut hole"—the point

TABLE 10.2

Health insurance coverage for persons aged 65 and over, according to type of coverage and selected characteristics, selected years 1992–2006 [CONTINUED]

[Data are based on household interviews of a sample of the civilian noninstitutionalized population]

	Medicare fee-for-service only or other[f]				
Characteristic	**1992**	**1995**	**2000**	**2005**	**2006**
Age			Number in millions		
65 years and over	2.9	3.1	3.5	4.3	4.9
			Percent of population		
65 years and over	9.9	10.5	11.5	13.3	13.9
65–74 years	9.7	10.7	12.6	14.9	14.8
75–84 years	10.1	9.9	9.9	11.9	13.1
85 years and over	10.8	11.3	12.1	11.6	12.5
Sex					
Male	12.2	12.6	13.3	16.2	16.0
Female	8.3	8.9	10.2	11.2	12.2
Race and Hispanic origin					
White, not Hispanic or Latino	7.7	8.7	9.6	12.2	13.1
Black, not Hispanic or Latino	26.7	25.0	26.1	21.9	21.6
Hispanic	18.3	17.1	16.7	13.9	13.6
Percent of poverty level[c]					
Below 100%	14.3	13.3	15.1	—	—
100%–less than 200%	12.9	13.1	12.7	—	—
200% or more	4.0	4.5	6.3	—	—
Marital status					
Married	8.5	9.0	10.5	12.1	12.9
Widowed	11.2	11.9	11.6	13.5	14.3
Divorced	15.7	15.1	16.1	17.9	17.9
Never married	*	13.1	16.8	20.4	14.1

*Estimates are considered unreliable if the sample cell size is 50 or fewer.
—Data not available.
[a]Enrollee has Medicare Health Maintenance Organization (HMO) regardless of other insurance.
[b]Enrolled in Medicaid and not enrolled in a Medicare risk HMO.
[c]Percent of poverty level is based on family income and family size and composition using U.S. Census Bureau poverty thresholds.
[d]Private insurance plans purchased through employers (own, current, or former employer, family business, union, or former employer or union of spouse) and not enrolled in a Medicare risk HMO or Medicaid.
[e]Supplemental insurance purchased privately or through organizations such as AARP or professional organizations, and not enrolled in a Medicare risk HMO, Medicaid, or employer-sponsored plan.
[f]Medicare fee-for-service only or other public plans (except Medicaid).
Notes: Insurance categories are mutually exclusive. Persons with more than one type of coverage are categorized according to the order in which the health insurance categories appear.

SOURCE: "Table 141. Health Insurance Coverage for Persons 65 Years of Age and over, by Type of Coverage and Selected Characteristics: United States, Selected Years 1992–2006," in *Health, United States, 2008. With Chartbook*, National Center for Health Statistics, 2009, http://www.cdc.gov/nchs/data/hus/hus08.pdf#listtables (accessed May 6, 2009)

when Medicare beneficiaries become responsible for the full cost of their drugs, which they must pay for out of pocket. According to Reschovsky and Felland, in 2007 the coverage gap began when a beneficiary incurred $2,400 in total drug spending and ended after out-of-pocket spending reached $3,850.

Medicare beneficiaries with employer drug coverage reported the lowest rate of unmet needs in 2007, just 2.5%. However, Reschovsky and Felland note that Medicare beneficiaries with employer drug coverage tend to be those with higher incomes and fewer health problems than beneficiaries with other types of drug coverage. Beneficiaries with employer-sponsored drug benefits generally do not have doughnut holes in coverage because they provide more generous coverage than Medicare Part D.

Medicare Faces Challenges

Like Social Security, the Medicare program's continuing financial viability is in jeopardy. The Social Security and Medicare trust funds are examined annually by the Social Security and Medicare Boards of Trustees, who publish an annual "report on the current and projected financial status of the two programs." This section reviews the origins of the challenges Medicare faces and the Trustees' findings in *Status of the Social Security and Medicare Programs: A Summary of the 2009 Annual Reports* (May 12, 2009, http://www.socialsecurity.gov/OACT/TRSUM/).

A NATIONAL BIPARTISAN COMMISSION CONSIDERS THE FUTURE OF MEDICARE. The National Bipartisan Commission on the Future of Medicare was created by

TABLE 10.3

Total Medicare beneficiaries with prescription drug coverage, February 2009

Description	Beneficiaries with drug coverage (millions)
Medicare beneficiaries eligible for part D	**45.24**
Medicare part D	**26.65**
Medicare stand alone drug coverage (part D)	17.48
Medicare Advantage with drug coverage (part D)	8.97
Other Medicare health plan types	0.20
Medicare Retiree Drug Subsidy (RDS)	**5.97**
Other drug coverage	**8.16**
TRICARE retiree coverage	0.97
FEHBP retiree coverage	0.99
Veterans Affairs (VA) coverage	1.57
Active workers with Medicare secondary payer	1.81
Multiple sources of creditable coverage[a]	0.77
Other retiree coverage, not enrolled in RDS[b]	1.50
Medigap and other individual insurance[b]	0.20
State pharmaceutical assistance programs[b]	0.02
Indian Health Service coverage[b]	0.03
Other sources[b,c]	0.30
Total Medicare beneficiaries with drug coverage	**40.78**

[a]Includes beneficiaries with more than one of the following: TRICARE (Defense Department insurance system for current or former military personnel, and dependents), FEHPB (Federal Employees' Health Benefits), VA, Active Workers.
[b]This information is only available at the national level.
[c]Includes: FEHBP spouses and dependents.

SOURCE: "Total Medicare Beneficiaries with Prescription Drug Coverage as of February 1, 2009," in "2009 Enrollment Information," *Prescription Drug Coverage—General Information*, Centers for Medicare and Medicaid Services, April 6, 2009, http://www.cms.hhs.gov/PrescriptionDrugCovGenIn/ (accessed May 20, 2009)

FIGURE 10.3

Expected decline in workers per retiree to fund Medicare, 1960–2040

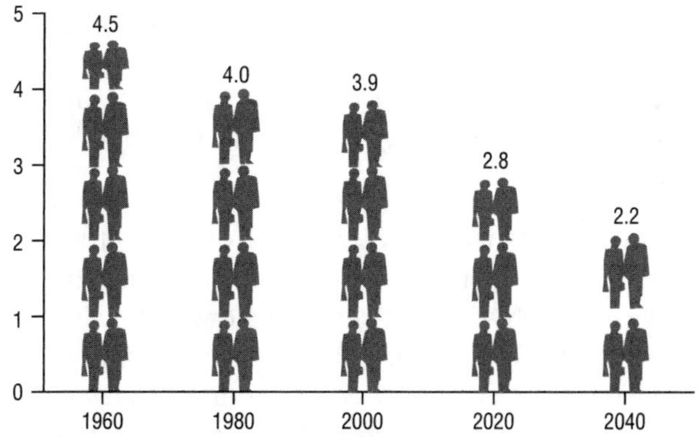

SOURCE: "Fewer Workers per Retiree to Fund Medicare," in *The Facts about Medicare*, National Bipartisan Commission on the Future of Medicare, 1999, http://thomas.loc.gov/medicare/factpage4.html (accessed May 20, 2009)

FIGURE 10.4

Increased Medicare enrollment, selected years 1970–2040

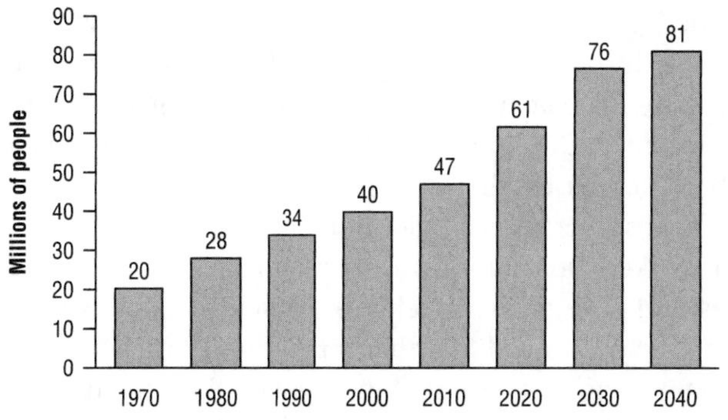

SOURCE: "Medicare Enrollment Soars," in *The Facts About Medicare*, National Bipartisan Commission on the Future of Medicare, 1999, http://thomas.loc.gov/medicare/factpage4.html (accessed May 20, 2009)

Congress in the Balanced Budget Act of 1997. The commission was charged with examining the Medicare program and drafting recommendations to avert a future financial crisis and reinforce the program in anticipation of the retirement of the baby boomers (people born between 1946 and 1964).

The commission observed that like Social Security, Medicare would suffer because there would be fewer workers per retiree to fund it. (See Figure 10.3.) It predicted that beneficiaries' out-of-pocket costs would rise and forecasted soaring Medicare enrollment. (See Figure 10.4.) Perhaps the commission's direst prediction was the determination that, without reform, the Medicare Part A fund would become bankrupt in 2008.

When the commission disbanded in March 1999, it was unable to forward an official recommendation to Congress because the plan it proposed fell one vote short of the required majority needed to authorize an official recommendation. The plan would have changed Medicare into a premium system, where instead of Medicare directly covering beneficiaries, the beneficiaries would be given a fixed amount of money to purchase private health insurance. The plan would have also raised the age of eligibility from 65 to 67, as has already been done with Social Security, and provided prescription drug coverage for low-income beneficiaries, much like the Medicare Prescription Drug, Improvement, and Modernization Act of 2003.

THE MEDICARE PRESCRIPTION DRUG, IMPROVEMENT, AND MODERNIZATION ACT AIMS TO REFORM MEDICARE. The Medicare Prescription Drug, Improvement, and Modernization Act of 2003 is a measure intended to introduce private-sector enterprise into a Medicare model in urgent need of a reform. Under the act, premiums and deductibles may rise quickly, because they are indexed to the growth in per capita Medicare expenditures.

Older adults with substantial incomes face increasing premium costs. According to the SSA, in *Medicare Part B Premiums: Important Information for People Newly Eligible for Medicare* (December 2008, http://www.socialsecurity.gov/pubs/10162.pdf), in 2009 older adults with annual incomes of $85,000 or less or couples earning $170,000 or less paid the standard premium. Individuals and couples with higher incomes paid additional income-adjusted amounts monthly, ranging from $38.50 to $211.90 per month.

The act also expanded coverage of preventive medical services. According to the CMS, new beneficiaries receive a free physical examination along with laboratory tests to screen for heart disease and diabetes. The act also provided employers with $89 billion in subsidies and tax breaks to help offset the costs associated with maintaining retiree health benefits.

Medicare's Problems May Be More Urgent Than Those of Social Security

Medicare costs forecasts show them outpacing Social Security costs because it is anticipated that per capita health care costs will continue to grow faster than the per capita gross domestic product (GDP; the total value of goods and services produced by the United States) in the future. In *Status of the Social Security and Medicare Programs*, the Social Security and Medicare Boards of Trustees project that Medicare expenditures will increase from 3.6% of the GDP in 2009, to 6.4% in 2030, to 11.4% by 2082. (See Figure 10.5.) According to the Trustees, Medicare paid out more in benefits than it collected in 2009 and that by 2017 it will be insolvent. The Trustees caution that if reforms to sharply control these cost increases are not implemented, then both taxes on workers and out-of-pocket payments from beneficiaries will have to rise much more quickly than incomes in the decades ahead. Furthermore, the Trustees call for prompt action, warning "the sooner that solutions are adopted, the more varied and gradual they can be."

FIGURE 10.5

Social Security and Medicare costs as a percentage of gross domestic product, 1970–2080

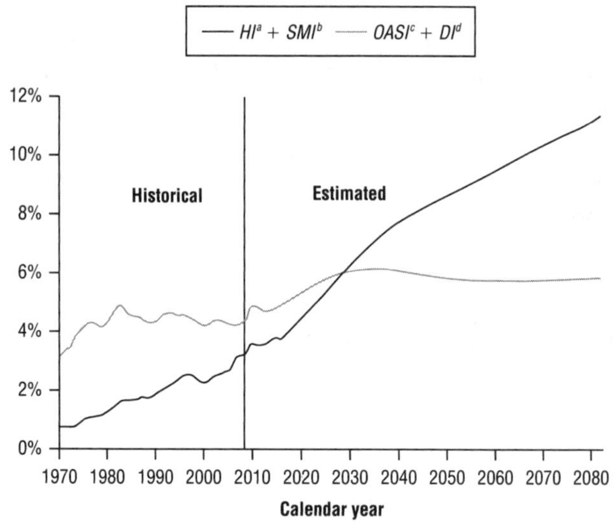

[a]HI = Health insurance.
[b]SMI = Supplemental medical insurance.
[c]OASI = Old age survivor insurance.
[d]DI = Survivor insurance.

SOURCE: "Chart B. Social Security and Medicare Cost as a Percentage of GDP," in *Status of the Social Security and Medicare Programs: A Summary of the 2009 Annual Reports*, U.S. Social Security Administration, Office of the Chief Actuary, May 12, 2009, http://www.socialsecurity.gov/OACT/TRSUM/ (accessed May 21, 2009)

MEDICAID

Congress enacted Medicaid in 1965 under Title XIX ("Grants to States for Medical Assistance Programs") of the Social Security Act. It is a joint federal-state program that provides medical assistance to selected categories of low-income Americans: the aged, people who are blind and/or disabled, and families with dependent children. Medicaid covers hospitalization, physicians' fees, laboratory and radiology fees, and long-term care in nursing homes. It is the largest source of funds for medical and health-related services for the United States' poorest people and the second-largest public payer of health care costs, after Medicare. In 2004 Medicaid provided coverage for 9% of adults aged 65 and older. (See Figure 10.2.)

Brian Burwell, Kate Sredl, and Steve Eiken report in "Medicaid Long-Term Care Expenditures in FY 2007" (September 26, 2008, http://www.hcbs.org/moreInfo.php/nb/doc/2374/Medicaid_Long_Term_Care_Expenditures_FY_2007) that Medicaid long-term care expenditures in fiscal year 2007 totaled $101.3 billion, approximately 32.5% of total Medicaid expenditures of $311.9 billion. Long-term care expenditures increased by 1.9% from 2006. Medicaid spending for nursing home expenditures decreased 1.5% in 2007, from $47.7 billion to $47 billion. Expenditures for services provided in intermediate care facilities decreased 3.7%, from $12.5 billion to $12 billion.

Medicaid is also the largest third-party payer of long-term care in the United States, financing about half of all nursing home care. Expenditures for community-based long-term care services continued to increase in 2007. According to Burwell, Sredl, and Eiken, total home and community-based services increased by 7.9%, to $42.3 billion. Expenditures for Medicaid home health care benefits increased 5.9%, to $4 billion, and expenditures under the Medicaid personal care services benefit increased 11.1%, to $10.4 billion. This trend is expected to persist as Medicaid programs continue to invest more resources in alternatives to institutional services.

VETERANS' BENEFITS

People who have served in the U.S. military are entitled to medical treatment at any veterans' facility in the nation. The U.S. Department of Veterans Affairs reports in *Analysis of Unique Veteran Utilization of VA Benefits and Services* (April 29, 2009, http://www1.va.gov/vetdata/docs/uniqueveteransMay.pdf) that in fiscal year 2008 about 8.5 million veterans received benefits and services, including health services, and of this total, 3.8 million were aged 65 and older.

The number of veterans aged 65 and older that received health care from the Veterans Health Administration (VHA) increased steadily from 1990 through 2006. (See Figure 10.6.) This increase may be attributable in part to the fact that VHA benefits cover services not covered by Medicare, such as prescription drugs (Medicare coverage began in 2006), mental health care, long-term care (nursing home and community-based care), and specialized services for people with disabilities. In 2006 approximately 2.4 million veterans aged 65 and older received health care from the VHA. An additional 1.1 million older veterans were enrolled to receive health care but did not use services in 2006.

LONG-TERM HEALTH CARE

The options for quality, affordable long-term care (LTC) in the United States are limited but improving. Nursing home costs range from $50,000 to more than $200,000 per year, depending on services and location. In *The MetLife Market Survey of Nursing Home and Assisted Living Costs* (October 2008, http://www.metlife.com/assets/cao/mmi/publications/studies/mmi-studies-2008-nhal-costs.pdf), the MetLife Mature Market Institute notes that in 2008 nursing home care cost an average of $77,320 per year for a private room. Many nursing home residents rely on Medicaid to pay these fees. In 2004 Medicaid covered 48% of nursing home costs for older Americans. (See Figure 10.2.) The second most common source of payment at admission is private insurance, the prospective resident's own income, or family support, followed by Medicare (which only pays for short-term stays after hospitalization). The primary source of payment changes as a stay lengthens.

FIGURE 10.6

Total number of veterans aged 65 and over who are enrolled in or receiving care from the Veterans Health Administration, 1990–2006

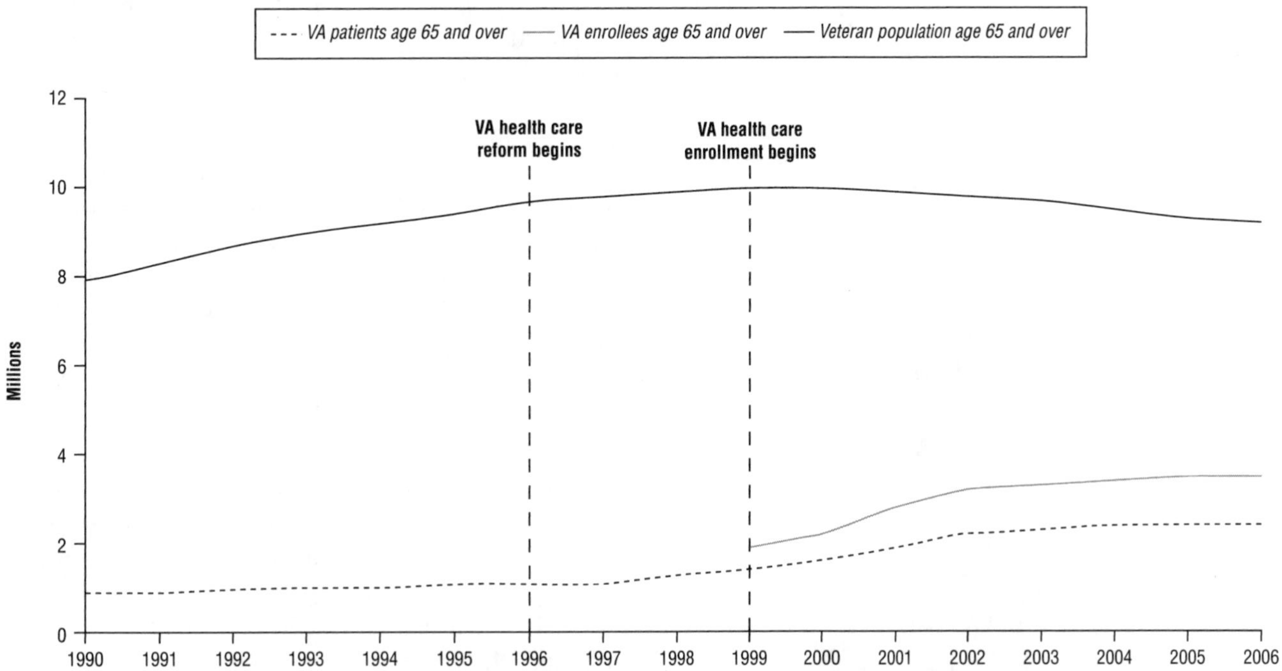

Note: Department of Veterans Affairs (VA) enrollees are veterans who have signed up to receive health care from the Veterans Health Administration (VHA). VA patients are veterans who have received care each year through VHA. Starting with 1999 data, the methods used to calculate VA patients differ from what was used in *Older Americans 2004* and *Older Americans Update 2006*. Veterans who received care but were not enrolled in VA are now included in patients counts. VHA Vital Status files from the Social Security Administration (SSA) are now used to ascertain veteran deaths.
Reference population: These data refer to the total veteran population, VHA enrollment population, and VHA patient population.

SOURCE: "Total Number of Veterans Age 65 and over Who Are Enrolled in or Receiving Care from the Veterans Health Administration, 1990–2006," in *Older Americans 2008: Key Indicators of Well-Being*, Federal Interagency Forum on Aging-Related Statistics, March 2008, http://www.agingstats.gov/agingstatsdotnet/Main_Site/Data/2008_Documents/OA_2008.pdf (accessed April 20, 2009)

After their funds are "spent down," nursing home residents on Medicare shift to Medicaid.

Even though nursing home care may seem cost prohibitive, an untrained caregiver who makes home visits can cost more than $25,000 a year, and skilled care costs much more. According to Amy Butler of the Bureau of Labor Statistics, in "Wages in the Nonprofit Sector: Healthcare, Personal Care, and Social Service Occupations" (April 15, 2009, http://www.bls.gov/opub/cwc/cm20090123ar01p1.htm), in 2007 the average hourly rate for home care aides was $11 per hour and homemakers/companions earned an average of $17 per hour. Licensed practical nurses and licensed vocational nurses earned more than $18 per hour and registered nurses earned about $30 per hour.

The National Clearinghouse for Long-Term Care Information (April 13, 2009, http://www.longtermcare.gov/LTC/Main_Site/Paying_LTC/Costs_Of_Care/Costs_Of_Care.aspx) reports an even higher average cost for homemaker and home health aide services: $18 and $29 per hour, respectively, in 2008. Many older adults cannot afford this expense and may exhaust their lifetime savings long before the need for care ends.

Who Pays for Long-Term Care?

Payment for LTC is derived from three major sources: Medicaid, private insurance (LTC insurance), and out-of-pocket spending. As Figure 10.7 shows, Medicaid pays the lion's share of LTC costs—48.9%—and Medicare contributes an additional 20.4%, under specific circumstances.

FIGURE 10.7

National spending on long-term care, 2005

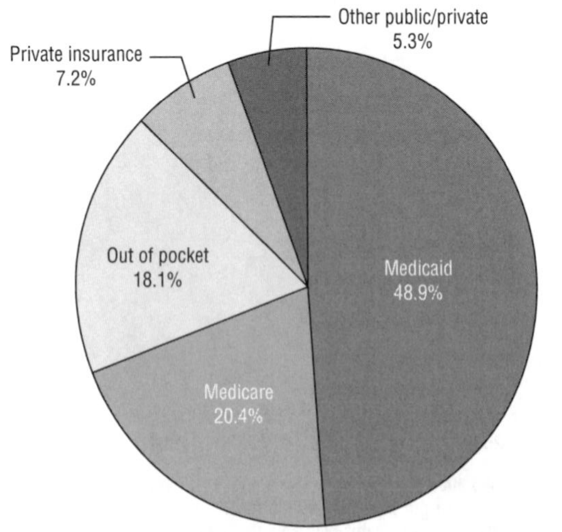

SOURCE: "National Spending on Long-Term Care," in *National Clearinghouse for Long-Term Care: Paying for Long-Term Care*, U.S. Department of Health and Human Services, Administration on Aging, April 13, 2009, http://www.longtermcare.gov/LTC/Main_Site/Paying_LTC/Costs_Of_Care/Costs_Of_Care.aspx (accessed May 22, 2009)

Eighteen percent of LTC costs are paid out of pocket, 7.2% are covered by private insurance, and 5.3% are paid by other public and private sources.

Medicare, Medicaid, and Long-Term Care

Medicare does not cover custodial or long-term nursing home care but, under specific conditions, will pay for short-term rehabilitative stays in nursing homes and for some home health care. Medicaid is the only public program with LTC coverage.

Medicaid, however, does not work like private insurance, which offers protection from catastrophic expense. Medicaid is a means-tested program, so middle-income people needing nursing home care become eligible for Medicaid only after they spend down their own personal income and assets.

Even then, Medicaid will not necessarily pay the entire nursing home bill. Nursing home residents must also meet income eligibility standards. In some states older adults with incomes too high for regular Medicaid eligibility, but with substantial medical bills, are allowed to spend down to become income-eligible for Medicaid. They must incur medical bills until their income for a given period, minus the medical expenses, falls below the Medicaid threshold.

Even though every state's Medicaid program covers LTC, each has made different choices about the parameters of its program. Eligibility rules and protection for the finances of spouses of nursing home residents vary widely, but federal law requires states to allow the community spouse to retain enough of the institutionalized spouse's income to maintain a monthly allowance for minimum living costs. The CMS (2009, http://www.cms.hhs.gov/MedicaidEligibility/Downloads/1998-2009SSIFBR052209.pdf) states that the allowance is set by the state according to federal guidelines—in 2009 no less than $1,821.25 per month and no more than $2,739. The community spouse is also allowed to retain joint assets—an amount equal to half of the couple's resources at the time the spouse enters the institution, up to a federally specified maximum ($109,560 in 2009).

Figure 10.2 shows the breakdown of LTC expenditures for older adults by the source of payment. In 2004 Medicaid paid the largest proportion of institutional expenses (48%), but nearly the same proportion (45%) was paid out of pocket. Medicare made the largest contribution (93%) toward home care services, whereas 1% of services were covered by Medicaid and 5% were paid out of pocket.

Private Long-Term Care Insurance

Another source of financing is LTC insurance. Private LTC insurance policies typically cover some portion of the cost of nursing home care and home health care services. The American Association for Long-Term Care Association (AALTCA) reports in the press release "Consumers Purchasing More Affordable Long-Term Care Insurance Protection" (February 25, 2009, http://www.aaltci.org/subpages/media_room/story_pages/media022509.html) that about 400,000 people purchased long-term care insurance in 2008, bringing the total number of Americans with LTC insurance to 8.2 million.

In the press release "180,000 Americans Receive Long-Term Care Insurance Benefits" (August 6, 2008, http://www.aaltci.org/subpages/media_room/story_pages/media080608.html), the AALTCA notes that the LTC insurance industry paid out $3.5 billion in benefits to about 180,000 Americans in 2007. Forty-three percent of claims were for home care services, 32.9% were for assisted living, and 24.1% were for nursing home care.

LTC insurance premiums take into account the cost of services and the risk that policyholders will need LTC as they age. According to Corey Rieck, in "Points to Make during the LTC Planning Conversation" (*Life and Health National Underwriter*, February 2, 2009), in 2009 the average LTC premium was $200 to $300 per month. The lower premiums offered to younger people assume that their risk of requiring LTC services is low and that they will pay premiums over a longer period than will people who obtain LTC insurance when they are older.

Premiums for private LTC insurance are tax deductible. The AALTCI explains in the press release "2009 Tax Deductible Limits for LTCi Announced" (October 16, 2008, http://www.aaltci.org/subpages/media_room/story_pages/media101608.html) that in 2009 the Internal Revenue Service increased deductibility levels to encourage the purchase of LTC insurance. The amount that may be deducted increases with advancing age. For example, people up to age 40 may deduct $320, whereas older adults aged 60 to 70 can deduct up to $3,180 and those aged 70 and older can deduct $3,980.

HOME HEALTH CARE

In *National Home and Hospice Care Survey (NHHCS) Public-Use Data File* (March 16, 2009, http://www.cdc.gov/nchs/products/elec_prods/subject/nhhcs.htm), the National Center for Health Statistics describes home health care as "provided to individuals and families in their place of residence for the purpose of promoting, maintaining, or restoring health or for maximizing the level of independence while minimizing the effects of disability and illness, including terminal illness."

Andrea Sisko et al. observe in "Health Spending Projections through 2018: Recession Effects Add Uncertainty to the Outlook" (*Health Affairs*, vol. 28, no. 2, 2009) that home health care grew by an estimated 9.1% in 2008, down from 11.3% growth in 2007. This slowdown is expected to continue through 2011. From 2013 through 2018 home health care spending growth is expected to remain steady, averaging 7.9% per year and reaching $134.9 billion in the next decade. Even though Medicare has been the principal payer for home health care, Medicaid is expected to become the largest payer of these services by 2010, as care continues to be redirected from institutions to home and community-based settings.

Community Housing with Home Care Services

Some older adults have access to a variety of home care services through their place of residence. Assisted living facilities, retirement communities, and continuing care retirement facilities are community housing alternatives that often provide services such as meal preparation, laundry and cleaning services, transportation, and assistance adhering to prescribed medication regimens.

In 2005 just 2% of Medicare recipients aged 65 and older lived in community housing that offered at least one home care service, and an additional 5% lived in LTC facilities. (See Figure 10.8.) The percentage of people residing in community housing that offered home care services was higher in the older age groups. Among people aged 85 and older, 7% lived in community housing with services and 17% lived in LTC facilities.

Older adults living in community housing with support services had more functional limitations than those living in the community but fewer than residents of LTC facilities. Twelve percent of older adults living in community housing with services had three or more activities of daily living limitations, compared with 6% of older adults living in the community and 64% of older adults in LTC facilities. (See Figure 10.9.)

FIGURE 10.8

Percentage of Medicare enrollees aged 65 and over residing in selected residential settings, by age group, 2005

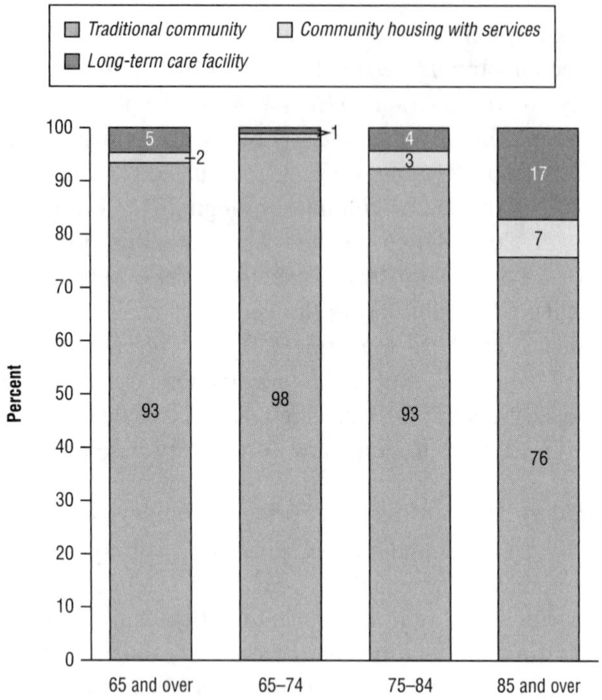

Note: Community housing with services applies to respondents who reported they lived in retirement communities or apartments, senior citizen housing, continuing care retirement facilities, assisted living facilities, staged living communities, board and care facilities/homes, and other similar situations, AND who reported they had access to one or more of the following services through their place of residence: meal preparation, cleaning or housekeeping services, laundry services, or help with medications. Respondents were asked about access to these services but not whether they actually used the services. A residence (or unit) is considered a long-term care facility if it is certified by Medicare or Medicaid; has 3 or more beds and is licensed as a nursing home or other long-term care facility and provides at least one personal care service; or provides 24-hour, 7-day-a-week supervision by a non-family, paid caregiver.
Reference population: These data refer to Medicare enrollees.

SOURCE: "Percentage of Medicare Enrollees Age 65 and over Residing in Selected Residential Settings, by Age Group, 2005," in *Older Americans 2008: Key Indicators of Well-Being*, Federal Interagency Forum on Aging-Related Statistics, March 2008, http://www.agingstats.gov/agingstatsdotnet/Main_Site/Data/2008_Documents/OA_2008.pdf (accessed April 20, 2009)

FIGURE 10.9

Percentage of Medicare enrollees aged 65 and over with functional limitations, by residential setting, 2005

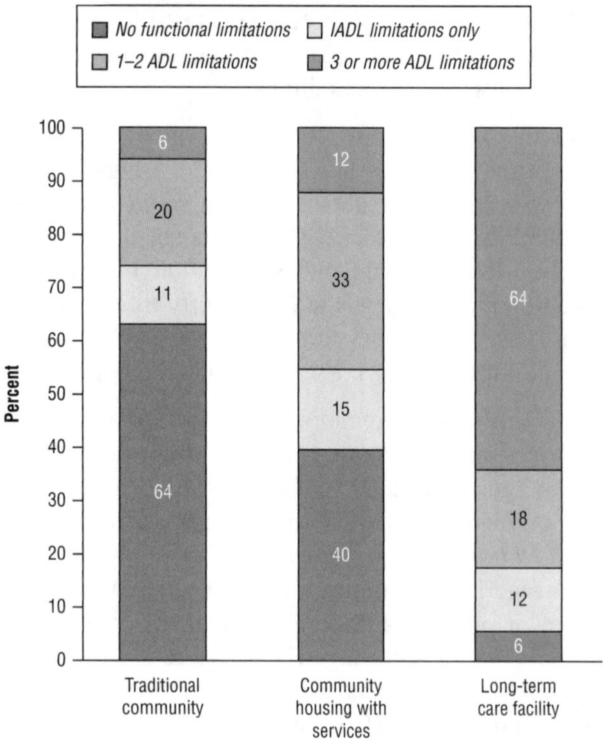

Note: Community housing with services applies to respondents who reported they lived in retirement communities or apartments, senior citizen housing, continuing care retirement facilities, assisted living facilities, staged living communities, board and care facilities/homes, and other similar situations, AND who reported they had access to one or more of the following services through their place of residence: meal preparation, cleaning or housekeeping services, laundry services, or help with medications. Respondents were asked about access to these services but not whether they actually used the services. A residence (or unit) is considered a long-term care facility if it is certified by Medicare or Medicaid; has 3 or more beds and is licensed as a nursing home or other long-term care facility and provides at least one personal care service; or provides 24-hour 7-day-a-week supervision by a non-family, paid caregiver. Activities of Daily Living (ADLs) limitations refer to difficulty performing (or inability to perform, for a health reason) one or more of the following tasks: bathing, dressing, eating, getting in/out of chairs, walking, or using the toilet. Instrumental Activities of Daily Living (IADLs) limitations refer to difficulty performing (or inability to perform, for a health reason) one or more of the following tasks: using the telephone, light housework, heavy housework, meal preparation, shopping, or managing money. Long-term care facility residents with no limitations may include individuals with limitations in certain IADLs: doing light or heavy housework or meal preparation. These questions were not asked of facility residents.
Reference population: These data refer to Medicare enrollees.

SOURCE: "Percentage of Medicare Enrollees Age 65 and over with Functional Limitations, by Residential Setting, 2005," in *Older Americans 2008: Key Indicators of Well-Being*, Federal Inter agency Forum on Aging-Related Statistics, March 2008, http://www.agingstats.gov/agingstatsdotnet/Main_Site/Data/2008_Documents/OA_2008.pdf (accessed April 20, 2009)

CHAPTER 11
CRIME AND ABUSE OF OLDER ADULTS

Elder financial abuse is a crime growing in intensity and, especially now, with the plummeting economy, elders will be unable to recover from such losses.

—Pamela Teaster, quoted in *Broken Trust: Elders, Family, and Finances* (March 2009)

The Professionals against Confidence Crimes (PACC), a nonprofit, nonpartisan organization of law enforcement professionals, states in "Fear of Crime" (2008, http://stopcon.org/Fear%20of%20Crime.htm) that older adults believe they are most susceptible to crimes such as murder, aggravated assault and rape, armed robbery, theft from their person, burglary, and fraud. Their fears are not, however, entirely consistent with reality. Older adults are the least likely to become victims of violent crimes. The crimes more often committed against older adults are purse snatching and pocket picking (theft of their purses or wallets), fraud and confidence crimes, mail theft, vandalism, and burglary.

PACC attributes older adults' misplaced fears in part to sensational media reports that do not correctly convey the real crime risks for older adults. As a result, older adults do not have an accurate understanding about the crimes that affect them. PACC contends that unless older adults understand the real risks, they will not take the proper steps to protect themselves.

CRIME AGAINST OLDER ADULTS

Michael R. Rand of the Bureau of Justice Statistics (BJS) reports in *Criminal Victimization, 2008* (September 2009, http://www.ojp.usdoj.gov/bjs/pub/pdf/cv08.pdf) that adults aged 65 and older experienced much less violence and victimization as well as fewer property crimes than younger people did between 1973 and 2008. Adults aged 65 and older had the lowest rates of violent victimization of any age group. According to Rand, violent crimes against older adults have steadily declined since 1995. He notes that adults aged 50 and older were victims of violent crime at lower rates than people in other age groups.

Like violent crimes, older adults also experienced low rates of property crimes in 2006, the most recent year for which data were available as of mid-2009. For example, older adults had the lowest rates of vehicle theft (3.1 per 1,000 households), compared with those aged 20 to 34 (14.6 per 1,000 households). (See Table 11.1.) Similarly, the rates of household burglary and theft decline with advancing age. In 2006 adults aged 65 and older had the lowest rates of property crimes (70.2 per 1,000 households) of all age groups. (See Table 11.2.)

Homicide

Older adults also have lower rates of murder than other age groups, and the number of homicides of older adults decreased between 1976 and 2005. James Alan Fox and Marianne W. Zawitz of the BJS indicate in *Homicide Trends in the United States* (July 2007,http://www.ojp.usdoj.gov/bjs/homicide/elders.htm) that in 2005 just 5% of all homicides were adults aged 65 and older. More older men were homicide victims than women of the same age. (See Figure 11.1.)

There has been a decline not only in the murder rate of older adults but also in the rate of older offenders. In 2005 the homicide victimization rate was 1.9 per 100,000 population and the offending rate was just 0.7 per 100,000 population for people aged 65 and older. (See Figure 11.2.)

Older adults are more likely to be killed during a felony than younger victims. In 2005 more than half of all murders of people aged 72 and older occurred in this circumstance. (See Figure 11.3.)

Women of all ages are more likely than male victims to be killed by an intimate—a spouse, family member, or friend. Table 11.3 shows that from 1976 to 2005 more than three times as many women over the age of 60 (21%) were murdered by an intimate as were men (6%).

TABLE 11.1

Number of victimizations and victimization rates of vehicle theft, by selected household characteristics, 2006

	Based on households			Based on vehicles owned		
Characteristic	Number of households	Number of thefts	Rate per 1,000	Number of vehicles owned	Number of thefts	Rate per 1,000
Race of head of household						
All races	117,858,380	992,260	8.4	226,697,560	1,067,590	4.7
White only	96,211,280	707,010	7.3	192,664,870	774,920	4.0
Black only	14,820,190	219,150	14.8	21,631,710	226,580	10.5
Other race only[a]	5,575,500	57,150	10.2	9,908,950	57,150	5.8
Two or more races[b]	1,251,420	8,950[c]	7.2[c]	2,492,030	8,950[c]	3.6[c]
Age of head of household						
12–19	1,073,350	21,570[c]	20.1[c]	1,637,280	21,570[c]	13.2[c]
20–34	26,665,840	388,650	14.6	47,337,260	418,090	8.8
35–49	36,364,320	311,690	8.6	77,787,030	339,710	4.4
50–64	30,165,640	196,500	6.5	64,352,370	211,060	3.3
65 and over	23,589,240	73,840	3.1	35,583,620	77,170	2.2
Form of tenure						
Owned or being bought	81,041,450	506,860	6.3	177,658,300	558,760	3.1
Rented	36,816,930	485,400	13.2	49,039,260	508,830	10.4
Locality of residence						
Urban	37,054,500	473,470	12.8	59,387,630	517,310	8.7
Suburban	51,586,630	413,950	8.0	105,060,940	430,400	4.1
Rural	29,217,260	104,830	3.6	62,248,980	119,890	1.9

Note: Due to changes in methodology, the 2006 national crime victimization rates are not comparable to previous years and cannot be used for yearly trend comparisons. However, the overall patterns of victimization at the national level can be examined. See *Criminal Victimization, 2006,* at <http://www.ojp.usdoj.gov/bjs/abstract/cv06.htm>. Detail may not add to total shown because of rounding.
The number of thefts based on vehicles owned is equal to or higher than the corresponding figure based on households because the former includes all completed or attempted vehicle thefts, regardless of the final classification of the event; personal crimes of contact and burglary occurring in conjunction with motor vehicle thefts take precedence in determining the final classification based on the number of households.
The term "Urban" is used to denote "Central cities."
The term "Suburban" is used to denote "Outside central cities."
The term "Rural" is used to denote "Nonmetropolitan areas."
[a]Includes American Indian, Eskimo, Asian Pacific Islander if only one of these races is given.
[b]Includes all persons of any race, indicating two or more races.
[c]Estimate is based on 10 or fewer sample cases.

SOURCE: "Table 18. Number of Victimizations and Victimization Rates on the Basis of Thefts per 1,000 Households and of Thefts per 1,000 Vehicles Owned, by Selected Household Characteristics," in *Criminal Victimization in the United States, 2006 Statistical Tables*, U.S. Department of Justice, Bureau of Justice Statistics, August 2008, http://www.ojp.gov/bjs/pub/pdf/cvus0601.pdf (accessed May 23, 2009)

The Physical and Emotional Impact of Crime

According to the BJS, most older Americans who are the victims of violent crime are not physically injured. However, physical injuries do not tell the whole story. Victimization and fear of victimization can have far more serious effects on the quality of older adults' lives than they might for younger people.

Older adults are often less resilient than younger people. Even so-called nonviolent crimes, such as purse snatching, vandalism, or burglary, can be devastating. Stolen or damaged articles and property are often irreplaceable because of their sentimental or monetary value. Furthermore, nonviolent crimes leave victims with a sense of violation and heightened vulnerability.

Older People Are Considered Easy Prey

Because of their physical limitations, older adults are often considered easy prey. They are less likely than younger victims to resist criminal attacks. Their reluctance to resist may be based on awareness that they lack the strength to repel a younger aggressor and that they are physically frail and at risk of injuries that could permanently disable them. The U.S. Bureau of Justice reports that crime victims over the age of 65 who try to protect themselves most often use nonphysical actions, such as arguing, reasoning, or screaming. Younger victims are more likely to use physical action, such as attacking, resisting, or running from or chasing offenders.

FRAUD

Older adults are also considered easy prey for fraud, deception, and exploitation. They are more readily accessible to con artists than other age groups because they are likely to be at home to receive visits from door-to-door salespeople, e-mails, or calls from telemarketers. Older adults who are homebound or otherwise isolated may not have regular contact with others who might help them to identify possible schemes or frauds. Law enforcement officials and consumer advocates assert that older people are targeted because:

- They are more likely than younger people to have substantial financial savings, home equity, or credit, all of which are tempting to fraud perpetrators.

TABLE 11.2

Victimization rates by type of crime and age of head of household, 2006

	Rate per 1,000 households				
Type of crime	12–19	20–34	35–49	50–64	65 and over
Property crimes	**366.5**	**214.4**	**190.1**	**140.5**	**70.2**
Household burglary	44.9	41.8	32.7	27.3	16.4
Completed	33.8*	34.7	26.7	20.1	13.2
Forcible entry	22.0*	13.8	10.1	5.8	3.7
Unlawful entry without force	11.8*	20.9	16.6	14.2	9.4
Attempted forcible entry	11.0*	7.1	6.0	7.2	3.2
Motor vehicle theft	20.1*	14.6	8.6	6.5	3.1
Completed	20.1*	12.2	6.6	5.2	2.0
Attempted	0.0*	2.3	1.9	1.3	1.2*
Theft	301.6	158.0	148.8	106.7	50.7
Completed	291.8	151.2	143.6	101.8	49.0
Less than $50	55.2	40.2	37.2	31.4	16.6
$50–$249	133.9	54.5	54.4	34.6	13.6
$250 or more	80.5	45.3	38.6	25.4	10.9
Amount not available	22.2*	11.2	13.3	10.5	7.9
Attempted	9.8*	6.8	5.2	4.9	1.7
Total number of households	1,073,350	26,665,840	36,364,320	30,165,640	23,589,240

Note: Due to changes in methodology, the 2006 national crime victimization rates are not comparable to previous years and cannot be used for yearly trend comparisons. However, the overall patterns of victimization at the national level can be examined. See *Criminal Victimization, 2006,* at <http://www.ojp.usdoj.gov/bjs/abstract/cv06.htm>. Detail may not add to total shown because of rounding.

*Estimate is based on 10 or fewer sample cases.

SOURCE: "Table 19. Victimization Rates by Type of Crime and Age of Head of Household," in *Criminal Victimization in the United States, 2006 Statistical Tables*, U.S. Department of Justice, Bureau of Justice Statistics, August 2008, http://www.ojp.gov/bjs/pub/pdf/cvus0601.pdf (accessed May 23, 2009)

FIGURE 11.1

Number of homicides of persons aged 65 and older by gender, 1976–2005

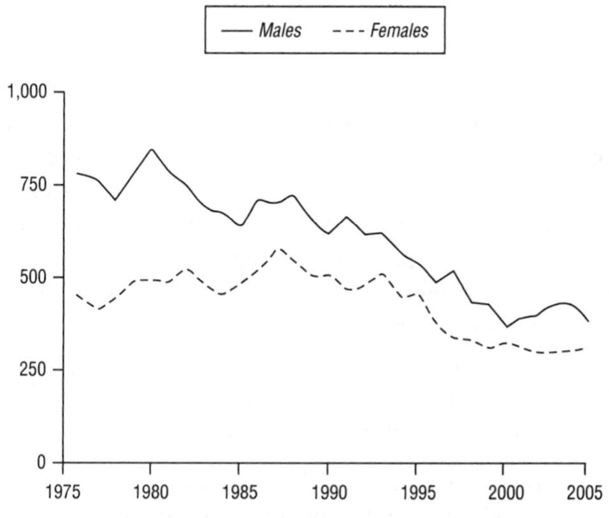

SOURCE: James Alan Fox and Marianne W. Zawitz, "Number of Homicides of Persons Age 65 and Older by Gender, 1976–2005," in *Homicide Trends in the United States*, U.S. Department of Justice, U.S. Bureau of Justice Statistics, July 2007, http://www.ojp.usdoj.gov/bjs/homicide/elders.htm (accessed May 23, 2009)

FIGURE 11.2

Homicide victimization and offending rates for persons aged 65 and older, 1976–2005

[Rate per 100,000 population]

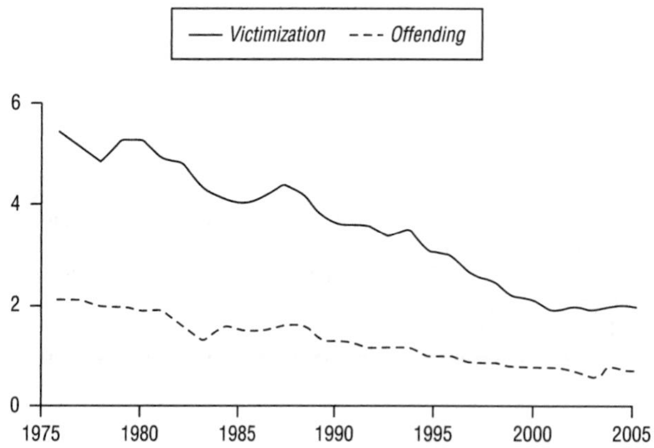

SOURCE: James Alan Fox and Marianne W. Zawitz, "Homicide Victimization and Offending Rates for Persons Age 65 and Older, 1976–2005," in *Homicide Trends in the United States*, U.S. Department of Justice, Bureau of Justice Statistics, July 2007, http://www.ojp.usdoj.gov/bjs/homicide/elders.htm (accessed May 23, 2009)

- They are often reluctant to be rude to others, so they may be more likely to hear out a con's story. They may also be overly trusting.
- Older adults are less likely to report fraud because they are embarrassed, they do not know how or to whom to report the crime, or they fear appearing incapable of handling their personal finances.

FIGURE 11.3

Percent of homicides committed during a felony, by age of victim, 1976–2005

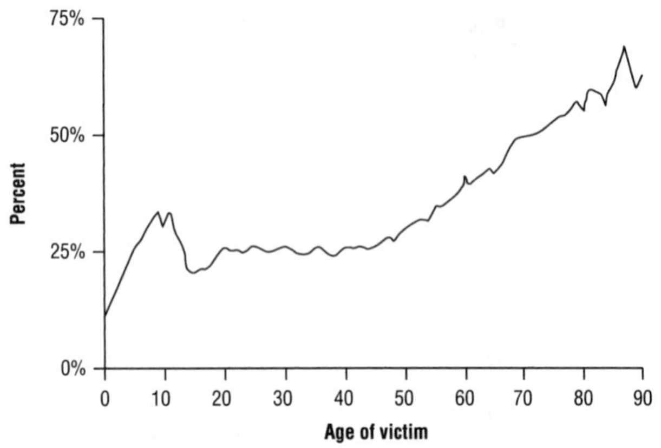

SOURCE: James Alan Fox and Marianne W. Zawitz, "Percent of Homicides Committed during a Felony by Age of Victim, 1976–2005," in *Homicide Trends in the United States*, U.S. Department of Justice, Bureau of Justice Statistics, July 2007, http://www.ojp.usdoj.gov/bjs/homicide/elders.htm (accessed May 23, 2009)

TABLE 11.3

Murder victims killed by an intimate, percentage by sex, 1976–2005

	Male victims	Female victims
12–17	—	5%
18–24	2%	29
25–29	4	37
30–34	6	41
35–39	8	43
40–44	9	42
45–49	10	40
50–59	10	32
60+	6	21

—Less than 0.5%

SOURCE: James Alan Fox and Marianne W. Zawitz, "For Every Age Group Female Murder Victims Are More Likely Than Male Victims to Have Been Killed by an Intimate," in *Homicide Trends in the United States*, U.S. Department of Justice, Bureau of Justice Statistics, July 2007, http://www.ojp.usdoj.gov/bjs/homicide/intimates.htm# intprop (accessed May 23, 2009)

- Older adults who do report fraud may not make good witnesses. Their memories may fade over the often protracted span of time between the crime and the trial, and on the witness stand they may be unable to provide detailed enough information to lead to a conviction.

In "The Effects of Loneliness on Telemarketing Fraud Vulnerability among Older Adults" (*Journal of Elder Abuse and Neglect*, vol. 20, no. 1, February 2008), Linda M. Alves and Steve R. Wilson indicate that the typical telemarketing fraud victim is a male between the ages of 60 and 70 who is divorced or separated and is college educated. Alves and Wilson suggest that loneliness and social isolation may increase an older adult's vulnerability to telemarketing fraud.

The Federal Trade Commission (FTC) is the federal government's lead consumer protection agency. FTC authority extends over practically the entire economy, including business and consumer transactions via telephone and the Internet. The FTC's consumer mission includes prohibiting unfair or deceptive acts or practices.

The U.S. Food and Drug Administration (FDA) and the FTC actively work to prevent health fraud and scams. These agencies identify products with substandard or entirely useless ingredients as well as those with fraudulent or misleading advertising to prevent the dissemination of unsubstantiated or deceptive claims about the health benefits of particular products or services.

The FTC acts not only to prevent consumer fraud but also to monitor its occurrence. In *Consumer Fraud in the United States: The Second FTC Survey* (October 2007, http://www2.ftc.gov/opa/2007/10/fraud.pdf), the FTC reports the results of a 2005 survey, which found that older consumers were significantly less likely to be victims of specific kinds of fraud such as weight-loss products, prize promotions, foreign lotteries, work-at-home programs, credit repair, and unauthorized billing for Internet services. Whereas 15.4 percent of adults aged 35 to 44 were victims of one or more frauds in 2005, just 11% of adults aged 55 to 64 and 5.6% of those aged 75 and older had been victims of fraud.

Health Fraud

Older adults may be particularly susceptible to false or misleading claims about the safety and efficacy of over-the-counter (nonprescription) drugs, devices, foods, dietary supplements, and health care services, because the marketing of such products and services often relates to conditions associated with aging. Also, many of these unproven treatments promise false hope and offer immediate cures for chronic (long-term) diseases or complete relief from pain. It is easy to understand how older adults who are frightened or in pain might be seduced by false promises of quick cures.

Working together, the FTC and the FDA combat deceptive advertising for health services such as false and unsubstantiated claims for dietary supplements. One example of their joint effort is the press release "FDA, FTC Warn Public of Fraudulent 2009 H1N1 Influenza Products" (May 1, 2009, http://www.fda.gov/NewsEvents/Newsroom/PressAnnouncements/ucm149576.htm), which warns consumers "to be wary of Internet sites and other promotions for products that claim to diagnose, prevent, mitigate, treat or cure the 2009 H1N1 influenza virus." The FDA warns that these deceptive products have not been proven to be safe or effective and are often sold over the Internet via illegitimate Web sites.

Financial Fraud, Abuse, and Exploitation

Financial crimes against older adults are largely underrecognized, underreported, and underprosecuted but are estimated to total losses of at least $2.6 billion each year. This section describes findings from *Broken Trust: Elders, Family, and Finances* (March 2009, http://www.metlife.com/assets/cao/mmi/publications/studies/mmi-study-broken-trust-elders-family-finances.pdf), a study about preventing financial abuse of older adults that was conducted by the MetLife Mature Market Institute, the National Committee for the Prevention of Elder Abuse, and the Center for Gerontology at Virginia Polytechnic Institute and State University. The study considers elder financial abuse as "the unauthorized use or illegal taking of funds or property of people aged 60 and older."

The study's principal findings include:

- Older adults' larger net worth—adults over age 50 control 70% of the net worth of U.S. households—and vulnerabilities, such as impaired cognitive abilities, loneliness, and social isolation make them prime targets for financial abuse.
- Aging of the population coupled with social changes such as families living at a distance and technological advances such as virtual social networks will act to sharply increase opportunities for financial abuse of older adults.
- Financial abuse generally occurs at the hands of someone the older adults trust—business and service professionals including paid caregivers, neighbors, and family members—rather than strangers.
- Financial abuse of older adults occurs among men and women of every race and ethnicity.
- A typical victim is a white woman aged 70 to 89, who is frail, cognitively impaired, and trusting, lonely, or isolated.

Financial abuse is considered the third most common type of abuse of older adults, following neglect and emotional/psychological abuse.

Medicare Fraud

Every year Medicare loses millions of dollars because of fraud and abuse. *Broken Trust* reports that Medicare and Medicaid fraud totaled $121.4 million in a three-month period (April to June 2008), during which researchers monitored Newsfeed media reports. The most common forms of Medicare fraud were:

- Billing for services not furnished
- Misrepresenting a diagnosis to justify a higher payment
- Soliciting, offering, or receiving a kickback
- Charging Medicare higher fees than normal for certain procedures
- Falsifying certificates of medical necessity, plans of treatment, and medical records to justify payment
- Billing for a service not furnished as billed

The Health Insurance Portability and Accountability Act of 1996 allocated funds to protect Medicare's integrity and prevent fraud. In one of the largest efforts in the history of Medicare, the program has undertaken a major campaign to help eliminate Medicare fraud, waste, and abuse.

To combat Medicare fraud at the level of the beneficiary, the U.S. Administration on Aging (AoA) provides grants to local organizations to help older Americans become more vigilant health care consumers so that they can identify and prevent fraudulent health care practices. The Senior Medicare Patrol, now known as the SMP program, trains community volunteers, many of whom are retired professionals, such as doctors, nurses, accountants, investigators, law enforcement personnel, attorneys, and teachers, to help Medicare and Medicaid beneficiaries become better health care consumers. In "Performance Data for the Senior Medicare Patrol" (May 18, 2008, http://www.smpresource.org/eSeries/Content/ahqaNavigationMenu/VolunteersMakeaDifference/oei-02-09-00170.pdf), Stuart E. Wright of the U.S. Department of Health and Human Services (HHS) indicates that between 1997 and 2008 the SMP program had recouped $105.7 million. According to the AoA, in *Online Performance Appendix—to the FY 2009 Congressional Justification for the President's FY 2009 Budget* (April 8, 2009,http://www.aoa.gov/AoARoot/Program_Results/docs/2009/AoAOnlinePerformanceAppendix012508Final.pdf), the number of SMP-trained volunteers increased by 62%, from 31,000 in 2002 to 50,220 in 2009. (See Table 11.4.)

ABUSE AND MISTREATMENT OF OLDER ADULTS

Domestic violence against older adults is a phenomenon that first gained publicity during the late 1970s, when Representative Claude Denson Pepper (1900–1989; D-FL) held widely publicized hearings about the mistreatment of older adults. In the three decades since those hearings, policy makers, health professionals, social service personnel, and advocates for older Americans have sought ways to protect the older population from physical, psychological, and financial abuse.

Magnitude of the Problem

It is difficult to determine exactly how many older adults are the victims of abuse or mistreatment. As with child abuse and domestic violence among younger adults, the number of actual cases is larger than the number of reported cases. There is consensus among professionals

TABLE 11.4

Target and actual numbers of older adults trained to serve in the Senior Medicare Patrol, 2004–09

#	Key outcomes	Fiscal year 2004 actual	Fiscal year 2005 actual	Fiscal year 2006 Target	Fiscal year 2006 Actual	Fiscal year 2007 Target	Fiscal year 2007 Actual	Fiscal year 2008 target	Fiscal year 2009 target
Long-term objective: Improve efficiency of Older Americans Act (OAA) by at least 35% by 2010.									
1.4	For Senior Medicare Patrol, increase the number of beneficiaries trained per million dollars of AoA funding.	46,229 (+49%)	47,758 (+54%)	37,200 (+20%)	42,767 (+38%)	48,980 (+58%)	Sept-08	49,600 (+60%)	50,220 (+62%)

Note: For presentation which ties to the budget Administration on Aging (AoA) highlighted specific measures that are most directly related to Aging Network Support Activities, however multiple performance outcomes are impacted by this program because AoA's performance measures (efficiency, effective targeting, and client outcomes) assess network-wide performance.

SOURCE: "Aging Network Support Activities," in *Online Performance Appendix—to the FY 2009 Congressional Justification for the President's FY 2009 Budget*, Department of Health and Human Services, Administration on Aging, April 8, 2009, http://www.aoa.gov/AoARoot/Program_Results/docs/2009/AoAOnlinePerformanceAppendix012508Final.pdf (accessed May 24, 2009)

and agencies that deal with issues of elder abuse that it is far less likely to be reported than child or spousal abuse. The challenge of estimating the incidence and prevalence of this problem is further compounded by the varying definitions of abuse and reporting practices used by the voluntary, state, and federal agencies, as well as the fact that comprehensive national data are not collected. Furthermore, research suggests that abuse often occurs over long periods of time and that only when it reaches a critical juncture, such as instances of severe injury, will the neglect or abuse become evident to health, social service, or legal professionals.

Even though the magnitude of the problem of abuse and mistreatment of older adults is unknown, its social and moral importance is obvious. Abuse and neglect of older individuals in society violates a sacred trust and moral commitment to protect vulnerable individuals and groups from harm and to ensure their well-being and security.

The National Center on Elder Abuse (NCEA) finds in *2004 Survey of State Adult Protective Services: Abuse of Adults 60 Years of Age and Older* (February 2006, http://www.ncea.aoa.gov/ncearoot/main_site/pdf/2-14-06%20FINAL%2060+REPORT.pdf), the most recent national statistics available as of mid-2009, that there was a 19.7% increase in the number of reports of elder and vulnerable adult abuse since 2000. With just 32 states reporting, Adult Protective Services received over 253,000 reports on people aged 60 and older. According to H.R. 448, the Elder Abuse Victims Act of 2009 (January 9, 2009, http://www.gop.gov/bill/111/1/hr448), "between 1–2 million Americans over the age of 65 have been injured, mistreated, or exploited by a caregiver. Data suggest that only 1 in 14 incidents are brought to the attention of authorities."

Types of Mistreatment

Federal definitions of elder abuse, neglect, and exploitation appeared for the first time in the Older Americans Act Amendments of 1987. Broadly defined, there are three basic categories of abuse: domestic elder abuse, institutional elder abuse, and self-neglect or self-abuse.

Most documented instances of elder abuse refer to a form of maltreatment of an older person by someone who has a special relationship with the older adult, such as a spouse, sibling, child, friend, or caregiver. Until recently, most data indicated that adult children were the most common abusers of older family members, but Pamela B. Teaster of the University of Kentucky indicates in *A Response to the Abuse of Vulnerable Adults: The 2000 Survey of State Adult Protective Services* (March 7, 2003, http://www.ncea.aoa.gov/ncearoot/Main_Site/pdf/research/apsreport030703.pdf) that the landmark 2000 NCEA survey found that spouses are the most common perpetrators of abuse and mistreatment. The major types of elder abuse and mistreatment include:

- Physical abuse—inflicting physical pain or bodily injury
- Sexual abuse—nonconsensual sexual contact of any kind with an older person
- Emotional or psychological abuse—inflicting mental anguish by, for example, name calling, humiliation, threats, or isolation
- Neglect—willful or unintentional failure to provide basic necessities, such as food and medical care, as a result of caregiver indifference, inability, or ignorance
- Material or financial abuse—exploiting or misusing an older person's funds or assets
- Abandonment—the desertion of an older adult by an individual who has physical custody of the elder or who has assumed responsibility for providing care for the older person
- Self-neglect—behaviors of an older person that threaten his or her own health or safety

Reporting Abuse

Like child abuse and sexual assault crimes, many crimes against older adults are not reported because the victims are physically or mentally unable to summon help or because they are reluctant or afraid to publicly accuse relatives or caregivers. Loneliness or dependency prevents many victims from reporting the crimes, even when they are aware of them, simply because they are afraid to lose the companionship and care of the perpetrator. When financial abuse is reported, the source of the information is likely to be someone other than the victim: a police officer, an ambulance attendant, a bank teller, a neighbor, or other family member.

In "Elder Abuse and Neglect: When Home Is Not Safe" (*Clinics in Geriatric Medicine*, vol. 25, no. 1, February 2009), Linda Abbey of the Virginia Commonwealth University reports that all 50 states require physicians and other social service professionals to report evidence of abuse, neglect, and exploitation when an older adult is in an institution and most also require reporting when abuse occurs in a private home. Abbey notes that most common reporters for older adults were family members (17%), social services (10.6%), friends/neighbors (8%), the older adults themselves (6.3%), long-term care staff (5.5%), law enforcement (5.3%), and nurses/aides (3.8%). Physicians represented just 1.4% of reporters. Abbey asserts that low physician reporting may be attributable to lack of awareness of the problem, lack of training about how to identify abuse, denial that the family may be abusing a loved one, concern about compromising relationships with the family, reluctance to become involved with legal proceedings, and time pressures that prevent the identification of instances of abuse. She also opines that physician discomfort with the problem may impede case finding and observes that "family violence does not fit neatly within the traditional medical paradigm of symptoms, diagnoses and treatment."

Causes of Elder Abuse

According to the NCEA, no single theory can explain why older people are abused. The causes of abuse are diverse and complicated. Some relate to the personality of the abuser, some reflect the relationship between the abuser and the abused, and some are reactions to stressful situations. Even though some children truly dislike their parents and the role of caregiver, many others want to care for their parents or feel it is the right thing to do but may be emotionally or financially unable to meet the challenges of caregiving.

STRESS. Meeting the daily needs of a frail and dependent older adult is demanding and may be overwhelming for some family members who serve as caregivers. When the older person lives in the same household as the caregiver, crowding, differences of opinion, and constant demands often add to the strain of providing physical care. When the older person lives in a different house, the pressure of commuting and managing two households may be stressful.

Stress may be a reality in the life of caregivers, but research does not support its role as the most significant contributing factor in abuse of older adults. Instead, Namkee G. Choi, Jinseok Kim, and Joan Asseff note in "Self-Neglect and Neglect of Vulnerable Older Adults: Reexamination of Etiology" (*Journal of Gerontological Social Work*, vol. 52, no. 2, February 2009) that research points to social and financial problems such as frail older adults' and their families' lack of resources to pay for essential goods and services and the inadequate health care and other formal support programs for older adults and their caregivers. Choi, Kim, and Asseff assert that inadequate public policy and supportive services rather than individual and family risk factors need to be considered as a significant cause of elder abuse.

FINANCIAL BURDEN. Caring for an older adult often places a financial strain on a family. Older parents may need financial assistance at the same time that their children are raising their own family. Instead of an occasional night out, a long-awaited vacation, or a badly needed newer car, families may find themselves paying for ever-increasing medical care, prescription drugs, special dietary supplements, extra food and clothing, or therapy. Saving for their children's college education, for a daughter's wedding, or for retirement may be difficult or impossible. Choi, Kim, and Asseff observe that financial strain may be a contributor to mistreatment of older adults.

CYCLE OF ABUSE. One theory of the causation of abuse of older adults posits that people who abuse an older parent or relative were themselves abused as children. Suzanne K. Steinmetz, the director of Resources for Older Americans at the University of Delaware and a recognized expert on domestic violence, finds support for this hypothesis in her landmark study of abusers, *Duty Bound: Elder Abuse and Family Care* (1988). She finds only 1 out of 400 children who were treated nonviolently when they were raised attacked their older parents; by contrast, 1 out of 2 children who were violently mistreated as children abused their older parents.

INVASION OF PRIVACY. In "Elder Abuse" (April 20, 2009, http://emedicine.medscape.com/article/805727-overview), Monique I. Sellas and Laurel H. Krouse indicate that a shared living arrangement is a major risk factor for mistreatment of older adults, with older people living alone at the lowest risk for abuse. A shared residence increases the opportunities for contact, conflict, and mistreatment. When the home must be shared, there is an inevitable loss of a certain amount of control and privacy. Movement may be restricted, habits may need to change, and rivalries between generations may follow. Frustration and anxiety may result as both older parent and supporting child try to suppress anger, with varying degrees of success.

SOCIAL ISOLATION. Sellas and Krouse note that social isolation is linked to abuse and the mistreatment of older adults. It may be that socially isolated families are better able to hide unacceptable behaviors from friends and neighbors who might report the abusers. Even though there are no data that support the corollary to this finding, it is hypothesized that mistreatment is less likely in families rooted in strong social networks.

ALZHEIMER'S DISEASE OR OTHER DEMENTIA. Claudia Cooper et al. assert in "Abuse of People with Dementia by Family Carers: Representative Cross Sectional Survey" (*BMJ*, vol. 338, January 22, 2009) that the diagnosis of Alzheimer's disease or other dementia is a risk factor for the physical abuse of older adults. Cooper et al. researched the prevalence of psychological and physical abuse by family caregivers of older adults with Alzheimer's or another dementia. They find that more than half (52%) of caregivers reported some abusive behavior, with verbal abuse reported most frequently. Only 1.4% of caregivers reported physical abuse.

According to Randy R. Gainey and Brian K. Payne, in "Caregiver Burden, Elder Abuse, and Alzheimer's Disease: Testing the Relationship" (*Journal of Health and Human Services Administration*, vol. 29. no. 2, fall 2006), "caregiver burden" (the stress associated with caring for older adults with dementia with limited community support services) is the most frequently cited explanation for the observation that people suffering from dementia are at a greater risk for mistreatment. The researchers looked at instances of mistreatment of older adults with Alzheimer's and those who were not cognitively impaired and found almost no difference in caregiver burden among those caring for older adults with or without dementia. Research has not pinpointed the relationship between dementia and the risk for abuse; however, it may be that dementia itself is not the risk factor but the disruptive behaviors that result from dementia. This hypothesis is consistent with research that shows that the disruptive behavior of Alzheimer's disease patients is an especially strong predictor and cause of caregiver stress.

REVERSE DEPENDENCY. Some sources believe that abusers may be quite dependent, emotionally and financially, on their victims for housing, financial assistance, and transportation than are nonabusing caregivers. They appear to have fewer resources and are frequently unable to meet their own basic needs. Rather than having power in the relationship, they are relatively powerless. From these observations, some researchers speculate that abusing caregivers may not always be driven to violence by the physical and emotional burden of caring for a seriously disabled older person but may have mental health problems of their own that can lead to violent behavior. Several studies specifically point to depression as a characteristic of perpetrators of elder mistreatment.

The Abusive Spouse

Edward O. Laumann, Sara A. Leitsch, and Linda J. Waite of the University of Chicago estimate in "Elder Mistreatment in the United States: Prevalence Estimates from a Nationally Representative Study" (*Journal of Gerontology Series B: Psychological Sciences and Social Sciences*, vol. 63, no. 4, July 2008) the prevalence of mistreatment of older adults using data from the National Social Life, Health, and Aging Project—the first population-based, nationally representative study to ask older adults about their recent experience of mistreatment. The researchers find that about 13% of older Americans had been abused and 26% identified a spouse or romantic partner as the abuser.

The high rate of spousal abuse among the older population is possibly because many older adults live with their spouses, so the opportunity for spousal violence is great. Violence against an older spouse may be the continuation of an abusive relationship that began years earlier—abuse does not end simply because a couple ages. Sometimes, however, the abuse may not begin until later years, in which case it is often associated with mental illness, alcohol abuse, unemployment, postretirement depression, and/or loss of self-esteem.

Intervention and Prevention

All 50 states and the District of Columbia have laws addressing abuse of older adults, but like laws aiming to prevent and reduce child abuse and domestic violence among younger people, they are often ineffective. The effectiveness of laws and the enforcing agencies vary from state to state and even from county to county within a given state. No standard definition of abuse exists among enforcement agencies. In many cases authorities cannot legally intervene and terminate an abusive condition unless a report is filed, the abuse is verified, and the victim files a formal complaint. An older adult could understandably be reluctant, physically unable, or too fearful to accuse or prosecute an abuser.

Clearly, the best way to stop elder abuse is to prevent its occurrence. Older people who know that they will eventually need outside help should carefully analyze the potential challenges of living with their families and, if necessary and possible, make alternate arrangements. All older adults should take action to protect their money and assets to ensure that their valuables cannot be easily taken from them.

Families or individuals who must serve as caregivers for older adults, voluntarily or otherwise, must be helped to realize that their frustration and despair do not have to result in abuse. Health and social service agencies offer myriad interventions including group support programs and counseling to help caregivers and their families. Many communities allocate resources to assist families to offset the financial burden of elder care, for example, through tax deductions or subsidies for respite care.

INSTITUTIONAL ABUSE—A FORGOTTEN POPULATION?

Abuse of the older population can and does occur in the institutions (nursing homes, board-and-care facilities, and retirement homes) charged with, and compensated for, caring for the nation's older population. The term *institutional abuse* generally refers to the same forms of abuse as domestic abuse crimes but is perpetrated by people who have legal or contractual obligations to provide older adults with care and protection. Even though the Omnibus Budget Reconciliation Act of 1987 states that nursing homes must take steps to attain or maintain the "highest practicable physical, mental, and psychosocial well-being of each resident," too many residents are the victims of neglect or abuse by these facilities or their employees.

Older adult residents of long-term care facilities or supportive housing are thought to be at higher risk for abuse and neglect than community-dwelling older adults. They are particularly vulnerable because most suffer from one or more chronic diseases that impair their physical and cognitive functioning, rendering them dependent on others. Furthermore, many are either unable to report abuse or neglect, or they are fearful that reporting may generate reprisals from the facility staff or otherwise adversely affect their life. Others are unaware of the availability of help.

There are federal laws and regulations that govern nursing homes, but there are no federal standards that oversee or regulate residential care facilities, such as personal care homes, adult congregate living facilities, residential care homes, homes for the aged, domiciliary care homes, board-and-care homes, and assisted living facilities. As a result, it is much more difficult than with nursing homes to estimate the prevalence or nature of abuse or neglect in these facilities. Despite reports in recent years that have raised the specter of widespread and serious abuse of institutionalized older people, as of 2009 there had never been a systematic study of the prevalence of abuse in nursing homes or other residential facilities.

However, Gerald J. Jogerst, Jeannette M. Daly, and Arthur J. Hartz of the University of Iowa identify in "State Policies and Nursing Home Characteristics Associated with Rates of Resident Mistreatment" (*Journal of the American Medical Directors Association*, vol. 9, no. 9, November 2008) state and nursing home characteristics associated with the rates of nursing home resident mistreatment. The researchers report that in 2004, 1.6% of the nursing home population was reported to be mistreated. The average rates per 1,000 residents were 16 reports, but rates varied widely between states. Incident report rates per 1,000 ranged from 0.04 in Virginia to 46 in Alabama and complaint report rates ranged from 0.42 in Hawaii to 52 in New Mexico. Higher rates of complaint and reports were associated with lower levels of staffing.

Types of Abuse and Neglect

Nursing home neglect and abuse can take many forms, including:

- Failure to provide proper diet and hydration
- Failure to assist with personal hygiene
- Over- or undermedication
- Failure to answer call lights promptly
- Failure to turn residents in their beds to promote circulation and prevent decubitus ulcers (bedsores)
- Slapping or other physical abuse
- Leaving residents in soiled garments or beds or failure to take them to the toilet
- Use of unwarranted restraints
- Emotional or verbal abuse
- Retaliation for making a complaint
- Failure to provide appropriate medical care
- Sexual assault, unwanted touching, indecent exposure, or rape
- Theft of the resident's property or money

Surveys conducted with certified nursing assistants (CNAs) who work in long-term care facilities are summarized in "Preventing Abuse and Neglect in Nursing Homes: The Role of Staffing and Training" (November 23, 2003, http://sp.srph.tamhsc.edu/centers/moved_SRHRC/PPT/nh2_gsa03.ppt) by Catherine Hawes, the director of the Southwest Rural Health Research Center at Texas A&M University. Hawes reveals that more than one-third of CNAs have witnessed abuses including incidents of physical and verbal or psychological abuse, such as:

- Aggressiveness with a resident and rough handling
- Pulling too hard on a resident
- Yelling in anger
- Threatening behavior
- Punching, slapping, kicking, or hitting
- Speaking in a harsh tone, cursing at a resident, or saying harsh or mean things to a resident

The CNAs also offered examples of neglect, which is often more difficult to detect and measure, including:

- Neglecting oral/dental care
- Failing to perform prescribed range of motion exercises
- Failing to change residents after an episode of incontinence

- Ignoring residents who are bedfast, particularly not offering activities to them
- Not performing prescribed wound care
- Failing to bathe residents regularly
- Performing a one-person transfer (move from bed to chair or wheelchair) when the resident required a two-person transfer
- Not providing cuing or task segmentation to residents who need that kind of assistance to maximize their independence
- Failing to perform scheduled toileting or helping residents when they ask
- Not keeping residents hydrated
- Turning off a call light and taking no action on the resident's request

Resident Risk Factors

Even though there has been scant research describing the factors that contribute to risk for abuse of institutionalized older adults, some studies indicate that the risk for abuse increases in direct relationship to the older resident's dependence on the facility's staff for safety, protection, and care. For example, Diana K. Harris and Michael L. Benson, in *Maltreatment of Patients in Nursing Homes: There Is No Safe Place* (2006), and Andrew C. Coyne of the University of Medicine and Dentistry of New Jersey, in "The Relationship between Dementia and Elder Abuse" (*Geriatric Times*, vol. 2, no. 4, July–August 2001), suggest that a patient with a diagnosis of Alzheimer's disease, another dementia, or some type of memory loss or confusion is at greater risk for abuse in the average nursing home population. In "Elder Abuse and Neglect in Long-Term Care" (*Elder Abuse and Neglect in Long-Term Care Clinics in Geriatric Medicine*, vol. 21, no. 2, May 2005), Seema Joshi and Joseph H. Flaherty of the St. Louis Veterans Administration Medical Center suggest that residents with behavioral symptoms, such as physical aggressiveness, appear to be at higher risk for abuse by staff; this finding is supported by interviews with CNAs.

Social isolation may also increase the risk for abuse. Residents who have no visitors are especially vulnerable, because they lack family or friends who could oversee their care, bear witness to and report any abuses, and advocate on their behalf.

Efforts to Identify and Reduce Abuse

In an effort to improve the quality of care and eliminate abuse in nursing homes, government regulations and laws have been enacted that require greater supervision and scrutiny of nursing homes. In 1987 President Ronald Reagan (1911–2004) signed the Omnibus Budget Reconciliation Act, which included protections for patient rights and treatment. The law went into effect October 1990, but compliance with the law varies from state to state and from one nursing facility to another.

In 1987 the AoA established the Prevention of Elder Abuse, Neglect, and Exploitation program. This program trains law enforcement officers, health care workers, and other professionals about how to identify and respond to elder abuse and supports education campaigns to increase public awareness of elder abuse and how to prevent it.

Many states have adopted additional legislation to help stem instances of institutional abuse and neglect. For example, in 1998 the state of New York enacted Kathy's Law, which created the new felony-level crime of "abuse of a vulnerable elderly person." At the state level there are many agencies involved in identifying and investigating cases of abuse and neglect. These agencies differ across states but may include ombudsmen (offices that assist patients who have complaints), adult protective services, the state survey agency responsible for licensing nursing homes, the state agency responsible for the operation of the nurse aide registry, Medicaid fraud units in the attorney general's office, and professional licensing boards.

LONG-TERM CARE OMBUDSMAN PROGRAM. Long-term care ombudsmen are advocates for residents of nursing homes, board-and-care homes, assisted living facilities, and other adult care facilities. The Long-Term Care Ombudsman Program was established under the Older Americans Act, which is administered by the AoA.

In "Long-Term Care Ombudsman Program" (July 7, 2009, http://www.aoa.gov/AoARoot/AoA_Programs/Elder_Rights/Ombudsman/index.aspx), the AoA reports that in fiscal year (FY) 2007 about 12,600 volunteers and 1,300 paid ombudsmen devoted over 670,000 hours to serving long-term care facility residents. Over 282,000 complaints by 186,403 individuals were investigated by the ombudsmen. More than three-quarters (79%) of all nursing homes and nearly half (46%) of all board-and-care, assisted living, and similar homes were visited regularly by state and local ombudsmen. Table 11.5 shows the target and actual numbers of complaints that were at least partially resolved by ombudsmen between FYs 2004 and 2009.

Table 11.6 lists the top complaint categories and shows that the number of nursing facility complaints increased from FY 1996 through FY 2005, but declined in FYs 2006 and 2007. Table 11.7 lists the top complaint categories and the steadily increasing number of board-and-care facility complaints investigated by ombudsman programs during the same time period.

TABLE 11.5

Target and actual numbers of complaints at least partially resolved by ombudsmen, 2004–09

#	Key outcomes	Fiscal year 2004 actual	Fiscal year 2005 actual	Fiscal year 2006 Target	Fiscal year 2006 Actual	Fiscal year 2007 Target	Fiscal year 2007 Actual	Fiscal year 2008 target	Fiscal year 2009 target
Long-term objective: Improve efficiency of Older Americans Act (OAA) by at least 35% by 2010.									
1.2	For Title VII Services, increase the number of Ombudsman complaints resolved or partially resolved per million dollars of AoA funding.	10,778 (+16%)	11,687 (+26%)	10,062 (+14%)	10,745 (+16%)	11,811 (+27%)	Sept-08	11,439 (+23%)	11,811 (+27%)
Long-term objective: By 2012, improve the Ombudsman complaint resolution rates in 35 states.									
2.7	Improve the Ombudsman complaint resolution rates.	26	26	15	27	15	Sept-08	30	32

Note: For presentation which ties to the budget AoA highlighted specific measures that are most directly related to Protection of Vulnerable Older Americans, however multiple performance outcomes are impacted by this program because AoA's performance measures (efficiency, effective targeting, and client outcomes) assess network-wide performance.

SOURCE: "Protection of Vulnerable Older Americans," in *Online Performance Appendix—to the FY 2009 Congressional Justification for the President's FY 2009 Budget*, Department of Health and Human Services, Administration on Aging, April 8, 2009, http://www.aoa.gov/AoARoot/Program_Results/docs/2009/AoAOnlinePerformanceAppendix012508Final.pdf (accessed May 24, 2009)

TABLE 11.6

Complaints about nursing facilities, by category, fiscal years 1996–2007

Group		Complaint categories	1996 Total	1996 %	1996 Rank	1997 Total	1997 %	1997 Rank	1998 Total	1998 %	1998 Rank	1999 Total	1999 %	1999 Rank	2000 Total	2000 %	2000 Rank	2001 Total	2001 %	2001 Rank
			144,680			**157,380**			**163,540**			**172,662**			**186,234**			**209,663**		
F.	41	Failure to respond to requests for assistance	5,441	3.76%	2	6,189	3.93%	1	7,026	4.30%	1	7,644	4.43%	1	8,676	4.66%	1	10,126	4.83%	1
C.	19	Discharge/eviction—planning, notice, procedure, implementation, including abandonment	4,110	2.84%	9	4,794	3.05%	6	5,407	3.31%	6	5,455	3.16%	7	5,762	3.09%	7	6,699	3.20%	6
D.	26	Dignity, respect—staff attitudes	4,882	3.37%	4	5,318	3.38%	4	5,710	3.49%	4	6,453	3.74%	4	7,351	3.95%	4	8,838	4.22%	2
J.	71	Food service—quantity, quality, variation, choice, condiments, utensils, menu	4,295	2.97%	8	4,082	2.59%	8	4,554	2.78%	9	5,063	2.93%	8	5,540	2.97%	8	6,161	2.94%	8
F.	40	Accident or injury of unknown origin, falls, improper handling	6,661	4.60%	1	5,701	3.62%	2	6,032	3.69%	3	6,804	3.94%	3	7,675	4.12%	2	7,810	3.73%	4
F.	42	Care plan/resident assessment—inadequate, failure to follow plan or physician orders	4,453	3.08%	5	5,445	3.46%	3	5,242	3.21%	7	6,412	3.71%	5	7,550	4.05%	3	8,572	4.09%	3
F.	44	Medications—administration, organization	3,123	2.16%	12	3,366	2.14%	12	3,885	2.38%	11	4,397	2.55%	10	4,914	2.64%	9	5,734	2.73%	9
F.	45	Personal hygiene (includes nail care and oral hygiene) and adequacy of dressing & grooming	5,301	3.66%	3	5,299	3.37%	5	6,411	3.92%	2	7,110	4.12%	2	7,279	3.91%	5	7,712	3.68%	5
I.	66	Resident conflict, including roommates	1,749	1.21%	29	1,713	1.09%	31	1,801	1.10%	31	1,759	1.02%	31	1,757	0.94%	32	2,028	0.97%	34
K.	79	Equipment/building—disrepair, hazard, poor lighting, fire safety, not secure	2,025	1.40%	24	2,400	1.52%	21	1,952	1.19%	26	2,541	1.47%	20	2,899	1.56%	19	3,472	1.66%	18
F.	48	Symptoms unattended, including pain, pain not managed, no notice to others of changes in condition	3,198	2.21%	11	3,529	2.24%	11	3,818	2.33%	12	4,077	2.36%	12	4,617	2.48%	10	5,075	2.42%	10
E.	38	Personal property lost, stolen, used by others, destroyed, withheld	3,598	2.49%	10	3,621	2.30%	10	3,993	2.44%	10	4,229	2.45%	11	4,227	2.27%	12	4,680	2.23%	12
D.	27	Exercise preference/choice and/or civil/religious rights, individual's right to smoke	2,211	1.53%	20	2,375	1.51%	22	2,851	1.74%	15	3,479	2.01%	13	3,803	2.04%	14	4,109	1.96%	15
K.	78	Cleanliness, pests, general housekeeping	2,242	1.55%	19	2,919	1.85%	14	3,123	1.91%	14	3,458	2.00%	14	3,832	2.06%	13	4,199	2.00%	14
M.	97	Shortage of staff	4,332	2.99%	6	4,351	2.76%	7	4,887	2.99%	8	5,740	3.32%	6	6,625	3.56%	6	6,664	3.18%	7
M.	100	Staff unresponsive, unavailable	2,376	1.64%	15	3,050	1.94%	13	3,248	1.99%	13	3,286	1.90%	15	3,700	1.99%	15	4,605	2.20%	13
A.	1	Physical abuse (including corporal punishment)	4,321	2.99%	7	4,080	2.59%	9	5,426	3.32%	5	4,591	2.66%	9	4,350	2.34%	11	4,842	2.31%	11
F.	49	Toileting, incontinent care	2,070	1.43%	23	2,193	1.39%	26	2,720	1.66%	16	3,022	1.75%	16	3,093	1.66%	17	3,377	1.61%	19
G.	53	Assistive devices or equipment	1,431	0.99%	35	1,792	1.14%	30	1,751	1.07%	32	1,944	1.13%	29	2,151	1.15%	28	2,354	1.12%	30
A.	6	Resident to resident physical or sexual abuse	2,532	1.75%	13	2,565	1.63%	17	2,577	1.58%	19	2,851	1.65%	17	3,034	1.63%	18	3,569	1.70%	17
K.	77	Air/environment: temperature, and quality (heating, cooling, ventilation, water, noise)	1,849	1.28%	27	1,835	1.17%	28	1,811	1.11%	29	2,030	1.18%	26	2,066	1.11%	30	2,439	1.16%	28
J.	70	Fluid availability/hydration	1,122	0.78%	44	1,282	0.81%	41	1,457	0.89%	39	1,655	0.96%	35	2,219	1.19%	27	2,531	1.21%	26
P.	120	Family conflict; interference	2,172	1.50%	21	2,342	1.49%	23	2,284	1.40%	23	2,222	1.29%	25	2,473	1.33%	23	2,713	1.29%	24
A.	3	Verbal/psychological abuse (including punishment, seclusion)	2,431	1.68%	14	2,676	1.70%	15	2,598	1.59%	18	2,601	1.51%	18	2,787	1.50%	20	3,171	1.51%	21
K.	83	Odors	1,874	1.30%	26	2,515	1.60%	19	2,493	1.52%	21	2,544	1.47%	19	2,472	1.33%	24	3,230	1.54%	20
P.	122	Legal—guardianship, conservatorship, power of attorney, wills	2,338	1.62%	16	2,275	1.45%	24	2,268	1.39%	24	1,974	1.14%	28	2,309	1.24%	26	2,465	1.18%	27
M.	101	Supervision	1,825	1.26%	28	2,202	1.40%	25	1,925	1.18%	27	2,325	1.35%	24	3,326	1.79%	16	3,607	1.72%	16
E.	36	Billing/charges—notice, approval, questionable, accounting wrong or denied	2,254	1.56%	18	2,419	1.54%	20	2,428	1.48%	22	2,497	1.45%	22	2,589	1.39%	22	2,755	1.31%	23
A.	5	Gross neglect	2,123	1.47%	22	2,648	1.68%	16	2,551	1.56%	20	2,331	1.35%	23	2,372	1.27%	25	2,591	1.24%	25
F.	52	Not used (other: care pre federal fiscal year 2007)	2,275	1.57%	17	2,543	1.62%	18	2,717	1.66%	17	2,521	1.46%	21	2,645	1.42%	21	2,776	1.32%	22

TABLE 11.6

Complaints about nursing facilities, by category, fiscal years 1996–2007 [CONTINUED]

Group		Complaint categories	2002 Total	2002 %	2002 Rank	2003 Total	2003 %	2003 Rank	2004 Total	2004 %	2004 Rank	2005 Total	2005 %	2005 Rank	2006 Total	2006 %	2006 Rank	2007 Total	2007 %	2007 Rank
			208,762			**226,376**			**227,721**			**241,684**			**221,486**			**218,773**		
F.	41	Failure to respond to requests for assistance	9,885	4.74%	1	11,240	4.97%	1	11,720	5.15%	1	14,391	5.95%	1	14,186	6.40%	1	13,932	6.37%	1
C.	19	Discharge/eviction—planning, notice, procedure, implementation, including abandonment	7,670	3.67%	5	7,465	3.30%	6	7,172	3.15%	7	7,942	3.29%	6	8,526	3.85%	2	9,517	4.35%	2
D.	26	Dignity, respect—staff attitudes	8,583	4.11%	3	8,326	3.68%	4	8,537	3.75%	4	9,062	3.75%	3	8,491	3.83%	3	8,778	4.01%	3
J.	71	Food service—quantity, quality, variation, choice, condiments, utensils, menu	6,185	2.96%	7	7,074	3.12%	7	8,034	3.53%	5	9,326	3.86%	2	7,459	3.37%	6	8,165	3.73%	4
F.	40	Accident or injury of unknown origin, falls, improper handling	8,082	3.87%	4	9,514	4.20%	2	10,078	4.43%	2	8,998	3.72%	4	7,736	3.49%	5	8,032	3.67%	5
F.	42	Care plan/resident assessment—inadequate, failure to follow plan or physician orders	8,842	4.24%	2	8,758	3.87%	3	8,638	3.79%	3	8,944	3.70%	5	8,408	3.80%	4	7,708	3.52%	6
F.	44	Medications—administration, organization	5,841	2.80%	8	6,931	3.06%	8	6,757	2.97%	8	7,735	3.20%	7	7,263	3.28%	7	7,397	3.38%	7
F.	45	Personal hygiene (includes nail care and oral hygiene) and adequacy of dressing & grooming	7,519	3.60%	6	7,531	3.33%	5	7,821	3.43%	6	7,554	3.13%	8	7,032	3.17%	8	6,877	3.14%	8
I.	66	Resident conflict, including roommates	1,958	0.94%	33	2,636	1.16%	29	3,864	1.70%	18	4,586	1.90%	15	4,888	2.21%	12	6,459	2.95%	9
K.	79	Equipment/building—disrepair, hazard, poor lighting, fire safety, not secure	3,657	1.75%	18	4,323	1.91%	14	4,753	2.09%	10	6,993	2.89%	9	5,541	2.50%	10	6,045	2.76%	10
F.	48	Symptoms unattended, including pain, pain not managed, no notice to others of changes in condition	4,886	2.34%	11	5,600	2.47%	9	5,172	2.27%	9	5,760	2.38%	10	5,776	2.61%	9	5,719	2.61%	11
E.	38	Personal property lost, stolen, used by others, destroyed, withheld	4,531	2.17%	13	4,919	2.17%	12	4,735	2.08%	11	4,878	2.02%	13	4,625	2.09%	14	5,079	2.32%	12
D.	27	Exercise preference/choice and/or civil/religious rights, individual's right to smoke	3,939	1.89%	15	4,237	1.87%	16	4,122	1.81%	14	4,844	2.00%	14	4,371	1.97%	16	5,003	2.29%	13
K.	78	Cleanliness, pests, general housekeeping	4,002	1.92%	14	3,912	1.73%	18	4,146	1.82%	13	4,538	1.88%	17	4,228	1.91%	17	4,857	2.22%	14
M.	97	Shortage of staff	5,503	2.64%	9	4,308	1.90%	15	3,968	1.74%	15	4,561	1.89%	16	4,760	2.15%	13	4,435	2.03%	15
M.	100	Staff unresponsive, unavailable	4,964	2.38%	10	4,627	2.04%	13	4,182	1.84%	12	5,050	2.09%	12	5,452	2.46%	11	4,392	2.01%	16
A.	1	Physical abuse (including corporal punishment)	4,777	2.29%	12	5,163	2.28%	10	3,858	1.69%	19	4,137	1.71%	19	3,770	1.70%	18	3,828	1.75%	17
F.	49	Toileting, incontinent care	3,107	1.49%	21	3,713	1.64%	19	3,919	1.72%	17	4,095	1.69%	20	3,587	1.62%	19	3,806	1.74%	18
G.	53	Assistive devices or equipment	2,497	1.20%	26	2,822	1.25%	23	3,240	1.42%	22	3,352	1.39%	24	3,273	1.48%	21	3,371	1.54%	19
A.	6	Resident to resident physical or sexual abuse	3,746	1.79%	17	5,010	2.21%	11	3,691	1.62%	20	3,372	1.40%	23	2,833	1.28%	25	3,346	1.53%	20
K.	77	Air/environment: temperature, and quality (heating, cooling, ventilation, water, noise)	2,456	1.18%	28	2,810	1.24%	26	3,951	1.74%	16	3,904	1.62%	21	3,026	1.37%	23	3,269	1.49%	21
J.	70	Fluid availability/hydration	2,458	1.18%	27	2,909	1.29%	22	2,847	1.25%	28	4,346	1.80%	18	3,227	1.46%	22	3,200	1.46%	22
P.	120	Family conflict; interference	2,440	1.17%	29	2,814	1.24%	25	2,886	1.27%	26	2,925	1.21%	28	2,842	1.28%	24	2,970	1.36%	24
A.	3	Verbal/psychological abuse (including punishment, seclusion)	3,256	1.56%	20	3,618	1.60%	20	2,932	1.29%	25	3,056	1.26%	25	2,809	1.27%	26	2,968	1.36%	25
K.	83	Odors	3,370	1.61%	19	3,127	1.38%	21	3,108	1.36%	23	5,370	2.22%	11	4,488	2.03%	15	2,896	1.32%	26
P.	122	Legal—guardianship, conservatorship, power of attorney, wills	2,588	1.24%	25	2,815	1.24%	24	2,641	1.16%	29	2,492	1.03%	29	2,396	1.08%	28	2,715	1.24%	27
M.	101	Supervision	3,872	1.85%	16	4,218	1.86%	17	3,273	1.44%	21	3,541	1.47%	22	3,532	1.59%	20	2,520	1.15%	29
E.	36	Billing/charges—notice, approval, questionable, accounting wrong or denied	2,616	1.25%	22	2,495	1.10%	30	2,224	0.98%	32	2,271	0.94%	33	2,203	0.99%	30	2,338	1.07%	30
A.	5	Gross neglect	2,610	1.25%	24	2,775	1.23%	28	2,056	0.90%	37	2,399	0.99%	31	2,166	0.98%	32	2,019	0.92%	33
F.	52	Not used (other: care pre federal fiscal year 2007)	2,135	1.02%	31	2,799	1.24%	27	2,934	1.29%	24	2,975	1.23%	26	2,168	0.98%	31	0	0.00%	116

SOURCE: "Top 20 Complaints by Category for Nursing Facilities (FFY 1996–2007)," in *2007 National Ombudsman Reporting System Data Tables*, U.S. Department of Health and Human Services, Administration on Aging, December 9, 2008, http://www.aoa.gov/AoARoot/AoA_Programs/Elder_Rights/Ombudsman/National_State_Data/2007/Index.aspx (accessed May 24, 2009)

TABLE 11.7

Complaints about board-and-care facilities, by category, fiscal years 1996–2007

Group		Complaint categories	1996 Total	1996 %	1996 Rank	1997 Total	1997 %	1997 Rank	1998 Total	1998 %	1998 Rank	1999 Total	1999 %	1999 Rank	2000 Total	2000 %	2000 Rank	2001 Total	2001 %	2001 Rank
			31,660			30,783			34,696			37,953			41,397			50,152		
J.	71	Food service—quantity, quality, variation, choice, condiments, utensils, menu	1,459	4.61%	1	1,499	4.87%	1	1,792	5.16%	1	1,816	4.78%	1	2,060	4.98%	1	2,736	5.46%	1
F.	44	Medications—administration, organization	1,154	3.64%	3	1,113	3.62%	2	1,433	4.13%	2	1,682	4.43%	2	1,844	4.45%	2	2,234	4.45%	2
C.	19	Discharge/eviction—planning, notice, procedure, implementation, including abandonment	915	2.89%	6	1,000	3.25%	5	1,216	3.50%	3	1,365	3.60%	3	1,421	3.43%	4	1,691	3.37%	4
K.	79	Equipment/building—disrepair, hazard, poor lighting, fire safety, not secure	952	3.01%	5	1,058	3.44%	4	1,023	2.95%	6	1,300	3.43%	5	1,261	3.05%	5	1,486	2.96%	5
D.	26	Dignity, respect—staff attitudes	978	3.09%	4	918	2.98%	7	1,129	3.25%	4	1,336	3.52%	4	1,491	3.60%	3	1,915	3.82%	3
F.	40	Accident or injury of unknown origin, falls, improper handling	676	2.14%	11	546	1.77%	16	698	2.01%	13	843	2.22%	10	886	2.14%	11	1,009	2.01%	13
F.	42	Care plan/resident assessment—inadequate, failure to follow plan or physician orders	531	1.68%	17	505	1.64%	18	664	1.91%	15	754	1.99%	15	1,025	2.48%	8	1,146	2.29%	9
K.	78	Cleanliness, pests, general housekeeping	718	2.27%	10	909	2.95%	8	927	2.67%	8	1,133	2.99%	6	1,091	2.64%	6	1,419	2.83%	6
E.	36	Billing/charges—notice, approval, questionable, accounting wrong or denied	649	2.05%	12	676	2.20%	11	724	2.09%	11	825	2.17%	13	928	2.24%	10	1,061	2.12%	11
E.	38	Personal property lost, stolen, used by others, destroyed, withheld	627	1.98%	14	576	1.87%	14	691	1.99%	14	789	2.08%	14	867	2.09%	12	1,080	2.15%	10
D.	27	Exercise preference/choice and/or civil/religious rights, individual's right to smoke	574	1.81%	15	539	1.75%	17	644	1.86%	16	719	1.89%	16	701	1.69%	17	1,009	2.01%	13
A.	1	Physical abuse (including corporal punishment)	1,291	4.08%	2	938	3.05%	6	1,044	3.01%	5	901	2.37%	9	847	2.05%	13	979	1.95%	15
I.	66	Resident conflict, including roommates	231	0.73%	44	241	0.78%	40	290	0.84%	37	269	0.71%	45	301	0.73%	40	375	0.75%	40
F.	45	Personal hygiene (includes nail and oral) and adequacy of dressing & grooming	912	2.88%	7	1,093	3.55%	3	940	2.71%	7	914	2.41%	8	1,061	2.56%	7	1,163	2.32%	7
K.	77	Air/environment: temperature, and quality (heating, cooling, ventilation, water, noise)	480	1.52%	20	477	1.55%	19	536	1.54%	20	612	1.61%	19	581	1.40%	21	772	1.54%	22
M.	97	Shortage of staff	636	2.01%	13	614	1.99%	13	720	2.08%	12	836	2.20%	12	1,001	2.42%	9	1,149	2.29%	8
E.	37	Personal funds—mismanaged, access denied, deposits & other money not returned	812	2.56%	9	728	2.36%	9	887	2.56%	9	929	2.45%	7	806	1.95%	14	1,012	2.02%	12
A.	3	Verbal/psychological abuse (including punishment, seclusion)	822	2.60%	8	652	2.12%	12	797	2.30%	10	843	2.22%	10	802	1.94%	15	895	1.78%	16
I.	64	Activities—choice and appropriateness	410	1.30%	24	454	1.47%	21	510	1.47%	22	554	1.46%	22	578	1.40%	23	782	1.56%	21
P.	121	Financial exploitation or neglect by family or other not affiliated with facility	444	1.40%	21	338	1.10%	33	403	1.16%	32	379	1.00%	34	526	1.27%	29	567	1.13%	30
P.	122	Legal—guardianship, conservatorship, power of attorney, wills	409	1.29%	25	440	1.43%	23	506	1.46%	23	458	1.21%	28	610	1.47%	19	591	1.18%	28
P.	120	Family conflict; interference	420	1.33%	22	365	1.19%	29	449	1.29%	27	395	1.04%	31	572	1.38%	25	604	1.20%	26
F.	48	Symptoms unattended, including pain, pain not managed, no notice to others of changes in condition	565	1.78%	16	464	1.51%	20	577	1.66%	17	644	1.70%	17	703	1.70%	16	895	1.78%	16
F.	41	Failure to respond to requests for assistance	255	0.81%	40	275	0.89%	36	331	0.95%	34	384	1.01%	32	548	1.32%	27	767	1.53%	23
M.	101	Supervision	365	1.15%	30	389	1.26%	25	460	1.33%	26	431	1.14%	29	581	1.40%	21	755	1.51%	24
A.	6	Resident to resident physical or sexual abuse	411	1.30%	23	348	1.13%	30	424	1.22%	30	329	0.87%	36	505	1.22%	32	529	1.05%	35
M.	100	Staff unresponsive, unavailable	400	1.26%	27	377	1.22%	28	465	1.34%	25	533	1.40%	24	552	1.33%	26	859	1.71%	18
M.	98	Staff training	386	1.22%	28	447	1.45%	22	483	1.39%	24	573	1.51%	20	603	1.46%	20	848	1.69%	19
L.	93	Offering inappropriate level of care	484	1.53%	19	571	1.85%	15	518	1.49%	21	534	1.41%	23	520	1.26%	30	731	1.46%	25
A.	5	Gross neglect	500	1.58%	18	705	2.29%	10	562	1.62%	18	614	1.62%	18	649	1.57%	18	798	1.59%	20

TABLE 11.7

Complaints about board-and-care facilities, by category, fiscal years 1996–2007 [CONTINUED]

Group		Complaint categories	2002 Total	2002 %	2002 Rank	2003 Total	2003 %	2003 Rank	2004 Total	2004 %	2004 Rank	2005 Total	2005 %	2005 Rank	2006 Total	2006 %	2006 Rank	2007 Total	2007 %	2007 Rank
			49,463			**56,470**			**57,190**			**61,646**			**60,767**			**60,801**		
J.	71	Food service—quantity, quality, variation, choice, condiments, utensils, menu	2,035	4.11%	2	2,350	4.16%	2	2,727	4.77%	1	3,221	5.22%	1	2,930	4.82%	2	3,240	5.33%	1
F.	44	Medications—administration, organization	2,335	4.72%	1	2,528	4.48%	1	2,497	4.37%	2	2,955	4.79%	2	3,094	5.09%	1	3,098	5.10%	2
C.	19	Discharge/eviction—planning, notice, procedure, implementation, including abandonment	1,867	3.77%	3	2,231	3.95%	3	2,280	3.99%	3	2,542	4.12%	3	2,699	4.44%	3	2,945	4.84%	3
K.	79	Equipment/building—disrepair, hazard, poor lighting, fire safety, not secure	1,358	2.75%	5	1,577	2.79%	5	1,742	3.05%	5	1,982	3.22%	4	2,181	3.59%	4	2,439	4.01%	4
D.	26	Dignity, respect—staff attitudes	1,787	3.61%	4	1,763	3.12%	4	1,856	3.25%	4	1,962	3.18%	5	2,022	3.33%	5	2,130	3.50%	5
F.	40	Accident or injury of unknown origin, falls, improper handling	1,059	2.14%	10	1,434	2.54%	7	1,419	2.48%	7	1,516	2.46%	7	1,731	2.85%	7	1,848	3.04%	6
F.	42	Care plan/resident assessment—inadequate, failure to follow plan or physician orders	1,278	2.58%	6	1,482	2.62%	6	1,576	2.76%	6	1,585	2.57%	6	1,804	2.97%	6	1,650	2.71%	7
K.	78	Cleanliness, pests, general housekeeping	1,109	2.24%	8	1,233	2.18%	8	1,236	2.16%	9	1,381	2.24%	10	1,314	2.16%	8	1,475	2.43%	8
E.	36	Billing/charges—notice, approval, questionable, accounting wrong or denied	1,133	2.29%	7	1,117	1.98%	13	1,136	1.99%	11	1,399	2.27%	9	1,304	2.15%	9	1,360	2.24%	9
E.	38	Personal property lost, stolen, used by others, destroyed, withheld	973	1.97%	14	1,151	2.04%	12	1,256	2.20%	8	1,298	2.11%	12	1,267	2.09%	10	1,344	2.21%	10
D.	27	Exercise preference/choice and/or civil/religious rights, individual's right to smoke	895	1.81%	16	1,154	2.04%	11	972	1.70%	17	1,150	1.87%	15	1,266	2.08%	11	1,342	2.21%	11
A.	1	Physical abuse (including corporal punishment)	1,076	2.18%	9	1,189	2.11%	9	1,041	1.82%	13	1,132	1.84%	16	1,198	1.97%	12	1,280	2.11%	12
I.	66	Resident conflict, including roommates	346	0.70%	43	492	0.87%	38	775	1.36%	26	805	1.31%	27	913	1.50%	24	1,228	2.02%	13
F.	45	Personal hygiene (includes nail and oral) and adequacy of dressing & grooming	965	1.95%	15	1,169	2.07%	10	1,139	1.99%	10	1,357	2.20%	11	1,100	1.81%	15	1,134	1.87%	14
K.	77	Air/environment: temperature, and quality (heating, cooling, ventilation, water, noise)	660	1.33%	28	789	1.40%	25	950	1.66%	19	1,274	2.07%	13	1,132	1.86%	13	1,119	1.84%	15
M.	97	Shortage of staff	1,029	2.08%	11	979	1.73%	18	959	1.68%	18	1,433	2.32%	8	1,031	1.70%	17	1,118	1.84%	16
E.	37	Personal funds—mismanaged, access denied, deposits & other money not returned	975	1.97%	13	955	1.69%	19	973	1.70%	16	1,025	1.66%	17	999	1.64%	18	1,114	1.83%	17
A.	3	Verbal/psychological abuse (including punishment, seclusion)	1,025	2.07%	12	1,023	1.81%	16	986	1.72%	15	1,014	1.64%	18	1,125	1.85%	14	1,103	1.81%	18
I.	64	Activities—choice and appropriateness	830	1.68%	18	811	1.44%	23	1,086	1.90%	12	926	1.50%	21	986	1.62%	19	1,101	1.81%	19
P.	121	Financial exploitation or neglect by family or other not affiliated with facility	608	1.23%	32	734	1.30%	27	807	1.41%	23	815	1.32%	26	950	1.56%	20	1,017	1.67%	20
P.	122	Legal—guardianship, conservatorship, power of attorney, wills	823	1.66%	19	903	1.60%	20	935	1.63%	20	851	1.38%	25	928	1.53%	22	994	1.63%	21
P.	120	Family conflict; interference	703	1.42%	25	801	1.42%	24	795	1.39%	24	967	1.57%	19	903	1.49%	25	959	1.58%	22
F.	48	Symptoms unattended, including pain, pain not managed, no notice to others of changes in condition	819	1.66%	20	1,029	1.82%	15	900	1.57%	21	873	1.42%	24	949	1.56%	21	913	1.50%	23
F.	41	Failure to respond to requests for assistance	617	1.25%	31	695	1.23%	29	737	1.29%	28	1,184	1.92%	14	927	1.53%	23	883	1.45%	24
M.	101	Supervision	854	1.73%	17	1,088	1.93%	14	992	1.73%	14	967	1.57%	19	1,050	1.73%	16	871	1.43%	25
A.	6	Resident to resident physical or sexual abuse	695	1.41%	27	997	1.77%	17	873	1.53%	22	906	1.47%	23	863	1.42%	27	842	1.38%	26
M.	100	Staff unresponsive, unavailable	795	1.61%	22	784	1.39%	26	746	1.30%	27	680	1.10%	32	761	1.25%	29	837	1.38%	27
M.	98	Staff training	808	1.63%	21	860	1.52%	22	781	1.37%	25	732	1.19%	29	753	1.24%	31	821	1.35%	29
L.	93	Offering inappropriate level of care	654	1.32%	29	658	1.17%	32	633	1.11%	32	610	0.99%	35	561	0.92%	37	811	1.33%	30
A.	5	Gross neglect	771	1.56%	23	868	1.54%	21	729	1.27%	29	761	1.23%	28	864	1.42%	26	788	1.30%	32

SOURCE: "Top 20 Complaints by Category for Board and Care Facilities (FFY 1996–2007)," in *2007 National Ombudsman Reporting System Data Tables*, U.S. Department of Health and Human Services, Administration on Aging, December 9, 2008, http://www.aoa.gov/AoARoot/AoA_Programs/Elder_Rights/Ombudsman/National_State_Data/2007/Index.aspx (accessed May 24, 2009)

IMPORTANT NAMES AND ADDRESSES

AARP (formerly American Association of Retired Persons)
601 E St. NW
Washington, DC 20049
1-888-687-2277
URL: http://www.aarp.org/

Alliance for Aging Research
2021 K St. NW, Ste. 305
Washington, DC 20006
(202) 293-2856
FAX: (202) 785-8574
E-mail: info@agingresearch.org
URL: http://www.agingresearch.org/

Alzheimer's Association
225 N. Michigan Ave., 17th Floor
Chicago, IL 60601-7633
(312) 335-8700
1-800-272-3900
FAX: 1-866-699-1246
E-mail: info@alz.org
URL: http://www.alz.org/

American Association for Geriatric Psychiatry
7910 Woodmont Ave., Ste. 1050
Bethesda, MD 20814-3004
(301) 654-7850
FAX: (301) 654-4137
E-mail: main@aagponline.org
URL: http://www.aagponline.org/

American Association of Homes and Services for the Aging
2519 Connecticut Ave. NW
Washington, DC 20008
(202) 783-2242
FAX: (202) 783-2255
E-mail: info@aahsa.org
URL: http://www.aahsa.org/

American Geriatrics Society
350 Fifth Ave., Ste. 801
New York, NY 10118
(212) 308-1414
FAX: (212) 832-8646
E-mail: info@americangeriatrics.org
URL: http://www.americangeriatrics.org/

American Heart Association
7272 Greenville Ave.
Dallas, TX 75231
1-800-242-8721
URL: http://www.americanheart.org/

Arthritis Foundation
PO Box 7669
Atlanta, GA 30357-0669
1-800-283-7800
URL: http://www.arthritis.org/

Assisted Living Federation of America
1650 King St., Ste. 602
Alexandria, VA 22314-2747
(703) 894-1805
FAX: (703) 894-1831
E-mail: info@alfa.org
URL: http://www.alfa.org/

The Boomer Project
2601 Floyd Ave.
Richmond, VA 23220
(804) 358-8981
FAX: (804) 342-1790
E-mail: matt@boomerproject.com
URL: http://www.boomerproject.com/

Centers for Disease Control and Prevention
1600 Clifton Rd.
Atlanta, GA 30333
1-800-232-4636
URL: http://www.cdc.gov/

Centers for Medicare and Medicaid Services
7500 Security Blvd.
Baltimore, MD 21244
(410) 786-3000
1-877-267-2323
URL: http://www.cms.gov/

Children of Aging Parents
PO Box 167
Richboro, PA 18954
1-800-227-7294
URL: http://www.caps4caregivers.org/

Civic Ventures
114 Sansome St., Ste. 850
San Francisco, CA 94104
(415) 430-0141
FAX: (415) 430-0144
E-mail: info@civicventures.org
URL: http://www.civicventures.org/

Eldercare Locator Directory
1-800-677-1116
URL: http://www.eldercare.gov/

Family Caregiver Alliance
180 Montgomery St., Ste. 1100
San Francisco, CA 94104
(415) 434-3388
1-800-445-8106
E-mail: info@caregiver.org
URL: http://www.caregiver.org/

Gerontological Society of America
1220 L St. NW, Ste. 901
Washington, DC 20005
(202) 842-1275
FAX: (202) 842-1150
URL: http://www.geron.org/

Gray Panthers
1612 K St., NW, Ste. 300
Washington, DC 20006
(202) 737-6637
1-800-280-5362
URL: http://www.graypanthers.org/

Insurance Institute for Highway Safety
1005 N. Glebe Rd., Ste. 800
Arlington, VA 22201
(703) 247-1500
FAX: (703) 247-1588
URL: http://www.highwaysafety.org/

Mature Workers Employment Alliance
826 Euclid Ave.
Syracuse, NY 13210
(315) 446-3587
E-mail: mwea4cny@mwea-cny.com
URL: http://mwea-cny.com/index.php

Medicare Rights Center
1224 M St. NW, Ste. 100
Washington, DC 20005
(202) 637-0961
1-800-333-4144
FAX: (202) 637-0962
URL: http://www.medicarerights.org/

National Academy of Elder Law Attorneys
1577 Spring Hill Rd., Ste. 220
Vienna, VA 22182
(703) 942-5711
FAX: (703) 563-9504
URL: http://www.naela.org/

National Alliance for Caregiving
4720 Montgomery Ln., Fifth Floor
Bethesda, MD 20814
E-mail: info@caregiving.org
URL: http://www.caregiving.org/

National Association for Home Care and Hospice
228 Seventh St. SE
Washington, DC 20003
(202) 547-7424
FAX: (202) 547-3540
URL: http://www.nahc.org/

National Caregiving Foundation
801 N. Pitt St., Ste. 116
Alexandria, VA 22314-1783
E-mail: info@caregivingfoundation.org
URL: http://www.caregivingfoundation.org/

National Caucus and Center on Black Aged
1220 L St. NW, Ste. 800
Washington, DC 20005
(202) 637-8400
FAX: (202) 347-0895
URL: http://www.ncba-aged.org/

National Center on Elder Abuse
C/o Center for Community Research and Services
University of Delaware
297 Graham Hall
Newark, DE 19716
(302) 831-3525
FAX: (302) 831-4225
URL: http://www.ncea.aoa.gov/ncearoot/Main_Site/index.aspx

National Center for Health Statistics Division of Data Services
3311 Toledo Rd.
Hyattsville, MD 20782
1-800-232-4636
URL: http://www.cdc.gov/nchs

National Citizens' Coalition for Nursing Home Reform
1828 L St. NW, Ste. 801
Washington, DC 20036
(202) 332-2276
FAX: (202) 332-2949
URL: http://www.nccnhr.org/

National Family Caregivers Association
10400 Connecticut Ave., Ste. 500
Kensington, MD 20895-3944
(301) 942-6430
1-800-896-3650
FAX: (301) 942-2302
E-mail: info@thefamilycaregiver.org
URL: http://www.thefamilycaregiver.org/

National Hispanic Council on Aging
734 15th St. NW, Ste. 1050
Washington, DC 20005
(202) 347-9733
FAX: (202) 347-9735
E-mail: nchoa@nchoa.org
URL: http://www.nhcoa.org/

National Hospice and Palliative Care Organization
1731 King St., Ste. 100
Alexandria, VA 22314
(703) 837-1500
FAX: (703) 837-1233
E-mail: nhpco_info@nhpco.org
URL: http://www.nhpco.org/

National Indian Council on Aging
10501 Montgomery Blvd. NE, Ste. 210
Albuquerque, NM 87111
(505) 292-2001
FAX: (505) 292-1922
URL: http://www.nicoa.org/

National Institute on Aging
Bldg. 31, Rm. 5C27
31 Center Dr., MSC 2292
Bethesda, MD 20892
(301) 496-1752
FAX: (301) 496-1072
URL: http://www.nih.gov/nia

National Osteoporosis Foundation
1232 22nd St. NW
Washington, DC 20037-1202
(202) 223-2226
1-800-231-4222
URL: http://www.nof.org/

National PACE Association
801 N. Fairfax St., Ste. 309
Alexandria, VA 22314
(703) 535-1565
FAX: (703) 535-1566
E-mail: info@npaonline.org
URL: http://www.npaonline.org/

National Respite Locator Service Chapel Hill Training-Outreach Project
800 Eastowne Dr., Ste. 105
Chapel Hill, NC 27514
(919) 490-5577
FAX: (919) 490-4905
URL: http://www.respitelocator.org/

National Senior Citizens Law Center
1444 Eye St. NW, Ste. 1100
Washington, DC 20005
(202) 289-6976
FAX: (202) 289-7224
URL: http://www.nsclc.org/

National Society for American Indian Elderly
200 E. Fillmore St., Ste. 151
Phoenix, AZ 85004
(602) 424-0542
E-mail: info@nsaie.org
URL: http://www.nsaie.org/

National Urban League
120 Wall St., Eighth Floor
New York, NY 10005
(212) 558-5300
FAX: (212) 344-5332
E-mail: info@nulexplore.org
URL: http://www.nul.org/

Older Women's League
1828 L St. NW, Ste. 801
Washington, DC 20036
1-800-825-3695
FAX: (202) 332-2949
URL: http://www.owl-national.org/

Pension Benefit Guaranty Corporation
1200 K St. NW
Washington, DC 20005-4026
(202) 326-4000
1-800-400-7242
URL: http://www.pbgc.gov/

Pension Rights Center
1350 Connecticut Ave. NW, Ste. 206
Washington, DC 20036-1739
(202) 296-3776
FAX: (202) 833-2472
URL: http://www.pensionrights.org/

SeniorNet
12801 Worldgate Dr., Ste. 500
Herndon, VA 20170
(571) 203-7100
FAX: (703) 871-3901
URL: http://www.seniornet.org/

Service Corps of Retired Executives
409 Third St. SW, Sixth Floor
Washington, DC 20024
1-800-634-0245
URL: http://www.score.org/

U.S. Administration on Aging
One Massachusetts Ave. NW
Washington, DC 20001
(202) 619-0724
FAX: (202) 357-3555
E-mail: aoainfo@aoa.hhs.gov
URL: http://www.aoa.gov/

U.S. Census Bureau
4600 Silver Hill Rd.
Washington, DC 20233
URL: http://www.census.gov/

U.S. Department of Veterans Affairs
Washington, DC 20011
1-800-827-1000
URL: http://www.va.gov/

RESOURCES

Many of the demographic data cited in this text were drawn from U.S. Census Bureau and Bureau of Labor Statistics publications, including "Older Americans Month: May 2009" (March 2009), *2008 Current Population Survey*, *2007 American Community Survey*, and "Census Bureau Reports on Residential Vacancies and Homeownership" (April 2009). A report prepared by the United Nations' Department of Economic and Social Affairs, *World Population Prospects: The 2008 Revision* (2009), provided comparisons of life expectancy and population aging throughout the world.

The report *A Profile of Older Americans: 2008* (Saadia Greenberg, March 2009) by the U.S. Administration on Aging and *Older Americans 2008: Key Indicators of Well-Being* (March 2008) by the Federal Interagency Forum on Aging-Related Statistics provided useful data about older adults. Additional population data were drawn from *The World Factbook* (2009) by the Central Intelligence Agency.

The *The 2009 Retirement Confidence Survey: Economy Drives Confidence to Record Lows; Many Looking to Work Longer* (Ruth Helman et al., April 2009) by the Employee Benefit Research Institute, the American Savings Education Council, and Matthew Greenwald and Associates, provided information about pension plans and other employee benefits. The U.S. Department of Labor and the National Economic Council Interagency Working Group on Social Security described trends in labor force participation. In "Myths about Older Workers" (March 2009), the North Carolina Collaboration on Lifelong Learning and Engagement described older workers' productivity. The Equal Employment Opportunity Commission offered information about age discrimination issues and claims. Peter Shapiro's *A History of National Service in America* (1994) detailed the establishment of a national senior service during the administration of President John F. Kennedy.

The American Association of Community Colleges (AACC) reported on students at the nation's community colleges. The National Center for Education Statistics report *Digest of Education Statistics* (Thomas D. Snyder, Sally A. Dillow, and Charlene M. Hoffman, March 2009) provided information about trends in adult education. The Pew Internet and American Life Project report *Generations Online in 2009* (Sydney Jones and Susannah Fox, January 2009) tracked Internet use by age. In *Staying the Course: Online Education in the United States, 2008* (November 2008), I. Elaine Allen and Jeff Seaman discussed online enrollment.

The National Highway Traffic Safety Administration, in *Older Population Traffic Safety Fact Sheet* (September 2008), documented the increasing numbers of older drivers. The U.S. Government Accountability Office (GAO) publication *Transportation-Disadvantaged Seniors: Efforts to Enhance Senior Mobility Could Benefit from Additional Guidance and Information* (August 2004) and Rhianna JoIris Babka, Jill F. Cooper, and David R. Ragland's *Evaluation of Urban Travel Training for Older Adults* (November 2008) explored ways to improve transportation options for older adults. The Insurance Institute for Highway Safety publication *Fatality Facts 2007: Older People* (June 2009) reported that even though the oldest and youngest drivers have the highest fatality rates on a per-mile-driven basis, older drivers involved in crashes are less likely than younger drivers to hurt others. In "Realizing Dignified Transportation for Seniors" (April 2009), Philanthropy New York reported that each year more than 1 million older adults stop driving because of declines in their fitness level, vision, and ability to think clearly. The American Medical Association and the National Highway Traffic Safety Administration developed the *Physician's Guide to Assessing and Counseling Older Drivers* (May 2003), which details medical conditions and their potential effect on driving skills.

The U.S. Department of Housing and Urban Development's Office of Community Planning and Development described in *The Third Annual Homeless Assessment*

Report to Congress (July 2008) the plight of homeless older Americans. The National Low-Income Housing Coalition report *Out of Reach 2009* (April 2009) documented rental housing cost data. *Public Housing and Supportive Services for the Frail Elderly: A Guide for Housing Authorities and Their Collaborators* (2006), by the Milbank Memorial Fund and the Council of Large Public Housing Authorities, described the percentage of low-income housing occupied by older adults.

The Social Security Administration provided information about the history and future of Social Security as well as benefits and eligibility in publications such as *Fast Facts and Figures about Social Security, 2008* (August 2008), "Social Security Basic Facts" (February 2009), and *The 2009 Annual Report of the Board of Trustees of the Federal Old-Age and Survivors Insurance and Federal Disability Insurance Trust Funds* (May 2009). The *Milliman 2009 Pension Funding Study* (March 2009) detailed recent losses in corporate pension plans. A report issued by the Center for Economic and Policy Research, *The Wealth of the Baby Boom Cohorts after the Collapse of the Housing Bubble* (David Rosnick and Dean Baker, February 2009), described economic losses suffered by the baby boom generation. The report *The Mature Market: Consumer Trends and U.S. Retail Markets* (March 2007) offered insight into the purchasing power of older consumers.

The Centers for Medicare and Medicaid Services (CMS) coordinates Medicare and Medicaid. The CMS provided information about the history, the beneficiaries, and the future of these entitlement programs. The Centers for Disease Control and Prevention (CDC) provided vital health statistics in publications such as *Health, United States, 2008*, "Deaths: Final Data for 2006" (Melonie Heron et al., April 2009), and *2008 National Health Interview Survey*. The Social Security Administration report *Status of the Social Security and Medicare Programs: A Summary of the 2009 Annual Reports* (May 2009) detailed the challenges both programs face.

In *The MetLife Market Survey of Nursing Home & Assisted Living Costs* (2008), the MetLife Mature Market Institute reported on the costs associated with nursing homes and assisted living. *Retooling for an Aging America: Building the Health Care Workforce* (2008) by the Institute of Medicine's Committee on the Future Health Care Workforce for Older Americans reported that an increasing number of Americans are hiring caregivers to assist with older relatives.

The AARP underwrites research about older Americans. Examples of its research cited in this text are *A First Look at Older Americans and the Mortgage Crisis* (September 2008) and *AARP Bulletin Survey on Expectations for the New Administration and Congress* (Gerard Rainville, December 2008).

Many organizations and publications provide information on specific health and medical problems of older adults. Among the many publications cited in this text are the American Heart Association's "Risk Factors and Coronary Heart Disease and Stroke" (January 2008), the American Cancer Society's *Cancer Facts and Figures, 2009* (2009), the CDC's "Falls among Older Adults: An Overview" (January 2009), and the Alzheimer's Association's *2009 Alzheimer's Disease Facts and Figures* (2009). The U.S. Department of Veterans Affairs (VA) provided demographic projections of the health and other needs of older veterans.

Similarly, many agencies, organizations, and professional organizations, notably the American Association of Homes and Services for the Aging, the National Center for Education Statistics, the Mature Workers Employment Alliance, and the American Geriatrics Society, offered data and analyses of myriad issues of importance to older Americans.

Professional medical journals offered research findings and information about health and disease among older adults as well as health service utilization and financing. Articles from the following journals were cited in this text: *Acta Psychiatrica Scandinavica, Addiction, Aging, Neuropsychology, and Cognition, Alzheimer's and Dementia, American Journal of Geriatric Psychiatry, Annals of Internal Medicine, Annals of Neurology, Annual Review of Public Health, Archives of Ophthalmology, BMC Health Services Research, BMJ, Clinics in Geriatric Medicine, Health Affairs, International Journal of Impotence Research, Journal of the American Medical Association, Journal of the American Medical Directors Association, Journal of Gerontological Social Work, Journal of Gerontology, Journal of Happiness Studies, Journal of Health and Human Services Administration, Journal of Personality and Social Psychology, Medical Clinics of North America, Medical Journal of Australia, Milbank Quarterly, Neurology, New England Journal of Medicine, Proceedings Baylor University Medical Center, Psychology and Aging, Seminars in Respiratory and Critical Care Medicine, Social Science and Medicine, The Gerontologist, Tracking Report No. 23, U.S. Pharmacist.*

Because the aging population affects nearly every aspect of society, from employment and housing to health care and politics, consumer publications frequently feature articles about and of interest to older adults. Articles cited in this volume were drawn from *FutureAge*, *New York Times*, *San Francisco Chronicle*, *Science Daily*, and *USA Today*.

Information about abuse and mistreatment of older adults was found in *Broken Trust: Elders, Family, and Finances* (March 2009) by the MetLife Mature Market Institute, the National Committee for the Prevention of Elder Abuse, and the Center for Gerontology at Virginia Polytechnic Institute and State University; *Consumer Fraud in the United States: The Second FTC Survey* (October 2007) by the Federal Trade Commission; and *2004 Survey of State Adult Protective Services: Abuse of Adults 60 Years of Age and Older* (February 2006) by the National Center on Elder Abuse. The Bureau of Justice Statistics' *Criminal Victimization, 2007* (Michael R. Rand, December 2008), *Criminal Victimization in the United States, 2006 Statistical Tables* (August 2008), and *Homicide Trends in the United States* (James Alan Fox and Marianne W. Zawitz, July 2007) provided data about fraud and abuse as did *A Response to the Abuse of Vulnerable Adults: The 2000 Survey of State Adult Protective Services* (Pamela B. Teaster, March 2003) and "Preventing Abuse and Neglect in Nursing Homes: The Role of Staffing and Training" (Catherine Hawes, November 2003).

We are very grateful to the Gallup Organization for permitting us to present the results of its renowned opinion polls and graphics and to the Commonwealth Fund for granting permission to cite data and reproduce graphics from "Culture Change in Nursing Homes: How Far Have We Come? Findings from the Commonwealth Fund 2007 National Survey of Nursing Homes" (Michelle M. Doty, Mary Jane Koren, and Elizabeth L. Sturla, May 2008).

INDEX

Page references in italics refer to photographs. References with the letter t *following them indicate the presence of a table. The letter* f *indicates a figure. If more than one table or figure appears on a particular page, the exact item number for the table or figure being referenced is provided.*

T

U

V

W